Langford has finally received his literary admirable biography ... an essential requ... pugilist-specialist-reader.
Boxing Monthly

Clay Moyle's fine, new book pulls together many of the myths and facts about Langford, and makes his worldwide pursuit of Johnson into a chase equal to Captain Ahab's stalking of Moby Dick.
The Ring

Here's a treasure ... a scholarly work, carefully compiled, but make no mistake: there is plenty of action, and a right education in this largely forgotten chapter of boxing history.
Inside Sport
Australia

Absorbing ... Clay Moyle has produced a prodigious book on Langford's life that is a must for any boxing fan with even the slightest interest in those early times.
Boxing News

... a fascinating study of a man and his desire to defy not only odds, but the sheer fear of him that existed in so many of his contemporaries.
www.badlefthook.com

... the most definitive biography of Sam Langford ever presented
... loaded with many rare details and excellent photographs
... an important read for historians and fans
Cyber Boxing Zone

... a journey through a tumultuous life filled with triumph and tragedy, accomplishment and disappointment, joy and pain ... Moyle's biography crowns Langford with glory.

Charles Saunders
Author of Sweat and Soul: The Saga of Black Boxers from the Halifax Forum to Caesars Palace

… *reads like a novel. It is one of the most detailed boxing history books I have read, yet it is never dry. … Any fan of the sport will enjoy the book.*

> Marc Lichtenfeld
> Host of Through the Ropes

… *makes the reader feel like they are with Sam Langford during his journey through life. If you can read, you must read this book.*

> Bill Calogero, Jr.
> Host of TalkinBoxing.com

Moyle has recovered a lost body of knowledge and rescued a piece of our history. His book is a model for all serious collectors, whatever their fields.

> David Chesanow
> Americollector.com

This is an excellent book. Thorough and scholarly, it has a fine eye for detail and anecdote. … I highly recommend this book.

> Steve Marantz
> Author of Sorcery at Ceasers (Leonard vs. Hagler)

The ultimate biography of one of the greatest boxers of all time. … A pleasure to read, every boxing fan needs to have this volume in his library.

> Johnny Griffin
> Ringmemorabilia.com

… *this is indeed a special book and well worth reading* …

> Mike Silver
> Former boxing promoter and inspector of the New York State Athletic Commission. Contributor of boxing articles for The New York Times, The Ring, Boxing Monthly, and ESPN and Seconds Out websites

All I can say is WOW. I have read a great deal on Langford, and I thought some of the writing by Nat Fleischer was great. You just set a new standard.

> Chip Hodgkins
> President of Pittsfield, MA radio station

… a great book that paid proper tribute to a fascinating ring legend.
                          Jack Hirsch
                          President of the Boxing Writers Association

… truly a book that was long overdue
                          Richard Scurti
                          Author of Boxing's Greatest Interviews

There is much to commend about this work … no doubt the definitive biography of Sam Langford for a long time to come.
        Adeyinka Makinde
        Author of Dick Tiger: The Life and Times of a Boxing Immortal

Reader Comments from retail websites and letters:

… a must read for any boxing fan. Anyone who likes boxing should read this book.

… An outstanding book with a lot of new great info for the avid boxing fan and a must read for anyone interested in the plight of the life of a black boxer just after the turn of the 20th century.

… A great book about one of boxing's best, Sam Langford. It truly is a compelling story!

… a superb example of what a boxing biography should be like.

I was held from the first page to the last – an example of what boxing biography should be!

… the best boxing book I have ever read.

… a book you didn't want to end

… superbly researched and well-paced.

… a long-needed and definitive life account of the great "Boston Tar Baby," Sam Langford. This is truly one MAGNIFICENT work!!!

… one of the best boxing books written. You've done a real service here, never mind that the book is a terrific read.

SAM LANGFORD

BOXING'S GREATEST UNCROWNED CHAMPION

CLAY MOYLE

B&H Bennett & Hastings Publishing

Copyright © 2006 by Clay Moyle

Paperback: First printing 2013. Revised with corrections August, 2013.

All rights reserved. No part of this book may be reproduced or transmitted in any form by any means, electronic or mechanical, including photocopying and recording, or by any information storage and retrieval system, except as may be expressly permitted by the 1976 Copyright Act or the publisher. Requests for permission should be made in writing to: Bennett & Hastings Publishing, c/o the address posted at www.bennetthastings.com.

Unless otherwise credited, photographs are from the author's personal collection.

Clay Moyle cmoyle@aol.com

www.prizefightingbooks.com

ISBN: 978-1-934733-70-7 This paperback edition provides revisions to the text issued in hardcover. This paperback edition is also available in eBook formats. Please contact the publisher if you would like assistance finding an eBook edition suited to your reader.

Hardback: ISBN: 978-1-934733-02-8 First printing May 2008. Second printing with revisions October 2008.

Cover photo: Sam Langford knocks Bill Lang on the ropes, National Sporting Club, London, England, February 21, 1911. Photo courtesy of Ben Hawes Collection.

Library of Congress Control Number: 2012955079

SAM LANGFORD

Boxing's Greatest Uncrowned Champion

Dedicated to my wife Margaret
and our children Grace and Caleb

And for Carol and Rosemarie

ACKNOWLEDGMENTS

Writing Sam Langford's story turned out to be a much bigger task than I ever imagined. As with most projects of this nature there are numerous parties to thank for their assistance, and many whose help was instrumental in the production of this story. First and foremost is Rosemarie Pleasant, Sam's great-great niece, and the great-great-granddaughter of Sam's brother, Walter. Rosemarie has been thoroughly researching Sam's life and career for a number of years now and generously shared the results of her labor in the form of photocopied materials throughout this project. Her assistance was invaluable and I thank her from the bottom of my heart. Thank you to Carol Doyle, Sam's great-granddaughter, for generously sharing her memories of Sam and his relationship with his family. I am very grateful for the valuable insight Carol provided during multiple phone interviews and for the additional photographs supplied. Carol is extremely proud of her great-grandfather as are Sam's great-great-grandsons, Arlin Foster, David Foster, and Brendon Foster. I am also deeply indebted to my aunt, Sheila Rabe, and my friend Joe Stack for all their editing advice, as well as that which I received from my friends Marina Licursi, John Cusimano, and John and Pamela Ochs to a lesser but no less important degree.

Ben Hawes, J.J. Johnston, and Barry Deskins were kind enough to share their extensive Sam Langford files with me. Ben also allowed me the use of many rare photographs from his fantastic collection. My cousin, Brian Robertson, translated a number of articles from numerous French boxing magazines related to the time Sam spent in France, and Arly Allen, Dave Bergin, Bob Carson, David Chesanow, Don Cogswell, Steve Compton, Monte Cox, Luckett Davis, Marvin Gilmore, Craig Hamilton, Bob Marchment, Ray McCormack, Brian O'Conner, Bill O'Loughlin, Charles Saunders, Tom Scharf, Don Scott, Harry Shaffer, Steve Shaw, Kevin Smith, Mrs. A.J. Spears, Claudia Thomas, Thelma Todd, Roberto Valero, Geoffrey Ward, and Richard

Zampetta each contributed to the project in some way or another ranging from copies of articles, photographs, research assistance, or in some cases advice on specific issues like publication.

A special note of thanks is due to Ray Beere Johnson II for his research that led to the identification of Langford's date of marriage and other notable events, and to Kevin Smith for graciously sharing some of his research information concerning Sam and a number of his opponents and for supplying Sam's middle name. (Kevin Smith's contributions are a result of his important three-volume series on the history of the black prizefighter from 1870-1930, titled *The Sundowners*.) I also want to thank Carol Sinclair from the King County Library Reference Center in Issaquah, Washington for all her help obtaining newspaper microfilm and copies of articles for me to research, and the Weymouth Visitor Information Center for the information they provided regarding the Sam Langford School. Lastly, I wish to thank my publisher, Bennett & Hastings I couldn't be more pleased with their efforts on this project. I can only hope that I have not forgotten anyone. If so, I sincerely apologize and beg their forgiveness.

CONTENTS

Foreword		11
Introduction		13
1	Weymouth Falls, Nova Scotia	21
2	Champion of Cambridge Street	27
3	Joe Gans "The Old Master"	39
4	Joe Walcott, "The Barbados Demon"	49
5	Tackling the Big Fellows	61
6	England	73
7	A Black Heavyweight Champion	87
8	The Iron Man	99
9	Chasing the Michigan Assassin	113
10	Encounter with a Razor	125
11	Ketchel	137
12	The Fight of the Century	157
13	The "Joplin Ghost"	189
14	The Rabbit Punch	199
15	Australia	217
16	Mastering McVea	237
17	Troubles Down Under	261
18	"Gunboat"	279
19	An End to Heavyweight Title Hopes	299
20	Passing of the Torch	323
21	"Heavyweight Champion of Mexico!"	357
22	Retirement	373
23	The Forgotten Man	391
24	Epilogue	403
Sam Langford's Professional Record		415
Sources: Abbreviations		430
Bibliography		431
Index		435

FOREWORD

I first heard the name Sam Langford when my mother, Marie Pleasant, called and asked if I had ever heard of him. I hadn't, so I looked in a few Canadian reference books, and sent Mom the little information I found. When I talked to her later she mentioned that he was related to my late father.

I had become interested in the family history and didn't think or know that there was anyone notable in the family tree, so I finally went off to the (then) National Library and Public Archives of Canada to start my research.

What I found was a wealth of material scattered in so many places that it was difficult to make sense of it. There was information on Sam, mostly in boxing collections and articles scattered through various magazines and newspapers. Many of the stories were the same, and repeated through the years with little new information.

I had no idea what I would do with what I found when I heard from Clay. He was generous about sharing/trading information and I was glad that he was planning this book. He sent me a copy of the manuscript to read.

Wow! He's made sense of Sam's career and put his life in order. He even found out Sam's middle name and marriage date.

Every two years there's a reunion held in Weymouth Falls (next one in 2008) where the Sam Langford Community Center is the focus, and the organizers try to keep Sam's memory alive. This book will be a great help and starting point for local historians and a reference for the younger people when they ask questions.

There are still Langfords living there (Walter Langford was my great-grandfather through my grandmother Flora) who are proud of their link to Sam.

On their behalf, thanks Clay.

ROSEMARIE PLEASANT

Thank you Clay, for answering so many of my unanswered questions in this amazing biography of my great-grandfather. In spite of Big Granny's gentle coaxing all I could squeak out when I was around him as a very young girl was a meek "hello."

My memory of him is so clear in my mind, it is like it was yesterday. I can still see him sitting at Big Granny's kitchen table, by the window next to the sink, with his bald head, large hands, dark glasses and cane. Thank you Clay. You have given me that voice, and I can say now with honor and love that only a few short steps from the shy little girl was one of the greatest boxers to ever enter the ring: Samuel Langford, "The Boston Tar Baby," my great-grandfather.

CAROL DOYLE
SAM LANGFORD'S GREAT-GRANDDAUGHTER

INTRODUCTION

In January of 1944 the *New York Herald Tribune* published "The Forgotten Man," a piece that was carried across the nation. It was a story about Sam Langford, a.k.a. "The Boston Tar Baby," one of boxing's greatest fighters during the first quarter of the 20th century, and it related how only eighteen years after his remarkable career Sam had completely disappeared from mainstream society and ended up blind and penniless.[1]

The prize-winning article reintroduced Langford to another generation of Americans and resulted in a drive that brought about the establishment of a small trust fund that ensured his basic needs were met for the remainder of his life.

Over sixty years later, Langford is once again relatively unknown among the general population, while the names of fighters such as Jack Dempsey, Jack Johnson, Joe Louis, and Sugar Ray Robinson are recognizable. Why is that the case? How could a man, who was arguably one of the greatest pound-for-pound fighters of all time, and feared by men such as Jack Johnson and Jack Dempsey, be overlooked?

To answer that question one must consider how difficult it was for a black-skinned man to make his way in American society during the early 20th century. Boxing was a microcosm of the general society, and Langford's plight was not unlike that suffered by a number of great African-American boxers during the early part of the 20th century. The era in which he fought was one in which many states outlawed bouts between men of different races; and in those locations where it was allowed, it was not at all uncommon for the best Caucasian fighters of the day to "draw the color line," a term used to describe the convenient practice of refusing to fight a dark-skinned man. It was also a time when many white Americans feared the ascension of blacks, particularly in any areas of social significance.

It was in horse racing and cycling that African-Americans first

---
[1] *New York Herald Tribune*, January 1944

achieved athletic prominence in the United States. As servants of the old south, they had been the first stable boys, trainers and jockeys. When the first Kentucky Derby was run in 1875, thirteen African-American jockeys dominated the field of fourteen. Isaac Murphy, the "Black Archer," was America's finest rider during the 1880s and 1890s. He won the Kentucky Derby three times. His counterpart, Willie Simms, won the Derby twice and was the first American jockey to ride in a crouch with shortened stirrups, as all riders do today. Major Taylor was the winner of the American bicycle sprint championship in 1898 and achieved worldwide recognition when that sport was at its zenith.

Prizefighting was the third sport in which African-Americans received significant newspaper attention. These three sports—horse racing, bicycling and prizefighting—provided the black community with their earliest popular heroes. The public appearances of men such as Jack Johnson, Sam Langford, Isaac Murphy, and Major Taylor always produced excited African-American crowds.

It was another story altogether with baseball, the nation's most popular sport and known as the national pastime. While African-Americans were playing the game as early as 1867, the National Association of Baseball Players formally excluded their participation. By 1887 there were seven "Negro" clubs playing professionally, but not against whites. They formally challenged the white players to a series of games to determine the national championship, but the white team declined to participate explaining that they could not afford to lose the white fans who would desert them. The color barrier remained in professional baseball until 1947, when Jackie Robinson joined the Brooklyn Dodgers.[2]

In 1895, only seven years before Sam's professional boxing career began, *New York Sun* editor Charles Dana wrote:

"We are in the midst of a growing menace. The black man is rapidly forging into the ranks in athletics, especially in the field of fisticuffs. We are in the midst of a black rise against white supremacy."[3]

---

[2] Roi Ottley, *Black Odyssey: The Story of the Negro in America*. New York: Charles Scribner's Sons, 1948

[3] William C. Rhoden, *$40 Million Slaves. The Rise, Fall and Redemption of the Black Athlete*. New York: Crown Publishers, 2006

The Dana article went on to say:

> Less than a year ago Peter Jackson (the black heavyweight champion from Australia) could have whipped the world—Corbett, Fitzsimmons, but the white race is saved from having at the head of pugilism a Negro ....[4]

Newspapers of the day were filled with racist drawings of black prizefighters, grossly exaggerating features and printing derogatory descriptions such as "gorilla-like," "coon," "shine," "dusky," and "skin as black as printer's ink," while occasionally using the term "a white heart" to describe a black man who they felt was particularly kind-hearted and caring toward his fellow man. In those days, the white press typically portrayed black fighters in a very primitive and unflattering manner. It was not unusual for quotes from black fighters to be printed using language such as "dem," "dat," or "dere," instead of "them," "that," or "there." As a result the reader will notice, throughout this book, a number of passages where newspapers quote Sam and other black men speaking in that manner. I made a conscious decision to include quotes exactly as they appeared in print at that time. Sam was not a highly educated individual, but he certainly was not as poorly spoken as he was often portrayed by the press.

A number of widely believed myths are also apparent in historical quotes. For example, many individuals believed that the skulls of black men were thicker than their white counterparts, making it difficult to hurt them with blows to the head. And yet, for some reason, they were believed to be more susceptible to blows to the stomach.

This was the social environment during Sam's fighting career, 1902-1926. It was next to impossible for a black man to obtain an opportunity to fight for a world championship. There were some notable exceptions: George Dixon held the featherweight title for most of the 1890s, Joe Walcott the welterweight title from December of 1901 to April of 1903, and the great black lightweight Joe Gans held that division's crown from 1902-1908, but the lower weight classes didn't carry the same level of esteem. Granting a black man an opportunity to win a title at one of those weights, while not favorably looked upon,

---

[4] Arthur R. Ashe, Jr., *A Hard Road To Glory. A History of The African American Athlete 1619-1918.* New York: Amistad Press, 1993

was not considered grossly offensive. The heavyweight champion of the world was considered the greatest fighting man in the world.

In 1908, Jack Johnson overcame those obstacles and became the first black heavyweight of the world when he defeated Canadian-born heavyweight Tommy Burns. Johnson worked hard to get the opportunity: he was granted a chance at the title only after chasing the champion across a number of continents and finally cornering him in Australia, where a local promoter offered Burns a tremendous sum of money to defend his title. Burns could not refuse.

Burns was later chastised by many Americans, including former heavyweight champion John L. Sullivan, for foolishly granting Johnson the chance to fight for the title. Unfortunately, Johnson's subsequent behavior—thumbing his nose at white society, cavorting with and marrying white women—served to strengthen the color barrier. Consequently other professional black fighters of the day were often denied opportunities to compete.

Making matters worse, during his reign as heavyweight champion Johnson himself—with one exception—refused to fight men of his own race. Publicly, he claimed that a match between two black men wouldn't draw well. Privately, Johnson admitted that there were plenty of other, easier "white hopes" for him to fight and that he had no desire to risk his title against Langford, who he felt had a chance to win against anybody.

There was certainly no other boxer during this period who deserved a chance to fight for a world championship more than Sam Langford. The fact that Sam fought at such a high level and from 1905 to 1926 *without* receiving that opportunity speaks volumes concerning the social climate black boxers had to contend with in those days.

When I began to research Langford's career I came to realize that not only was he one of the game's greatest fighters of all time, but he was also one of its most colorful. There were all those wonderful nicknames that were hung upon him, "Old Ho Ho," "The Boston Bone Crusher," "The Weymouth Wizard," and of course the most famous of all "The Boston Tar Baby." And he called his shots long before a precocious young man by the name of Cassius Clay burst upon the boxing scene.

Sam officially fought hundreds of bouts over his twenty-four year career, and it is likely he fought many more that went unrecorded. Standing no more than 5'7" inches tall and weighing between 170-180 pounds in his prime, Sam routinely met and defeated taller and bigger fighters all over the world. He became recognized as the heavyweight champion of England, Australia, and Mexico before blindness finally forced his retirement from the ring at age forty. He never received the opportunity to fight for another world title after his fight with Joe Gans.

Sam came from humble beginnings in the Canadian province of Nova Scotia. His mother died when he was only twelve, and his father, a stern disciplinarian, made his living working a modest farm. Sam received very little in the way of formal education before running away from home at age thirteen.

He found work wherever he could, ultimately bumming his way to the city of Boston. There, as fate would have it, he would eventually gain employment performing various duties for a pharmacist who operated a small boxing gymnasium. It was there that Sam received his first instruction as a fighter and found his calling.

In many ways Sam never really grew up. He loved life and was always in search of a good time. Once he began making money in the fight business he indulged his fancies for flashy clothing, jewelry, and long black cigars. Eventually, he developed an appetite for alcohol, automobiles, and gambling, whether it was dice, cards, or playing the horses. Confiding to one of his trainers that he didn't expect to live a long life, Sam spent his money as fast as it came in.

At the same time, he was extremely generous and considerate toward others. And when the money was gone, he was perfectly content, so long as he could pay for food and basic shelter, with a little bit left over for his tobacco and gin. There are some who believe that Sam's happy-go-lucky attitude was more of an act than a characteristic. But there were just too many reporters and others involved in the fight game who knew him well and described him as the former for me to believe that. With the exception of a charge of domestic violence, I uncovered nothing that would indicate otherwise.

While writing Langford's biography I found that separating fact from fiction was impossible in some cases. For example, most Langford fans are probably well aware of the story of how Sam agreed to carry a particular opponent only to have that individual start to take advantage of the situation. When the next round began, Sam came out and extended his hand to the opponent as is customary prior to the final round. "But this isn't the final round," his surprised opponent said. "It is for you," Sam reportedly replied, and then proceeded to knock out his wide-eyed opponent. It's a great story, and one that I believe is true. However, during my research I found that particular story connected to no fewer than four different opponents. Unable to determine for sure whether the story was true, and if so, to which opponent it applied, I felt I had no choice but to leave it out.

Then there's another story about how one of his frequent opponents, Bill Tate, reportedly bragged to *New York World* sportswriter Hype Igoe that he was Sam's master and could flatten him any time he wanted. It's said that Sam learned of this and developed a plan. Allegedly, when he followed Tate into the ring for their next fight, instead of going to his corner he walked over to a point about three feet in front of Tate's stool and stopped. Without looking at Tate, Sam stared at the canvas in front of him. Then he stopped, smiled, and motioned for his second who quickly produced a tape measure for Sam. Sam placed it on the spot he'd picked out and, with his second's assistance, stretched it out to a length of 6'2", which was Tate's height. The task completed, Sam looked Tate in the eye and then up and down. Then he looked back at the measurement on the canvas and back up at Tate. Sam was telling Tate and everyone else exactly where he was going to drop Tate. According to the story, Sam came out like a house afire, and poor Tate couldn't get over the transformation in his foe. In the fifth round, Sam pulled Tate into a clinch and let him know that he thought he was about ready for the spot he'd picked out for him. Then as they came out of the clinch, he hit him with a left hook to the body, followed with a right uppercut that sent him crashing to the boards in the general area that Sam had measured out for him. Tate was counted out. Again, another great story, but if it really happened I wasn't able to confirm it in any of the newspaper accounts of Sam's many fights with Bill Tate. So it wasn't included either.

The omission of a few stories like these shouldn't matter much though, because what is known about Sam's life and boxing career, from his own mouth and from those who knew him personally or fought against him, and from those who covered his contests for newspapers throughout the world, provided more than enough material to tell the story of one of the greatest and most colorful fighters in boxing history.

Sam's story is typical of the injustices and discriminatory practices that blacks in general suffered during the early 20th century, including prizefighters. But the injustices that Sam suffered in his chosen field of endeavor were even more so when one considers his greatness and the level of esteem to which he was held by his counterparts and the most knowledgeable parties within the sport.

Despite the fact that Sam ended up blind and broke, I am convinced that the statements he made to various individuals during the latter part of his life about being perfectly content with his lot in life were genuine.

I leave it up to you to decide for yourself based upon the ensuing story. It's a story that is long overdue. I hope that you will enjoy reading it as much as I did writing it.

SAM LANGFORD'S BOYHOOD HOME
1950s
CAROL DOYLE COLLECTION

"HE USED TO BEAT THE HELL OUT OF ME WHEN HE CAME HOME DRUNK."
~ SAM LANGFORD

CHAPTER 1

WEYMOUTH FALLS, NOVA SCOTIA

His money and eyesight were long gone, but Sam was a millionaire in memories. Yes, old Sam had his memories... and what memories they were! Over the course of a long boxing career he had traveled the world and fought some of the greatest names in fistic history, including Stanley Ketchel, Joe Walcott, Joe Jennette, Sam McVea, Harry Wills, "Tiger" Flowers, the great lightweight champion Joe Gans, and Jack Johnson.

To his dying day, Sam believed that if he had been granted an opportunity to fight Johnson for the heavyweight crown he would have defeated him. He wasn't alone. Many respected individuals in the boxing fraternity thought the knowledge Sam had acquired during the pair's only bout (when Sam was a young twenty-year-old) and the ring skills and physical maturation he gained later would have enabled Sam to turn the tables on Johnson. If only he had received the chance.

Sam Edgar Langford entered the world fists clenched on March 4, 1886, born to Charlotte and Robert Langford in the small community of Weymouth Falls, Nova Scotia. The actual date of Sam's birth was often a subject of debate in later years, probably because he began fighting at such an early age. Many people assumed he must be older, but the man who became his fight manager, Joe Woodman, ultimately tracked down Sam's birth certificate in Nova Scotia and confirmed the date.

Sam's mother was Charlotte Langford, a tiny woman standing just 5'0" tall. Sam may have inherited his fighting spirit from his father,

Robert, a big strapping man, 6'3" tall and known to possess a quick temper. Robert was a mariner and well known as a scrapper. Many residents of Weymouth Falls were fond of saying that Robert Langford would rather fight than eat. There is evidence that a Weymouth heavyweight fighter named Michael McGowan died from a head injury suffered in a fight with Robert.[1]

The Langford family's path to Nova Scotia can be traced back to the American War of Independence. During the war the leader of the British forces, Sir Henry Clinton, promised freedom to any slaves who would flee their masters and fight for the British king. Over 2,000 black slaves took him up on the offer. Escapees from plantations joined the British Army in New York City to battle against their oppressors. When the war ended in 1783, the British soldiers evacuated New York by ship, taking the black soldiers with them. Thousands of people loyal to the British crown left for Europe, England, and other communities in British North America. Nova Scotia was one of those destinations. Weymouth was one of many coastal towns that received a large number of settlers.[2] It was around this time that Sam's great-grandfather, William Langford (enslaved to Captain Langford of Shrewsbury, New Jersey), is said to have escaped and sailed to Nova Scotia in one of the captain's "borrowed" boats.[3]

Fishing was the primary industry in Weymouth, but the lush and fertile landscape also proved an ideal place for raising crops such as apples. In 1896, S. Fawes Smith of Philadelphia, Pennsylvania built a pulp mill near Weymouth. It became the mainstay of the local economy for almost half a century. The sale of slaves took place in Canada, just as it did in the United States. It wasn't until England abolished slavery in the colonies in the 1830s that immigration to Nova Scotia for the purpose of slavery ended entirely, and it wasn't until the start of the 19th century that those sales disappeared in Nova Scotia.

As late as 1949, sociologist Ruth Wilson described Canadian racial prejudice as varying in the same degrees as patterns found in Mississippi and New York. She identified Nova Scotia as the Canadian Province with the greatest concentration of blacks and also the one

---

[1] J.W. Philbrick, compiler. *Descendants of Michael McGowan of Liverpool, Queens County, Nova Scotia.* (Natick, Massachusetts, 1973)
[2] Martyn Franklin, talk given in series titled *Canadian Athletes*, 25 Jan 1948
[3] *Digby Courier*, 22 July 1938

with the most discrimination.[4] A dual school system for blacks and whites was maintained in Nova Scotia until the late 1950s, although some exceptions were made. The environment of Sam's youth in Nova Scotia was in many ways not that much different than the one he encountered later when he migrated to Boston, Massachusetts.

Sam was the sixth of seven children. He had three brothers: Charles (1879); William, who went by the name Walter (1883); and Robert, who went by the name Amos (1888); and three sisters: Annie (1874), Sophia (1877), and Ellen May (1881). At his full height of only 5'6½" inches, Sam was the tallest of the boys. Later in life he would claim that his sisters were 6'0" or taller.[5]

The family lived in a small bungalow-style house, comprised of two ground floor rooms and an attic where the entire family slept. Sam didn't receive a lot of schooling and said that was the case for many folks in Weymouth at that time. Education was viewed as an interference with work.

Sam was only twelve years old when his mother passed away in October of 1898. Subsequently, Sam was turned loose from school to look for work and his older sisters assumed more responsibility around the household. This included giving direction to Sam. He found it difficult to accept this "bossing" from his older sisters, and the loss of his mother undoubtedly created a void that could not be filled.[6]

Not much later, while running with some slightly older boys Sam was involved in the theft of some eggs. The group was arrested and the bigger boys all said that Sam had given them the eggs. The judge's verdict against Sam was a $15.00 fine or fifteen days in jail. Sam's father had the money but decided Sam needed to learn a lesson, so he refused to pay the fine. When Sam's fifteen day sentence was up, he found his father waiting for him. "I guess there will be no more stealing," said his father. Sam readily agreed. He had no desire to experience the inside of a jail cell again.[7]

However, Sam continued to struggle at home. His father, who surely had his hands full raising the children without a mother, was a stern

---

[4] *The Nova Scotia Historical Quarterly* Vol. 4, No. 3, September 1974

[5] *Halifax Herald*, 12 August 1924

[6] 1891 census, Nova Scotia, District no. 31, Digby, Subdistrict #22, Weymouth Bridge, p. 7, no. 24

[7] *MacLeans*, February 1955

disciplinarian and Sam, like many young boys, was prone to getting himself in trouble. When this occurred he suffered consequences at the hands of his father. Also, according to Sam his father drank a lot and used to "beat the hell out of [him] when he came home drunk."[8]

Reports vary as to Sam's exact age at the time of the significant falling out with his father, but it seems directly related to an incident that occurred when Sam was about twelve years old. The family was in need of some groceries so Robert sent young Sam to town with some cash and the specifics as to what he was to purchase. Along the way, Sam met up with some other boys, started playing with them, and forgot all about the groceries. When he returned home empty handed, his father gave him a whipping. For Sam, this had become all too frequent. The next morning he took his father's oxen into the woods, where he had been sent to cut up some logs, but instead of tackling the job he simply tied up the oxen and headed for the nearby town of Weymouth.[9]

Eventually, Sam ended up in Digby, some twenty miles away from Weymouth. He found a job there, working through the winter as an ox-driver and log-hauler. It paid $1.25 per week plus room and board. When spring arrived, Sam returned on foot to Weymouth, but not to home. Quoted later, his father would say, "The home was here for him, but he didn't see fit to come back, and I didn't ask him. He could please himself."[10]

For a number of months, Sam took up odd jobs, eating and sleeping when and where he could, sometimes in barns and other times aboard various vessels that were in port at the time. Next, he ventured to Grand Manan where he stayed and fished for a couple of months, finding work first as a cabin boy aboard a haddock fishing vessel named *Sally Ellen,* and then as a sailor on a steamer carrying lumber. The last job came to an abrupt end when the vessel was wrecked during a storm off the New Brunswick coast. The crew survived only by virtue of the lifeboats. This experience helped convince Sam that the life of a mariner was not for him.[11]

Sam returned to the woods of Nova Scotia, drifting from one place to another, until he found employment as a kitchen helper in a log-

---

[8] newspaper clipping, unknown source
[9] *MacLeans,* February 1955
[10] *Halifax Chronicle,* 22 June 1909
[11] Martyn Franklin, talk given in series titled *Canadian Athletes,* Jan 25, 1948

ging camp. He remained in the logging camp for the next three years, working at a rate of $5.00 per month plus room and board. Towards the latter part of the third year he met Dr. Blodgett, who practiced at the Massachusetts General Hospital in Boston. The doctor visited the lumber camp often and ultimately offered Sam a job on his farm in Lincoln, New Hampshire. Weighing the offer against his immediate prospects, Sam accepted.

Each morning Sam would take the doctor by horse and buggy to the train, go back to work on the farm during the day, and then meet the train to pick up the doctor. While working for the doctor Sam heard about Bob Fitzsimmons defeating Jim Corbett for the heavyweight championship of the world. Sam made a connection between Bob Fitzsimmons and his own father, Bob Langford. He always liked the name Bob, and he started telling the other boys who worked on the farm that a man named Bob or the son of any man named Bob, could whip almost anybody. One of the boys decided to challenge Sam. While the two were standing together in the barn the boy placed a chip on his own shoulder, challenging Sam to knock it off. Sam did, the boy punched him, and Sam hit him back. The short contest ended after Sam's opponent suffered a bloodied nose and blackened eyes.

After word of the fight spread among the other boys on the farm, some of the older and bigger boys began to pick on Sam. Sam responded with his fists. He found he enjoyed fighting, like his father.

The doctor, however, didn't find it amusing. One day the doctor found Sam fighting another boy behind the barn:

"What's this all about?" asked the doctor.

"Oh, we're just playing a little," Sam said.

"So you're the cause of all these beaten up boys eh," said the doctor. "Well you're all through playing around here. Pack your clothes and get."[12]

Sam walked to the town of Cambridge, Massachusetts, where he found a job working in a brickyard among a number of tough boys who told him that nobody could work in the brickyard unless he proved he was a fighter. That suited Sam fine. He fought anyone put before him and more often than not came out on top.

---

[12] *Halifax Herald*, 12 August 1924

One day he broke a brickyard rule about fighting during work hours, the boss caught him, and Sam found himself unemployed again. He bounced around briefly from job to job. He worked for a time selling newspapers on the street and found he had to fight to keep his papers, and to hang onto the money he got for selling them. He also picked up some spending money grooming horses in a stable where he slept.

Eventually, one of his friends at the brickyard told him he might be able to find work cutting down trees in the woods of New Hampshire. Sam worked there until he was again fired for fighting. From there he hiked to Boston, where he could get a room for thirty-five or forty cents and an occasional meal from his sister who lived there. Sam didn't know it at the time, but Boston was to become the town of his destiny. It was 1901, and he was fifteen years old.

"FIGHT THAT MAN THE WAY YOU DID THE ONE IN MY SALOON SAM, YOU CAN BEAT HIM THAT WAY."

~MIKE FOLEY

CHAPTER 2

CHAMPION OF CAMBRIDGE STREET

Jobs were hard to come by and Sam's need for food and shelter drove him back to the docks. He even considered working at sea again, but there was no work available.

Passing through a tough Irish section of town, Sam asked a bartender standing outside of a saloon if he could use a hard working boy. The bartender, named Mike Foley, gave Sam a job cleaning the saloon, provided him with a place to sleep, food to eat, and a little spending money to boot.

One day Mike had to leave the saloon to attend a funeral, and he left Sam in charge. Shortly thereafter a stocky fellow walked in and in quick order finished off a number of beers. He then got up and started to walk out without paying. Sam moved quickly to catch him before he reached the door, and asked for the money.

The customer pushed Sam away and replied, "You don't belong to the bartender's union. You're just a scab. I don't pay scabs."

He started for the door again as Mike walked in. Mike asked Sam what the ruckus was about. Sam told him that the customer owed Mike for the beer.

Mike, deciding that Sam needed to learn how to fight his own battles, grinned and said, "Sam, he doesn't owe me anything. If any money is owing it's owing to you, and you have got to collect it if you can." So Sam turned to the customer and demanded, "Give me the money."

Unknown to Sam, this fellow was considered the undisputed champion of Cambridge Street. He weighed in the neighborhood of 170 pounds, and he had no intention of paying Sam for the beers. As soon as Sam demanded payment the second time, the "champ" took a swing at him. Sam avoided the punch and landed one of his own on his foe's chin: down he went. The "champ" got up and rushed Sam and Sam hit him again, dropping him for the second time. He climbed to his feet only to be deposited on his seat for a third time. Sam told him to get up for more.

The ex-"champ" looked up sadly at Sam while reaching for his wallet and said, "I don't think I'll get up for awhile. I can pay you just as well from here as I can standing up. How much do you have coming?"

Sam told him, and the ex-champ paid the bill, got up, and walked out.

Mike laughed himself silly and asked Sam how old he was. "I'm fifteen," replied Sam. Mike couldn't get over it. Sam had to weigh all of 125 pounds, and he had just soundly whipped a grown man of 170 pounds who had been considered the toughest man in the local area. Sam had become the new champion of Cambridge Street.[13]

Unfortunately for the new champion, this job also soon disappeared when business slowed. He found himself back on the street, struggling to find work again. It was becoming more and more difficult to put together enough money for two square meals per day. However, that didn't prevent Sam from sharing what little he had when a small, yellow, mangy-looking dog crossed his path one day.

The little dog immediately became Sam's new companion. He followed Sam everywhere as Sam continued his search for work, nourishment, and a place to sleep at night. In return for the companionship, whenever Sam was able to rustle up something to eat he was always sure to share a small part of it with his newfound friend.

A few weeks passed and Sam woke up one morning stiff and sore after a restless November night spent on a park bench. He found a newspaper and read a story about the results of a fight that had taken place the night before at a local club. Sam decided the club was as good a place as any to approach next in his search for work. So after a quick stretch to work the kinks out of his stiffened body, off he went, his little yellow mutt trailing close behind.

---

[13] *Halifax Herald*, 13 August 1924

When they reached the club, Sam knocked sharply on the door and awaited a response. After a short time, a janitor named Dowzer Dowling opened the door and asked what he wanted. Putting on his best face and standing up straight, as the little dog sat at attention at his side, Sam looked Dowling in the eye and said, "I want a job doing anything. But most of all I would certainly love to clean up the floors of your building."[14] He was hoping that a few of those customers attending the fight the night before might have accidentally dropped some loose change, which he and his companion could use to buy some food.

Dowzer quickly sized up Sam and told him to sit tight, that he'd let him know shortly. Then he shut the door on Sam.

Not much time passed before the door opened again, and Sam got his first look at the club's owner, a Mr. Joe Woodman. In addition to running the fight club, Mr. Woodman also owned a drugstore business. It must have seemed like an insignificant meeting at the time, but it represented the beginning of a long and mutually beneficial relationship.

Joe took in the pitiful sight before him. Sam was wearing an old, ragged, oversized overcoat with a rope tied at the waist to hold it closed. His pants were worn and baggy, his hat badly frayed, his toes showed through the end of his shoes, and he looked like he hadn't eaten in days. To complete the picture, seated at Sam's feet was a scrawny little dog, whining and nosing here and there in search of a scrap of food. Joe couldn't remember the last time he'd seen a sorrier sight. He asked Sam if he was a good worker. Sam told him he was and that he wouldn't be sorry if he gave Sam a try. Joe indicated he'd do just that, but after taking another hard look at Sam he asked him when he last ate. Sam told him it had been a couple of days. Joe gave him fifty cents and told him to go get himself something to eat before he began working.

As Joe closed the door again, Sam glanced up and down the street in search of a place to get something to eat. Just a few doors away he spied a bakery. So he and his little yellow dog ventured into the bakery to see what they could get with their newfound wealth. After

---

[14] *Halifax Herald*, 14 August 1924

careful deliberation, Sam chose a large bag of broken cakes for 25 cents. Back at the club, Sam found a glass for himself and a pail for his friend, filled each with water, and divided up the cakes between them. That was a meal Sam would never forget. After going two days without food, Sam thought those cakes were the best thing he'd ever eaten. His little friend apparently felt the same way, quickly wolfing down his share.

Sam had the place all cleaned up when Mr. Woodman returned later in the day, and he overheard Dowzer tell Mr. Woodman what a good worker Sam was. Mr. Woodman asked Sam where he was living. When Sam told him that he slept wherever he could, but mostly in parks, Woodman asked him if he'd like a job working as a porter for the club. He also offered to let Sam sleep in the club at night. Woodman thought it would be a good idea to have the boy serve as a pseudo night watchman for the club in addition to his daily duties. A wrestling mat in the corner of the gym would serve as his bed. It might not have been as comfortable as a mattress and box spring, but it sure beat sleeping outside in the elements.

Each day Sam performed a variety of tasks as outlined by Dowzer and Mr. Woodman, including cleaning and helping set up and break down for shows. He was even called upon occasionally to serve as a sparring partner when nobody else was available.

One evening, a fighter scheduled on the evening's fight card failed to appear, and Sam asked Woodman for a chance to take the fighter's place. Joe told him that before he could box with professionals he'd need to learn how to fight. If he was serious, Joe would arrange for him to box at the Roanoke Athletic Club with amateurs closer to his own ability and experience.

True to his word, Joe cleared the way for Sam to fight on an amateur card and even provided him with the required entry fee and some fighting gear. He didn't figure on Sam as much of a prospect though, and didn't bother to go watch him that first night. Sam won a few bouts that evening and was awarded a watch by the officials for his efforts. The next day, he surprised Woodman by showing up wearing a new watch. Sam was disappointed to learn that Mr. Woodman hadn't seen him fight, but Joe promised Sam he'd attend the following week. Joe was unable to attend the following week, but that didn't prevent Sam from picking up more victories and another watch. He was even happier about the watches when he found that they could be sold for as much as $17.00 to $20.00 each.

Enjoying fighting, and figuring there were more watches and money to be won, Sam decided he could afford to spend some of the money he'd earned. He bought himself a fancy new suit, a pair of bright yellow shoes, socks, a cane, two pink shirts, suspenders, some ties, and a derby hat. He also paid two weeks in advance for a hotel room, and he went out and celebrated with a big chicken dinner.

After living high on the hog and not showing his face around the club for a few days, Sam reappeared in his brightly colored new attire. Despite his pugilistic success he wasn't quite ready to give up his day job, and he resumed his normal duties at the club.

A young bantamweight by the name of Jimmy Walsh, who would go on to claim the American version of the bantamweight title and ultimately capture the featherweight title from Johnny Kilbane in 1912, was also fighting out of Boston at this time. Sam expressed his desire to become a fighter to Walsh's manager, Eddie Keevin. Eddie agreed to let Sam work with Walsh.

Relating the story to a reporter in 1911, Walsh claimed that he took it to an inexperienced Langford, landing punches at will against the game but awkward fighter. But Sam was determined and kept coming back for more. Over the course of several months Walsh showed him how to hit, feint, and get inside of punches.

As Sam's amateur success continued, Joe began to pay closer attention. He decided that he should give Sam a chance to fight in his own club, so he matched him for an amateur fight with a fighter named Jack McVicker. They were to fight three rounds. On January 13, 1902, Sam entered the ring in Woodman's club for the first time. His old boss, saloon keeper Mike Foley, was there in his corner for the occasion.

Years later, in an interview Sam would say that when he went up against McVicker that day he ate more leather than he had ever seen in his life in those first two rounds.

> "You see," said Sam, "I had been trying to box McVicker, and I couldn't get in a decent punch against the more experienced man. I thought I was supposed to box scientifically, and I was not as advanced as McVicker in that regard."

When Sam returned to his corner after the second round he told his former boss, Mike Foley, that he was a beaten man.

"Fight that man the way you did the one in my saloon Sam. You can beat him that way," said Foley. "Forget all the scientific boxing and tear into him."

"Is that rough business allowed here?" Sam responded in surprise.

"Hell yes, it is," replied Foley.

When the bell rang for the third round, McVicker found himself fighting a new man. Sam threw caution to the wind and initiated some spirited exchanges that earned him the decision. He had learned a valuable lesson. Sam would say years later, "I thought you had to be clever to win. Man! Talk about being green."[15]

He followed up this win with two more three-round amateur victories, including another over McVicker.

Those successes encouraged Woodman to declare Sam a professional, and he matched him for a longer contest on April 11, 1902, with McVicker again. However, before this contest, Woodman had a few things to say to Sam. He felt that Sam hadn't beaten McVicker as impressively as he should have in their two previous three-round encounters.

"This business of winning decisions isn't enough. Stop being so nice with these fellas. Knock em dead, that's the thing. That's what you said you were going to do. Now I'll get you McVicker again, and this time you go out and knock him out."

That's exactly what happened. Sam knocked McVicker out in the sixth round, earning $25.00 for his first fight as a professional.

"Now you're doing something, knock em out, that's the thing. And remember, the quicker you do it the less work you have to do. Never work any harder than you have to," said Joe.[16]

Shortly after that fight, there was an accident at Woodman's boxing club. A young boy died after one of the fights, and the club was closed. Sam lost his job. He heard that a New Hampshire lumber camp was hiring, so he hurried on up there without telling Woodman that he was leaving town.

---

[15] *San Francisco Chronicle*, 18 January 1927
[16] *Halifax Herald*, 15 August 1924

Sam landed a job in the lumber camp and worked there through the summer. That November the weather turned cold and Sam remembered what it was that he disliked most about the lumber business. He packed up and returned to Boston where he looked up Joe Woodman in his drugstore. There wasn't much difference in his appearance from the first time Joe had seen him, except that this time there was no scrawny yellow dog with him. Somewhere along the line the two had parted company.

"Where have you been?" asked Joe.

Sam explained that he had gone to New Hampshire to work in a lumber camp.

"Well, the next time you decide to take a run out let me know. I think you have the makings of a good fighter, and if you stick around here and don't go running your fool head off, maybe I can get you some fights and make you some money."

That sounded fine to Sam. "Are you going to manage me?" he asked Joe.

"Yes," replied Joe, "Somebody's got to stop you from running into the woods whenever you get spring fever."[17]

Joe would be Sam's manager for the next fifteen years, though unofficially they would remain connected for much longer. Sam's fighting career would take them to many parts of the world including Canada, England, France, Australia, Panama, and the Argentine. They never wrote out a contract, but they agreed that Joe's cut would be 25% of Sam's ring earnings. As far as Sam was concerned, it was Joe's job to line up opponents and Sam's job to knock them out.

Around this time, veteran boxer George Byers, a black middleweight considered a serious title contender only a few years earlier, gave Sam his first real instruction on how to hit. Sam was anxious to please Joe Woodman by knocking out his opponents, but he found he couldn't seem to hit them just right. He worried that Joe would give up on him if he didn't start producing knockouts.

One day, George noticed Sam looking worried and asked what was the problem. Sam explained that he didn't seem to be able to put enough steam behind his punches to put his opponents down. George told him he wasn't setting when he hit. He then offered to give Sam a few lessons, and Sam quickly accepted.

---

[17] *Halifax Herald,* 15 August 1924

Those few lessons turned into many. George showed Sam how to trick his opponent into a position where he could hit him. He showed Sam how to "set" in an instant and how to put all his force into his blows. He showed him how to throw powerful short punches. For the first time, Sam also learned something about the art of defense. Before George started working with him, Sam would just wade into the other fighter slinging leather and catching it in return, until somebody dropped or the fight was over. George showed Sam ways to avoid getting hit, and he told Sam:

> "Always remember that the best thing in this fight game is to not get hit. It doesn't matter if you can hit hard enough to knock down a building if you can't avoid getting hit. Because how do you know that the other fella ain't gonna knock you down before you can hit him? Always remember, don't get hit any more often than you can avoid."[18]

Sam resumed his fighting career on January 15, 1903, winning a second-round knockout against Arthur Pratt. Sam fought another twenty-six bouts that year! It would have been more, but Joe wasn't able to find more men who wanted to fight Sam. He fought for any kind of purse Joe could get for him, the highest being one hundred dollars, a figure he fought for twice that year.

Most of Sam's early professional bouts took place in and around Boston, usually at the Armory Athletic Association where billiard tables were removed to make way for ringside chairs and bleacher seats. The fights were primarily attended by club members and their friends. This was the norm in the early part of the 20th century: there were small clubs all over the country, and the vast majority of fights took place in these venues.

Sam found he wasn't able to correctly apply the hitting lessons he'd learned from George right away. He'd win the fights alright, but he couldn't quite hit them hard enough to put them away. Eventually, he began to get the knack of it, especially in regards to throwing the left hook the way George taught him. Results came with repetition.

It wasn't until the night of November 25, 1904, in a fight against Tommy Sullivan in Marlboro, Massachusetts, that Sam really finally learned the knack of hitting. Sam had taken this fight in the first place

---

[18] *Halifax Herald*, 15 August 1924

as a last minute replacement when another fighter by the name of Jack Blackburn took ill.

> "I'll never forget that night," said Joe, his manager. "Quite by accident, Sam snapped his wrist as he delivered a right to Sullivan's jaw and at the same time leaned into the punch. No one was more surprised than Sam when Sullivan dropped to the canvas unconscious. From then on he was the killer he wanted to be."[19]

Sam suffered a couple of setbacks in the ring in 1903. The first of those was against a fighter by the name of Andy Watson. Nicknamed "Professor" because of his skill, Watson's earnings in the ring enabled him to purchase a building in Boston where he opened an athletic club. The popularity of his gym and his reputation as a trainer eventually led to an appointment as chief boxing instructor at Harvard. He was a seasoned veteran when Sam faced him for the first time on April 20th of 1903, and that experience carried him to a twelve-round popular newspaper decision.[20]

Sam's other setback of note during 1903 was against a lightweight by the name of Danny Duane on June 26th. With all his success that year, Sam was gaining notoriety around the Boston area. When a couple of New Yorkers heard some Bostonians bragging about him, they claimed that they had just the man who could whip Sam. Joe Woodman accepted the challenge.

Danny advised he wouldn't fight Sam unless there was a side bet of $500. Although Joe had never seen him fight, he had enough confidence in Sam's abilities that he didn't hesitate to make the bet.

As Duane climbed through the ropes, Sam remembered looking over, seeing a nice looking boy, and thinking what a shame it was that he was going to have to mess his face up. However, once the opening bell rang Sam found he was in the ring with a whirlwind. Duane was so fast that Sam could hardly follow him. He was peppered with punches that he found himself unable to effectively counter. Sam lost both the decision and Joe's $500 side bet.

Sam never saw Duane again. Danny only fought three more times, including a second-round knockout victory over Jack Blackburn in

---

[19] John Jarrett, *Dynamite Gloves* (London: Robson Publishing, 2001)
[20] Kevin Smith, *The Sundowners: The History of the Black Prizefighter, Volume II, Part 3, 1870-1930* (unpublished manuscript)

March of 1904. There is a story that Danny's best friend, also a fighter, fought a fellow in New York not too long thereafter and, when the other fellow died after the fight, both Danny and his friend decided to quit the ring. In any case, Duane hung his gloves up early in 1905, and Sam never did get a rematch with the fighter he called the fastest man he ever fought in his life.

Two weeks later, Sam defeated Belfield Walcott in a twenty-round decision. At the time, Belfield's brother, Joe Walcott, was the welterweight champion of the world. The brothers sparred frequently with one another, and Sam's performance against Belfield in 1903 and again on January 27, 1904, as well as those against other notable fighters such as Jack Blackburn and Joe Gans, no doubt helped set the stage for a September 1904 pairing between Sam and the great Joe Walcott. Sam and Belfield also became friends, and Belfield, who had learned his boxing tricks from his brother Joe, passed them along to Sam. This knowledge came in handy when he eventually fought the welterweight champion.

GEORGE BYERS

CA. 1890

AUTHOR'S COLLECTION

"A WONDER OF WONDERS, THAT WAS JOE GANS."
~SAM LANGFORD

CHAPTER 3

JOE GANS "THE OLD MASTER"

The highlight of 1903 for Sam was a very surprising fifteen-round decision victory on December 8th over the great lightweight champion, Joe Gans, a.k.a. "The Old Master." Gans, born Joseph Gaines in Baltimore, Maryland on November 25, 1874, was considered a complete fighter: highly skilled at blocking punches, counter punching, feinting, and delivering a wallop with either hand. Fighting men of his day sang his praises. Even old John L. Sullivan begrudgingly declared that Gans was the greatest lightweight the ring ever saw.

On December 4th, it was announced that Gans had accepted Sam's recent challenge to meet in a fifteen-round bout, on the condition that in addition to the purse there would be a side bet of $500. Once word got out that the match was set, it seemed that everyone Sam ran into felt the need to tell him what a terrific hitter and fighter Gans was. That didn't have much effect on Sam however, because at the time he didn't know enough about Gans to be overly concerned. In fact, in a newspaper interview years later, Sam said that he considered himself lucky to have been so ignorant of Gans' greatness at the time; because when it came time to face Gans he was much calmer than he would have been otherwise.

Joe Gans had become the first African American to win a world championship when he captured the world lightweight championship crown in 1902 with a one-round knockout of Frank Erne. Two years earlier Gans had lost a twelfth-round knockout to Erne. George Dixon, another black man, had won a world championship earlier, but he was a Canadian citizen. Gans held the title until 1908, finally relinquishing it in the seventeenth round of a bout with "Battling" Nelson. At that time, Gans was already battling against the early stages of tuberculosis, a fight he would eventually lose on August 10, 1910, when only thirty-five years old.

In 1903, Gans was having difficulty getting fights with men his weight, so he began fighting slightly heavier men in the welterweight division. Sam was seventeen, while Joe was twenty-nine years old and tipped the scales at 131½ pounds.

Regardless of the outcome Gans would receive a fee of $700 while Sam would accept $250. It was agreed that the men would weigh no more than 138 pounds.[1] On the day of the fight Gans weighed 135¼ pounds, while Sam came in two pounds over at 140 pounds.[2] One of the conditions for the fight was that Sam could not exceed the agreed upon limit without having to pay a forfeit, rumored to be anywhere from $200 to $500. Luckily for Sam, Gans refused to collect the agreed upon forfeit despite the urging of his manager, Al Herford. Still, that extra weight would come back to haunt Sam.

Sam entered the contest in excellent shape. Gans on the other hand, made the mistake of underestimating the seventeen-year-old. His friends had convinced him that Sam would give him little trouble. Gans agreed and figured he would put Sam away within a couple of rounds. He openly boasted that he would do so. Rumor has it that an overconfident Gans spent the night before playing cards and drinking while en route to Boston from Philadelphia, where he had engaged in a six-round bout against tough Dave Holly.

Gans opened up the match quickly, firing lightning jabs mixed with swift left hooks. Several of them landed, considerably shaking Sam. One hook staggered Sam, and Gans followed it up with a terrific right hand punch that landed full on Sam's mouth.

Gans continued to force the fight in the second and third rounds, as Sam focused on trying to avoid Gans' leads. Gans could hit alright, and he was clever. Years later, in a 1927 newspaper interview given to columnist Ed Hughes, Sam said that Gans showed him stuff he had never dreamed of before.

---

[1] *The Evening Times* (Pawtucket, R.I.), 4 December 1903
[2] *Boston Daily Globe*, 9 December 1903

"Gans was the coolest, calmest fighter I ever met, or saw. No matter what was happening to him he never lost his temper, never changed the expression on his face. Many fighters, when hurt, show it in their faces. Joe never did. Many fighters, when ready to hit, tighten their lips, half close their eyes, or give a tip-off in some way as to what's going to happen. Joe never did. A wonder of wonders, that was Joe Gans," said Sam.[3]

During the first three rounds, Sam kept his distance and avoided any infighting. It was in the third round that Sam began to realize that although Gans' punches were landing frequently, they were not seriously hurting him. Additionally, when the pair clinched or fought on the inside, Sam was encouraged to learn that he was a lot stronger than the champion.

In the fourth round, Gans launched a furious attack and battered Sam all about the ring. At one point Sam appeared ready to fall, but he managed to pull Joe into a clinch and hold on until the bell sounded. During the break, Sam's corner worked feverishly on him with smelling salts and a wet sponge to get him ready for the fifth session.

The seventeen-year-old Sam recovered quickly and came out strong for the beginning of the fifth. From this round on the tables turned. Sam became the aggressor. The much more experienced champion found himself having to dig deep into his bag of tricks to stand up to Sam's offensive tactics.

Though both fighters focused on landing blows to the head throughout the fight, Sam was the more successful of the two with body blows. When Sam landed one of the body blows, those at ringside could tell that Gans felt the effects.

As the contest progressed, there were a number of times when Gans appeared to be almost out on his feet, but Sam seemed content to play it safe and simply outpoint him in order to gain the victory by decision. He wisely avoided taking any unnecessary chances with Gans. Despite tiring badly as the fight progressed, Gans continued to display wonderful defense as he successfully slipped or blocked the majority of Sam's heavy punches.

When the fight was two-thirds along it was becoming apparent (to the delight of the hometown crowd) that Sam was winning more of the

---
[3] *San Francisco Chronicle*, 19 January 1927

rounds, and Gans might need a knockout to avoid defeat. *The Boston Globe* reporter covering the fight felt that after the third round Sam beat the champion in a manner that left no doubt to the crowd as to who was the better man.[4]

When the bell sounded to end the fight, Sam appeared to have won the majority of the rounds. Many felt Gans won both the first two and last two rounds. Some felt the fight was close enough to warrant a draw. When the verdict was received from the referee, the announcer raised his hand to silence the crowd and announced, 'The winner and new lightweight champion of the world, Sam Langford of Boston!" The crowd erupted with cheers. Gans later acknowledged his agreement with the decision and his regret for underestimating Sam.

Years later, Sam told the brilliant writer A.J. Liebling that once he was back in his dressing room he asked George Byers, the old middleweight who'd taught him how to hit harder, how he'd looked. Byers told him that he was strong but didn't know a thing.

In his book, *A Neutral Corner,* Liebling writes that rather than becoming offended by Byers' comment, Sam asked Byers how much he'd charge to teach him what he felt he needed to know. Byers said, "Ten dollars," and Sam paid it to him.

"And then what happened?" Liebling asked Sam.

"He taught me. He was right. I didn't know nothing. I used to chase and punch, hurt my hands on hard heads. After George taught me I made them come to me. I made them lead," replied Sam.

"How?" Liebling asked.

"If they didn't lead I'd run them out of the ring. When they led I'd hit them in the body. Then on the point of the chin. Not the jaw, the point of the chin. That's why I got such pretty hands today," said Sam.

A few hours later, flush from his victory, Sam celebrated his big win at a local cabaret with some of his friends. It was the very same establishment that Joe Gans had chosen as a place to nurse his wounds. Gans spied Sam first, from a few tables away. Without a moment's hesitation, he walked over to Sam's table and shook his hand saying:

---
[4] *Boston Globe,* 9 December 1903

"Boy, you're going to be a great fighter someday. You're the first man that ever puffed my lips. Take care of yourself, don't get a big head and nobody can keep you from being a champion."[5]

After telling Sam that he had no intention of fighting him again because he was too tough, he extended an offer to show him a few things in regards to how to hit. Gans told Sam that if he had already known what Gans planned to show him, Sam would have been able to win by knockout.

Sam had been extremely impressed with the skills that Gans had exhibited in the ring earlier that evening, so he gladly took Gans up on his offer. The two eventually got together and Joe spent an hour showing Sam his hitting faults, and how he could change them to hit more like Joe did. Sam would later say:

"In my opinion, Joe Gans was the greatest all around fighter, when you consider brains, boxing coolness, speed, and ability to take it and power to give. I learned more from him than any fighter I ever faced in my fight with him, and from the knowledge he shared with me afterwards."[6]

Sam's reign as lightweight champion was short lived. The day after the fight it was announced that the lightweight title still belonged to Gans by virtue of Sam's failure to scale down to the 135-pound lightweight limit. Victory was his, but the title had eluded him as a result of his failure to drop that last little bit of weight. It would be another 4½ years before Gans would eventually lose again, relinquishing his title to "Battling" Nelson on July 4, 1908.

The *Chicago Journal*, while noting that for several rounds Sam was a bit scared, published a lively account of the change that had come about. They wrote that after discovering that Gans couldn't hurt him, Sam gained confidence and soon set to work in so masterly a fashion "that Gans ran eleven miles around that ring and received the unholiest licking of the season." The *Journal* then proclaimed Sam "the real thing and the man they all want to see. Give him the credit due, black though he may be!"[7]

---

[5] *San Francisco Chronicle*, 19 January 1927
[6] *Halifax Herald*, 19 September 1924
[7] *Hamilton Spectator*, 10 December 1903

There was no rematch, despite the fact that Gans' manager badly wanted another crack at Sam and, a week later, offered a side bet of $1,000. Said Herford:

> "I do not wish to detract from his (Sam's) reputation, as he is a very good man. But he should not take credit for a thing which does not belong to him. Gans was not in as good shape as he has been in other important battles, but excuses are odious, and we don't care to make them. If Langford is sincere he can have a fight without much trouble."[8]

But once that fight was over, Sam advised his manager that he was finished reducing weight to fight lighter fellows.

Sam decided that he didn't enjoy the process of trying to drop weight, and that lightweight men weren't much fun to fight since they were usually very fast: you had to chase them too much to get a chance to land any punches.

Sam ended the year with one more impressive outing, this one on December 23rd, against a tough 135-pound lightweight named Jack Blackburn. Although he went on to achieve greater fame as the trainer of heavyweight champion Joe Louis, Jack Blackburn, whose real name was Charles Henry Blackburn, was a great fighter in his own right. In 1903 he was considered one of the most scientific boxers in the game. He possessed an excellent jab and powerful left hook, was very fast and was outstanding at blocking and countering blows. His style was a bit awkward, but at the time he and Sam met he held a big advantage on Sam in terms of experience inside the ropes.

Prior to the scheduled twelve-round contest it was agreed that if both men were on their feet at the end the bout would be ruled a draw. Although it was reported that Blackburn had the better of the proceedings, Sam's performance against the cagey veteran was considered noteworthy. But Sam still had a lot to learn. The *Police Gazette,* well known for their coverage of boxing at the time, reported that Blackburn easily outclassed Langford and at times made him look like a novice. Their reporter felt that it was only Sam's ability to withstand hard punishment that saved him from a knockout.

Still, Sam's fights with Joe Gans and Jack Blackburn, more than any others up to that point, demonstrated that there was greatness

---

[8] *Halifax Spectator,* 16 December 1903

ahead for him. No one was more convinced of this than Joe Woodman, who not long afterwards gave up his drugstore to focus on a full-time career managing Sam.

Sam and Jack Blackburn would go on to face each other five more times over the next twenty-two months. As Sam would later explain it, he kept on thinking that he was a little better than Jack, so he kept challenging him. And he found a willing partner in Blackburn.

Their second fight took place only a few weeks later on January 11, 1904 in Jack's hometown of Philadelphia. It was ruled a six-round draw. There was some question as to whether this meeting was on the level. One newspaper account of the fight indicated that the match was so dreary that at the end of the third round the referee walked to the ropes and announced that unless the pair got together and gave the spectators a run for their money he would put on an extra bout and deduct the cost from their share. The announcement seemed to inspire the pair briefly, but midway through the third round they fell back to their former tactics. Langford didn't appear to deliver a punch with serious intentions the whole evening, and in general the fight was said to have consisted of one series of clinches after another.

Afterward, it was reported that Blackburn had been suffering from dysentery for some time, and that he was physically incapable of doing himself justice. Based upon this revelation there was rumor that the pair had come to an arrangement beforehand to avoid losing out on a payday.

The third meeting was a fifteen-rounder that took place at the Highland Athletic Club in Marlboro, Massachusetts. In this one, Sam decided he was going to try and put Jack away quickly. So when the opening bell rang he rushed out to meet Jack and landed a hard left hook that sent Blackburn to the deck for a count of nine. Sam caught him again a short time later with a right hook that sent Blackburn down for another count of nine. Jack landed on the canvas one more time, his third count of nine during the first round, before he heard the welcome sound of the bell ending the session.

When Sam returned to his corner, Woodman suggested that he slow up a little to ensure he gave the crowd a run for their money and didn't put Blackburn away too early. But Sam was having none of that. He was determined to knock Blackburn out and administered a severe beating to him over the next six rounds. Blackburn visited the canvas many more times. However, around about the eighth round, Sam began to tire and Blackburn got his second wind. Reversing the trend of the previous seven rounds Jack began to give Sam a taste of his own medicine. Once he hit Sam so hard that Sam swore he saw eighteen Blackburn's flying around the ring for a minute. When Sam returned to his corner after that eighth round, Joe advised him that he'd better quit playing now and finish Blackburn.

"Listen Joe, if you see that boy hit me again like he did in that round, just drop everything you are doing and get me an undertaker," replied Sam.[9]

Sam didn't receive another blow as bad as that one, but for the rest of the fight Jack busted Sam up and sent him to the canvas a number of times. In the last two rounds, too tired to try and escape Jack's attacks, Sam stood toe-to-toe with him slugging it out.

When the fight ended, the referee ruled it a draw. That surprised Sam, who figured he'd won at least ten of the rounds. So did most of the crowd. The *Police Gazette* reported that it would have been difficult to pick a winner on points. They cited Sam as having the better of the first eight rounds, his two fisted attack making him look like a sure winner, but they inexplicably stated that Blackburn had evened things up by taking the last two rounds.[10]

A similar fight took place between the two on August 18, 1905 in the Leiperville Athletic Club. Blackburn had been scheduled to fight Joe Walcott, but Sam filled in when Walcott was unavailable. This time, the two men boxed in a tent with less than one half of the available seats filled with spectators. Once again, Sam built up an early advantage as he assumed the role of aggressor carrying the fight to his lighter opponent. Each time Sam got in close he punched Jack severely about the body. A game Blackburn came on strong from the tenth to the fifteenth sessions and steadily ate away at Sam's early lead. Blackburn fought at a furious pace in the thirteenth round and had Sam on the defensive in the fourteenth. At the finish it was the

---

[9] *Halifax Herald*, 20 August 1924
[10] *Police Gazette*, 27 December 1904

opinion of those present that Sam had a shade better of the bout by a small margin, but no official decision was awarded.

The last fight between the pair took place October 7, 1905 in Philadelphia. Sam was to have faced George Cole, who fought out of that city, but when the latter took ill Blackburn stood in for him and took the fight with Sam on short notice.

Early in the first round, Sam caught Blackburn with a hard punch on the jaw but failed to follow up on his advantage. A wary Blackburn chose not to pursue Sam, and unlike the previous five contests between the two, the first three rounds slowed to a crawl. By the fourth round, with neither fighter showing any inclination to initiate exchanges and the crowd yelling to stop the fight, the referee stepped in and ruled the bout no contest. The crowd jeered both fighters as they returned to their dressing rooms. It was a strange ending to a fierce two year rivalry with a man Sam felt had a greater fighting heart than any opponent he ever faced in the ring.

Blackburn's own ring career was interrupted in 1909 when he shot and killed three people, including his wife, during a heated argument. He was found guilty of manslaughter and received a prison sentence of ten to fifteen years, but he was ultimately released for good behavior after four years, eight months.

After retiring from the ring in 1923 Jack became a very good trainer and worked with champions like Sammy Mandell and Bud Taylor prior to achieving greater fame as Joe Louis' trainer. Jack taught Joe everything he knew, and Louis always credited Jack for making him into the fighter he became.

JOE WALCOTT

CA. 1900

AUTHOR'S COLLECTION

"WATCH THIS WELL BUILT NEGRO! HE LOOKS LIKE A SURE THING TO WIN EITHER THE WELTERWEIGHT OR MIDDLEWEIGHT CHAMPIONSHIP."

~ARTHUR LUMLEY, NEW YORK ILLUSTRATED NEWS

CHAPTER 4

JOE WALCOTT, "THE BARBADOS DEMON"

The engagements with Jack Blackburn in 1904 and 1905 were two of several serious ring tests Sam participated in during those years. He fought twenty-four more bouts on top of his five meetings with Blackburn. In February of 1904, he faced a tough, young twenty-year-old welterweight named Willie Lewis and stopped him in the second round. That performance prompted Woodman to match him with Dave Holly, an awkward but clever twenty-three-year-old veteran lightweight. Holly hadn't begun his professional career until 1900, yet he had already participated in at least eighty official fights, possibly as many as one hundred, by the time he met Sam. His résumé included a popular decision over lightweight champion Joe Gans in a non-decision bout, though Gans would later defeat him several times.[1]

Sam met Holly on April 11, 1904, the first of four meetings between the pair over a one year period. Holly fought out of a crouch and with a defensive style that Sam found difficult to penetrate. Even though Sam landed the heavier punches in their first meeting, he found himself on the short end of a decision when Holly outfought him in the final round. The *Philadelphia Item* reported the contest as a draw.[2]

---

[1] Kevin Smith, *The Boston Tar Baby: The Life and Legend of Sam Langford* (unpublished manuscript)

[2] *Philadelphia Item*, 12 April 2004

Before Sam received a chance to even the score with Holly he fought two other opponents of note that year. The first of those was George "Elbows" McFadden, a fighter who had acquired his nickname based on the effective use of his elbows to block his opponent's blows. Sam faced McFadden on July 29th at the Pastime Athletic Club of Manchester, New Hampshire in a bout scheduled for fifteen rounds.

Sam wasted no time establishing his superiority over McFadden, assuming the role of the aggressor from the outset. He dropped "Elbows" to the mat partway through the opening session with a beautiful left hook, and then repeated the feat with another tremendous left hook in the second session. The latter blow reportedly landed flush on McFadden's jaw, lifting him off his feet and dumping him on the canvas.

At that point McFadden's corner decided they had seen enough. They tossed in the sponge, and the referee immediately halted the bout.

That year's second opponent of note was the welterweight champion of the world, Joe Walcott, nicknamed the "Barbados Demon" after his native land in the West Indies. Walcott was born in Demarara, British Guyana on March 13, 1873. He stood approximately 5'2", but he had long arms, a powerful physique and a punch like the kick of a mule. He was a tireless fighter able to absorb a lot of punishment. During his career he fought, and more than held his own, against many much heavier opponents. Many knowledgeable boxing historians consider the "Barbados Demon" the greatest welterweight of all time, and *The Ring* included him in their list of the one hundred greatest punchers of all time.[3] Sam faced Walcott in an open air arena in Manchester, New Hampshire.

A newspaper story during the lead-up to this fight recorded one of the earliest known incidents behind Sam's nickname, "Boston Tar Baby." It is said that Tad Dorgan, a leading newspaperman and famous sporting cartoonist of the day, in search of a story, sought out a number of fans prior to the fight and asked for their thoughts regarding the outcome of the match. He asked a group of young black women and they replied, "Why, our baby of course," or something close to that.

---

[3] *The Ring*, Collectors Special Issue, Vol. 82 No. 10, 2003 Yearbook

"Walcott?" Tad asked.

The girls laughed and replied, "Don't you know that Sam Langford is our baby?" Tad reportedly combined that tag line with Sam's dark skin and the fact that Sam was fighting out of Boston to come up with "The Boston Tar Baby." The nickname stayed with Sam for the rest of his life.[4]

Aware of Joe's reputation and victories over several bigger opponents, Sam later admitted to having some fear of him. When the pair entered the ring, Walcott tried to rattle Sam by pointing to some trees outside the arena and remarking:

> "See those trees over there Sam? I guess you do. Well then, you black monkey, just wait a few minutes and I'll make you jump right out from the middle of the ring onto one of the top branches, and you'll have to use your tail then to hang on with."[5]

Sam assumed this was meant to be a reflection on his color and his African ancestry. He didn't respond, but he was determined to make Walcott pay for the insult.

Arthur Lumley, editor of the *New York Illustrated News* and a leading sports authority, who was seated ringside that night, provided the following report the next day:

> Joe Walcott, world welterweight champion and Sam Langford of Cambridge, Massachusetts, fought a vicious fifteen-round draw at the Coliseum. The fight was witnessed by a fair-sized gathering. The spectators were much displeased by the decision, as the rounds story was one clearly in favor of Langford. He had earned that right and should have gotten the decision. That, at least, was the general opinion, and it was voiced freely after the fight.
>
> After a fine even opening round, the honors were all in Langford's favor from then on through the seventh. Sam shot his left hand jab regularly to Walcott's face, and despite the crouching tactics employed by Walcott, Langford had no difficulty in reaching his face often, and shooting in terrific right hand uppercuts and swings to the body. In the eighth, Walcott,

---

[4] *Fight Stories*, Winter 1948
[5] *Washington Post*, 11 March 1911

urged on by his manager, set about in grand style to overcome the handicap. He was told that he had to fight at top speed if he wanted to win and he gave the spectators a thrill by obeying the command. He hit Langford often and tried to beat him down. Sam showed much cleverness and avoided the traps, though he was severely punished about the body.

Although Walcott carried the fight to Langford from the seventh to the finish, Sam's counter blows scored heavily, and he even out-boxed Joe. Seldom was there a close exchange of punches, each being satisfied to box and toss blows at long range. Langford received two hard rights to the chin in the thirteenth round that jarred him and one under the heart that almost took him off his feet.

Those punches were the hardest struck in the fight and had the most telling effect. But Langford came out for the fourteenth round with an abundance of confidence, and acted as if he had not even been hit in the previous session. He leaped forth at the clang of the gong and caught Walcott with a beautiful right hand swing that landed with a crash against Joe's body, and followed with two straight lefts to the mouth that brought the claret and a right uppercut jolt that struck with a thud. Those punches seemed to have angered the champion, for from then to the finish of the round, he forced the milling and for the first time in the fight the spectators were treated to a thrilling encounter. When the bell sounded for the final session, Walcott's anger was still with him, for he refused to shake hands and was razzed for his poor sportsmanship. The round was hectic, with honors about even. Each landed often and hit hard, but Langford's straight lefts had such sting to them that they showed their work when the end of hostilities were announced.

The decision of a draw was not well received, and it is safe to say that Walcott's retention of his welterweight championship hung by a thread. My personal opinion is that Langford was entitled to the verdict. Watch this well built Negro! He looks like a sure thing to win either the welterweight or middleweight championship, though he may outgrow both divisions before he reaches his peak![6]

---

[6] *New York Illustrated News*, 6 September 1904

Lumley's concluding words proved prophetic. Sam's own recollections of the fight painted a much fiercer picture. He came away from the fight with the highest level of respect for Walcott.

> "My oh my, wasn't Joe Walcott a tough boy! He was the hardest hitter I ever met. Never before or never since then have I been hit as hard and as often as that night, and I never landed more blows on a fighter in fifteen rounds than I hurled into Joe Walcott that night. The house was in an uproar before the first round ended and from then until the end of the fight the customers never sat down," said Sam.[7]

Sam didn't seem to mind the decision of a draw near as much as the customers did, but approximately six years later he advised a reporter with a great deal of satisfaction that towards the end of the fight when he felt sure he was going to win, he whispered quietly to Joe, "Say, Joe, don't think I shall jump in those trees—why don't you try instead?"[8]

Sam said that Walcott didn't reply, but the look he shot back spoke volumes. When the fifteenth round ended, Sam was just glad the fight was over and he was still alive.

Walcott's career almost ended six weeks later when he was tragically involved in an accidental shooting. While attending a dance in Boston, Walcott was showing a revolver to a man by the name of Nelson Hall, and the gun discharged. The bullet passed through Walcott's right hand and hit Hall in the heart killing him almost instantly.

Walcott didn't fight again until mid-1906 when he twice attempted to regain the welterweight title against Honey Mellody. He lost the first fight by decision over fifteen rounds, and then suffered a twelfth-round knockout in the rematch. He fought on until the end of 1911 and then retired from the ring.

Sam received another crack at Dave Holly on September 30, 1904 in Baltimore, Maryland, and came away unsatisfied again as the fifteen-round fight was ruled a draw. He didn't have to wait long for a third chance at him as they met again in Philadelphia on November 4th.

---

[7] *Halifax Herald*, 18 August 1924
[8] *Washington Post*, 11 March 1911

The third meeting was hotly contested from the beginning to the end, but once again at the end of this scheduled six-round contest there was little to merit a choice between the pair. Sam appeared the stronger of the two at the conclusion of the fight, and although no official decision was rendered most in attendance felt that Sam had won.

Andy Watson became Sam's next victim when the pair met on November 24th for a twelve-round bout at the Lakeside Athletic Club in Webster, Massachusetts. Sam drove Watson all over the ring, twice knocking him through the ropes. Although no decision was given the *Washington Post* reported that Sam was the better man.[9] He followed that up one day later with a three-round technical knockout of Tommy Sullivan in Marlboro, Massachusetts.

Sam's bachelor days came to an abrupt end on December 7, 1904 when he married Martha Burrell, a pretty twenty-year-old, in Cambridge, Massachusetts. Martha, born in Philadelphia, Pennsylvania, was living in Boston at the time and making her living as a dressmaker. She was a tiny, sweet and gentle woman, standing barely 5' tall, with very smooth skin of a pale brownish tone, soft grayish-brown eyes and beautiful black hair.[10] While it's not known how the two originally met, one can easily imagine that Sam's growing obsession with fine clothing may have provided the setting for the initial meeting between the couple. It's not difficult to picture Martha being easily impressed by the relatively affluent and gregarious eighteen-year-old athlete who was making such a name for himself in the city.

Sam was a busy man inside the ring at this point in his career. In fact, the third of his fights with Jack Blackburn (covered in the previous chapter) occurred only two days after his marriage to Martha.

A fourth and final meeting took place between Sam and Dave Holly on February 13, 1905 at the Apollo Athletic Club in Salem, Massachusetts. Holly weighed in for this fight at 137 pounds, the agreed upon weight. Sam, obviously overweight, refused to weigh in, and Holly agreed to go forward with the match only upon the condition that if both men were on their feet at the end of fifteen rounds the contest would be declared a draw.

---

[9] *Washington Post*, 25 November 1904
[10] Carol Doyle (great-granddaughter of Sam Langford). Telephone interview, October 21, 2007

In the first five rounds Sam found many of his blows landing on the top of Holly's head, the result of the crouch that Holly fought out of, but as the fight continued Sam's superiority became evident. He did his best to put Holly away over the course of the fight, but Holly proved his ability to withstand punishment. When both were still standing at the sound of the final bell, there was no choice but to call it a draw. Newspapermen in attendance reported that Sam would have been declared the winner had it not been for the stipulation that called for a draw verdict if both men were still standing at the end.

Sam followed up the match with Holly with a nine-round no-contest bout versus George Cole on March 4th and a twelve-round decision over George Gunther on March 13th. His next bout was held two months later on May 16th against Bogardus Hyde in Webster, Massachusetts. It resulted in a technical knockout when Hyde's seconds threw in the sponge after the conclusion of the third round. The event was so poorly attended that the club announced that it would have no further boxing in Webster. On May 26th, Sam fought "Young Peter Jackson," a.k.a. the "Baltimore Demon," for the first of what would ultimately be six matches between the two. Jackson, born Sim Thompkins, was twenty-seven years old at the time and considered an accomplished welterweight.

Sim got the name of "Young Peter Jackson" in Denver in the year of 1895. He had been boxing as an amateur in Colorado City. After defeating all of the boys in that city he ventured to Denver where he introduced himself to a local promoter named Reddy Gallagher. Gallagher agreed to give him a fight against a boxer named Eugene Turner. Sim was tickled pink.

Later that evening a number of newspapermen asked Gallagher for the names of the participants in his upcoming show. Gallagher reeled off the names, but when it came to the show's feature bout he could not remember the name of the man who was to box Turner. Unable to recall Sim's name he told the reporters that the fighter was a dead ringer for the great Australian heavyweight Peter Jackson, only not as large. The next morning the papers told of the contest to take place between Turner and "Young Peter Jackson."

Sim read one of the newspapers and immediately sought out Gallagher:

"Say, Mr. Gallagher ... I thought you were going to give me that fight with Turner," said a heartbroken Sim.

"Well, you are to fight him," replied Gallagher.

"The papers say that some fellow by the name of Jackson is going to box with him," said Sim.

Gallagher had to explain how he couldn't remember Sim's name and what had happened. Sim went on to defeat Turner and from that time on became known as "Young Peter Jackson."[11]

When Sam faced the hard-hitting and dangerous Jackson, the latter was coming off a recent win over Larry Temple and had knocked out Joe Walcott in the fourth round of a contest only eleven months earlier. Sam earned a fifteen-round decision in this meeting.

He demonstrated that the victory over Jackson was no fluke by repeating the trick on June 17th before the Douglas Athletic Club in Chelsea, Massachusetts. In another fifteen-round contest, Jackson reportedly absorbed tremendous punishment and was all but out on his feet when the fight ended.

Sam suffered a brief setback in his next outing, July 4th versus New Yorker Larry Temple. Temple was awarded a ten-round decision victory at the Highland Athletic Club in Marlboro, Massachusetts.

Temple, known as the "Black Cyclone," was a stable mate of Joe Walcott and had proven himself a formidable opponent in his performances versus fighters such as Walcott, Jack Johnson, "Young Peter Jackson," "Philadelphia" Jack O'Brien, and "The Dixie Kid." He was viewed as a larger version of Joe Walcott, though nowhere near as nasty as the welterweight champion. He was discovered and managed by Tom O'Rourke, the same man who had managed the careers of Joe Walcott and the great featherweight George Dixon. He also had extremely large hands and feet, his boxing shoes having to be custom made to accommodate his size sixteen feet.[12]

The pair fought again on September 7th before the club members in the Marlboro Theatre, this time to a fifteen-round draw. The newspaper report indicated that it was an even fight throughout, though

---

[11] *The Trenton Times,* 7 February 1902

[12] Kevin Smith, *"The Sundowners: The History of the Black Prizefighter, Volume II, Part 3, 1870-1930"* (unpublished manuscript)

Temple was the primary aggressor. The draw decision was well received by those in attendance.

Sam met Young Peter Jackson for a third time on September 29th in Baltimore. It was a bout that was ruled a draw by the referee, but the newspapers reported Sam won. Sam had pounded Jackson's left eye to a pulp and hammered him with straight, hard blows almost at will throughout the bout. Jackson twice appealed to the referee that he'd been hit low, but the referee witnessed no such infraction.

Sam continued to enjoy greater ring success and the size of his purses increased, as did his stature on a local basis. Never one to shy away from spending, the paper and coin passed through Sam's hands like water. A good portion of it went into his ever expanding wardrobe and towards satisfying a newfound taste for jewelry. In fact, Sam developed quite an appetite for sparkling stones. It was not unusual to see Sam out about town sporting a variety of ornaments including large diamond rings, horseshoe shaped pins and watches decorated with expensive stones.

There is a story that a few years later, while riding a train with his manager one day, Sam found himself sitting next to a gentle looking man who, upon recognizing Sam as a fighter, began a conversation with him. When Sam and his manager departed the train, Sam commented on what a nice fellow he'd been seated near.

"That fellow was J.P. Morgan, the richest man in the world!" said Joe.

"My god, the richest man in the world. He didn't have a single diamond on him!" replied Sam.[13]

Supposedly, this made such an impression upon Sam that he discontinued his practice of wearing diamond jewelry shortly thereafter.

Sam's last fight of the year took place Christmas Day at the Unity Cycle & Athletic Club in Lawrence, Massachusetts. It was an ambitious one. He tackled the first of the really big men he would fight during his career, and it would have been difficult to find one much tougher. Sam was matched with the very formidable, black, twenty-six-year-old heavyweight, Joe Jennette. Joe, whose birth name was

---

[13] Roland Pete, "The Extraordinary Mr. Langford," *Boxing & Wrestling*, December 1957

Jeremiah, was only thirteen months into his professional career, but he'd already logged fourteen fights—including three that same year against future heavyweight champion Jack Johnson. This would be the first of fourteen times he and Sam would face one another in the ring!

Somehow Sam had come to believe that it was easier to beat the bigger fellows than the ones around his own size. That contributed to his finding himself facing a man five inches taller and forty to forty-five pounds heavier.

When the fight started, Sam tried to use the same tactics against Joe that he used against opponents his own size, but after two rounds he realized his jabs and hooks were landing ineffectively on Jennette's shoulders, while Joe was returning fire with punches that were inflicting a significant amount of punishment upon Sam.

Sam decided to change his tactics by focusing on blows to the body, in addition to trying to land a few well placed uppercuts. When the third round began, he slipped a left jab from Jennette and launched an uppercut that surprised Joe right on the point of his jaw. Joe wasn't the only one surprised. Sam was momentarily taken aback that he had been able to land the punch so easily. When Joe tried to respond, he left himself wide open for a body blow, and Sam landed a hard right to the stomach that produced a loud grunt from Jennette.

From that point on, Sam targeted Joe's stomach. When the opportunity presented itself, Sam managed to throw in a few more uppercuts that found themselves a home on Jennette's chin. However, Sam continued to take a beating throughout most of the fight. He did manage to send Joe to the floor during one round when he landed a hard uppercut. There was also a point in the fifth round where he looked like a possible winner when he was battering Jennette about the ring, but after that round Joe began to establish his superiority by landing many heavy blows to Sam's face.

In the sixth round Joe hit Sam twice on the eye, followed by a right hook to the jaw that sent Sam reeling into the ropes. In the seventh, Sam did manage to land a hard right to the stomach that hurt Jennette badly and caused him to cling to Sam until he recovered sufficiently. But these successes were far and few between for Sam in the later rounds. Joe had things all his way in the eighth round, opening a deep cut on Sam's eye with one blow that caused blood to flow down Sam's face. When that round ended, Sam returned to his corner barely able to see out of badly swollen eyes. Realizing there was little chance of a win, and that Sam would most likely suffer a lot more punishment and risk permanent damage, Sam's corner threw in the sponge.

Far from being disheartened by this defeat, Sam felt that he had learned some valuable lessons on how to fight effectively against bigger men. He knew it would serve him well in the future: he was confident the result would be different the next time the two met.

JOE JENNETTE

CA. 1906-1907

BEN HAWES COLLECTION

"SAM LANGFORD WAS THE TOUGHEST LITTLE SON OF A BITCH THAT EVER LIVED."

~JACK JOHNSON

CHAPTER 5

TACKLING THE BIG FELLOWS

Sam began the year 1906 by avenging a loss he'd suffered against a tough, black welterweight named Larry Temple. Temple had defeated Sam in a ten-round decision on July 4, 1905. It was the only loss Sam had suffered during 1905 beside the one to Joe Jennette, and he was eager to even the score.

He got his revenge and then some on March 1st when he knocked Temple down three times in the eleventh round, and finally put him down for the count in the fifteenth. The two faced each other two more times: once in 1907 and again in 1908, but after this meeting Sam clearly had Temple's number.

Sam defeated "Black Fitzsimmons" next, by way of an eleven-round technical knockout on March 19th. Fitzsimmons, whose real name was Ulysses Cannon, came by his fighting name as a result of his lanky and powerful build, which was along the lines of the white champion, Bob Fitzsimmons.[1]

Three weeks later, Sam fought Joe Jennette for a second time. In this April match he put the lessons he had learned in their first fight to use, focusing on attacking Joe's body from the outset of the contest. He pounded away at Joe's midsection throughout the contest while Joe tried his best to keep him at bay with jabs and straight rights to the face.

In the tenth round, Sam picked up his pace, and there was a

---

[1] Kevin Smith, *The Sundowners: The History of the Black Prizefighter Volume II, Part 1 1870-1930.* Boston: CCK Publications, 2006

moment when it appeared he might drop Jennette. The latter staggered around the ring with Sam in hot pursuit, but Joe was able to remain on his feet. In the twelfth round the two went at it hammer-and-tongs until Joe gave in and sought relief by drawing Sam into a clinch. Sam then won the thirteenth and fourteenth rounds setting the stage for the fifteenth and final round.

That final round was a humdinger! Sam launched a two fisted attack and battered Joe with punches to the face and body. Joe tried desperately to stave them off. Shortly before the end of the round, Sam landed a heavy right to Joe's jaw and the big man looked like he would crash to the canvas as he swayed to and fro, but the bell rang and his seconds immediately ran out to catch him and help him back to his corner.

Sam was declared the victor on points. That win, combined with a number of victories over heavier opponents (including two 1905 wins over Young Peter Jackson) set the stage for a match with another top heavyweight contender, a black man by the name of Jack Johnson. Johnson had rung up a number of impressive victories and was being hailed as a top contender for the heavyweight championship of the world. In 1905-1906, Johnson and Jennette had fought each other six times, Jennette matching up quite well against Johnson, and Sam had just decisively defeated Jennette. It seemed reasonable to match Sam with Johnson.

Consequently, on April 16th it was reported that the two had been matched to meet on April 26th. "You go and get Johnson and I'll meet him,"[2] a confident Langford had replied in response to the question posed him as to whether he'd be willing to face the bigger man. Sam knew he was taking on a considerable task, but he thought he'd be able to tie the big fellow up in knots. He planned to tear into Johnson and not allow him to box. He wanted to be the one to defeat Johnson before anyone else did, thinking it would greatly enhance his reputation.

Most of the local boxing experts didn't give Sam much chance of winning. According to the *Boston Globe* no one expected the bout to last the scheduled fifteen rounds because Johnson would be too big for Sam.[3] Both parties trained hard for the bout.

The contest took place in the Lincoln Athletic Club's Pythian

---

[2] *Boston Globe*, 16 April 1906
[3] *Boston Globe*, 23 April 1906

Rink, a facility that fully-seated, could accommodate up to 2,000 fans. It had small exits, camp chairs and was surrounded by wooden plank bleachers. The place was considered a firetrap, and in fact did burn down, two years later.

The little arena was filled to the brim on fight day. Many attendees were anxious to see how Sam would fare against the bigger Johnson. Among them were fighters George Dixon, Sandy Ferguson, and Johnson's friend Joe Walcott, all of whom gave advice to Johnson throughout the contest. Johnson had traveled with Walcott a few years earlier as a sparring partner. Sam had done so well against both Walcott, whom Johnson had a high regard for, and the great lightweight Joe Gans, that Johnson didn't take him lightly, but Johnson had an even greater amount of respect for his own abilities. Before the fight began, he stated that he wouldn't fight unless Sam would agree to bet $250 against $500 that he could last the full fifteen rounds with Johnson. Sam accepted the wager.

Other bets were being offered around the ring that Sam wouldn't last ten, twelve or the full fifteen rounds, but there were few men willing to wager that Sam would last that long, regardless of their respect for his abilities.

Sam entered the ring first, wearing a big smile, and red trunks with a green sash. He received a thunderous ovation from the hometown crowd. He was seconded by George Byers and Andy Watson. Johnson entered next, to cheers, waving to the crowd and wearing long, dark, tight trunks.

Before getting underway the two advanced to the ring's center to receive instructions from the referee. The twenty-eight-year-old Johnson standing 6'1" towered over the 5'6" twenty-year-old Langford. He also had approximately forty pounds on Sam. It looked like a gross mismatch. Both men smiled confidently as they returned to their respective corners to await the bell that would open the evening's proceedings.

When the fight got underway, the two men circled each other warily, flicking out the occasional jab. Although Johnson was very confident, he'd heard enough about Sam's abilities to know better than to get careless.

As the round continued, Johnson offered a smiling invitation to Sam. "Come get me Sambo."

To which Sam replied, "I'll get you when I'm good and ready," as he dropped his arms to his side and stuck out his tongue at Johnson, bringing a roar from the crowd.[1]

There was little action to speak of in either of the first two rounds. Johnson seemed puzzled as he experienced difficulty hitting the crouching little man, but suddenly near the end of the second frame he began to rock Sam with jabs and hooks.

In the third round, Johnson started to take charge. He rained seven or eight blows on Sam's head for every one Sam successfully returned to the body. Employing a strategy similar to the one he had utilized against Jennette, Sam continually sought to slip under Johnson's left jab in order to deliver blows to Johnson's body. It was a tactic that was successful at times and resulted in Johnson's retreat. At one point in this round Johnson hit Sam with a terrific left hook that bloodied his mouth and shortly thereafter stunned Sam again with a strong uppercut. Momentarily losing his cool, Sam carelessly waded in to retaliate, only to receive a stiff right to the body, prompting him to cover up instead.

In the fourth round, Johnson routinely landed hooks to Sam's body and head, and before long one of Sam's eyes began to swell. Although he continued to be on the receiving end of more punches than he was able to deliver, Sam exhibited his gameness and was able to land a hard right to the jaw when Johnson dropped his guard in response to a feint to the body by Sam.

Some six to seven years later, Sam told Australian trainer Duke Mullins that he dropped Johnson for a count of nine near the end of the fifth round, and that the bigger man refused to mix it up with him for the balance of the fight. There is no mention of that knockdown in any of the Boston newspaper accounts of the fight, but Johnson himself seems to substantiate being knocked down, as he mentions suffering a knockdown in his 1910 book *Mes Combats*. He also mentioned it to Mullins in 1908, although he indicated to the latter that it was the result of being caught off balance.

---

[1] Seth Kantor, "When Johnson Met the Tar Baby," magazine article, source and date unknown

The Ring founder and editor, Nat Fleischer, later wrote that his father-in-law, A.D. Phillips, who attended the bout told him that Johnson went to the mat in the fifth round as a result of a slip when he missed with a big swing aimed at Sam's jaw, but Sam reportedly caught him at the same time with a terrific blow just above the heart.

Sam picked up his pace in the sixth round, but Johnson drove Sam into the ropes. There, he landed a volley of punches, punctuated by a hard uppercut to the jaw that sent Sam crashing to the boards for a count of nine.

Sam managed to struggle to his feet and attempted to clinch with Johnson until he regained his senses, but Johnson was too strong for him. He freed himself and dropped Sam for another count. Struggling to his feet, Sam fought back gamely and the *Boston Morning Journal* reported that when the round concluded "Johnson was exhausted and weak from punching."[5]

By the end of the seventh, it appeared that Johnson was pitching a shutout: he would only need to win one more round to be assured of a victory on points should the contest go the distance. He was relatively unmarked and sat smiling during the intermissions, while Sam's corner worked furiously to prepare him for each coming round. One of Sam's eyes had been closed by that time and his face evidenced the punishment he'd been taking. The only question now seemed to be whether or not Sam could go the distance.

In the eighth, Johnson moved easily about the ring as Sam began to slow. Sam tried to retreat, but Johnson caught him with an overhead right on the mouth, staggering him and knocking him back towards the ropes. Johnson followed Sam into the ropes, raining a series of blows and ending with a hard left hook, knocking Sam to the canvas.

The referee began to count, and Jack stood by waiting to hit Sam again should he rise. After what seemed to many in attendance like a very slow count, Sam rose at "nine" by grasping the rope and pulling himself upright. A combination of punches and pushes sent Sam back to the mat. It looked like he was finished, but with the crowd urging him on, Sam dug deep, hurried to his feet and came in for more. Johnson tried to finish him, but shortly before the bell Sam

---

[5] *Boston Morning Journal*, 27 April 1906

successfully ducked under a punch and landed a heavy punch to Johnson's bread basket. At the bell both fighters trudged back to their corners.

In the ninth round, Sam shot a left hook to Johnson's body: it caused Jack to drop his hand and gasp like a man taking his dying breath. Sam was unable to capitalize, and Jack recovered and boxed carefully the rest of the round.

Whenever he needed a breather, Johnson clinched and leaned his big body on Sam. As the fight continued, Sam found himself tiring from his efforts to push back against the heavier and stronger man. In the latter part of the tenth round, as Johnson attempted to initiate a clinch, Sam managed to catch him with a left hook to the jaw that jarred him badly. But before Sam could follow up on his advantage, Jack latched onto him and hung on for dear life until the bell rang, ending the round.

Sam was tiring badly. The burden of wrestling around the ring with Johnson in clinches was taking its toll, but Sam did little clinching himself and was more than willing to continue mixing it up with Johnson throughout the fight.[6]

At the end of the twelfth round, Sam's nose was bleeding and his other eye was also closing. Johnson had done everything he could to put away Sam, including holding him with one hand while whaling away with the other on a few occasions. At the end of the round, Sam's corner men rushed out to help him to his corner. Johnson was bleeding from the mouth.

Throughout the fight, heavyweight contender Sandy Ferguson sat near Johnson's corner trying to divert Sam's attention by hurling insults. He was so conspicuous that the next morning's *Boston Globe* said that Ferguson should have been ejected.[7]

In the fifteenth and final round, Sam looked like he was running on fumes. The crowd cheered him for the courage he had exhibited and exhorted him to continue. Sam wasn't the only one exhausted. Johnson looked tired as well, though not as badly damaged as Sam. Neither was able to hurt the other in this last round, and both men finished on their feet.

---

[6] *Boston Globe*, 27 April 1906

[7] *Boston Globe*, 27 April 1906

At the end of the fight, Johnson appeared disappointed. He had failed to prevent Sam from going the distance. There was no doubt that Johnson had won the fight. He still looked relatively unmarked, while Sam's face was very badly bruised and puffed. Johnson was tired, and Sam was clearly exhausted. Sam took some solace in the fact that Johnson now owed him $500, and he was wildly cheered by the crowd for the courage he exhibited. Wrote the *Globe*, "There is one thing sure: that when Langford left the ring the spectators did not call him the names that they did when Sandy (Ferguson) fought Johnson at the same club."[8]

There was no disagreement over whether Johnson had won the fight. Various reports made it clear the affair had been one sided, but there was much admiration expressed for the smaller man's fighting spirit.

According to the *Police Gazette*:

> With a gameness and capacity for punishment that seemed beyond the powers of a human being, Sam Langford, the colored fighter, weighing 156 pounds, battled fifteen rounds at the Lincoln A.C., of Chelsea, Mass., on April 26, with Jack Johnson who outweighed Sam by about thirty pounds. Johnson gave Langford a terrible beating and was awarded the decision.[9]

The Boston Globe reported:

> Though Sam Langford was beaten by Jack Johnson, he is held in high regards by the fans. He proved beyond doubt that he is one of the gamest fighters that ever stepped in the ring. Badly handicapped as he was, he put up a good battle against the odds, and he gave the fans a big bump by staying the limit.[10]

The *Boston Morning Journal* wrote that Sam provided a superb exhibition of grit and courage, making other local exhibitions of gameness in the ring seem insignificant. The *Journal* indicated that Johnson would have been an easy mark for Jeffries if the champion had chosen to accept his challenge.[11]

---

[8] *Boston Globe*, 27 April 1906
[9] *Police Gazette*, 12 May 1906
[10] *Boston Globe*, 27 April 1906
[11] *Boston Morning Journal*, 27 April 1906

The *Boston Herald* reported that the fight did little to aid Johnson's campaign for the heavyweight crown:

> He was unable to stop Langford, who was nearly 40 pounds lighter and fully a foot shorter... even though Langford took a real hammering. The fight was completely one-sided, and only Langford's gameness and ability to stay for the full fifteen rounds warranted the crowd's enthusiasm.[12]

Fourteen years later, English writer and boxing enthusiast A.G. Hales wrote:

> Sam made one mistake in that battle which he did not realize until too late, he fought for Johnson's belly instead of punching under the heart. He started in to rectify this mistake about half-way through the battle, but by that time a lot of the crispness was gone from his punches, and a fair amount of his speed had left him but his heart punches when they did come along disturbed the giant a great deal, and had Sam adopted those tactics from the very first I think it quite probable he might have won. A man may have a cast iron jaw, a chin of adamant, and a belly of brass but no man can control the action of the heart. It may be a long job before the heart begins to flutter, but when it does flutter it ceases to pump properly, and the brain clouds and the end is not far off.[13]

In his 1910 French biography, *Mes Combats,* Johnson wrote of his fight with Sam:

> I found him one of the toughest adversaries I ever met in the ring. I weighed 190 pounds and Langford only 138. In the second round the little Negro hit me on the jaw with a terrible right hand and I fell as if upended by a cannon ball. In all my pugilistic career, not before and not afterwards, have I received a blow that struck me with such force. It was all I could do just to get back on my feet just as the referee was about to count "Ten!" I made it, but I assure you that I felt the effects of that punch for the rest of the fight. I recovered, but I would have to take my hat off to him if I hadn't had so much science at my command. In the fifteenth round I was declared the winner on points.

---

[12] *Boston Herald,* 27 April 1906
[13] *Topical Times,* 17 April 1920

Many years later, in the 1940s, when asked what he thought of Sam Langford, Johnson told Kevin Aylwood, a trustee of the New England Sports Museum, "Sam Langford was the toughest little son of a bitch that ever lived."[14]

At the time, Sam had no way of knowing that he would never be able to get Jack Johnson to officially meet him in the ring again. He did however, face him in an exhibition that was arranged to benefit the April 18th San Francisco earthquake survivors. The day after the fight with Johnson, Sam was asked if he'd be willing to appear in an exhibition that coming Saturday night at the Hub Theatre. When he accepted, they asked if there was anyone special he'd like to box, and he told them it didn't matter but if they could get Jack Johnson he'd be much obliged. And that's exactly who they lined up.

The exhibition against Johnson was just one of many that had been arranged for the benefit, and it was reported on the morning of the 28th that based upon advance sales the theatre probably would be unable to accommodate all who wished to attend.

The program included twenty-one boxing bouts, two wrestling bouts and six vaudeville acts. All of the bouts were reportedly lively and evoked considerable applause from the crowd. There were no ropes and no ring; the boxers simply exhibited their skills on a theatre stage.

The exhibition proceedings were briefly halted while Johnson was presented with a watch and chain, supposedly given by some admirers. A short acceptance speech by Johnson followed. Sam claimed to know the watch wasn't from anybody but Johnson himself, and that Johnson had staged this little event in an effort to make himself appear popular. This annoyed Sam, who was also angered because he had heard that the day after their fight Johnson had issued a statement saying that he had taken it easy on Sam during their match.

Sam claimed that when the first exhibition round began, he made it a point to get Jack into a clinch and let him know it wasn't going to be an exhibition. This was going to be a real fight.[15]

As soon as he broke loose of the clinch, Sam went after Johnson, slinging leather fast and furious. Johnson tried to hold off the onslaught

---

[14] Glenn Stout, "Fighting Blind," *Boston*, February 1987
[15] *Halifax Herald*, 13 September 1924

as Sam rushed him across the stage, punching all the while. Quickly realizing Sam was serious, Johnson started to respond in kind.

The pair fought from one side of the stage to the other, back to the curtains and forward towards the front of the stage, each determined to knock the other out. Before the round concluded they had knocked over their water buckets, chairs and anything else in their path. The referee became the invisible man.

Midway through the second round, Sam drove Johnson into the stage scenery, and they clinched as they fell into it. A second later the scenery fell upon them, splitting the canvas where their bodies poked out of it. Pushing the scenery to the floor, the pair emerged to resume fighting as furiously as ever! The crowd was in an uproar at the sight before them.

They continued to battle this way into the third round, maneuvering their way around a cluttered floor. At one point they clinched and tried to toss one another. When that failed, they went back to brawling until someone called time, and the so-called "exhibition of the art of boxing" came to an end.

That was Sam's version of the exhibition. The next day's coverage of the event by local area newspapers reported that a number of the matches were very lively but failed to confirm Sam's version. *The Boston Post* wrote that Johnson was careful not to do further damage to Sam's eye, which had been closed during their match only two days earlier.[16] The *Boston American* reported, "Big Jack Johnson and his late opponent Sam Langford, just to show there wasn't any hard feelings over their last encounter, squared off and showed the fans some clever boxing."[17]

In any event the benefit was a huge financial success.

A month and a half later, Sam suffered a technical knockout to Young Peter Jackson in Southbridge, Massachusetts, under somewhat mysterious circumstances: Sam sat down on his stool in the fifth round and refused to continue. He declared that he had been struck a low blow and injured, but the referee claimed not to have witnessed it and proceeded to count him out while he remained in his corner. Many believed that Sam's contention must have been correct, as he

---

[16] *Boston Post*, 29 April 1906
[17] *Boston American*, 29 April 1906

had nothing to fear from Young Peter and should have been able to put him away. In any case, the result was Sam's second loss in a row.

Sam avenged the loss to Young Peter Jackson with a fifteen-round decision over him, November 21st in Rochester, New York.

It was Sam's third win over Jackson in the past two years. Sam was the aggressor at all times during this fight. He got off to a fast start, drawing first blood and closing Jackson's left eye by the end of the first round. Jackson clinched throughout the fight in an effort to avoid punishment and last the distance. There was no doubt but that Sam had won the fight when the bell rang ending the fifteenth round.

Sam finished the year with a third-round knockout, and his fourth successive victory. On November 29th, he fought George Gunther, a tough middleweight from Melbourne, Australia dubbed "The Australian Kangaroo." In that fight, Gunther's seconds threw in the sponge to prevent their fighter from incurring any further punishment.

SAM LANGFORD ARRIVES IN ENGLAND

MARCH 1907

PICTURED L TO R: ENGLISH SPORTSWRITER JAMES BUTLER; UNKNOWN; SAM LANGFORD; AMERICAN BANTAMWEIGHT FIGHTER AL DELMONT; UNKNOWN; AND SAM'S MANAGER, JIM MCQUILLAN

BEN HAWES COLLECTION

"I DON'T KNOW WHO WILL BE LANGFORD'S NEXT CUSTOMER, BUT WHOEVER IT MAY BE HE WILL KNOW HE HAS BEEN IN THE RING BEFORE HE HAS FINISHED WITH LANGFORD."

~JAMES BUTLER
ENGLISH SPORTSWRITER

CHAPTER 6

ENGLAND

By 1907 Sam was a full-fledged middleweight, and that class was loaded with talent. In addition to Sam, notable middleweights included Hugo Kelly, Stanley Ketchel, and Billy Papke. After going the distance with highly-regarded heavyweight Jack Johnson in April of 1906, Sam expected promoters would be beating down his door with fight offers. He was half right. A number of promoters were very interested in having him fight out of their club, but all of a sudden a lot of fighters found that they had previous engagements, which prevented them from being able to face Sam.

Sam's plight was wonderfully expressed in the poem "Who'll Fight Sam Langford! (A Pugilistic Nursery Rhyme)" written by W.O. McGeehan:

I.

Who'll fight Sam Langford?
"Not I," said Stanley K.,
"Britt has taken me away
And I'm signed to do a play.
Then I'm going to the hay.
I'll not fight Sam Langford."

II.

"Who'll fight Sam Langford?
"Not I," said Jack the Twin.
"I am careful of my chin
And I'm pretty near all in,
And suicide's a sin.
I'll not fight Sam Langford."

III.

Who'll fight Sam Langford?
"Not I," is Papke's wail,
"I'm a lily white and pale
And my life is not for sale;
Why I'd sooner go to jail.
I'll not fight Sam Langford."

IV.

Who'll fight Sam Langford
"Not I," said Kid McCoy;
"I'm a pretty game old boy,
But this unrefined employ
I will leave for hoi polloi.
I'll not fight Sam Langford."

V.

Who'll fight Sam Langford?
"Not I," said poor old Fitz.
"Though I'd fight for just six bits,
Still I haven't lost my wits;
I'll preserve my speckled mitts.
I'll not fight Sam Langford.

VII.

Who'll fight Sam Langford?
"Not I," said Hugo Kelly.
"He would pound me to a jelly
And I'd lose some vermicelli.
Not for me. What ta helli?
I'll not fight Sam Langford."

VII.

Who'll fight Sam Langford?
"Not I," said Joe da Grim.
"I no like to fight with him
Cause he shutta up my glim
And da chances are too slim
I'll notta fight Sam Langford."

VIII.

Who'll fight Sam Langford?
"Not I," Al Kaufmann said.
"You are crazy in the head.
Chase yourself and go to bed.
I ain't anxious to be dead.
I'll not fight Sam Langford."

IX.

"Who'll fight Sam Langford?
"Not us." The low brows cried.
And they turned around to hide.
"Nix: the color line is wide,
And we're going to stay inside.
We'll not fight Sam Langford."[1]

When the promoters had difficulty finding opponents for him, Sam took it upon himself to look up various fighters and ask them to lace up the gloves with him. He found no takers. One reporter who heard about how Sam was running around trying to convince various parties to fight him wrote a story for a local Boston daily, referring to Sam as "Beggar Sam," thus adding another nickname to the growing list.

Sam's manager was able to find two fights for him during the month of January. The first of those was a third meeting with heavyweight Joe Jennette on January 11th in the Unity Club in Lawrence, Massachusetts. The pair fought to a twelve-round draw in a contest described as evenly and stubbornly fought. But not all his opponents were worthy or willing. Right after the Jennette fight Sam's next

---

[1] W.O. McGeehan, "Who'll Fight Sam Langford!" 1907 brochure, noted "Compliments of Sam Langford. Under Management of J.A. Woodman"

scheduled opponent, Sailor Burke, backed out of a contest by drawing the "color line."

The club manager found a substitute, a fighter named Kid Williams, who was announced to the crowd as being Sailor Burke. Sam and Joe Woodman played along with the deception.

The fight almost didn't come off though, because the imposter announced—just prior to the contest—that he would not fight because there was not enough money in the house. The crowd shouted insults at him, calling him yellow and a quitter, and he relented. He agreed to proceed as long as he was paid his fee of $250 in advance. Once that amount was handed over, the fight, or rather "the chase," was on.

Williams, the man the crowd thought was Burke, fought like a frightened amateur. He literally ran from Sam throughout the bout! The disappointed crowd booed the imposter's effort and rained insults upon him from all parts of the arena. Williams was saved by the bell while sitting on the floor at the end of the fifth round. After Sam delivered two hard rights to the body in the sixth, Williams decided to drop to the floor. He refused to get up while the referee counted him out. The promoter was forced to admit his deception once the morning papers ran their stories about "Sailor Burke's" disgraceful performance.

In February, frustrated by the inability to line up more fights, Sam went to see Doc Almy. Doc worked for a Boston daily newspaper and also served as the American correspondent for sports publications in England, Ireland, and France. He was a regular contributor to England's popular periodical *The Mirror of Life and Boxing World*.

When Sam walked into Doc's office he told him that he and Joe Woodman had parted ways over a disagreement. Sam needed money, and he asked if Doc could get him a fight. Doc told him that he thought he could but that it would have to be outside of the country because he didn't want to step on Joe Woodman's toes. Doc asked Sam if he'd be willing to fight in England. Sam replied that he'd be willing to fight anywhere and against anybody.

Doc then cabled A.F. "Peggy" Bettinson, the manager of London's famous National Athletic Club, requesting a booking on Sam's behalf. Bettinson replied with an offer of $1,500 plus expenses for Sam to fight at the club on April 22nd against a middleweight named "Tiger" Smith. The offer was quickly accepted.

Doc had confidence in Sam's abilities, so he immediately went to work to line up additional fights throughout Europe for Sam, pending a victory over Smith. Unfortunately for Doc, he found that it was impossible to get two months personal leave to accompany Sam. He had no choice but to find another party to act as Sam's manager. Jim McQuillan, who was managing a local bantamweight fighter named Al Delmont, was offered the opportunity. He accepted with the condition that a fight be lined up for Delmont as well. This was communicated to Bettinson, and it was arranged for Delmont to fight on the undercard of the Langford-Smith fight.

As the date of sailing was approaching rumors began circulating: Sam had run up a number of debts, and some of the parties he owed money to might try to prevent him from leaving the country while his bills remained unpaid. Doc hatched a plan for Sam to be smuggled on board the Cunard Liner *Ivernia* early, to avoid any parties looking to prevent his boarding. On the date of the ship's departure Doc arrived early as planned, but Sam did not appear. It started to look like Sam would miss the ship's sailing.

Finally, minutes before the scheduled departure, Doc heard a lot of exuberant voices coming from the end of the pier. He spied Sam headed toward the ship, followed by a small group of men. Every one of them was carrying baggage of some sort. As the group came nearer it became clear that they were drunk. An obviously very drunk Langford announced loud enough for anyone nearby to hear, "I'm Sam Langford, I'm going to England to fight 'Tiger' Smith. I can lick any fighter in the world!"

"So much for smuggling Sam on board," Doc thought to himself.[2] He hurriedly boarded Sam and removed him from sight.

Sam had led his drunken entourage to believe they would be accompanying him on the trip at Doc's expense. Once it became apparent to the men that Doc had no intention of allowing them to board, they began to create a scene. Not much time passed before a loudly laughing Sam reappeared at the rail of the ship, stuck out his tongue and gave the group the raspberry. Only then did the gang realize they'd been had.

---

[2] Harry Pegg, *The Veteran Boxer*, Issue # 11 1952

The whistle sounded, the gangplank was pulled up, lines were cast, and Sam was on his way to England with McQuillan and Delmont, who had both boarded the ship much earlier.

Sam's arrival in England was a newsworthy event. When the *Ivernia* crossed into English waters, she welcomed aboard two British sportswriters who had been commissioned by Bettinson to charter a boat and board the liner before she docked. One of those sportswriters was James Butler. Reporting on Sam's arrival in the March 23rd issue of *The Mirror of Life and Boxing World,* Butler said that he had envisioned a giant Negro, and upon first impression thought Sam a little man. But on second glance he recognized Sam's tremendous build; the width of his shoulders, his deep barrel-like chest, and long arms that hung loosely at his side. Sam's massive frame was exaggerated by the fact that he was wearing a very loud, checkered suit. A flat nose spread across Sam's face, sometimes obscured by a cloud of smoke puffed out from Sam's big, black cigar. To top off his loud suit, Sam also wore a brown bowler.

Butler explained Bettinson's plans for the group over the remainder of the journey and convinced the men to accompany him to see Mr. Bettinson once the ship docked.

Butler observed that Sam's loud attire created a mild sensation as they walked through the streets of London. He noted that Negroes were seldom seen in the street those days, and that the way Sam was dressed drew a lot of attention. They hadn't walked more than a hundred yards before they were surrounded by a number of youngsters singing out "I see you've got your old brown hat on!"

Sam took it all very good-naturedly. He began hamming it up, turning and tipping his hat and flashing a big smile: Butler observed that whenever a party approached them from the opposite direction Sam kept walking out into the street. Butler pointed out to Sam that there was no need for him to do this and that he had as much right to walk on the sidewalk as anyone else. Sam was very surprised by this and remarked, "You really allows colored folks to walk with white people? Why, where I come from, you know we're considered nothing but poor black trash!"[3]

---

[3] James Butler, *The Mirror of Life*, 23 March 1907

Sam impressed Butler as being very happy-go-lucky and unpretentious in his behavior. But while nobody in England had heard much about Sam before his arrival, by the next morning he was the talk of the town.

Sam and his group set up camp at Stonebridge Park to train for their upcoming fights. One day Sam received word that Frank Craig, a.k.a. "The Harlem Coffee Cooler," a well respected fighter rapidly approaching his thirty-seventh birthday, was coming over to watch Sam work out. Sam enlisted McQuillan to convince Craig to spar three rounds. Sam hit the Coffee Cooler so hard that Craig decided two rounds was more than enough for him.

A representative of *The Mirror of Life* observed Sam's training. His initial impressions were that Sam hit with tremendous power but appeared slow in his footwork and delivery. The reporter also felt that Sam's defense was lacking, especially in regards to leaving openings to the stomach area. The idea that a black fighter was much more susceptible to a blow to the stomach than a white fighter was a misconception shared by many people in and around the fight game at that time.[4]

A subsequent report on Sam's progress by *The Mirror of Life*, published just two days prior to his April 22nd contest with Smith, pronounced Sam exceptionally fit and praised him for the quickness he exhibited while sparring with bantamweight Vince Coleman. The reporter was also very impressed with Sam's judgment of distance and his ability to hit with either hand, seemingly from any position. The same report advised that "Tiger" Smith had never looked better. Smith, very confident in himself, felt sure he would defeat Sam.

Prior to the date of the contest, the National Sporting Club matchmaker asked to meet with Sam regarding the selection of a referee. They were taken aback when Sam informed them that he had brought his own referee along with him. Incredulous, they advised Sam that was completely out of the question. Sam just gave them a big smile, raised his right fist in the air and announced, "Here's my referee, a referee that can give the right decision every time."[5]

---

[4] James Butler, *The Mirror of Life*, 6 April 1907
[5] Nat Fleischer, "The Langford Legend," *The Ring*, March 1956

Sam's meaning was clear. It didn't concern him who they selected as the referee because he was confident no decision would need to be awarded. Sam would eliminate the need for a decision with his fists. Famed British sportsman Eugene Corri was selected to serve as the referee.

The fight took place as scheduled on April 22nd. It was announced as a contest for the middleweight championship of England and a purse of $2,000. Sam was a 3:1 betting favorite. "Tiger" entered the ring first and received a tremendous ovation. Sam's entrance received a mild but polite response from the crowd.

When the opening round began Sam received a bit of a surprise. Smith was a southpaw. Sam found this awkward at first. Smith went after Sam in a furious manner, slinging leather in rapid succession, but Sam exhibited skillful footwork and neatly blocked or slipped all of Smith's blows. Somewhat puzzled, Smith stepped back to plan his next advance and Sam quickly sprang forward. He staggered Smith with a left over the right eye, opening a deep cut from which blood immediately began to pour.

Sam became the aggressor while Smith tried his hand at defending himself. Smith quickly realized he was unable to successfully defend himself against Sam's attacks, so he resumed his offensive tactics. He rushed Sam, only to be met by a hard right to the mouth. Undeterred, Smith rushed in again and found himself on the receiving end of a hard, left uppercut as Sam stepped aside to avoid Smith's rush. Shortly thereafter the bell rang, ending the round.

Sam was careful not to look too good during the early rounds while McQuillan was doing his best to get some bets down. Noted ringside observer James Butler wrote: "He (Sam) missed wild leads and swings by feet, with the result that McQuillan soon made a bet."[6]

The second and third rounds were more of the same, though Sam knocked "Tiger" to the canvas near the end of the second with a left hook. As the third round drew to a close the pair was in a clinch near Sam's corner. At that point, Sam looked over Smith's shoulder and called out to McQuillan, "Is it on yet?" meaning "were Sam's bets down?" McQuillan nodded in confirmation, and the bell rang immediately afterwards, ending the round.

---

[6] *The Illustrated Sporting Budget,* 4 February 1911

The end came fifty-seven seconds into the fourth round as Sam went after Smith in earnest. He poured in lefts and rights with such power and speed that Smith seemed completely unable to defend himself. He fell to the floor glassy eyed and bleeding. At that point Corri stepped in and called out, "That's enough: stop boxing."

British sportswriter James Butler wrote:

> No man living could stand up to such a barrage, and "Tiger" game though he was, was just being scientifically slaughtered when the referee stepped in and stopped the one-sided farce.

Five minutes after the fight, Sam sat in his dressing room calmly smoking a long black cigar while entertaining reporters. When he departed the club he pulled out another cigar and took a nice walk to relax.

Butler reported:

> I don't know who will be Langford's next customer, but whoever it may be he will know he has been in the ring before he has finished with Langford.[7]

A.F. Bettinson, the club's manager, later wrote of Sam and the match:

> Langford was no ordinary man, in a way he was a freak. Even as Negroes go, he was facially forbidding; his general physical make-up was gorilla like, for his arms were inordinately long; his craftiness uncanny; his sense of distance was phenomenal, while his capacity to hit with either hand was tremendous; it was from the first ridiculously one-sided.

The members of the club were so impressed with Sam's performance that one of them called for three cheers for Sam Langford, the real heavyweight champion of the world. Tommy Burns held the title at the time. The cheer wasn't completed, because Sam interrupted them and said, "Say boss, that's not me. There's a big smoke back home called Jack Johnson who is unbeatable. He licked me in Massachusetts last year and he's improving every month."[8]

That was the first time most in Britain had heard anything about Johnson's abilities. Over the next two years, they would learn much more.

---

[7] James Butler, *The Mirror of Life*, 27 April 1907

[8] James Butler, *The Fight Game*. London: The World's Work, 1954

Following his impressive victory over Smith, Sam was matched with Geoff Thorne for a bout on June 3rd. Thorne had been a one-time sparring partner of Bob Fitzsimmons. The taller Thorne proved no match for Sam, falling before him in the first round.

After delivering these two impressive performances Sam again faced a lack of opponents. He was unable to find any welterweights or middleweights in England willing to face him. McQuillan issued a challenge on Sam's behalf, offering to meet any fighter in England, preferably England's heralded heavyweight "Gunner" Moir. Nobody stepped forward. Moir reportedly preferred to wait for a fight with "Philadelphia" Jack O'Brien, who would arrive from America.

Sam managed to earn a few more paychecks in England by performing in a number of England's music halls. This was a good sideline while waiting for a fight, but it couldn't hold him for good. Having run out of opponents, Sam ultimately decided to return home $4,600 richer. He had made a very favorable impression upon the English boxing fraternity, and they made it very clear he would be welcomed back with open arms.

When Sam reached home he and Woodman patched up their differences. Joe resumed his efforts to line up paydays for Sam. The first fruit of his efforts was a fight on August 27th against Larry Temple in Chelsea, Massachusetts. Although no official decision was rendered in this ten-round contest, Sam clearly demonstrated that he was the superior fighter. Temple was game, but Sam staggered him several times. It was only by stalling and frequently falling into a clinch that Temple was able to get through many of the rounds.

Sam's next fight initiated what would ultimately become a long series of battles between him and a colorful fighter by the name of Jim Barry. Barry was a protégé of the great John L. Sullivan. Sam's first fight with Barry was a six-round bout held on September 25, 1907 at the Sharkey Athletic Club in New York.

Tad, a great cartoonist and leading boxing authority of the day, witnessed the fight. He reported that Barry had weight, reach, and height on Langford. Barry tore into Sam midway through the opening round, punishing him with numerous blows to the body. Relentless in his attack, Barry eventually delivered a right on the ear that dropped Sam for a count of nine before the round was over.

As the men returned to their corners the crowd was in an uproar, calling wildly for Barry to finish Sam in the next round. Sam had sprained his ankle, which would seriously hinder his movement for the rest of the contest.

Barry came out fast in the second round, absolutely determined to finish the job he'd begun in the opening session. But Sam met his rush with a right to the jaw. Barry was sent crashing to the floor head first, where he suffered his own count of nine before rising. Sam gave Barry a terrible beating for the balance of the round and had him reeling all over the ring, clinching and stalling whenever possible.

In the third round, Sam dropped Barry with another hard right, and it became clear that Barry had shot his bolt in the first round. The fight continued for the full six rounds, but Sam dominated the balance of the fight, and Tad reported that, "Sam was the better boxer, and harder hitter, and proved to be the better man."[9]

Sam's fight with Barry had proved so entertaining that the two were matched to meet again only eighteen days later for a ten-round bout in Chelsea, Massachusetts. As was so often the case for Sam, and true over his long career, he was more successful against an opponent when they met the second time. Sam apparently possessed a greater ability than most when it came to figuring out the other party's weaknesses. In their second meeting, Sam clearly showed himself Barry's master. Sam had Barry puzzled from the start and clearly out pointed him. Barry claimed that he dislocated his left wrist in the sixth round. The *Police Gazette* backed this up, reporting that had that not been the case Barry would have emerged victorious.

To get more fights, Sam traveled to the West Coast. There, he faced Young Peter Jackson in a twenty-round contest, November 12th, before the Pacific Athletic Club in Los Angeles.

Sam did all the forcing in this contest, showing a willingness to fight at all times while Jackson spent the majority of time covering up.

Toward the end of the fight, hopelessly outclassed, Jackson attempted to convince the referee that some of Sam's hard left hooks had landed foul. But the blows were clean and Referee Eyton openly laughed at this claim. Jackson was unpopular with the majority of the

---

[9] *Winnipeg Evening Tribune*, 2 November 1926

crowd and was roundly booed for his reluctance to mix it up with Sam. Many fans left before the end of the bout.

Sam finished the year with a contest against Jim Barry, in Los Angeles at the Pacific Athletic Club. This fight took place on December 17th and was held under the guidelines of a new Los Angeles law that set a limit of ten rounds with six-ounce gloves. The law further stipulated that no decision be given.

Barry came out fast, determined to try and take Sam out early. Failing to accomplish that objective, Barry tired badly and Sam took control. By the end of the match, although no formal decision could be awarded, the general consensus was that Sam had clearly out pointed Barry. Later, this was confirmed by Barry, who blamed his defeat upon a lack of conditioning.

JACK JOHNSON

CA. 1905-1906

CHARLES DANA PHOTO/BEN HAWES COLLECTION

"THERE AIN'T ANY OF EM COULD DO THAT TO ME, NOT EVEN JACK JOHNSON, AND THE ONLY WAY I CAN EXPLAIN IT IS THAT HE HAPPENED TO GET ME JUST RIGHT."

~ "FIREMAN" JIM FLYNN

CHAPTER 7
A BLACK HEAVYWEIGHT CHAMPION

Sam fought five times in the first four months of 1908: meeting Jim Barry in a no-decision bout that the *Milwaukee Evening Press* judged Barry had the better of;[1] stopping Black Fitzsimmons in four rounds; fighting to a draw with Joe Jennette; outclassing Larry Temple in a no-decision bout; and knocking out Barry in the second round of a return bout.

On May 19th, Sam met another big heavyweight, a twenty-eight-year-old rugged fighter named Sandy Ferguson. Their bout was at the Armory in Boston. Despite being almost a foot shorter and considerably lighter, Sam gave Ferguson a beating. Ferguson had rolls of fat around his midsection, and by the end of each round he was breathing heavily. Ferguson had difficulty landing on Sam with any degree of consistency. Sam, as had become his norm against bigger foes, focused his attack on the body and followed up with occasional uppercuts to the jaw. One of those blows to the jaw sent the badly tiring Ferguson to his knees in the tenth round. Sam was badly tired himself, from pushing the bigger man around the ring throughout the fight, but he was able to put his opponent down again near the end of the twelfth and final round. The big fellow was being counted out when the bell rang, ending the contest.

Sam followed that performance with another quick win over Jim

---
[1] *Milwaukee Evening Press*, 15 January 1908

Barry, on June 19th at the Fairmont Athletic Club in New York. This time, he knocked Barry out with a right hand uppercut in the third round of an action-packed contest.

Sam's only child, a daughter, was born less than a month later, on July 18, 1908. Sam and his wife, Martha, named the newborn Charlotte Elizabeth, after Sam's mother.

There was little time for Sam to enjoy the occasion. Only three days later he was back on the road and in action against a Chicago heavyweight named John Wille. Sam made quick work of the big man, knocking him out in the second round with a murderous short right hand.

Tony Ross was Sam's next victim. When they met in New York on August 7th Ross, a.k.a. "The Italian Bearcat," spent about as much time lying on the canvas as he did standing on his feet. Sam learned something from Ross though, for whenever Ross dropped to the canvas he made sure that when he got back to his feet he had maneuvered himself out of the immediate range of any further punches. This unique talent only delayed the inevitable. Sam floored him twice in the fourth round, then delivered a smashing left hook in the fifth, knocking Ross halfway across the ring and over onto his side. Ross struggled to his feet only to be dropped to the canvas with another left hook. Although he managed to beat the count, he became the victim of a technical knockout when his second mercifully flung the sponge into the ring.

Sam met Joe Jennette in New York on September 1st at the National Athletic Club. The six-round scheduled contest was to Sam's advantage, since he seemed to tire out when having to battle a bigger foe over longer periods of time. Sam knocked Joe to the canvas three times during the lively bout. Although no official decision was given, it was clear that Sam would have been the winner if one had been rendered.

Learning of middleweight champion Stanley Ketchel's quick victory over Joe Thomas in mid-September, Sam issued a challenge to Ketchel. He said he would agree to come in at no more than 158 pounds if Ketchel would agree to fight him. To further entice him, Sam offered to accept the loser's end of the purse if he failed to stop Ketchel within ten rounds, or to give him the entire purse if he failed to stop Ketchel within twenty. At the same time he reiterated his desire to meet either Tommy Burns or Jack Johnson.

Sam was to face "Philadelphia" Jack O'Brien in a six-round contest October 30th at New York's National Athletic Club, but it was called off when it was learned that the police might interfere. At the time Section 1.710 of the State Penal Code forbade charging money for the reservation of seats or places for a boxing event. A number of clubs successfully circumvented this law on occasion, under the guise of providing the entertainment solely for its members inclusive of their membership dues. Even so, there was always the danger of a police raid, especially when it came to a well publicized or controversial bout. This cancellation was somewhat of a surprise because many believed that the club's political ties were strong enough to enable them to proceed, but the risk of a raid and the resulting embarrassment to the club was deemed too great. In early November *The New York Times* reported that the National Athletic Club would discontinue its weekly boxing shows until it was determined whether they could reinstitute them without any fear of future police interference.[2]

As prospective opponents in the East dried up Sam and Joe Woodman turned their attention to the West, where they found a willing opponent in one "Fireman" Jim Flynn. It was agreed that the pair would face each other December 21st in San Francisco at the Washington Athletic Club. The bout would be promoted by Sam Berger.

Langford and his manager left for the West Coast, and by December 9th Sam had begun training for the match. Flynn, however, was confident of a victory. He was training also, but he was sure his height and weight advantage would be too much for Langford. Flynn said:

> "There is not a nigger smaller than I that I can't lick. Each of these colored gents have a little yellow in them, and if Langford is built on this plan the yellow flag will be hoisted early in the game. I will go after him and get him."[3]

Upon being informed of these comments, Sam just smiled to himself.

---
[2] *New York Times*, 2 November 1908
[3] *San Francisco Chronicle*, 21 December 1908

The night before the fight Sam went out and got himself good and drunk. An old featherweight named Charley "Kid" Bell accompanied him and ultimately, it was said, put him to bed. Many years later Bell told *San Francisco Examiner* sports columnist Eddie Muller that he didn't think Sam would even be able to show up the next day, let alone fight.[4]

Sam not only showed up, he showed up as healthy as if he had spent the previous night at home. There was little, if any, effect from the previous night's partying.

Legend has it that on the way to his dressing room he spied, through an open door, Flynn's chief second busily cutting up oranges. Puzzled, Sam stopped and asked:

"What are you dishin' all of them oranges for?"

"Why," replied the second, "Jim has a yen for them, and when he's fighting he likes to suck on oranges between rounds."

There were a dozen oranges in view. Sam studied them for a moment, then remarked, "My goodness, you've done wasted time and money. He won't be needing all that fruit."[5]

Not realizing what Sam meant, the second just gave Sam a puzzled look.

Sam felt that Flynn, who bore in straight ahead, was made to order for him. He just smiled and continued on to his own dressing room.

As Sam readied himself for the fight, Joe informed him that he would only be receiving $700 for the event while Flynn was going to get $2,500. This made Sam very angry. When Sam Berger, the fight's promoter, visited Sam's dressing room to wish him good luck and ask him to provide the customers a good show, Sam replied, "He's getting $2,500, while I'm getting $700. Mr. Berger, this is going to be the shortest fight you ever did see!"[6]

As soon as the contest got under way it became obvious that Flynn was in trouble. It's quite likely that the significance of Sam's remarks about the oranges may have hit home with Flynn's second about that

---

[4] *San Francisco Examiner*, 5 February 1956
[5] Harold Ribalow, "Sam Langford: Boston Tar Baby," magazine article, source and date unknown
[6] Roland Pete, "The Extraordinary Mr. Langford." *Boxing & Wrestling*, Dec. 1957

time as well. Sam began proceedings with a hard right to the body. He followed up with a left to the face. As expected, Flynn rushed in, but Sam greeted him with a hard combination to the body. After two minutes of fighting, Sam feinted with his right and quickly brought up a left uppercut that landed on the Fireman's jaw with such an impact that it was heard all about the arena.

Flynn fell with a thud, his face twisted in pain. He rolled onto his back and then, as if trying to find a position that would ease the pain, turned onto his side. The count of ten passed without any sign of recognition from Flynn. He remained helpless on the floor as his seconds came to his aid. After a few minutes they dragged him to his corner.

It was five minutes before Flynn was able to say anything that made any sense, and he mumbled "What hit me?" Shortly thereafter, he was helped to his dressing room where it was learned that both his nose and jaw had been broken.

Once he'd regained his senses and was available to talk to reporters Flynn issued the following quote:

> "A man gets it in the first round once in a while, I got mine quick. He is a demon. I thought I had a chance with him, but I guess I didn't figure at all. I stayed eleven rounds with Johnson, and this fellow gets me in the first. I have not decided what I will do, but I guess nobody wants to see any return match. He is a square fighter, all right, and a good natured coon.[7]
>
> "I can't see yet how it was done. He got me just on the right spot and what could I do when I got it handed to me that way? If he had knocked my eye out or smashed my nose clear off my face, I'd have put my head down and gone right after him just the same, but you can't fight when you are knocked senseless.
>
> "I would make a match with him again tomorrow, for I can't help but feel that he happened to get those two punches across on me. He made a play for my stomach and before I saw that kind of work, he steps back and lets me have his right on the jaw, and before I could get set again he rips in his left and it's all over for me. There ain't any of em could do that to me,

---

[7] *San Francisco Chronicle,* 22 December 1908

not even Jack Johnson, and the only way I can explain it is that he happened to get me just right."[8]

"Langford is a marvel and a hard man to beat," added the fight's referee.[9]

Wrote one reporter after the fight:

> Now is the time for Ketchel and, yes, even Tommy Burns to draw the color line tight and put up reinforced concrete fences around it. The lily white champions had better keep themselves lily white for some time to come. There is a dark man looming up their horoscopes and they had better duck him.[10]

The Boston Globe wrote that Sam would likely find it even more difficult to find willing opponents as a result of this performance.[11]

Meanwhile, in Sydney Australia Tommy Burns' short reign as heavyweight champion was about to come to an end. Tommy had done his best to avoid accepting the ongoing challenges of Jack Johnson, but in Australia he ran into a promoter willing to provide his guaranteed price (6,000 pounds), and a public that demanded he finally face his challenger.

Johnson had followed Burns to England where the National Sporting Club had tried to arrange a meeting between the pair, but they wouldn't meet Burns' asking price. When Burns went to Australia, promoter Hugh "Big Deal" McIntosh, offered to guarantee Burns' price, but Johnson found himself short of the cash necessary for a trip to Australia. McIntosh sent them the fare for their travel. Mr. Bettinson of the National Sporting Club in London also advanced Johnson and his manager some funds to cover their expenses on the understanding that Johnson would double back to fight Langford in London after the Burns contest. Johnson agreed to this and wrote the following prior to departing for Australia:

---

[8] *Los Angeles Times*, 22 December 1908
[9] *San Francisco Chronicle*, 22 December 1908
[10] *Los Angeles Times*, 21 December 1908
[11] *Boston Globe*, 23 December 1908

Gentlemen,

I undertake and agree to carry out my contest with Sam Langford on the 22nd February 1909, on the same terms and conditions as already arranged with Langford, viz., 1000 pounds purse and one third of the interest in any bioscope pictures that may be taken. At the same time allow me to tender my thanks to you for the courtesy you have extended to myself and my manager, Mr. Sam Fitzpatrick, whilst we have been in this country.

I am, gentlemen,

Yours faithfully,

J. Johnson[12]

When Johnson arrived in Australia, he immediately obtained the services of an Australian boxing trainer named Duke Mullins. Duke had trained Johnson when he had visited the country in early 1907. Then he had faced thirty-seven-year-old black Australian heavyweight Peter Felix and an inexperienced Australian heavyweight named Bill Lang. The Aussie trainer and Johnson had hit it off and prior to his return to the States, Johnson had promised Mullins that when he eventually fought for the title he would send for him to assist with his preparation. Neither could have predicted that the title fight would be fought on Mullins' native soil.

In his memoirs, published many years later, Mullins said that while he found Johnson to be very prideful he also thought Johnson good mannered and courteous. Mullins came to know Johnson as "a great big inoffensive boy who loved his mother, loved life, and had a wholesome regard for his fellow men." In Mullins' view Johnson appeared a bully only when repaying people for the insults they heaped upon him.[13]

Commenting on Johnson's attitude towards women, Mullins advised that while Johnson had an eye for beauty, he was too tactful to say anything in front of a third party. Early on, Jack told Duke how he respected the cleverness of Abe Attell—the great American

---

[12] *New York Times*, 10 April 1909
[13] *The Sporting Globe*, 25 September 1937

featherweight, who was also known for his good looks. Another fighter he spoke to Duke about was Sam McVea, who Jack said was the ugliest fighter ever born. Duke shared that information to further illustrate how carefully Johnson discussed women he observed when the pair was together. Often, when he saw a pretty girl, Jack would stick an elbow in Duke's side and say, "Duke, wasn't that Abe Attell a wonderful fighter?" If on the other hand a shapely woman with a much less attractive face crossed their paths, Johnson would say something along the lines of, "Duke couldn't that Sam McVea take punishment like a glutton?"[14]

It was a private joke between the pair. Others in their company were simply left to wonder why Johnson chose to comment so frequently about Attell and McVea.

In the weeks leading up to the fight with Burns, Johnson seethed with anger whenever he read the comments the champion was handing out to the press. Burns would talk about the colored man having a yellow streak. Johnson promised Duke that he'd punish Burns badly for his insults when they finally met in the ring.

On December 26, 1908, Johnson and Mullins were in the dressing room preparing for the bout when Johnson asked where Burns was "housed." Mullins told him not to worry about Burns.

"Worry about him," Johnson replied, "why I know a few middleweights who could beat him."

Langford was no doubt one of the middleweights Johnson was referring to. Once, while training Johnson for the bout with Burns, Duke had asked him how he thought Little Sam would do against Burns.

"It wouldn't be a match, Langford would finish him off in no time," was Jack's reply.

While Duke was bandaging Johnson's hands the door of their room was pushed open by Burns, who inquired, "Are you there, Johnson?"

"Sure I'm here and waiting Tahmy," replied Johnson.

"I thought you were so yellow that you wouldn't turn up," Burns said, trying to get Johnson's goat.

Johnson flashed with anger and prepared to rise, but Duke seized his arm and urged him to pay the champion no mind. Johnson immediately brought himself under control and laughingly said, "Some of

---

[14] *The Sporting Globe*, 16 October 1937

you boys keep an eye on Burns. He might sneak out of the building now he knows I'm here."[15]

The contest itself proved to be anticlimactic. Johnson immediately established his superiority. He toyed with the smaller man throughout the fight. Burns was game but no match for the challenger, who taunted and appeared able to knock out the champion whenever he was ready. When Johnson returned to his corner at the end of the seventh round, his trainer confronted him and asked him why he didn't knock out Burns and get it over. Replied Johnson, "I couldn't repay him in seven rounds for what he has said about me in the last few weeks. I'm the one doing the fighting and I'll go on as I please."[16]

And so it continued. At the end of the tenth round Johnson advised Duke that when Burns quit talking he'd knock him out and finish it. Tommy finally quit talking by the end of the thirteenth round. Johnson came out for the fourteenth intent on finishing him, but it was clear that Burns was defenseless and a local official stepped in the ring and stopped the lopsided contest. Jack Johnson had become the first official, black heavyweight champion of the world.

It looked like Sam would be fighting for the title in a few short months.

It wasn't to be. After winning the title and being reminded of his obligation to the National Sporting Club, Johnson reneged. He wrote:

The offer of the Club was absolutely ridiculous. Being a champion, I don't see why the National Sporting Club has a right to dictate to me as to how much I will receive for my appearance and boxing ability. If they don't want to give me my price, which is 6,000 pounds win, lose, or draw, they can call things off. I am a boxing man and can now get my price, and I don't care what the public thinks.[17]

Although Johnson received only 1,200 pounds from McIntosh for his end of the fight, he received close to another 2,000 pounds from grateful gamblers who'd won handsomely by betting on him. He was also immediately signed up by the Tivoli Theatre to make a tour of Australia. That meant he would be making easy money, appearing before the thousands of people who were eager to see the new champion.

---

[15] *The Sporting Globe*, 2 October 1937

[16] *The Sporting Globe*, 8 October 1937

[17] TB Bennison, *Giants on Parade*. London: Rich & Cowan Ltd., 1936

The London club's president, Mr. Bettinson, knew that Johnson could not be forced to carry out his original agreement and suspected that Johnson was looking to avoid a meeting with Langford. While acknowledging it was impossible to know what would have happened had the two met again, the club representatives believed that many would have favored Langford, whom they considered a murderous puncher and Johnson's equal in cleverness.

Although Sam and Woodman desperately wanted a match with Johnson for the heavyweight crown, they knew it would be foolish to put all their eggs in that basket. They continued fighting their efforts to lure Stanley Ketchel into a match for the middleweight title.

During January of 1909, the newspapers were filled with articles speculating on the possibility of a Ketchel-Langford fight.

San Francisco boxing writer W.W. Naughton wrote:

> In powers of assimilation Stanley compares with Sam much as a spotted fawn compares with a rhinoceros. If ever a man possessed head, neck and upper frame that bade defiance to the ordinary punches of pugilism, Langford is the man. In the matter of natural bulwarks poor Ketchel is vastly inferior to the solidly built Negro and when it was all over I would understand thoroughly if someone said, "Ketchel is the greater fighter, but Langford won." It would be quite possible for a bruiser favored by nature as Langford to take a record hammering and then go in and conquer.[18]

Despite the efforts of various parties over the next forty-five days, no agreement was forthcoming, and Sam left for Boston in late February.

Sam and Joe continued to hold out hope that an opportunity for Sam to fight Johnson in England might arise. Sam was confident that he'd fare much better with Johnson a second time. On February 20th, Sam said of his chances against Johnson:

> "Jack beat me in that Chelsea fight. There's no disputing that. I didn't have the experience then, and above all else, I hadn't really learned the trick of beating men bigger than myself. I'll make Jack Johnson fight harder than he did with Burns, if he beats me in twenty rounds which we are scheduled

---

[18] *Vancouver World*, 6 January 1909

to go. I realize that Johnson is taller and heavier, but he isn't any faster, and I know I have a harder wallop than he has."[19]

Tiring of accusations that he'd gone back upon his word to the National Sporting Club, Johnson declared that he had never signed any such document. Rather, he said, Fitzpatrick (his former manager, whom he had broken with after his victory over Burns) had signed it without his authorization.

The club learned of this claim from its American matchmaker, Charles F. Mathison, and they cabled back, "Johnson's statement untrue. Contract signed by him. Not Fitzpatrick. Am sending photograph of agreement."[20] The photograph arrived shortly thereafter and was reproduced by the sporting editor of *The Morning World*.

But Johnson had his sights set on a bigger payday: a possible match with retired heavyweight champion James J. Jeffries. Perhaps he could be convinced to try and reclaim the title for the white race.

---

[19] *Washington Post*, 21 February 1909
[20] Charles Gillespie, "When Langford Hunted Johnson," *The Ring*, 1931 (month unknown)

"Iron" Hague vs. Sam Langford

May 24, 1909

National Sporting Club, England

> "I HAVE NEVER SEEN THIS NIGGER. I BELIEVE HE IS VERY STRONG. BUT IF I HIT HIM, HE'LL GO DOWN LIKE THE REST."
>
> ~"IRON" HAGUE

CHAPTER 8

THE IRON MAN

Unable to secure a match with either Johnson or Ketchel, Sam resumed action on March 17, 1909 with a six-round no-decision contest against Jim Barry. The two men met in Philadelphia, the city of brotherly love, but none was apparent here. This was a bitterly fought contest, with the two men refusing to shake hands and exchanging words upon conclusion of the fight. Though no decision was officially rendered, *The New York Times* stated that Sam so outclassed Barry that he had the better of every one of the six rounds.[1]

Sam then defeated a hard hitting black heavyweight named Morris Harris. Sam and Morris met March 29th before the Marathon Athletic Club in the Clermont Avenue Rink, Brooklyn, N.Y. Morris was expected to give Sam a tough battle, and Stanley Ketchel (the middleweight champion) was on hand to witness the action. The end came suddenly in the seventh round: Sam sent in two hard rights to the body and Harris clamped down on the second delivery, pinning Sam's right glove under his arm. Without hesitation, Sam brought up a booming left hand swing that started from his left hip and landed flush upon Harris' chin. Harris staggered and lost hold of Sam's right arm. With his right, Sam immediately delivered a knockout blow to Morris' chin.

Sam followed that up on April 3rd with a second round knockout of heavyweight John Wille before the National Athletic Club in Philadelphia.

---
[1] *New York Times*, 18 March 1909

On April 11th, Jack Johnson issued a statement advising that at noon the following day he would be at a New York sporting center, intent on arranging preliminary fight details with an open field. Johnson said that he was tired of listening to the insults issued by parties who claimed he was ducking a fight with them. He said Ferguson, Jeffries, Kaufmann, Ketchel, Langford, or any other heavyweight would be welcome, and he went on to say that nobody was barred. Johnson said he would be ready to fight anybody by September.

At that time Jeffries was in New York, as were Kaufmann, Ketchel and Langford.

The proposed meeting ended up taking place April 13th, with managers Willie Britt representing Ketchel, Joe Woodman representing Sam, and Billy Delaney representing Al Kaufmann. Also in attendance were a large number of newspapermen.

Without waiting for an invitation, Britt immediately took the floor and stated his case on behalf of Ketchel.

Delaney jumped up next, sputtering, and then they all started talking.

"Why don't you fight my little baby, Sam?" yelled Woodman.

"Yes, Britt, why doesn't he?" said Delaney. "Let him fight Langford, and we'll thrash the winner with Kaufmann."

"I'll fight Langford, and I'll fight Kaufmann, too," was Britt's retort.

"I'd be willing to fight you fellows, winner take all," Johnson broke in. "I don't want to hurt anybody's feelings, and I'll give all those boys a chance. Suppose they fight it out, and I'll take on the winner."[2]

Britt objected to that idea and suggested that Johnson should accept the challenger who could raise the largest purse.

At the close of the meeting, Australian fight promoter, Hugh D. McIntosh, offered a return match for Johnson and Burns. Johnson advised that he would accept on the terms demanded by Burns in the first fight: $30,000 win, lose, or draw.

This was declined by McIntosh. He advised he would attend a

---

[2] *Winnipeg Free Press*, 13 April 1909

meeting two days later, at which time, he would offer to match Burns against either Kaufmann, Ketchel, or Langford.

Johnson announced that he would not decide whose challenge to accept for a few days. The reason for this was that Al Kaufmann was to box Tony Ross that evening, and Johnson wanted to see how Kaufmann looked as a possible drawing card.

The meeting adjourned shortly thereafter with nothing decided, but with plans to meet again and further discuss some of the proposals.

Later that day, Kaufmann blew any chance he had to meet Johnson in the ring when he defeated Ross on points but looked unimpressive in doing so. He was criticized for lacking aggression and speed, and the general feeling was that he would stand little chance in a fight against either Johnson or Ketchel.

Meanwhile, Billy Delaney started spreading word that Johnson had secretly agreed to fight Ketchel that October or November in James Coffroth's club. Coffroth, (who had arrived in New York on the 12th) confirmed this rumor, telling a number of friends that he had received verbal agreements from both fighters and stating that fight articles would be signed within a few days. He was convinced that a Johnson-Ketchel bout would draw better than any other, outside of a Johnson-Jeffries.

While all this wheeling and dealing was going on, Sam continued to pick up spending money by fighting lesser fighters who were willing to face him.

On April 14th, Sam again met Jim Barry, this time in Albany, New York. The crowd was small enough that, at first, the two men refused to enter the ring, and it looked as though the fight would have to be cancelled. A collection was taken up among the crowd, and eventually the two fighters were induced to go forward. This was a ten-round contest that Sam won by decision, but it was so slow, some questioned whether it was on the up-and-up. Sam, it was said, appeared unmotivated to put forth his best effort. He seemed content to taunt Barry and stall throughout the contest, one time going so far as to clearly let Barry hit him in the stomach a number of times.

Only three days later, Sam met Al Kubiak, a.k.a. "The Michigan Giant" in a six-round match at Philadelphia's National Athletic Club. (This contest had been scheduled for a week earlier, but Kubiak had insisted on an extra week of training to better prepare himself. As it turns out, the extra week didn't do him much good.) Sam gave him a terrific beating over the duration of the contest and clearly held the advantage in this no-decision affair.

That same day, the press reported Woodman's protest against an agreement reported to have been reached between Ketchel and Jack Johnson, setting them up to fight in California later that year. Woodman alleged that Ketchel and his representatives had agreed not to make a match with Johnson until they had met with Langford and his representatives on the 17th. He was greatly dismayed to learn that Ketchel and Johnson had reportedly agreed to terms for a bout to take place on October 12th.

With little prospect of arranging a significant fight in the States, Sam and Joe again turned their attention to England.

On April 21st, it was announced that articles had been signed for Sam to meet Britain's latest heavyweight champion, a twenty-three-year-old named James William "Iron" Hague, at the National Sporting club in London on May 24th.

Hague had become Great Britain's heavyweight champion by virtue of a first round victory over "Gunner" Moir on April 19th. He stood 5'10" tall and weighed approximately 190 pounds. Former champion, Bob Fitzsimmons, had proclaimed him a "coming champion" after participating in a three-round exhibition with the young man the previous December.

The story behind James Hague's nickname "Iron" was communicated to English author Frank Vernon, who interviewed Hague's daughter, Agnes Ruecroft, in September 1986. According to Agnes the tag was applied to James by his mother. She used to hit him when he did anything wrong, but she couldn't seem to get through to him; nothing hurt him. Out of desperation, one day she tried hitting him with a folded up clothesline. After receiving the first blow from his mother James reportedly said, "You'll never hurt me mother?" His mother, agreeing, replied, "No! Because you're like iron!" The nickname stuck with him the rest of his life.[3]

Arrangements were made so that Sam would reach England early enough to allow him time to make a few music hall appearances and

---

[3] B. Chambers, *Iron Hague, A Champion's Diary*. Privately published, 1997.

pick up some extra coin, then have two weeks to train for the bout. Sam later claimed that he was offered $10,000 plus expenses for the fight itself. If true, it turned out to be the most money he was ever offered for a single fight.

Prior to departing for England Sam decided to accept an April 27th Boston rematch with Sandy Ferguson. The pair had fought the previous May, when Sam had defeated the taller and heavier man in a twelve-round decision. To the great surprise of most parties in attendance, on April 27th Ferguson earned a draw with Sam.

The *Police Gazette* reported that many excellent judges of pugilism felt the draw verdict was incorrect and had emphatically declared that Sam had won all the way. If the fight had gone to a finish Ferguson would have been knocked out. The crowd booed the referee's decision and left convinced that Sam was not only Ferguson's master but was capable of giving Jack Johnson all that he could handle.[4]

The referee's verdict of a draw left a sour taste in Sam's mouth as he prepared to set sail for London. Sam departed for England aboard the steamer *Deutschland* accompanied by manager Joe Woodman, sparring partners Bob Armstrong, John "Liver" Davis, and trainer George Byers, where he began preparing for the fight with Hague.

Shortly before the fight, Sam met Australian trainer Duke Mullins for the first time. Sam was in the London streets with his sparring partners when one of them recognized Mullins and gave Sam a nudge. Sam, whom Mullins recognized from photos he had seen of him, approached the Aussie.

"You're Duke Mullins who looked after Jack Johnson in Australia ain't you?" Sam said. "Come meet my friends."

Mullins joined the men. Sam asked him if he'd seen Hague in action. Mullins had, and noted that Hague was as slow as cold molasses, but could hit hard.

"I'se likes em slow," grinned Sam, as he fondled the knuckles of what Duke thought were very small hands for a light heavyweight.

Near the end of their meeting Langford fumbled in the pocket of his trousers and pulled out a large key that Mullins estimated to be nearly 10" in length and weighing close to a pound.

---

[4] *Police Gazette*, 27 April 1909

"Say boys, I don't think I can give this to Mr. Mullins," said Sam.

Duke didn't know what Sam was talking about, but an explanation followed. He was told that upon departing America Sam was handed the key by a friend and told that if he ever met an uglier man than himself he should pass the key to him.

Two years later, Duke saw Sam give the key away. They were in Paris, where Sam had arrived to fight Sam McVea. The main men of French boxing, including Sam McVea, had gathered at the *Gare du Nord* to welcome Langford. McVea was decked out in his best clothes for the occasion. He came strutting into the room, and the moment Langford laid eyes upon him he turned to his friend and long-tine sparring partner John "Liver" Davis, and excitedly said, "That's him! Where's my key?"

He then walked up to McVea and forced the key into his hand saying, "Golly, McVea, you'll have some trouble getting rid of that key." Someone then gave McVea an explanation of the story behind the key.

"Holy smoke!" exclaimed McVea. "Mrs. McVea's son Sammy ain't never won any beauty contests. I guess I'll carry that piece to the grave."[5]

On the day of the fight with Hague, Sam felt extremely confident. He and Woodman decided they wanted to place a big bet. They appointed John "Liver" Davis to act on their behalf and go get a $10,000 bet down at even money, on Sam to win. Since they hadn't yet collected the purse for the fight, they didn't have the money to put up, but in England at the time an oral bet was all that was required as long as the bookies felt the party was creditworthy.

Davis successfully located a party with whom to place the bet. He told them who he was and who he was representing, providing letters to prove it, and announced, "I want to bet ten thousand on Langford." The bet was quickly accepted and Davis left to give the good news to Sam and Joe.

Meanwhile, Hague and Sam were resting in adjacent rooms in the National Sporting Club. England's famous referee, Eugene Corri, had been assigned to officiate the contest, and he visited Hague prior to the fight. Said Hague to Corri, "I have never seen this nigger. I believe he is very strong. But if I hit him, he'll go down like the rest." Hague then

---

[5] *The Sporting Globe*, 23 October 1937

expressed a concern regarding Sam's hand bandages and shared his suspicion that Sam might put on hard bandages instead of soft ones.

"You needn't worry, Dr. Matthews is putting them on Langford now. They are the usual soft bandages. Come with me and take a look for yourself," said Corri.[6]

Hague accompanied Corri to Sam's room. They found Sam stripped to the waist. Corri saw a look of astonishment on Hague's face as he looked upon Sam for the first time. Corri was not surprised, as Sam was the most muscular boxer that he'd ever seen.

When Hague asked to see the bandages Sam laughed and responded, "Did you think I was going to put in a horseshoe for luck?"

Corri introduced the two and they shook hands.

"You look pretty strong," said Hague to Sam.

"I'm all right, you don't look too bad yourself," said Sam.

Hague's mission accomplished he returned to his own room to resume preparations for the fight.

Davis returned to Sam's dressing room at the club just twenty minutes before the fight. He had gotten lost on his way back, but he happily announced that the bet was down. "Here you go, ten thousand on you to win at even money," Davis said as he handed Sam the ticket.

Sam took a look at the ticket and a look of shock came over his face. Woodman grabbed the ticket and produced a look of astonishment as well.

"What's the matter, isn't it alright?" asked Davis. In a shaky voice Woodman responded, advising Davis that the bet he had placed was for 10,000 pounds, not 10,000 dollars, and 10,000 pounds was the equivalent of 50,000 dollars.

"If Sam doesn't win this fight tonight, we lose $50,000. We can't pay that much, and we'll be sent to jail," said Joe.

Now it was Davis' turn to experience shock.[7]

Sam was badly rattled as he made his way to the ring. He wasn't afraid of Hague, but the size of the bet and the fact that they didn't have the money to back it up had him legitimately worried. What if he accidentally lost the fight on a foul? Or he was unable to knock

---

[6] Eugene Corri, *Fifty Years in the Ring.* London: Hutchinson & Co., 1933.
[7] *Halifax Herald,* 25 August 1924

Hague out and an unfair decision were rendered? Any number of things could go wrong!

Hague entered the ring next.

For reasons that remain unknown, once Hague was in the ring Sam sauntered over to Hague's corner and raised an objection regarding the bandages on Hague's hands. Maybe this was an attempt on Sam's part to rattle Hague, or maybe it was simply Sam's way of needling Hague for having previously questioned the bandages on Sam's hands. Whatever Sam's reasons, a long argument ensued, during which Sam carried his stool over and seated himself until the matter was hashed out to everyone's satisfaction.

Immediately prior to the beginning of the first round, Mr. Bettinson made a remarkable announcement from the center of the ring. He said that, in the opinion of many good judges of pugilism, the contest about to take place was for the world championship. The basis for this belief he explained, was the fact that Johnson had failed to live up to his agreement to return to the club and face Langford. Thus, in the opinion of many the contest between Hague and Langford featured the man Johnson had forfeited to (Sam) and the current undisputed champion of England (Hague).

At the invitation of Bettinson, Duke Mullins was on hand to witness the event. In fact, Mullins had attended the weigh-in, where Hague's backers were excited to discover their man held a twenty pound weight advantage over Langford. Many of them immediately offered to bet 2:1 on their man. Recalling that Jack Johnson had said Langford could best half the heavyweights he knew, Mullins helped himself to a little of that action.

When the fight started, Sam was so worried about the bet Davis had placed that his mind wasn't on the task at hand. Hague came out fast, showing little interest in trying to get a feel for how Sam would handle the bout. Sam was worrying about the bet, while Hague was doing his best to deliver some immediate punishment. Hague's initial focus was clearly on Sam's body. Hague believed, as did many of the era, that you couldn't hurt a black fighter by hitting him in the head but you could hurt him with blows to the stomach. Sam didn't like a hard blow to the stomach, but what fighter did—white or black?

Hague threw many powerful blows in the first two rounds, but most either missed their mark or were blocked by Sam. He did however land a couple of blows to Sam's head in the second round. After one of those Sam slipped and went over on his hands, but he immediately jumped back up. Encouraged, Hague rushed Sam and scored with several more blows. The grin of bravado that Sam had exhibited at the beginning of the fight disappeared.

In the third round, Hague hit Sam on the point of the chin with a right hook, and Sam went down. British author Harry Preston recalled later that when Sam hit the deck, the club members gasped and excitedly looked at one another. "At last we have a real white hope," many in attendance thought at that point.

"Hear, hear!" the crowd yelled loudly.

Five seconds were counted before Sam crawled up onto one knee. But before getting into that position, Duke Mullins, who was sitting near the ring, saw Sam wink to his seconds. At the count of six he shook his head as if to clear out the cobwebs.

Hague looked on in astonishment, amazed that Sam was able to get back on his feet after receiving such a blow. He confidently rushed forward and threw a wild punch at Sam's head. Had it landed, it might have finished the job. But it missed badly, and it became clear that Hague was tiring from his efforts earlier in the round. After a few more frantic offensive efforts on Hague's part, the bell rang and both fighters retired to their corners for a well needed rest.

As he sat down on his stool Sam asked his trainer what the "hear, hear" business was all about. "That's English applause," he was told.[8] This was a revelation. The thought of applause for the punishment he had received in the previous round made Sam's blood boil. He forgot all about the $50,000 bet.

Sam came out for the fourth round like a house afire, delivering three rapid left jabs in succession. The third jab drew a lead left to the body from Hague, which Sam immediately countered with a perfectly timed right cross that landed on the point of Hague's chin.

"Hague dropped like a stricken ox," reported England's *Boxing World*.[9]

"There, there!" shouted Sam.[10]

---

[8] *Boxing*, 11 September 1909
[9] *Boxing World*, 3 March 1910: 57
[10] *Boxing*, 11 September 1909

As Preston recalled, the punch that Sam delivered was one of the most tremendous blows he had ever seen. It lifted Hague clean off his feet. Preston said he had never seen a fighter with a more extraordinary reach or a better sense of judgment. Preston always regretted that Peggy Bettinson, the club's matchmaker, never was able to bring Sam and Jack Johnson together for a match.

As the timekeeper began his count on Hague, Sam walked away. While the crowd yelled for Hague to get up, Sam stood with his back to his fallen opponent and spoke loud enough for all at ringside to hear, "Say boys, he'll never get up. That baby's out!"[11]

When the formal count was finished, Sam walked over and helped carry Hague back to his corner.

British sportswriter and author James Butler, who witnessed the fight against Hague as well as many others of Sam's, also felt that Sam was the most remarkable colored fighter of all time. Butler maintained that without hesitation Sam was the greatest glove fighter he ever met, and he always thought that if Sam had been matched a second time with Jack Johnson he would have defeated him.

After the fight, a bewildered Hague remarked to the referee Eugene Corri, "That nigger can fight. I'm not surprised that Johnson didn't want to meet him. I've had enough of him."[12]

Later in the club's lounge, Hague approached Sam and asked what in the hell he hit him with. "Your chin and my fist travelin' different ways, that's all, Mr. Hague," said Sam respectfully.[13]

Hague never could understand how a man that much smaller could pack such a wallop.

When Mullins caught up with Sam he asked how he had been knocked down in the third round.

Sam told Duke that he saw the big right hand coming and "jes' popped up my shoulder to stop the punch, and it am loaded with dynamite."[14] As Sam discovered, Hague could indeed hit.

Unfortunately for Hague, his fighting game never developed much further. Corri felt that Langford had broken his spirit. A number of

---

[11] James Butler, *Kings of the Ring.* London: Stanley Paul, 1936

[12] Eugene Corri, *Gloves and The Man.* London: Hutchinson & Co., 1928

[13] John B. Kennedy, "Tar Baby. An Interview with Sam Langford," *Colliers, The National Weekly,* 21 May 1927

[14] *The Sporting Globe,* 23 October 1937

men whom Hague had previously beaten defeated him in future bouts. Everything had been going Hague's way until he faced Sam. After that, Hague just wasn't the same.

The day after the fight British fans, still bitter at Johnson for backing out of his agreement to fight at the National Sporting Club, declared that Langford was the better man of the two. Many immediately claimed Sam was the new world heavyweight champion.

Sam immediately issued another challenge to meet Johnson in London, but, Johnson—who had been booked to appear in vaudeville for six weeks or more in London—suddenly cancelled those arrangements and issued a statement saying he intended to meet an opponent in the United States the next month.

That same day Woodman collected the $50,000 in winnings and the $10,000 purse, along with a handsome championship belt from the National Sporting Club. Sam made a few appearances in London music halls, billed as "the champion heavyweight of the world" and then the party set sail for home.

Harry Preston told an interesting story about one of Sam's experiences during this trip to England: one night in the bar of the National Sporting Club, Preston found one of the general members entertaining Sam and inquired how the two had met. It seems that a night or two before, Sam had been at the club around closing time. Coming out, there was a big crush, and one of the club members thought somebody was shoving him. Turning around, he saw a short, broad-shouldered "Negro" at his back. Immediately leaping to the conclusion that the "Negro" had pushed him, and being a man of action, he had punched the colored gentleman bang on the nose.

"Don't shove!" said he.

The "Negro" looked mildly surprised. He snorted through his affronted organ, shook his head, and said quietly, "You're very fresh tonight, mister."

It was Sam Langford. Being a quiet and inoffensive man, he could take a little thing like a punch on the nose in good spirit, and he chose not to retaliate.

When the member had come into the club the next Monday night, he saw the stocky black fellow there again and asked another member to identify who he was. When he learned it was Langford he'd assaulted he went over, apologized, and insisted on Sam breaking a bottle of champagne with him.

"It isn't often I get a chance to bang a man of your caliber on the nose, let alone get away with it," he told Langford.[15]

---

[15] Harry Preston, *Leaves From my Unwritten Diary*. London: Hutchinson & Co., 1936

SAM LANGFORD

ca. 1908-1909

Ben Hawes Collection

"LANGFORD IS CONSISTENT, HAS THE PUNCH, KNOWS THE GAME AND CAN WHIP THEM ALL RIGHT NOW, ONE AFTER THE OTHER."

~JOHN L. SULLIVAN

CHAPTER 9

CHASING THE MICHIGAN ASSASSIN

Sam's fame was slow to reach his hometown of Weymouth Falls, Nova Scotia. Eager to dig up information about the new heavyweight champion of England's boyhood, a reporter for *The Halifax Chronicle* traveled there on assignment. He was surprised to learn that most folks in Weymouth Falls were not interested enough to keep track of Sam's career. Even his father, when approached by the reporter, asked when Sam had last fought and with whom. However, the locals remembered Sam as a boy, and they spoke well of him. They remembered him as having a sunny disposition but being tough as hickory, and they said he rarely came out on the short end of any scrap involving other boys around his own age.

In 1909, the sport of boxing and pugilists themselves were looked down upon by many people. In fact, a Canadian newspaper, the *Truro Daily News* ran an editorial describing Sam as a "disgusting mill," and expressing the hope he get a beating that would keep him in bed for weeks—so he would neither interest young men in boxing nor disgrace his hometown by causing it to become known as the home of the heavyweight champion of the world. Over time, that would change, and Sam's career become a great source of pride for the folks of Weymouth Falls, but it certainly wasn't the case in 1909.[1]

In late June, Sam and his manager arrived in New York on board the *Lusitania*. Although the National Sporting Club had declared

---
[1] *Halifax Chronicle*, 22 June 1909

him the world champion, he didn't want the title that way, and he announced he had come home to fight any man in the world, Johnson, Ketchel, or Al Kaufmann preferred:

> "Ketchel's the man I'm after, as well as Johnson," said Sam. "But I suppose I'll have to wait until they have settled their differences in California in October. I'll challenge the winner of that fight, however, and will bet $10,000 on the side, if it is agreeable. If Johnson has really turned down Kaufmann, I will take up the match and fight him forty-five rounds at Colma whenever Coffroth says the word. I am in better condition than ever, and feel confident that I can beat any man in the ring today."[2]

July through September the newspapers were filled with stories of efforts on the part of various promoters and athletic clubs to match Sam with Ketchel that year. The efforts proved futile, some simply from the standpoint of inadequate purses and at least one because of the proposed revenue split.

While efforts along those lines continued, Sam accepted a match against a lightly regarded fighter named "Klondyke" Haines. Klondyke, who fought out of Chicago, was known to possess a big punch but have a problem landing it. His main claim to fame was a fifth-round technical knockout of Jack Johnson early in Johnson's career in 1899.

On July 13th, an out-of-shape Langford defeated Haines by decision in an unimpressive six-round performance in Pittsburgh, PA. According to the *Milwaukee Free Press,* Klondyke took a nine-count six times during the contest, and Sam was down twice. The *Free Press* report went on to say that Klondyke took a terrible beating and fouled Langford several times to avoid being knocked out.

Approached that same month about a possible meeting with Sam, former middleweight champion Billy Papke made it clear he was not interested: "I'm willing to meet Ketchel again any time that a purse is hung up. But that talk about a match with Sam Langford is all wrong. I will never meet a colored boxer under any circumstances."[3]

Sam's poor performance vs. Haines did little to dampen public

---

[2] *Hamilton Spectator,* 26, June 1909

[3] *Hamilton Times,* 27 July 1909

interest in a bout between he and Ketchel. It began to look as though there was a real possibility of a match in either Philadelphia or New York, before Ketchel faced Johnson that fall.

The popular ex-heavyweight champion, John L. Sullivan, was asked for his thoughts on Ketchel, Papke and Langford. He said that he believed Ketchel, if right, could trim Papke seven times a week, and that he could and would battle Jack Johnson to the floor when they met in October. He went on to say that he didn't believe Jim Jeffries would come out of retirement to face Johnson:

> "Jim has gone the pace that forbids him to face a young, strong fellow like Johnson and he will never enter the ring again. Sam Langford is the world's best and he can trim Johnson, Ketchel, Papke and the rest, one after the other. Johnson knows this and is sidestepping his fellow fighter at every turn of the road. Langford is consistent, has the punch, knows the game and can whip them all right now, one after the other. Kauffman is too slow, slow as a coach horse, and the others are outclassed; so it's up to Ketchel or Langford to turn the trick, and my bet is either will do it."[4]

By July 31st, New York's Fairmont Athletic Club had emerged as the agreed upon site for a September meeting between Langford and Ketchel. Preparations for the contest continued throughout the month of August and as anticipation for the event grew, New York sportswriter, Hype Igoe wrote an article in which he included the following physical comparisons between the two fighters:

> Perhaps few people realize how nearly equal Stanley Ketchel and Sam Langford are in their physical make-up. The men are splendidly built, and in many cases are very nearly alike.
>
> Ketchel has the better of the reach by a scant inch and a half. Both have a seventeen-inch neck. Three quarters of an inch makes up the difference in their thighs, with Ketchel on the small end; there is one inch difference in their calves, a quarter of an inch difference in the measurement of the ankles. Ketchel has the best of the forearm figures and the worst of the wrist, by an inch and a half in each instance.

---
[4] *Vancouver Province*, 24 July 1909

> The greatest difference in the tape measurement is in the chest and height. Ketchel stands 5'11", peering down on Sam from an eminence of four and a half inches. But Sam evens it up when the tape is whipped around that giant chest of his. The great darkey has a 44" chest normally, and when he throws it out with pride he adds two inches and a half. Sam has it on Ketchel by seven inches in the chest measurement.
>
> Both have small wrists when compared to the breadth of their shoulders. Langford is thicker through than Ketchel by two inches. Both men are growing, evidently, and there is no telling just what great changes may occur in their table of figures in a few years. Langford, with his naturally stubby build, can hardly hope to ever be as large. He resembles a heavyweight only in the heft of his punch.[5]

Meanwhile, Jack Johnson was on the West Coast preparing for his own October match with Ketchel, and he strongly objected to the idea of Ketchel going forward with plans to fight Langford that September. Asked for his thoughts on the planned match, Johnson replied:

> I think it is the most foolish thing in the world for Ketchel to go to New York to fight Langford. It is plain on the face of things that if Ketchel fights me and is defeated, he can still fight Langford who is a middle-weight. But if he loses to Langford, it will simply call off our fight. Ketchel ought to understand that.

Ketchel, undeterred by Johnson's comments, replied:

> "I expect to go ahead with my agreement to fight Langford in New York. Johnson needn't be afraid of my losing to Sam Langford. I know I can beat that Boston middleweight when in condition, and I am surely in tip-top shape."[6]

New York was anticipating one of the grandest bouts of recent years.

A damper was placed upon their enthusiasm when New York Police Commissioner Baker and District Attorney Jerome told William Gibson, of the Fairmont Athletic Club that the fight would not be tolerated, and that even bidding for such a bout was in violation of New York law. They pointed to Section 1.710 of the Penal Code of the State

---

[5] *Winnipeg Tribune*, 24 August 1909

[6] *Vancouver Province*, 28 August 1909

of New York, prohibiting the charging of a fee for the reservation of seats or places for a boxing exhibition.

Despite the warning, the club was confident the fight would take place and that they would successfully skirt the law by charging club members and sponsored guests alike, under the guise of club membership fees.

Ketchel arrived in New York during the first week of September. He reportedly appeared extremely fit, save for his right hand which he claimed was broken during his last fight with Papke. One reporter indicated that the bones had clearly not knitted properly and that there was a large ridge across the back of the hand.

Well known New York sportswriter Bob Edgren sat down for an interview with "The Assassin." Asked if he'd seen Langford and pressed to size him up, Ketchel smiled and replied:

> "He's slow. Langford is a dangerous man in the first round, or so. Sam is a hard hitter, and, like all Negroes, he's a great man when he's winning. I'll take the heart out of him. I'm a nervous sort of fellow. Being nervous makes me fast. I'll hit Langford whenever I want to. We'll try that out right from the start, and see who weathers the storm. I have as much endurance as he has—perhaps more. Langford has always fought men who were afraid of him. I'm not. That helps. I know I can drop any man I hit on the right spot, no matter how big he is. I figure Langford as being easy to hit. I've seen him fight, and I know to an inch just how fast he can go."[7]

Suffering from a lack of confidence was never a part of Ketchel's makeup. He had a boyish charm about him that won him a lot of friends, and it was clear he would be the public favorite in the matchup with Sam.

On September 16th, another conference between city officials and the Fairmont Club took place. Afterward, the club announced that the fight would be held that Friday night, as an "athletic entertainment for the members and guests of the club." District Attorney Jerome, however, went on record and reiterated his stance that the bout was in violation of Section 1.710 of the Penal Code of the State of New York.[8]

---

[7] *Winnipeg Tribune*, 15 September 1909
[8] *New York Times*, 16 September 1909

Jerome did not state a course of action, but his statement cast a cloud of doubt over whether the bout would take place.

The club restated its view that there would be no violation of the law, as interpreted by the courts, defining the liberties and rights of club members in their private entertainments. They claimed there would be no trouble since only members or properly sponsored guests of the same would be admitted to the event.

A day later, New York State Governor Hughes put an end to the planned bout when he telegraphed D.A. Jerome, Police Commissioner Baker and Sheriff Foyel stating that it was their duty to see that the law was not violated. Jerome subsequently gave his opinion that the club would be in violation of the law if the fight were carried out and advised the police to take action accordingly.

Police Commissioner Baker replied by quoting an injunction, signed by Justice Seabury of the State Supreme Court, restraining the authorities from interfering. Baker declared that he had no wish to run foul of any court injunction. He was told, in kind, that if the authorities were convinced that it was the intention of the club to violate the law, the club officials could be arrested and placed under bail. If the club proceeded with holding the fight, that course of action was considered open to the police and D.A.

A large contingency of policemen were ready to raid the club should the fight proceed, and the D.A. advised the police to secure warrants for the arrest of Ketchel and Langford. The club's Board of Directors hastily called a meeting and voted to call off the event, even though the decision caused the club to lose a considerable amount of money.

It was initially thought that the actions would kill boxing in New York. The Fairmont Club was thought to be the most politically connected of all the New York clubs, and if they couldn't pull off a fight like this, what hope would there be for any of the others?

The general consensus among those in the sporting community was that the Fairmont had made a big mistake when they announced the Ketchel-Langford fight. As long as the clubs operated under the radar, so to speak, they had been able to put on their boxing exhibitions under the guise of membership entertainment and city officials could look the other way. The Fairmont Club had been too blatant in promoting of the event.

Once the bout was called off, *The New York Times*, poked fun at the club by pointing out that the club members had been promised they'd get their money back. Wrote *The Times:*

> What money? Their dues? Why? Such is not the custom of other clubs when plans they have formed for an evening's entertainment fall through. But then, athletic clubs are different, some athletic clubs, that is.[9]

Ketchel immediately departed for San Francisco so he wouldn't risk his $5,000 forfeit for the match with Johnson. When asked if Ketchel would fight Langford for the same amount of money in Philadelphia, Ketchel's manager, Willus Britt replied, "Sure, but not until after the Johnson fight."[10]

On September 24th, *The New York Times* reported that the action to call off the fight between Ketchel and Langford had really been initiated by a number of well-known, local sporting men who feared for their bets.

As a matter of fact, Ketchel, the favorite, hurt his arm in training, or at least a report that he had hurt his arm was circulated quietly. There happened to be a group of prominent men around Forty-Second Street and Broadway who had wagered big sums of money on Ketchel to win.

Fearing that if their man went into the ring with a crippled arm he would be licked by the Negro, these men set to work to deliberately break up the bout. They succeeded in arousing certain anti-fight advocates without letting their interest in the matter be known to the reform element, and, as a result, strong representations were made to the governor that the law was about to be violated.[11]

Whether the story was true or not isn't known, but many people thought it very strange the way the fight was called off at the last minute.

Once the Ketchel bout fell through, Sam settled on Aaron Brown, a.k.a. "The Dixie Kid." The pair were matched to meet on September 28th at the Armory Athletic Club in Boston.

The Kid arrived in Boston on a hot streak, his last loss having

---

[9] *New York Times,* 17 September 1909
[10] *Winnipeg Tribune,* 17 September 1909
[11] *Hamilton Spectator,* 24 September 1909

been to "Philadelphia" Jack O'Brien in November of 1904. The Kid was a very clever fighter who often fought with his hands at his sides and chin sticking out, inviting his opponent to lead. He was swift on his feet, an accomplished defender, and he packed a wallop that many larger men would have been proud to possess. Five years earlier he'd gone twenty rounds with Joe Walcott, ultimately winning the welterweight title on a foul. He ended up relinquishing the title as a result of outgrowing the weight. Nat Fleischer, famous editor of *The Ring* magazine, ranked The Kid as the fifth greatest welterweight of all time.

The Kid was a master of the feint, and British sports writer Trevor Wignall claimed that he was most dangerous when he appeared on the verge of collapse from exhaustion. He would feign grogginess to such a degree that crowds would sometimes shout to the referee to stop the fight. When he dropped his head to his chest and appeared about to collapse to the canvas was when his opponent needed to be most alert. That was the time The Kid would suddenly come alive and attempt to land a haymaker on his unsuspecting opponent. Another of his favorite tricks was to crash into the ropes and come off them like a torpedo.

The Dixie Kid had plenty of reason to be confident, but when he finally got in the ring with Sam he sure didn't look it. A counter puncher by nature, The Kid made no attempt to lead and either covered up or jumped away whenever Sam launched a punch. In the opening round a hard right from Sam to The Kid's jaw nearly finished him, but he managed to survive the round.

In the third session Sam briefly appeared worried when he received a series of body punches and jabs to the face, but he landed a hard hook to The Kid's stomach. In the fourth, he punished The Kid severely, and it was more of the same in the fifth. The Kid was floored early in that round: he landed with a thud in his corner after receiving a heavy body punch from Sam, just prior to the bell.

Before the sixth round could begin The Kid's seconds threw in the sponge, saving their man from a certain knockout.

On October 16, 1909, middleweight champion Stanley Ketchel met Jack Johnson in Colma, CA. He was knocked out in the twelfth round. The well known story surrounding this fight is that an agreement had been made prior to the match stating that Johnson would not attempt to knock out Ketchel; but when Ketchel tried to double cross the heavyweight champion with a failed knockout blow of his own, he was knocked out by an angered Johnson.

Sam immediately reissued his challenge to Ketchel for a forty-five round contest for the middleweight crown. He said that he would agree to any fair division of the purse and a $5,000 side bet, and that he would stop Stanley in quicker fashion than Johnson had.

Sam also continued to hold out hope that the Johnson-Jeffries match wouldn't come off. If it didn't, Johnson might finally agree to set a match with Sam again.

Around the same time, Sam learned that John "Klondyke" Haines was publicly boasting of having stayed the limit with him in their six-round meeting in Philadelphia two months earlier. Sam felt there was just one thing to do: he would fight him again. This time they met in Boston on November 2nd.

Despite Klondyke's recent boasting, the *Milwaukee Evening* reported that "the big colored man from Chicago" appeared badly frightened by Sam. Sam dropped his opponent three times in the second round before landing a heavy right that ended the bout for good.[12]

Sam then made quick work of Mike Schreck in Pittsburgh on November 23rd. Schreck was expected to give Sam a tough fight, but Sam beat him so badly within the first minute of the opening round, that the local police superintendent stepped in and ordered an end to the contest.

Jack Johnson was also in Pittsburgh, playing a week's engagement at a local theatre. On November 24th, Sam and his manager posted the $10,000 forfeit that Johnson had been insisting as a prerequisite to fighting Sam again. They hoped this would embarrass the champion into accepting a match. There was little chance of this, because it was becoming clear that Jeffries would meet Johnson that coming summer.

At that point any chance of Johnson risking his title against Sam, or any other fighter, quickly disappeared. Johnson and Jeffries ultimately signed articles on February 1, 1910 to meet on July 4th of that same year.

Rebuffed again in his efforts to make a match with Johnson, Sam accepted another match with The Dixie Kid, to take place in Memphis,

---

[12] *Milwaukee Evening*, 3 November 1909

TN. At the time, the city of Memphis only allowed matches between fighters of the same race. Sam got a firsthand dose of the south's racial landscape. After being met at the rail station by several hundred black admirers he attempted to check into a first rate Memphis hotel and was refused. Rather than cause a disturbance of any kind, Sam simply picked up his belongings and moved along to a hotel that had no such restrictions.

It was later learned that in conjunction with Sam's trip to Memphis the Pullman Company was indicted by the grand jury of Paducah, KY for violating Jim Crow law. A "Jim Crow Law" was any of the laws that enforced racial segregation in the United States' southern states between the end of the formal Reconstruction period (1877) and the beginning of a strong civil rights movement (1950s). "Jim Crow" was the name of a minstrel routine—actually "Jump Jim Crow"—performed beginning in 1828 by its author, Thomas Darmouth "Daddy" Rice, and by many imitators. The term came to be a derogatory epithet for blacks and a designation for their segregated life.

From the late 1870s, Southern state legislatures, no longer controlled by carpetbaggers and freedmen, passed laws requiring segregation of whites from "persons of color" in public transportation. Generally, anyone of ascertainable or strongly suspected black ancestry in any degree was for this purpose a "person of color." The segregation principle was extended to schools, parks, cemeteries, theatres, and restaurants in an effort to prevent any contact between blacks and whites as equals.

A few days prior to Sam's match with The Dixie Kid in Memphis, several white Paducahians on their way from Louisville, KY to Paducah occupied berths in a Pullman sleeper car. They testified before the grand jury that two "Negro" boxers whom they figured were Sam Langford of Boston and another "Negro" fighter en route to Memphis, left the "Negro" coach, and, guided by the "Negro" porter, were led to berths in a Pullman sleeper on the Illinois Central Railroad. The Kentuckians had no objection to them as fighters but rebelled at traveling with "Negroes," who had no legal right to enter a coach occupied by white people.[13]

---

[13] *Milwaukee Evening*, 17 January 1910

The fight took place on January 10th in the Phoenix Athletic Club and wasn't much of a contest. The Dixie Kid seemed frightened from the start and was floored a number of times in the first two rounds. Despite yells from the crowd to stop the one-sided match the referee let the contest continue into the third round, when Sam delivered the knockout with a right hand blow to the Kid's midsection.

According to a story later told by sportswriter Al Laney, after the fight the Kid asked Sam why he always went for his body instead of his head. According to Laney, Sam told him it was because his head had eyes, implying it was easier to land blows to the body.

With no immediate opportunities available to Sam in the East on the horizon, Sam and Woodman headed West in search of willing opponents.

"Fireman" Jim Flynn and Sam Langford
squaring off in San Francisco prior to their 12/21/1908 match
Charles Dana photo/Richard Self Collection

"I HAVE SEEN MEXICANS CUT EACH OTHER INTO RIBBONS WITH BOWIE KNIVES, BUT THIS IS TOO STRONG FOR ME."
~FAN OBSERVATION AT LANGFORD-FLYNN MATCH

CHAPTER 10

ENCOUNTER WITH A RAZOR

Once Sam arrived on the West Coast arrangements were made for a rematch with "Fireman" Jim Flynn. They met on February 8, 1910 in Vernon, California.

Since Sam had knocked out the "Fireman" in the first round of their previous encounter (December of 1908) the general consensus was that he'd have an easy time of it. In fact, *Los Angeles Times* reporter Harry Carr wrote that Flynn had "about as much chance as a woodpecker would against a pile driver."[1]

But Flynn produced one of the biggest surprises of the year when he out-boxed Sam over the course of the scheduled ten-rounder. While no official verdict was given, the general consensus was that Flynn was the clear winner. He showed no hesitancy to mix it up with Langford, crouching low throughout the fight and repeatedly rushing into clinches as Sam attempted to set himself. Flynn also seemed to have the best of the infighting throughout the fight. Sam suffered a deep cut over his right eye in the third round, producing a steady flow of blood. The middle rounds reportedly belonged to Flynn, and he also appeared to get the better of the action in the last couple of rounds. Even so, Langford laughingly mocked him after receiving a light left lead at the beginning of one round, asking Flynn if he thought he "could knock [him] out."[2]

---

[1] *Los Angeles Times*, 6 February 1910
[2] *The Boxing World*, 3 March 1910

Promoter Tom McCarey, who had attended the fight and sat ringside, offered this view to a reporter:

> "Jim Flynn won that night for the simple reason that he was in the best shape of his career. On the other hand, I have reason to doubt that Langford was at his best. Langford, in my opinion, regarded Flynn as easy, and evidently for that reason neglected his training.
>
> "I can explain my knowledge of Langford's condition. It chanced that I sat back of Sam's corner when Joe Woodman, Langford's manager rushed from his seat and bawled out Bob Armstrong, who was seconding Langford. Bob Armstrong, by the way, was to my mind a very efficient second.
>
> "Woodman called out, 'Why don't you send Sam in and stop this fellow?'
>
> "I will never forget Bob's answer. 'Mister Joe, you done hired me to look after this matter and you is paying me pretty good money for what you thinks I know. You go down and tend to that door and look after the money. I am going to try my best to see that our Sammy is there at the end of ten rounds, instead of sending him in to stop Mister Flynn. I'se discovered that our Sam isn't in good condition and it takes some very good work to keep up our end. Now don't bother me no more, Joe, don't bother me.'
>
> "Sam had him (Flynn) on the floor twice in the first and second rounds, or second and third, I don't remember which, but Flynn was in such great shape that he managed to weather them through, and it was very hard on Sam, because he thought he had him and over-exerted himself a little. Therefore, from then on Sam had an awful battle on his hands, and Flynn received the verdict, which I think he deserved."[3]

Sam would later state, in his own defense, that there weren't a lot of men willing to face him at the time and it didn't seem like very good business on his part to kill them all off too soon, so he allowed Flynn to go the distance.

Letting Flynn go the distance was one thing, but Sam's performance didn't help his case for a match with Johnson. In fact, it raised

---

[3] Tom McCarey, "When Jim Flynn had Sam Langford on the Floor Four Times." newspaper article, source and date unknown

a lot of doubt in the minds of the general public regarding the validity of Sam's claims that he could defeat Johnson. Some suggested that his ring skills might be starting to decline.

Sam's pride was stung when he learned that Flynn's supporters were voicing the opinion that his knockout of Flynn in their first match had been a fluke. Los Angeles sports writer Beany Walker wrote that he'd been easily beaten by Flynn. Sam immediately demanded that Joe seek a rematch.

On February 10th, it was announced that Woodman and promoter Tom McCarey had reached an agreement for a third match between Flynn and Sam. It would be a forty-five round contest to take place on St. Patrick's Day, March 17th, in the Vernon Arena.

That business taken care of, Joe and Sam made plans to travel to Cheyenne, Wyoming for a February 22nd twenty-round match with Nat Dewey, Wyoming's reigning light heavyweight champion. Although Nat was rumored to be a fearsome prospect, Sam and his manager assumed the trip would be relatively uneventful. It turned out to be anything but.

Sam and Joe arrived in Cheyenne three days before the fight. The weather was extremely cold, and Sam later joked that every time he blew out a breath a cake of ice would fall on his feet, and sometimes it would be two or three cakes. He claimed that each morning when he awoke he had to get an axe and chip icicles off himself.

Sam's bout with Nat was scheduled to begin at 10 p.m. He had promised the promoters he'd go easy on Nat for awhile in order to ensure the locals got a run for their money. But when Joe came into his room an hour before the fight and told him that a train going back to Los Angeles was three hours late and would be coming through about 10:45 p.m., Sam immediately changed plans. Before Joe could finish suggesting that Sam end the evening's activities as soon as possible, Sam interrupted and said, "We're gonna catch that train. They ain't going to bury a chunk of black ice here tomorrow morning."[4]

Sam broke the news to the fight's promoters, who begged him to carry Dewey for at least a few rounds. Sam answered that while he'd like to oblige them, it was just too cold.

---

[4] *Halifax Herald,* 28 August 1924

When the preliminary matches concluded early the main event schedule was moved up, and the two fighters appeared in the ring at about 9:40 p.m. Sam looked Nat over as they came to the center of the ring to receive the referee's instructions. Nat was big and powerful looking, but Sam was confident he'd be able to take him out quickly. When he returned to his corner Sam told Joe that he was going to get Dewey early and for Joe to go get on the train—Sam would meet him on it.

When the bell rang both parties sprang to the center of the ring. Dewey landed several short jabs to Sam's face to no effect. Sam landed two hard lefts, one to Dewey's jaw, and the other to the stomach. Dewey came back and attempted to mix it up with Sam, covering his face and attempting to duck under Sam's punches, but Sam was able to reach over Dewey's guard with a left to the jaw that sent him reeling, and he stumbled to the floor twice.

Dewey was game though, and he rose for more. Sam landed a vicious right to the face that sent him down hard. Dewey managed to beat the count again, but his legs were shaky and it only took a light punch to the head to put him down for the count. The end had come only 1 minute and 50 seconds into the opening round.

Sam jumped down from the ring and started shoving his way up the aisle.

As he neared the back of the hall he suddenly heard a number of shouts and noticed people scattering in all directions. When he turned to see the cause of the ruckus he immediately spied a woman racing up the aisle toward him with an open razor in her hand. It was none other than Nat's wife who had been watching from ringside, and she was rapidly closing the distance between herself and Sam. Already in a hurry to make the train, Sam now had even greater incentive to make a quick exit.[5]

He immediately turned and raced into his dressing room, quickly locking the door. Throwing on his overcoat, he grabbed the remainder of his clothes, tucked them under his arm, opened a window, propelled himself into the cold night air, and ran through the town to

---

[5] It must be noted that the author found no newspaper accounts to substantiate Sam's story about being chased up the aisle by a woman with a razor following the conclusion of the fight.

reach the train station where he met up with Joe just before the train's departure.[6]

The story spread, and there were a number of times before future bouts when a spectator would holler out prior to the beginning of the contest, asking Sam whether he had a train to catch that night.

Back in Los Angeles, Sam began preparations for his March 17th fight with Jim Flynn. On the day of the fight, despite the recent loss to Flynn, he entered the ring a 10 to 4 betting favorite. The general line of thinking was that although the February meeting appeared to have been on the level, Sam had not come into that fight in very good condition. With both fighters appearing to be fit for this meeting the general opinion was that Sam would emerge victorious.

Before the contest began, Sam asked Joe where Los Angeles sportswriter Beany Walker was sitting. "Over there," Joe replied pointing to a man sitting in the first row on the opposite side of the ring. Sam identified the man who had written how easily Flynn won the last encounter and then turned his attention back to the business at hand.

A crowd estimated at 7,000 looked on in eager anticipation in the Vernon Arena. The fighting was fierce in the first five rounds. It is believed that Sam broke Flynn's nose in the second round, producing a steady flow of blood. Sam smiled throughout the round, seemingly playing for the benefit of the moving-pictures that were being filmed. In the third round, he dropped Flynn with a hard wallop on the jaw, and Flynn barely managed to beat the count. By the end of the fourth session, Flynn was bleeding freely from both the nose and mouth and one eye was nearly closed.

In the sixth round, it became clear to even Flynn's most ardent supporters that Sam was his master. Up until this point, Flynn had given his fans reason to hope that he might be able to fight his way to a decision victory, but from this round forward his only hope was to land a lucky blow that would produce a knockout. Flynn began the round cautiously, carefully covering up, and attempting to work on Sam's body, but Sam countered with a beautiful uppercut to the mouth. At one point, the right hand punches from Sam began to land with such frequency that Flynn's seconds urged their man to cover up, and Flynn heeded their advice as the round came to a close.

---

[6] *Halifax Herald*, 28 August 1924

As the end of the seventh round neared, Sam initiated a clinch and maneuvered Flynn over toward a corner near sportswriter Beany Walker's seat. Sticking his head out from under Flynn's arm Sam looked at Walker and said, "The first punch I hit your man with in the next round is going to put him right into your lap."[7] When the pair separated Flynn landed several hard body punches, but they appeared to have little effect on Sam. Towards the latter part of the round Sam landed a number of hard lefts and rights to Flynn's head. Flynn lost his temper and tried to respond in kind, and in the course of doing so continued to punch Sam after the bell. This infuriated Sam, and he had to be restrained by his seconds. He continued to stew while he sat on his stool waiting for the next round to begin.

When the eighth round opened it was clear that Flynn was looking to slow down the action a bit. Early in the round Flynn rushed Sam to the ropes near the press box, and somebody seated in the section yelled, "Why don't you drop him and let us go home?"

"What do you want me to do, murder him?" Langford replied.

Shortly thereafter, Flynn reverted to previous form, rushing into a clinch with Sam and trying to land short blows on the inside. The blows had little effect on Sam, who struggled mightily to push himself free of Flynn. Accounts of what happened next vary somewhat.

Sam said that while the pair wrestled toward the ropes Flynn continued to pound at his ribs and stomach with his free hand. While in this clinch Sam leaned over Flynn's shoulder and announced to Beany Walker, "Hey Mr. Walker, sir, I come to give you back your champion."

Harry Carr of the *Los Angeles Daily Times* reported that in one last burst of desperation Flynn had flown at Langford, rushing him to the ropes and beating at him frantically with both fists. Langford in response laughed and pushed his blood-soaked opponent back with a look of contempt.

"What's the matter, why don't you fight?" Flynn snarled at Langford.

Carr wrote that at that point Langford looked over Flynn's shoulders at the sportswriters and said, "I'm going to get him in a minute,"

---

[7] *Halifax Herald*, 27 August 1924

and that almost involuntarily Flynn turned his head for one fatal instant, to see who Langford was talking to.

What happened next is clear. Sam freed himself of Flynn's grip, and as Flynn tried to come forward for another clinch Sam met his advance with a powerful, swinging right hand uppercut that landed with full force on Flynn's jaw.

Flynn staggered forward and pitched face first to the canvas. His jaw had been broken by the force of the punch. Badly hurt and dazed he struggled to regain his footing. "Don't let me kill you!" yelled Sam while his opponent continued his effort in vain. Not waiting to see what would happen, Sam simply turned and walked away, a small smile of amusement on his face. He leaned over the ropes to shake hands with a supporter while Flynn continued his struggle.

When the referee reached the count of ten he awarded the victory to Sam, and Flynn's seconds came out to help their barely conscious man back to his corner. Once there, Flynn stood swaying uneasily.[8]

Sam crossed the ring and offered his hand to the defeated fighter. Thinking the fight still on, the confused Flynn desperately raised his guard. Sam laughed and stepped out of range of any potential blows.

Flynn's seconds helped him to his stool where he proceeded to lose consciousness. They sprayed water in his face and waved ammonia under his nose to bring him around. When he came to he tried to rise, and asked why they had stopped the fight. Then he lost consciousness again. The scene repeated itself a number of times before Flynn finally regained full consciousness.

Wrote Carr:

> It was horrible-sickening. I sat next to an old Californian who averted his head and held his hat before his face during the last few rounds. "I have seen Mexicans cut each other into ribbons with bowie knives he said, but this is too strong for me." It was cold, deliberate slaughter. Langford, the cave man, would put his left hand against the white man's bleeding face and push him away to arms length, his little red pig eyes running critically over the maimed white body, a connoisseur selecting a vital spot, then his fists would drive in with a crash. The impact of the blows so terrible they could be heard

---
[8] *Los Angeles Times*, 18 March 1910

all over the pavilion. Flynn fought with the helpless ferocity of a wounded lion. Sometimes he seemed to land heavily, but the fight was painfully unequal. It was a raw, clumsy, savage blunderer, trying to defend himself against the skill and strength of a jungle animal.[9]

Carr wasn't the only reporter to write of Sam in that manner. Another referred to him as the "gorilla of the ring," and a "throwback to cave dwellers." In this second writer's opinion, when Sam removed his hat his head had the appearance of having been severed with an ax and was "as flat as the plains of Nebraska." He told his readers that Sam was an arrested development and a throwback of ages, rather than generations, going all the way back to the days of cave dwellers and the saber toothed tiger.[10]

The gate receipts for the fight were $19,155. Flynn and Langford reportedly received a little more than $5,700 each for their trouble.

A number of years later Flynn said that Sam was the hardest hitter he ever faced:

> "I fought most of the heavyweights, including Dempsey and Johnson, but Sam could stretch a guy colder than any of them. When Langford hit me it felt like someone slugged me with a baseball bat. But strangely enough it didn't hurt. It was like taking ether, you just went to sleep. There was a peculiar and kindly thing about him. When he knocked someone out he always stayed around until the poor bum opened his eyes. Then he'd say, 'I'm sorry son, ah didn't mean to hit you so hard.' And, I think he really meant it, he never realized how hard he could punch."[11]

Sam resumed action a month later on April 14th, when he was matched against Jim Barry for a twenty-five round go in Los Angeles. Although there was no pre-fight weigh-in Barry was presumed to have an advantage of approximately thirty pounds. Despite the fact that Sam was always able to take Barry's measure he maintained a healthy respect for him. He felt that while there were many fighters who could hit harder and who were faster and smarter, there were none with a greater fighting heart than Barry.

---

[9] *Los Angeles Times,* 18 March 1910
[10] *The Post Standard,* 5 April 1910
[11] *The Hammond Times,* 29 August 1923

The early rounds were filled with action, both men exchanging terrific blows and the infighting fierce. Barry threw Sam around roughly in the clinches but received the worst of it when the two fought at long range. There were several times when the pair was booed by the crowd for spending so much time wrestling one another around the ring.

The tenth round was the beginning of the end for Barry. Sam landed lefts and rights freely on his body and jaw. A straight right by Sam sent Barry down for a count of eight. As soon as he rose, Sam landed three more rights to the jaw, sending Barry back down for a count of seven. He was saved by the bell ending the session.

In the eleventh round, Barry excited the crowd when he knocked Sam down against the ropes, but Sam was unhurt and quickly resumed the battle.

The end came in sensational fashion. It was the sixteenth round. By this time Barry was bleeding freely from the nose and mouth and his left eye was swollen shut. Sam tried to land a hard hook to Barry's chin and Barry, avoiding the punch, caught Sam with his own right hook, dropping Sam awkwardly to the floor.

Sam felt a searing pain shoot through his ankle. He braced himself on the floor with his hands and propelled to an upright position, placing the bulk of his weight on the opposite leg.

Barry excitedly rushed in to deliver the coup de grace and let fly a vicious right hook ... but he'd telegraphed the swing. Sam rocked back on his good leg, and as Barry's swing missed by inches, Sam rocked forward and launched a murderous right of his own. The impact was not unlike that of two locomotives colliding head on. Sam's punch had all his weight behind it, and it landed on Barry's chin just as he was coming forward full-force.

Barry's eye's rolled back in his head, and he crumpled to the floor, blood dripping from his mouth. Sam tried to balance himself on his one good leg, while Barry made a game attempt to rise before dropping again and rolling onto his back. It was no use: he was done for the night. Sam tried to hop to his corner but lost his balance. His seconds caught him and helped him back to his stool. Sam, in great pain, thought the ankle broken for sure—but he had merely twisted it badly.

Sam felt extremely fortunate to have escaped with a victory, but not everyone realized how difficult the fight had been for him. The

San Francisco Chronicle wrote "Langford had absolutely no trouble in defeating Barry, knocking him out in the early moment of the sixteenth round after having administered severe punishment in every preceding round.[12]

Barry was quoted after the fight as saying that he was finally convinced that he could not defeat Sam, this being the ninth time Sam had defeated him, and the third time he had knocked him out.[13]

After only three fights on the West Coast Sam had run out of willing opponents.

Woodman, while working to find Sam worthy opponents in the heavyweight ranks, had simultaneously continued his efforts to secure a match with Stanley Ketchel for the middleweight championship of the world.

West Coast promoter James Coffroth was very interested in staging a fight between the two men and presented a proposal to Ketchel's managers. Ketchel was co-managed at the time by Wilson Mizner and Hype Igoe. Unfortunately, the pair wanted more than what Coffroth offered Ketchel for his end of the fight.

Believing that if they held out for awhile and found a way to generate more interest in the proposed match Coffroth might increase his offer, Ketchel's managers approached Woodman and asked him to agree to a six-round, no-decision bout between the two fighters to take place in Philadelphia. They promised Joe that if he and Sam would accept the offer to fight Ketchel in Philadelphia on April 27th they would agree to give Sam an opportunity to fight Ketchel for the title on the West Coast in a longer contest regardless of whether Coffroth ended up increasing his offer.

While not happy with the idea of having to face Ketchel in a no-decision, non-title fight of only six rounds for far less money, Joe felt it their only opportunity to secure an eventual title fight. So he and Sam accepted the proposal, packed up and headed East. Sam was finally going to face "The Michigan Assassin."

---

[12] *San Francisco Chronicle*, 15 April 1910
[13] *Evening World*, 15 April 1910

STANLEY KETCHEL

Author's Collection

"THE FIGHT WAS A FINE PIECE OF UP-TO-DATE
PUGILISTIC ACTING."

~"HONEST JOHN" KELLY

CHAPTER 11

KETCHEL

Stanislaus Kaicel was born in Grand Rapids, Michigan, on September 14, 1887. Better known today as Stanley Ketchel, many boxing historians rate him as the greatest middleweight of all time. Those who don't rate him that high generally consider him among the best in that weight class. His two-fisted, attacking style enabled him to win 46 of 61 fights by knockout, and earned him his nickname, "The Michigan Assassin."

When Stanley Ketchel arrived in Philadelphia to face Sam Langford in April of 1910, he wore the mantle of Middleweight Champion of the World. This, by virtue of his eleventh-round stoppage of "The Illinois Thunderbolt" Billy Papke in the rubber match of their three epic battles that took place in San Francisco on November 26, 1908.

The Ketchel-Langford bout was scheduled for only six rounds and was designated as a no-decision contest, the only type allowed in Philadelphia at the time. Respected boxing writer W.W. Naughton, of *The San Francisco Examiner*, wrote that while Sam's manager, Joe Woodman, was not thrilled with a six-round bout, he and Sam had pleaded a long time for a crack at "The Michigan Assassin," and would have to be content with whatever they could get.[1]

It was Naughton's expressed opinion that it was in long distance bouts that Ketchel had won distinction, and the fact that he and his

---

[1] *Milwaukee Free Press*, 26 March 1910

manager, Willus Britt, were holding Langford to a six-round match was virtual admission that he felt Sam would prove too good for him over the distances generally selected when ring superiority was to be determined.

Nat Fleischer, future editor of *The Ring* magazine attended the Langford-Ketchel contest and, thirty years later, wrote a biography of Stanley Ketchel. In it, he expressed a similar opinion, writing:

> Sam and his manager Joe Woodman pleaded with Willus Britt, manager of the champ, to give Sam a shot at the crown. But Britt thought too much of Langford's ability and settled for a six rounder, no decision affair in the Quaker City.[2]

Sam and Woodman weren't the only parties disappointed by the six-round, no-decision arrangement. In addition to promoter James Coffroth, there was another individual who had attempted to match Ketchel and Langford for a longer bout. James Griffin, matchmaker of the Broadway Athletic Club in San Francisco, had announced on March 29th that he was going to make another bid for the two to meet in San Francisco on July 2nd, the same week as the upcoming Jeffries Johnson match. Griffin was willing to guarantee in the neighborhood of $25,000, and there were other reports that indicated Ketchel had been presented a guaranteed offer of $10,000 to meet Sam in that contest. Ketchel, however, sent word to the promoters that he had no interest in making the type of effort that would be required for him to prepare for twenty-round meeting with Langford.

Ketchel was widely criticized for his stance by San Francisco sporting men, who without a doubt, were disappointed that their hometown had not landed such a match. At the time Ketchel's reputation was already suffering among California boxing fans. Ketchel had disappointed them by going the full, scheduled twenty rounds with Billy Papke, rather than knocking him out to reclaim the middleweight championship. Ketchel's knockout at the hands of heavyweight champion Jack Johnson, in a choreographed contest, didn't help either.

More recently, Ketchel had engaged middleweight Frank Klaus in a six-round contest that was reported as a slow and uninteresting match for the spectators. It had ended in a no-decision draw. In fairness to Ketchel, it should be noted that he claimed to have broken

---

[2] Nat Fleischer. "The Michigan Assassin," *The Ring*, 1946

his left hand in the early rounds of the match with Klaus. That bout had taken place March 23rd. On April 3rd, the media reported that Ketchel had departed for New York where he would immediately begin training for the Langford fight. They also indicated that during his stay in Pennsylvania, "Ketchel had been having his left hand, which he broke in his recent fight here with Frank Klaus, treated by local specialists."[3]

Sam, on the other hand, was held in high regard by San Francisco's sporting crowd. They considered him the logical opponent for Jack Johnson, should Johnson defeat Jeffries in their July 4th match up.

For his part, Sam expressed confidence in a Jeffries victory. He said that Johnson lacked gameness and that if Jeff was fit and could hit like he used to the champion would quit under fire. Sam also indicated that he would not challenge Jeffries if he won, because he felt he would have no chance to defeat the former champion. This statement is the only evidence that this author found of Sam expressing reluctance to face another fighter. It raises the question: did Sam really believe he was no match for Jeffries or was he just stating that in an effort to appease white Americans who were eager for their champion to reclaim the title? Sam added that if Johnson were to succeed, he would continue to hound him for a match.

Joe Woodman made it known that he had recently visited Jim Jeffries' camp and offered Sam's services as a sparring partner. Sam was offering to help Jeffries, the former champion, prepare for his upcoming fight with Johnson. Jeffries accepted the offer.

A rumor soon circulated that the short fight between Sam and Ketchel in Philadelphia was really only a warm-up for a forty-five round meeting that would take place between the pair later that summer in San Francisco. Years later, at 83, Joe Woodman met boxing magazine writer Mike Sherry in New York City's fabled Stillman's Gym and gave an interview that confirmed that rumor as fact. Stated Woodman:

> "Philadelphia the night of January 27, 1910, was the last place in the world Sam and I wanted to be. But it would have been just plain stupid to be anywhere else.

---

[3] *Philadelphia Public Ledger*, 3 April 1910

"We wanted the San Francisco fight, with Ketchel's title riding on the line and our chunk of (promoter James) Coffroth's $30,000. Unfortunately Wilson Mizner and Hype Igoe, who co-managed Ketchel at the time, decided on keeping Coffroth guessing in hopes he would raise his bid to $40,000, which was the figure they set for a dangerous threat like my Sam. Igoe told me he would take the $30,000 if Coffroth held out, but that he wouldn't accept unless I agreed to the Philadelphia six-rounder. Of course I was dead against it. We had nothing to gain except a few thousand dollars and we were risking the big opportunity if anything went wrong.

"But I had no alternative. Mizner and Igoe held all the trumps, they had the title. All I had was Sam, the greatest fighting man who ever sucked a breath."[4]

In his memoirs, printed in a newspaper in the early 1920s Sam confirmed that plans for a second match influenced him during the Philadelphia fight.

Sam said that a couple of days before the Philadelphia fight, he received a telegram asking whether he would consider meeting Ketchel on the Pacific Coast in May or June, providing neither party was soundly whipped—or something along those lines—in the Philadelphia match up. Sam knew that Ketchel was a great draw on the Pacific Coast, and he figured that the folks out west liked him too. He estimated that an open air, West Coast fight between he and Ketchel would draw a gate of at least $50,000 ... as long as nobody got knocked dizzy in Philadelphia.

Sam said he reached a decision right then and there, on his own. He decided he would attempt to make the meeting in Philadelphia a good, fast fight with an outcome that appeared about even. That way, everybody on the Pacific Coast would want to see a re-match with more rounds between the pair. When the two met a second time Sam could knock Ketchel senseless and pick up a lot of money for himself, along with the middleweight title.

As if the potential West Coast match were not sufficient cause for distraction, a couple of years after the fight, Sam told Australian

---

[4] Mike Sherry. "Greatest Fights of The Century. Stanley Ketchel vs. Sam Langford," unknown magazine source ca. 1956

trainer Duke Mullins that, prior to the bout, he was contacted by a man who told him that if he put Ketchel on the floor he would never fight again. "Just this once will do," Sam replied. After all the chasing he'd done to get him inside the ropes, Sam was thinking he would have some fun with Ketchel. Sam wasn't prepared for what he heard next. The man told him that a couple of gunmen from New York would have him covered from the moment he entered the ring. Sam told Duke that when he and Ketchel met in the ring he fought with one eye on Ketchel and another looking for the gunmen.[5]

During the week leading up to the match both parties expressed their confidence regarding the outcome. Said Ketchel:

> "I expect to beat Langford. I've always wanted to fight him. I was disappointed when our match here previously was cancelled, and right after that I signed a set of articles for a finish fight with him in Nevada. I've got them up in my trunk now, but Langford wouldn't sign. I talked this fighter over with (Jack) Johnson out West. Johnson has no reason for wanting to lie to me and he told me that I can beat Langford sure if I force him to make weight. This is at catch-weights, but I intend to beat him just the same."[6]

The day before the fight the *Philadelphia Public Ledger* reported that when Ketchel entered the ring the next night he would wear on his wrist a tiny band of elephant hair, joined by a miniature gold clasp. The strand of hair reportedly came from the tail of a very large elephant killed in Africa. This good luck charm, as it was considered by the natives, was presented to Ketchel by Edgar Beecher Bronson, an author and hunter who traveled the African hunting grounds. Bronson told Ketchel:

> "The Negroes in Africa believed that the man who wore a strand of elephant hair will bear a charmed life. He could come to no sad ending, and often his enemy was routed when the little band of hair was flashed before their eyes. The Negroes were extremely superstitious regarding the token and had always respected the wearer of such a charm."

---

[5] *The Sporting Globe*, 4 December 1937
[6] *Philadelphia Record*, 24 April 1910

Bronson vowed that Langford's courage would wither at the sight of the charm on the evening of the fight.

The *Public Ledger* predicted that Ketchel would have his hands full when he met Langford, pointing out that Sam was regarded as one of the most dangerous men in the ring. While Ketchel continued to express his confidence, a greater number of the better judges of pugilistic prowess at the time thought that Sam hit just as hard, if not harder, and was also the more finished boxer. A number felt that Sam's infighting skills would enable him to deliver a knockout blow against Ketchel and his rushing tactics. As a result, Sam entered the ring that evening as a 10 to 8 betting favorite.[7]

The fight was well attended. More than 4,500 enthusiastic spectators crammed themselves into the old armory that was the home of the National Athletic Club. Ticket prices of $2, $5, and $10 were gladly paid by those fortunate enough to get an opportunity to view the pair in action. Total gate receipts reported included figures such as $18,750 and $24,000, either of which represented a record in the city of Philadelphia up until that time.

Ketchel, a magnificent fighter, showed himself to be no slouch as a businessman either, negotiating a fee of 50% of the total gross gate receipts instead of accepting the promoter's offer of a guaranteed flat fee of $7,500 beforehand.

Sam, by comparison, received a lesser purse of $5,000. At that time, black fighters had no choice but to accept lesser compensation than their white opponents. Still, this represented a very nice pay day for Sam. It would have been for most fighters in 1910.

Sam entered the ring first wearing pea-green silk tights. He was accompanied by former world lightweight champions Joe Gans, George Byers, George Cole, and "Young Mississippi." Sam weighed 178 pounds, giving him a 19-pound advantage, but at 5' 7 ½" he gave up an inch and a half in height to "The Michigan Assassin." *The Philadelphia Evening Bulletin*'s reporter indicated that Sam appeared uncomfortable as he awaited Ketchel's arrival and noted that he bit his lips.

Ketchel then entered the ring, weighing in at 159 pounds and accompanied by Eddie Baun, Jimmie Kelly, and Nick Muller. He wore

---

[7] *Philadelphia Public Ledger*, 26 April 1910.

an overcoat, and when he disrobed he revealed his customary red trunks. Reports regarding his apparent level of fitness varied. At least one report indicated he looked to be in real fine condition, while another said that he did not look to be well trained and appeared nervous and worried. *The Evening Bulletin* noted that despite wearing a smile when entering the ring and shaking hands with Sam, Ketchel appeared just as nervous as Sam. While he sat in his corner awaiting the call to the center of the ring he wore a very serious expression.[8]

Despite Stanley's claim that he would knock Sam out, he had a couple of ready-made excuses should Sam instead emerge victorious. First, he insisted on weighing in under the middleweight limit. If defeated he would be able to prove that he was under the middleweight limit, while Sam was clearly well above it. That alone would assure that—even if he were to be knocked out in the no-decision contest—there would be no question of the title changing hands. If that wasn't enough, Ketchel also advised that his hand, hurt in his fight with Frank Klaus, was still not 100%. He made it known that his hand was shot full of cocaine before the fight in order to diminish any pain that he might experience while landing punches during the fight with Sam.

When the bell rang to open the first round, Sam proceeded with his plan to avoid landing any blows with malicious intent. One newspaper report out of Philadelphia described this round as "having a slight odor of rat to it."[9] There were a number of jeers from the crowd who anticipated more action from these highly touted combatants.

At one point after some light sparring between the pair, Ketchel started one of his famous shifts. Ketchel's shift was similar to a move previously employed by former heavyweight champion Bob Fitzsimmons. He would feign the delivery of a right hand blow that had no chance of landing, but then step forward with his right foot with the specific purpose of shifting the weight onto that leg. The result would often be that he was then in a position to immediately deliver a heavy blow with the left hand to his surprised opponent.

Ketchel never finished his shift, though. Before he could deliver the blow he discovered Sam was no longer standing in the place where the punch was aimed. With a grin on his face, Sam had demonstrated

---

[8] *Philadelphia Evening Bulletin,* 27 April 1910
[9] Billy Hicks, "Ketchel Wins Because Langford is Under Pull," newspaper article, source and date unknown

his defensive cleverness, stepping neatly to the side and flicking out a left jab to Stanley's face. Then Sam rushed in and threw three quick uppercuts aimed at Stanley's jaw, but none of these punches landed.

During that round, Sam showed an ability to effectively block most of Stanley's offensive attacks, but the ones that got through gave Sam a taste of his opponent's power and he suffered a slight cut on the lip.

More dissatisfaction was expressed by a number of the fans when the bell rang to end the round.

The Philadelphia Evening Bulletin wrote that while "no damage was done, Langford had demonstrated that he was the cleverer and had the better jab."[10]

The action picked up in the second round. Stanley's punches packed some kick behind them. In the interest of self preservation, Sam loosened some of the wraps he had placed upon himself. He staggered Stanley with a left to the face, and the two men fell into a clinch. Ketchel butted Sam in the head and Sam responded in kind. The referee immediately warned both to stop it. Stanley threw a hard left that caught Sam while he was turning away from it. The impact sent Sam spinning away from Stanley, but Sam immediately rejoined the battle with a smile on his face.

The crowd began to cheer as the action increased. Stanley was clearly the aggressor, but Sam continued to demonstrate an ability to avoid or neatly block Stanley's blows while retreating. As the round came to a close, Sam stepped forward and landed a short left hook and then a right to the side of Stanley's head. Overall the round appeared fairly even, though it could be argued it belonged to Sam for landing two heavy punches to the jaw.

In the third round, Sam matched Stanley's level of intensity. Stanley continued to be the aggressor, but Sam began to catch him, coming in with some well-placed blows that had plenty of steam behind them. At one point, as Sam retreated he suddenly stopped and rushed forward. Stanley attempted to land a vicious right uppercut with all he could muster behind it, but Sam neatly avoided the blow and responded by landing two left hooks to Stanley's head. The second of these landed on Ketchel's nose and mouth, and he began to bleed freely. His face and chest were soon covered with blood.

---

[10] *Philadelphia Evening Bulletin,* 27 April 1910

The damage inflicted by Sam did little to slow the champion, and Ketchel continued to be the aggressor. At one point he caught Sam carrying his left shoulder a little low and whipped over a wild, right hand swing that landed and cut Sam's ear.

Although Stanley pressed forward with the attack during the bulk of this round, Sam began to land punches with more force and increasing frequency. He employed the uppercut to greet Stanley each time he came in close. Stanley continued to try and utilize his shift and enjoyed some measure of success, landing twice with it, to the great enjoyment of the crowd.

Near the end of the round, Sam avoided a wild rush by Ketchel and delivered a stinging left to the jaw that stopped the stunned champion dead in his tracks. To everyone's surprise, Sam made no attempt to follow up on his advantage even though it appeared that he could have inflicted serious damage. Some were sure that Sam had purposely passed up an opportunity to knock his opponent out.

Sam's failure to follow-up gave Stanley the time he needed to shake the cobwebs from his head, and he immediately resumed the offensive. The pair were busily exchanging blows when the bell rang to end the round, but they continued to swap a few after the bell. One of Sam's punches landed flush on Stanley's nose and renewed the stream of blood.

As Sam returned to his corner, he figured he'd shaken Stanley up a few times and that Stanley probably wasn't as comfortable as he was after the first two rounds. As his seconds tended to him, Sam decided he should ease up a little bit for fear of ruining his chances of securing a bigger title fight in California. So when the fourth round began Sam put himself under wraps again. With a stiff left, he produced a flow of blood from Ketchel's nose again, and twice he shook him with rights to the heart followed by left jabs to the face. Ketchel continued to bleed from the nose and mouth for the rest of the fight splattering both fighters.

Ketchel appeared tired and worried at times during this round, but nonetheless remained on the offensive. His punches appeared to have little effect on Sam until Sam made a near fatal mistake, allowing him to get through with a beautifully performed double shift. While focusing his efforts on fending off the furious attacks of Ketchel, Sam thought he had once again avoided one of Ketchel's attempted shifts, only to realize too late that the first two blows and initial shift only served to put Stanley in position to deliver a vicious right hand swing under Sam's heart. The punch caught Sam completely by surprise, jarring him terribly, and it was immediately followed with a left hook to Sam's chin. Sam's mouth flew open, his eyes closed and his knees buckled. It looked as though he was ready to drop at any moment.

Ketchel had hurt him, and he knew it. Sam would later say that it was at this point that Stanley made a terrible mistake. Instead of forcing Sam to fight at long range, which Sam would have been hard pressed to do in his sudden condition, Stanley sprang forward to finish Sam with short head and body punches. Sam still had enough of his wits about him to take the most sensible action available to him at that time. As Ketchel came forward, Sam grabbed Ketchel and held on for dear life.

Ketchel did everything he could to pry himself loose of Sam's hold, but Sam wasn't about to let him loose until his head cleared and he regained the strength in his legs. When they finally came out of the clinch the danger had passed for Sam, and although Stanley pursued Sam with a vengeance he was unable to inflict further damage. For the most part, Sam played it safe for the remainder of the round. At one point Ketchel missed three lefts and Sam hooked a left to his jaw. Ketchel was bleeding hard the last minute of the round, and appeared to be tiring from his earlier efforts. Just before the bell sounded to end the round Sam landed a hard right uppercut to Ketchel's jaw.

The *Philadelphia Evening Record* reported that while Sam was staggered by Stanley during the round, the fighting for the most part during this round was in Sam's favor. He successfully blocked most of Ketchel's blows and rushes, while getting home with some hard punches himself. The Record reported that Ketchel was tired and bleeding as he went back to his corner. Still another Philadelphian paper pointed out that at one point during this round when Langford landed two short hard lefts to Ketchel's face, Stanley appeared to be in bad shape, but Sam once again failed to follow-up on his advantage.

While recovering in his corner during the break between the fourth and fifth sessions Sam had another little heart-to-heart with himself. Reflecting back on this moment years later Sam said he told himself:

"Sammy, this boy is tougher than a hock shopkeepers' heart. It's bad business to be wearing wraps around here any longer. Here's where you forget all about that California brawl and you go out and break his neck, or he'll be breaking yours. Yes, sir, little Sammy, that's just what he'll be doing."[11]

Ketchel came out for the fifth round with blood dripping from his nose but immediately began to force the fighting. He showered Sam with lefts and rights, while Sam backed away and attempted to ward off the torrent of blows. Then Sam stopped and landed a stiff jab on Ketchel's nose, which started the steady flow of blood once again. Ketchel continued to force the fight throughout and although it was clear he wasn't hurting Sam, he landed enough punches to make him the clear winner of this round on points.

A Philadelphian newspaper suggested that Sam again passed up some opportunities in the fifth round, but it also appeared to some that Sam was tiring. Near the end of the round, Sam stopped and swung a murderous right that would have badly hurt Ketchel if it had landed. The punch failed to land and Sam's momentum caused him to pitch forward on his knees and elbows, producing a humorous sight that caused even Sam to laugh as the bell rang.

Tad Dorgan, the great *New York Journal* reporter and cartoonist openly burst into laughter when Sam missed with the wild right and fell to his knees. Turning to a colleague Tad reportedly said, "Who is Sam trying to kid? He couldn't miss that badly if he was drunk and had one leg cut off."[12]

The *Philadelphia Evening Record* report of the fifth round indicated that while Ketchel landed frequently to Langford's body with both hands, they did not have much steam, and Sam made little attempt to block the blows while smiling to his seconds.

When the pair came out for the sixth and final round, they met and shook hands, and then Ketchel quickly resumed the offensive shooting both hands to the body, followed by several missed swings. The crowd was in an uproar as Sam retreated, dodging and side-stepping to avoid Ketchel's attack. After an exchange of body punches, and

---

[11] *Halifax Herald*, 1 September 1924
[12] Joseph Friscia. "The Forgotten Fight Between Sam Langford and Stanley Ketchel," *Boxing Illustrated*, August 1964

another clinch, Sam again landed a stiff jab to Ketchel's nose, starting the blood again. They clinched again and Ketchel struggled to land to Sam's body, but Sam held him off and laughed. They broke away and Sam landed two jabs on Ketchel's nose producing even more blood. Stanley whipped over a left to Sam's stomach and the pair exchanged jabs to the face. Ketchel was always on the offensive but to some appeared more showy than effective.

In a special report to *The New York Times* from Philadelphia it was reported that in the middle of the round, Sam stepped in and landed a left and right that staggered Ketchel, but he was back at the little "Negro" like a bull. Sam resumed a defensive mode and Ketchel pressed for an advantage. Sam immediately countered an attack with a hard punch but didn't follow it up in the manner his fans were accustomed to. Ketchel continued to press forward, forcing the fighting.[13]

The *Philadelphia Evening Record* reporter wrote that it was noticed that Langford was only using one hand (his left), and that it looked to those close to the ring as if he was not exerting himself very much. Ketchel fought like a demon trying to get to Sam in this final round, sending punches in wildly, but Sam blocked almost every effort and occasionally shot out a straight left to the face. His right was always busy blocking punches, and he never attempted to follow up any of the openings that presented themselves.

The *Record* did express the opinion that it was in Sam's best interests to avoid throwing right hands in the final round, for had he done so he would have left himself open to one of Ketchel's murderous rights. Still, Ketchel was leaving himself wide open during this round, apparently operating under the philosophy that the best defense was a good offense. One had to wonder if Sam couldn't have taken advantage of this fact had he chosen to do so.[14]

One Philadelphia newspaper, while expressing the opinion that the final round was the best of the fight, wrote that while the crowd roared its approval, thinking Langford's lack of response to Ketchel's attacks meant that Sam was all in, it was in reality Sam playing possum. They felt Sam simply let Ketchel fight away, sent in a light punch once in a while to let people know he was there, and while Ketchel roughed it at close quarters, blocked his blows and stalled him off.

---

[13] *New York Times*, 28 April 1910
[14] *Philadelphia Evening Record*, 28 April 1910

They were doing this when the fight came to a close in Sam's corner, with Sam holding Ketchel's arms to his sides. When the bell rang Sam smiled. Later, he revealed that he whispered into Ketchel's ear, "See you in San Francisco, Mister Ketchel."[15]

The newspaper accounts of the outcome of the fight were all over the board. The *Philadelphia Record* published the following headline:

Langford Bests Stanley Ketchel, Boxing Entirely on the Defensive the Black Man Landed Most Blows — White Boy Made Fight — Forcing the Contest in Every Round and Was Well Winded at Finish

In a paragraph in the same article titled "Langford Did Not Try His Best" the reporter wrote:

Just what Langford could have done to Ketchel last night, had he cut loose, can be surmised, but he surely did not try his best to gain a decisive victory last evening, apparently being well content to block and counter and wait to gather the persimmon that he must surely feel is his, in a longer and better paying contest on the Pacific Coast.

Some of the spectators seemed to think that Ketchel, having forced the fighting, should be given credit for a victory, but it is difficult to see how that could honestly be done since a great majority of his blows did not land.[16]

Another paper out of Philadelphia ran the following headline: "Ketchel Wins Because Langford is Under Pull." Wrote Billy Hicks,

Stanley Ketchel, the Michigan Assassin, defeated Sam Langford in their six round bout at the National Athletic Club. Had Langford willed it, he could have "assassinated" the man from Michigan.

The fight went the six rounds, was a great bout to look at, full of sensational incident, but when the final bell rang, there were few at ringside who were not convinced that Langford wasn't up to his old tricks of saving a man he could have licked to use him as a meal ticket later. Langford got a pretty big chunk of money for the fight and he did not give full value for the coin. With him it was clearly a case of saving Ketchel for

---

[15] Joseph Friscia. "The Forgotten Fight Between Sam Langford and Stanley Ketchel," *Boxing Illustrated*, August 1964.
[16] *Philadelphia Record*, 28 April 1910

another time. They will probably meet in a finish' bout on the coast out of which both will get fat sums.[17]

"Honest John" Kelly, a veteran referee who had presided over many famous battles during the bare knuckle era of the late 1800s, sat ringside for the fight and offered the following observation:

> "The fight was a fine piece of up-to-date pugilistic acting. Langford did all he could to help Ketchel make a showing that would leave the winner of the contest in doubt.
>
> "A fight for a big purse on the coast is responsible for the spectacular side of the bout. These short, snappy punches that Langford has delivered against nearly every man he has met in earnest were held back to permit Ketchel to come forth with his swings."[18]

The *Philadelphia Public Ledger* headline read:

Ketchel Wins By a Shade Over Langford—Force Bout and Landed Greater Number of Blows on Clever Opponent—Negro Did Not Try—Man Who is After Johnson Was Content to Hold His Opponent Safe[19]

The *Milwaukee Free Press* printed that Ketchel outclassed Sam, and that with a ripping, throw caution to the wind finish, Ketchel earned a clear verdict over Sam in what was, up to the final round, either man's fight.[20]

Perhaps the report most pointedly in Ketchel's favor came from Bob Edgren, a respected reporter for the *New York World*. That paper ran the headline "Ketchel Wins Fight, Gives Sam Langford Terrific Beating" under which Edgren wrote the following:

> Stanley Ketchel, middleweight champion, whipped Sam Langford decisively last night at the A.C., in this town (Philadelphia).
>
> It was in a terrific two-round drive at the finish that he

---

[17] Billy Hicks. "Ketchel Wins Because Langford is Under Pull," newspaper article source and date unknown

[18] *Washington Post,* 29 April 1910

[19] *Philadelphia Public Ledger,* 28 April 1910

[20] *Milwaukee Free Press,* 28 April 1910

beat the Negro. Nothing could stop or even hinder Ketchel in those last rounds. He was a red-trunked, blood-spattered fury, one mad with fighting.

At the end, Langford, his confident grin wiped out, blood running over his black shoulders in a shiny stream from a cut behind the ear made by Ketchel's good right hand, weary, disheartened, was clinching for his life and trying to hold those arms with which the middleweight champion was delivering such crushing, flail-like blows. In the last round the Negro, fought fairly off his feet, ran around and around the ring, and whenever he halted for a second to try to stop the slaughter with wild swings and uppercuts Ketchel was on him in a flash, beating him about until he ran again or clinched desperately.[21]

After the fight, Ketchel stated that he had tried for a knockout, but that Sam just had too much weight on him. He said the next time they fought he would insist Sam come down and meet him in weight, and that he would stop him before the limit in that contest.

A number of years later Sam wasn't sure who had won the fight:

"I was sure after it was over that my neck wasn't broken and that if I fought that boy again there wasn't going to be any taking it easy, as he had me all but murdered.

"Stanley Ketchel was the most aggressive man I ever faced in the ring. I learned from him what an elegant thing it is to just sort of run in like a wildcat and hit the other boy so fast and so often that he just can't get out of his own way."[22]

This comment seemed to lend some credibility to those who felt Sam's lack of offensiveness had as much to do with a need to fend off Ketchel's continual attacks as with Sam simply holding back.

Sam never did get a second meeting with Ketchel. Stanley fought only three more times, in May and June of 1910, winning all three contests by knockout before his untimely death on October 15th of that same year.

During the last year of his life Ketchel had purchased 32,000

---

[21] *New York Evening World*, 28 April 1910
[22] *Halifax Herald*, 1 September 1924

acres of timber land and another 800 acres of farmland in the Ozarks. He was making plans to earn his living off that land.

Although he had no previous business experience he and Col. Dickerson, a good friend, made plans for Ketchel to gain some experience managing Dickerson's ranch in Conway, Missouri. At the same time, Ketchel would train and prepare himself for an upcoming fight with Sam McVea in Paris, which he claimed would be his last and for which he would receive a guaranteed purse of $30,000.

Dickerson went through a local employment agency and hired a ranch hand and a housekeeper, Walter Dipley and Goldie Smith, to assist Ketchel in running the ranch.

Although not married the pair represented themselves as man and wife. When they arrived in Conway they were introduced to Ketchel by Dickerson and told that Ketchel would be their boss.

After Dickerson had departed and while Dipley was working outside Ketchel allegedly tried to force himself upon Goldie. She later testified that Ketchel threatened to kill both her and Dipley if she ever told anyone. Later that evening Goldie said that she shared the details of what had transpired with Dipley.

At the time it was Ketchel's habit to carry a .45 Colt pistol which he kept tucked in the front waist band of his pants. The next morning while seated for breakfast with his back to the kitchen entrance, Stanley Ketchel was shot in the back by Walter Dipley with a .22 caliber rifle. Dipley and Smith later testified that the shooting was in self defense.

Ketchel did not die immediately. He rose from his chair and stumbled forward into the middle room where he fell onto his bed. Goldie and Dipley both ran out of the house. Dipley returned and, while Ketchel lie helpless, took his .45 revolver. Either he or Goldie also took whatever money he had on him at the time.

Immediately after the shooting, Col. Dickerson was summoned by one of the ranch hands. When Dickerson arrived at the ranch Ketchel was still alive and able to name his killer.

A local doctor who had been summoned to the ranch advised Dickerson that Ketchel's wound was fatal. Nevertheless, the decision was made to take Ketchel to Springfield where better medical care was available. Col. Dickerson undertook a frantic effort to arrange for a special train that could carry Ketchel from Conway to Springfield.

A carpenter who was repairing a barn on the ranch came into the house and stayed with Ketchel throughout most of the morning. The bullet had struck a major blood vessel in Ketchel's right lung and the pleural cavity was filling with blood, making it difficult for him to breathe or talk.

Ketchel hung on until a little past 7 p.m. He was pronounced dead a month past his 24th birthday.

Dipley and Smith were ultimately captured and tried for murder. A jury agreed with the prosecution's contention that Ketchel had been approached from behind and assassinated. The pair was found guilty of murder in the first degree. Life in prison was recommended for both. The case was appealed to the Missouri Supreme Court. Goldie Smith was freed after spending seventeen months in the penitentiary because the State failed to show evidence of a conspiracy to kill Ketchel, and she had taken no part in the shooting. Dipley's life sentence was confirmed. He was paroled in 1934 after serving twenty-three years. He died from kidney disease in 1956.

When Sam received news of Ketchel's death he remarked simply, "Poor Steve (Stanley's nickname), he went to his grave thinking he could really lick ol' Sam."[23]

Three years later when Sam was asked who he considered the best white man he ever fought he replied:

> "Stanley Ketchel, of course. He was one of the greatest fighters that ever climbed into a ring, and it is a pity that he was murdered, for if he had lived he would have defeated all of these 'white hopes' that they talk about these days."[24]

The fact that Sam didn't get a second opportunity to fight Ketchel bothered him for many years, because he could not prove his superiority to those who felt Ketchel was the better man.

In late 1910, Sam got so upset about an article that Bob Edgren (noted sports writer and cartoonist of *The New York Evening World*)

---

[23] Mike Sherry. "Greatest Fights of The Century. Stanley Ketchel vs. Sam Langford," Unknown magazine source c 1956

[24] *San Francisco Call,* 27 July 1913

wrote about his fight with Ketchel that he sat down and wrote Edgren a letter. Edgren referred to this in his November 3, 1916 column writing:

Sam Langford writes intimating that he held back a K.O. punch in the six-round bout with Ketchel in Philly:

>Dear Mr. Edgren,
>
>I am always glad to see you or any other person giving Stanley Ketchel a boost. He deserves it. Your boost for the late Stanley Ketchel last week read all right excepting for the part where you said he nearly knocked me out in our six-round rumpus in Philadelphia. To be real frank with you, I will say that you are greatly mistaken, for the simple reason that he never had a chance. I could say much more, but rest most assuredly I told you a mouthful.
>
>Respectively yours,
>Sam Langford[25]

As big a fan of Ketchel as Nat Fleischer was, he later wrote in one of his books, "I am convinced that, as great as Ketchel was, the colored man would have beaten him in an honest-to-goodness scrap."[26]

---

[25] *New York Evening World*, 3 November 1916

[26] Nat Fleischer. "Black Dynamite IV Fighting Furies," *The Ring*, 1939, 161

JAMES JEFFRIES

CA. 1915

BEAGLES POSTCARD/AUTHOR'S COLLECTION

"I AM NO GOOD AS A FIGHTER ANY LONGER. I COULDN'T COME BACK BOYS. I TRIED AND I COULDN'T."

~JAMES J. JEFFRIES
FORMER CHAMPION

CHAPTER 12

THE FIGHT OF THE CENTURY

After Sam's contest with Ketchel reports circulated of a possible match between he and Tommy Burns. Rumor was it was being set up to be held in San Francisco that coming summer. Discussions never reached a level serious enough to convert the rumor to fact. Instead, arrangements were made for Sam to meet with a heavyweight named "Battling" Jim Johnson.

Jim Johnson stood 6' 3" and weighed approximately 240 pounds. He was a big man and a strong fighter, and his ability to withstand punishment was known. A few years after his first match with Sam, Jim would achieve a measure of acclaim for fighting a ten round draw against Jack Johnson in Paris, France. Sam was matched to meet Jim Johnson on May 14th of 1910 in Philadelphia. That fight with Langford was the first in what would become a long series of matches between the two men: they would meet twelve times over the next eight years.

When they first met the much taller Johnson reportedly looked down upon Sam and remarked:

"Look out boy, I is bad medicine. I was born with boxing gloves on my hands."

Sam smiled and replied, "That's nothing big boy. First time I hit you, you is going to die with em on!"[1]

---

[1] Bob Edgren. "What Makes a Champion?" *The Ring* article of unknown date

Although he appeared chubby and out-of-shape, Sam emerged the victor in his first contest with Jim. It was a no-decision points victory in the opinion of those in attendance, including a *New York Times* fight reporter who wrote that Sam pretty much had everything his own way throughout the fight.[2]

Only three days later, Langford went face-to-face with another opponent much taller and heavier than he: Al Kubiak. The match took place in New York's Fairmont Club. Reporting on the fight, the *Evening World* advised that Kubiak, a.k.a. "The Michigan Giant," wore an anxious and worried expression prior to the beginning of the contest. In sharp contrast, Langford stood smiling and laughing with his seconds in his own corner.

Sam's confidence was not misplaced. He assumed control of the bout at the sound of the opening bell. His performance, right out of the gate, left little doubt as to the eventual outcome of the fight.

Shortly into the first round, Sam landed a hard left hook to Kubiak's breadbasket. One witness described it as sounding like a large, hard potato being thrown into an empty barrel. At the moment the sound was heard, a spectator from the gallery was reported to have emphatically yelled, "Good night!"

Sam, however, was in no hurry to send the spectators home. He worked deliberately throughout the balance of the opening round, walking in without any regard to possible threats from Kubiak and landing blow after blow at will upon the big heavyweight.

In the second round Kubiak was sent crashing to the canvas two times, the second meeting with the mat resulting from a right uppercut. The referee then stepped in and brought an end to the lopsided affair.[3]

One reporter in attendance at this fight raised the question of how long Ketchel would have lasted against Sam in their match a month earlier, had Sam put forth the same type of effort he had just shown versus Kubiak. He then stated an economic factor for his readers to consider: Sam—like a number of other great fighters of his race, such as Walcott, Gans, and Johnson—had no choice but to "put on the brakes occasionally to keep hay in the barn."[4]

---

[2] *New York Times*, 15 May 1910

[3] *Evening World*, 18 May 1910

[4] newspaper article, source unknown, 25 July 1911

After the Kubiak fight, Sam and Woodman headed west to see the Johnson-Jeffries fight and make good on Woodman's offer that Sam would provide sparring partner services for Jeffries.

After originally giving his word that he would do everything in his power to ensure the success of the bout, California's Governor Gillette succumbed to public pressure and issued an injunction preventing the fight from taking place in the state. The fight between Johnson and Jeffries ended up being moved to Reno, Nevada, a rugged mining town at the time.

Reno was busting at the seams from all the activity in the weeks building up to the event. Fight-related stories and rumors of stories kept the citizens and press people abuzz.

In late June, it had been reported that Sam had purchased a Selden automobile, which he and Woodman arranged to have shipped to Jeffries' training headquarters out West. (The pair were giving serious consideration to the idea of driving the car from San Francisco all the way back to Boston after the big fight took place. They believed that this would be the first ocean-to-ocean trip a fighter ever made in an automobile. Sam and Joe thought that this would bring Sam some measure of fame as a tourist in addition to his renown as a fighter. Woodman, being the more experienced driver, was reportedly the party who would actually be driving.) At Joe's urging, Sam continued to come up with ideas aimed at pushing Johnson into the ring. Their tool bag included just about anything that might publicly embarrass or antagonize Johnson into booking a fight between the two men. There was a story making the rounds that while Johnson was doing his roadwork, one of Sam's tricks was to occasionally quickly drive down the road in front of Johnson, raising all the dust he could so it would blow in Johnson's face as he continued his run.

As the date of the fight grew nearer, reports surfaced that Joe Woodman had been thrown out of Johnson's training camp after he showed up to witness filming of Johnson in training. Woodman was a partial owner of the filming rights and felt entitled to witness the event as a result. Johnson discovered that Woodman was at the camp prior to the camera crew's arrival, and—there being no love lost between the two as a result of Joe's involvement in activities aimed at inducing Johnson to book a fight with Sam—the champion instructed one of his bodyguards to tell Woodman to leave. Woodman prepared to go, but before he could depart Johnson himself appeared, and he also asked Joe to leave. When Joe asked to know the reason, Johnson simply replied that Joe knew very well the reasons why. Joe departed shortly thereafter without any further incident.

When Sam heard about this he told Joe he wanted to head over to Johnson's camp immediately and dare the champion to order him away, as he had ordered Woodman. Joe objected to that idea.

"If ah want to go to that niggah's camp," said Sam "and he orders me away from that place, ah'll smash him in the jaw, that's what ah'll do."[5]

In this case, however, Woodman persuaded Sam to stay away from Johnson.

During the week prior to the Johnson-Jeffries fight Sam and Tommy Burns had an opportunity to be introduced to each other. Burns was at Jeffries' training camp in Moana Springs, Nevada, discussing the upcoming fight with a number of reporters when Sam appeared on the scene. A reporter for *The Denver Post* named Otto Flotto spotted Sam and nudged Burns.

"There's your friend," said Flotto.

"No friend of mine, I never saw him before, who is he?" replied Tommy.

"Why that's Sam Langford," replied a number of writers, "Don't you know him?"

"No. Bring him over and introduce me," replied Tommy.

Otto talked to Sam, and Sam walked over and offered his hand to Tommy. The conversation between the two great fighters was reported as beginning with a humble exclamation from Sam:

"I'm mighty glad to meet you, Mister Burns."

"I had an idea you were a bigger man," replied Burns looking Sam over from head to foot.

"You don't look as big as I thought you would be," Sam responded.

"I guess Johnson thought I was pretty small," said Tommy.

---

[5] *Lincoln Evening News*, 1 July 1910

Sam then pointed in the direction of Jeffries and replied, "I guess our friend over there will be big enough for Johnson." This evoked a grin from Burns.

Both men expressed their belief that Jeffries would defeat Johnson. Burns, recalling that he had sent Johnson to the hospital to have his ribs attended to after their fight in Australia, speculated as to how much more damage Jeffries might do to him. And with that the brief and cordial introductory meeting between the two fighters came to an end.[6]

By this time, excitement was running high in the little mining town, which was full of eyes and ears seeking back stories to the big fight. In the last few days leading up to the Johnson-Jeffries showdown a rumor circulated that Sam would be heading over to Jeffries' training camp. It was believed that the pair were planning to spar on the evening of July 1st. Around that time, when someone reported that Sam had been seen leaving his hotel carrying a large bag—possibly containing his fighting gear—the numerous fight correspondents in town for the event rushed over to the training camp to catch the event. It turned out to be a false lead, and the rumor of a July 1 sparring date lost some of its steam. Still, the reporters and locals kept abreast of Sam's whereabouts and movements.

Around the time of the fight itself no reports surfaced of an actual Langford-Jeffries sparring session taking place, but such a story did emerge about 2½ years later. The following article ran in the January 18, 1913 issue of the British publication *The Mirror of Life and Boxing World:*

When Sam Langford Knocked Out Jim Jeffries
by George Almy (American correspondent)

According to "Biddy" Bishop, the old-time fight manager and sports writer, now located out in Tacoma (WA), Jim Barry is the father of an interesting story that pertains to the tragedy at Reno two years ago.

As my fellow-townsman, Sam Langford, figures as one of the principals, the story may be of interest to Post readers, so I am handing it to you via "Biddy" Bishop and Jim Barry for what it may be worth. The story follows:

---

[6] *Washington Post*, 2 July 1910

That Jim Jeffries was knocked out in four rounds in a private bout with Sam Langford just a few days before his memorable battle with Jack Johnson at Reno, which was no doubt responsible for the nervous breakdown, and which aided largely in his defeat, is the assertion of Jim Barry, Chicago heavyweight boxer, at present in Tacoma.

The impromptu contest, between Jeffries and Langford was arranged as a sort of tryout for Jeff. The big boilermaker wanted to test his fighting strength on the eve of the big battle. It took place at Moana Springs and was witnessed by only half a dozen people, all of them trainers of Jeffries. Joe Woodman, Langford's manager, and the colored boxer himself, were the only ones present outside of Jeff's own handlers. The little affair has been kept a secret all these months, only to be disclosed by Langford's manager, who confided it to Barry, who gave out the information to the writer lately at the Donnelly Hotel.

"That's as sure as you're a foot high," said Barry. "Joe Woodman told me all about it and I know he would not string me, for Joe and I have been close friends for a long time. I'm telling you this on the quiet."

Barry says the tryout match was framed up about a week before the Reno battle. A large room at the hotel where Jeff was staying at Mona Springs was cleared of its furniture, and the men went at it on the floor with no ring. Five ounce gloves were used. Woodman handled and cared for Langford in the bout, while there were four men who attended Jeffries: Bob Armstrong, Sam Berger, Jim Corbett, and the former champion's old friend, Dick Adams. No one else around the training quarters knew of the bout, and to this day Jeffries' other trainers, Roger Cornell and Farmer Burns, do not know that it took place, so carefully was the secret guarded.

"I did not see the scrap myself, but Woodman told me confidentially that Jeff had no chance with Langford, and that the Tar Baby knocked him out in the fourth round," says Barry. "Twice in the third round Langford floored Jeffries. Jeff didn't punish Sam very much. The big fellow was slow and couldn't hit well."

It was probably this as much as the great strain on the former champion, brought about by excessive training and other worries, that caused his mental collapse and made him a mark for the big black champion.

Knowing that a man much smaller than Johnson had whipped him had its effect. Fearing defeat, Jeffries entered the ring with Johnson more than two-thirds beaten, but a shell of his former greatness. So to Sam Langford Johnson probably owes his present lofty seat in the realm of pugilism.

Interesting as this story is, one has to question how this event, if it were true, could have been so successfully kept a secret by the many parties involved.

Another factor that makes the story difficult to believe is a story that appears in Jeffries' 1929 biography, *Two Fisted Jeff*, Jeffries tells how his brother, Jack, tried to talk him out of going through with the Johnson fight. It was just two days prior to the bout, and Jack felt his brother was nowhere near the fighter he had been when he'd retired from the ring six years earlier. Jim said that when Jack realized he could not talk him out of going through with the fight, Jack pulled aside Jim's large sparring partner, Bob Armstrong, and asked him if he would try to knock Jim out in a sparring session. Jack was convinced that Bob could do it, and he thought that the experience would then convince his brother that he had no chance against Johnson. Bob agreed to take part in the plan, but the timing didn't work out. When Bob approached Jim to spar with him, Jim said he was too tired to do any more work that day and that there would be no more sparring before the fight with Johnson. In *Two Fisted Jeff*, Jim said that had his brother and Armstrong succeeded in their plan and knocked him out that day, it would have been unlikely that he would have gone ahead with the fight against Johnson.[7]

Since Langford was certainly held in higher regard than Bob Armstrong, one would be inclined to believe that if Jim had truly done so poorly in a sparring session with Sam a few days before the Johnson fight, the impact would have been similar. Jim would probably have chosen to forego the fight with Johnson.

---

[7] Hugh Fullerton, *Two Fisted Jeff*. Chicago: Consolidated Book Publishers, 1929

Interestingly, Stanley Ketchel, a friend and admirer of Jeffries visited Jim's training camp during the lead up to the fight, and he shared Jim's brother's opinion of the former champion's chances against Johnson. After watching his friend train, Ketchel walked away in silence with his companion Wilson Mizner. After some time, Mizner asked Ketchel what he thought.

"He's licked," replied Ketchel.

Ketchel knew what Johnson was capable of doing, and the Jeffries he had just seen in training camp was nowhere near the fighter he had been six years earlier. There was no doubt in Ketchel's mind that Jeffries stood zero chance against Johnson.

Many years later Mizner said that the night before the fight Ketchel devised a plan to prevent Jeffries from the disgrace he was sure he would suffer at the hands of Johnson. Ketchel knew that he would be introduced in the ring prior to the beginning of the bout, and he told Mizner that when he went over to Jim's corner to shake his hand and wish him luck he would knock him cold. There wasn't the slightest doubt in Mizner's mind that Ketchel was serious.

> "I don't care what they think about it. It will save old Jeff from the worst hole he's ever been in, or any fighter has. I can say that he insulted me or threatened me, but I've figured out just how to get out of that arena in the excitement and I don't care what happens about it," said Ketchel.[8]

Mizner said that he tried to talk Ketchel out of this plan. When that failed he told promoter Tex Rickard and others about Ketchel's intention. Mizner, Rickard, and the others then made sure that on the day of the fight Stanley could get nowhere near Jeffries when being introduced in the ring. After the fact, Mizner let Ketchel know that he had let the others in on the plan. A disappointed Ketchel always felt the plan was sound, and he regretted he had not had the opportunity to carry it out.

The fight proved to be a thoroughly one-sided affair. Jack Johnson dominated Jim Jeffries before the largest crowd that had ever witnessed a prizefight up until that point in boxing history. Only the intervention of Jim's seconds in the fifteenth round prevented him from

---

[8] Edward Sullivan, *The Fabulous Wilson Mizner*. New York: Henkle Co., 1935

a certain knockout by Johnson, who openly taunted the former champion and his seconds throughout the fight.

Greatly disappointed afterward, Jeffries said "I am no good as a fighter any longer. I couldn't come back boys. I tried and I couldn't. Ask Johnson if he will give me his gloves."

In a 1911 issue of French magazine *La Vie Grande Air*, Jack Johnson reflected on the fight saying:

> "I never thought for an instant that Jeffries would be able to find again his previous stature of strength. I had examined him in his athletic exhibitions, all the while the crowd applauded him and acclaimed him but I had found him in a perfectly poor condition."[9]

There was a great deal of racially charged turmoil in the wake of Johnson's victory over "The Great White Hope." Hundreds of people of both races were injured and nineteen people were reported killed during the riots and/or incidents that followed.

The day after the fight, while preparing to travel to Chicago for a well-earned rest at his mother's home, Jack Johnson made it clear that he did not take Sam's challenge for the title seriously. His immediate plans were to continue on to New York for a series of vaudeville appearances.

That statement and schedule didn't prevent Johnson from teasing Langford and Woodman. On July 6th, as he passed through Cheyenne, Wyoming, Johnson issued a statement that he would be willing to meet Sam in Cheyenne that August, during the Great Frontier Celebration, if Sam would post a $20,000 side bet. In response, Wyoming's governor advised that he would not permit the pair (nor any other prizefighter) to fight in the state of Wyoming. Never one to let the other party get the last word in, Woodman wired that he would post the $20,000 once Johnson arrived in New York and posted his money.

Films of the Johnson-Jeffries contest quickly became the focal point of a heated debate taking place throughout the country. Various city and religious officials quickly moved to ban viewing of the films, on the basis that they would promote racial hatred and violence. Four days after the fight one New York paper voiced the opinion that the

---

[9] *Galveston Daily News*, 5 July 1910

fight could never have stirred up such racial hatred had it not been for the sensationalism of publicists concerned only with selling papers. They reasoned that if a telegraphic account of what occurred could stir up such strife the actual sight of the mill would promote a state bordering on war.

Debate over the films spread around the world. There was widespread demand for their prohibition as far away as South Africa and India for fear of their potential effect upon the natives. Word came from Toronto, Canada that the Provincial Executive surely had authority to protect the public from the "demoralizing exhibitions" if it chose to prohibit its showing. Ten days after the fight, word came from London, England that a motion prohibiting exhibition of the fight film in London music halls had been carried by a vote of 45-20 at the London City Council. (Johnson claimed he had sold his share, or rights to the film, for $50,000 and a bonus of $14,000.)

Johnson's mother was asked for her opinion regarding the riots that followed her son's victory. Speaking from her Chicago home, Johnson's mother stated that she deplored the riots that had resulted from it, but that the riots were due to an unwillingness on the part of many white persons to let a Negro express himself.

Johnson reached Chicago on July 8th. He was greeted at the station by throngs of admirers who excitedly congratulated him on his victory and escorted him to his mother's home.

When reporters questioned Johnson about his future, the champion implied that he might quit the ring.

By mid-July, however, *The New York Times* wrote that Johnson had indicated a willingness to meet any opponent for the title, providing it was for a $50,000 purse and a side bet of $20,000. In his opinion, Al Kaufmann was the best among the current heavyweight contenders.[10]

On July 20th, William Gibson of the Fairmont Athletic Club in New York issued a statement saying that he didn't believe anyone could pay Jack Johnson enough to fight Sam Langford. He claimed to have been present in a sporting resort when Langford came in and found Johnson there. According to Gibson, Sam rushed towards Johnson, and Johnson ran out of the establishment to avoid having any interaction with him.

---

[10] *New York Times*, 12 July 1910

In fairness to Johnson, stories of this nature—or some variation of them—surfaced continually at the time. In all likelihood many were probably planted by Woodman in an attempt to embarrass Johnson into fighting Sam. Woodman told anyone who would listen that he intended to follow Johnson all over the world if that's what it would take to get him to agree to a match.

Three days later Johnson announced that it might be a year before he fought again. He felt that a fortune awaited him in the form of theatrical appearances and that he would be foolish to pass up such a strong financial opportunity. The prospect of earning a great sum of money on the stage had to appeal to the champion a great deal more than the opportunity to risk his title against Sam (or anyone else) for twenty or thirty thousand dollars.

It was around this time that Woodman was successful in arranging a six-round, no-decision bout between Sam and Al Kaufmann, scheduled to take place in Philadelphia on August 10th. This was a match that Woodman had originally tried to make happen on the West Coast while he and Sam were on-hand, but at the time it hadn't generated much interest because of all the focus on the Jeffries-Johnson fight.

Now, the match made some sense. Sam and Woodman had tried every tactic they could think of in their efforts to convince Johnson to book a fight with Sam. Nothing had worked. Johnson, however, had fairly recently stated that he considered Kaufmann the best white heavyweight contender. It seemed that Sam would only strengthen his case for a match with the champion should he convincingly defeat Kaufmann.

The Langford-Kaufmann fight was scheduled to take place in the open air at the Phillies' ballpark, but it ended up being cancelled.

A story circulated that the cancellation was the result of financial trouble between Woodman and Sid Hester, of San Francisco. Hester allegedly claimed that he was owed money by Woodman, and he had come to Philadelphia ready to attach any money that might be coming to Langford. The rumor was that when Woodman learned of this he reportedly called off the bout.

The September 17th issue of the London magazine *Boxing* ran a different story regarding the fight's cancellation: the article was titled,

"Is Langford a Faker?" According to that article, Sam had planned on little more than a six-round exhibition with Kaufmann. When informed that he needed to be prepared to fight to win, Sam claimed that he was in no condition to fight six hard rounds with such a big fellow. He asked for an additional week's time to train. When that request was denied he asked for more money and a guarantee that it would be paid prior to the contest.

At that point the fight's promoter, Harry Edwards, involved the local police. The Assistant Superintendent of Police reportedly replied:

> "You tell Langford and his manager that I will be at the ringside. I know boxing when I see it. He will deliver the goods, and he will do it without getting his money beforehand. If he fakes I will run him in. Several fighters are now serving time in the West for pulling off what Langford plans to do. He will not get away with it here in Philadelphia. So long as I am in office and connected with the Department of Public Safety the sport of boxing will be kept clean."

When the message was carried to Sam he reportedly fled town, and Woodman followed later in the day.

Edwards called off the fight and advised that Langford and Woodman would never again be permitted to take any part in a boxing contest in Philadelphia.

In either case, Sam's failure to fight Kaufmann and make a good showing against him certainly didn't help his effort to gain an opportunity to fight the champion. It was another seven years before he fought again in Philadelphia.

Returning to his hometown of Boston, Sam convincingly defeated his old rival Joe Jennette by way of a fifteen-round decision, September 6th, in a bout promoted by Billy Pierce and refereed by Charlie White.

Not long afterward, Charlie White voiced his opinion that Sam was the right man to challenge Johnson for the title, saying:

> "Langford is a terrific puncher, and besides, can hit from any angle. One thing I am sure of, if those two ever meet, the fight will be a much better one than the Jeffries-Johnson contest at Reno was, for Langford fights so fast that Johnson would have his own troubles trying to escape his blows. I have

always considered Langford a wonderful fighter, and I only hope Johnson meets him. I am not saying that Sam can whip him, but I know from seeing him in action with Jennette that he can make the champion go some to beat him. Never in my experience in the ring have I witnessed such punching by a fighter as Sam put over in Boston.

"He is a wonder, and a match between him and Johnson would draw almost as big a gate as did the Johnson-Jeffries fight."[11]

---

[11] Charlie White. "Charlie White Thinks that Sam Langford Has a Chance," *Ottawa Journal*, 17 September 1910

SAM LANGFORD
ca. 1908
Don Scott Collection

172 Sam Langford: Boxing's Greatest Uncrowned Champion

Sam Langford
December 1908 at Millet's training camp, San Francisco
Ben Hawes Collection

JACK BLACKBURN

CA. 1905

RICHARD SELF COLLECTION

GEORGE GUNTHER

CA. 1905

AUTHOR'S COLLECTION

SANDY FERGUSON

CA. 1908

AUTHOR'S COLLECTION

P.O. CURRAN

CA. 1910

AUTHOR'S COLLECTION

LANGFORD GROUP PHOTO

L TO R: LANGFORD, GEORGE BYERS, BOB ARMSTRONG, "LIVER" DAVIS, UNKNOWN, AND JOE WOODMAN

BEN HAWES COLLECTION

KETCHEL VS. LANGFORD TICKET STUB

RARE TICKET STUB TO APRIL 27, 1910 FIGHT HELD IN PHILADELPHIA

JOHN GAY COLLECTIONS

**SAM LANGFORD AND
TONY ROSS**
NO DATE
CRAIG HAMILTON COLLECTION

**SAM LANGFORD, SAM BERGER, JAMES J. JEFFRIES,
JIM CORBETT, ABE ATTELL AND OTHERS**
AT JEFFRIES' TRAINING CAMP
PRIOR TO THE JULY 4, 1910 JIM JEFFRIES-JACK JOHNSON FIGHT
CRAIG HAMILTON COLLECTION

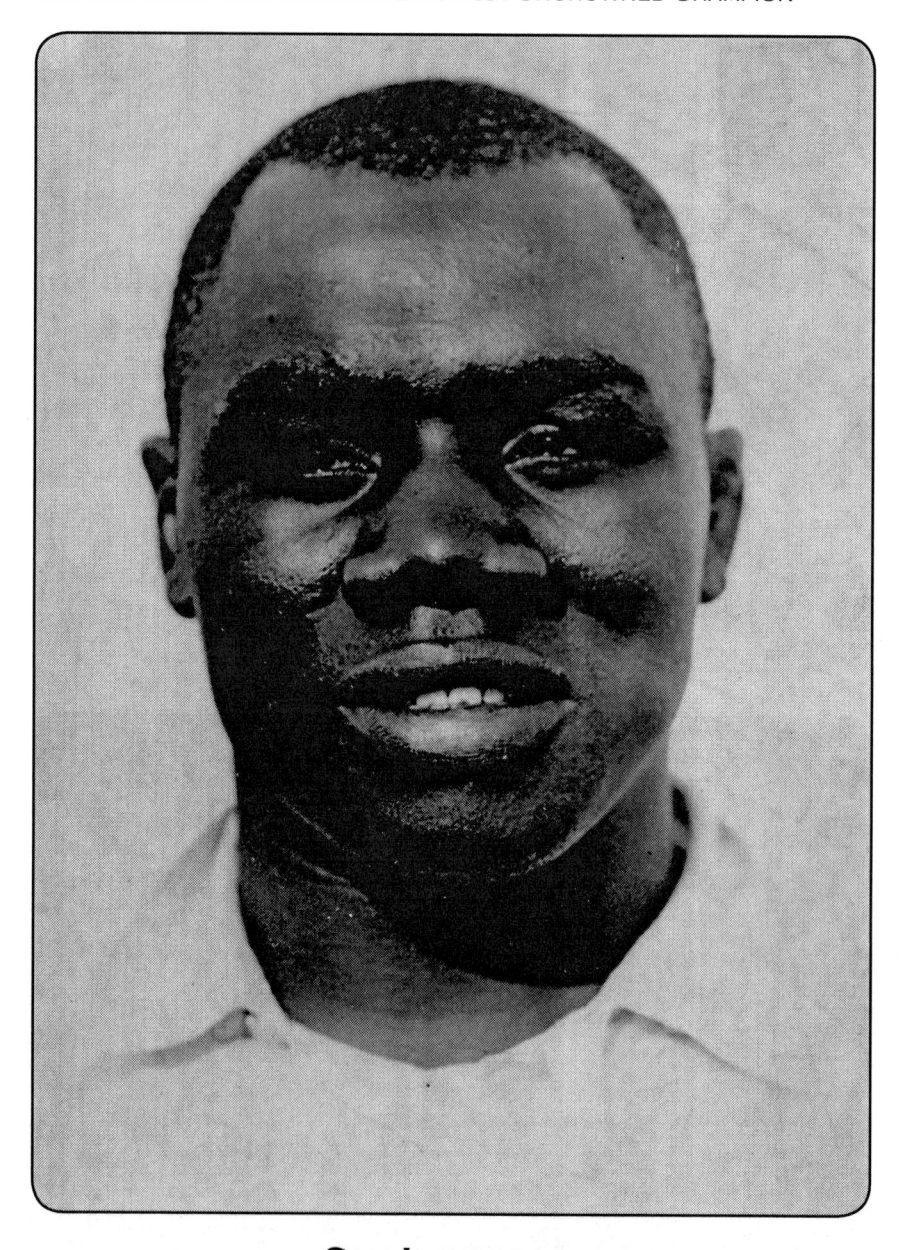

176 SAM LANGFORD: BOXING'S GREATEST UNCROWNED CHAMPION

SAM LANGFORD

WHILE IN TRAINING FOR 9/1/1908 NEW YORK FIGHT WITH JOE JENNETTE

BEN HAWES COLLECTION

**JOE JENNETTE
IN CATCHER'S MASK**
CA. DEC. 1909

**JOE, JOSEPH, AND
AGNES (BLANCHE)**
PARIS, FRANCE
CA. 1909

JOE JENNETTE
PARIS, FRANCE
IN TRAINING ROBE
CA. DEC. 1909

BEN HAWES COLLECTION

JOE JENNETTE SIGNED CARD

CA. 1909

BEN HAWES COLLECTION

SAM LANGFORD TRAINING AND POSING
WHILE TRAINING FOR MAY 24, 1909 FIGHT WITH "IRON" HAGUE
BEN HAWES COLLECTION

"IRON HAGUE" VS. SAM LANGFORD
MAY 24, 1909
NATIONAL SPORTING CLUB, ENGLAND
AUTHOR'S COLLECTION

LANGFORD LANDS A LEFT AGAINST "IRON" HAGUE
MAY 24, 1909
AUTHOR'S COLLECTION

SAM LANGFORD K.O. OVER "IRON" HAGUE
MAY 24, 1909
BEN HAWES COLLECTION

"IRON" HAGUE IS CARRIED BACK TO HIS CORNER AFTER BEING KNOCKED OUT BY LANGFORD
MAY 24, 1909
BEN HAWES COLLECTION

JIM BARRY
1908
BEN HAWES COLLECTION

1905-1910 183

JIM BARRY KNOCKING DOWN SAM LANGFORD
APRIL 14, 1910
CRAIG HAMILTON COLLECTION

SAM LANGFORD AND JIM BARRY
UNDATED
BEN HAWES COLLECTION

"Liver" Davis, Joe Woodman, Jimmy Walsh, Eddie Keevin, Sam Langford

1909 Health & Strength booklet titled
"Life & Battles of Sam Langford"

Author's Collection

Sam Langford and his Training Staff

ca. 1909

L to R: "Dusty" Coleman, George Lawrence, Joe Woodman, Langford, Jolly Jumbo, Jimmy Walsh and "Liver" Davis

Author's Collection

SAM LANGFORD

MARCH 1910

TAKEN AS SAM WAS TRAINING IN ARCADIA, CALIFORNIA FOR HIS REMATCH WITH JIM FLYNN

PHOTOGRAPHER: DINGMAN/BEN HAWES COLLECTION

186 SAM LANGFORD: BOXING'S GREATEST UNCROWNED CHAMPION

"BATTLING" JIM JOHNSON
NO DATE
BEN HAWES COLLECTION

JEFFREY CLARKE A.K.A. "THE JOPLIN GHOST"

CA. 1919

"I'LL FIGHT JOHNSON BEFORE ANY CLUB, OR I'LL GO DOWN INTO A CELLAR WITH HIM AND HAVE IT OUT."

~SAM LANGFORD

CHAPTER 13

THE "JOPLIN GHOST"

A chance meeting took place between Sam and Jack Johnson on September 20, 1910, and it gave local Boston area fans hope that the pair might fight each other again. The two fighters both attended a contest between Jimmy Walsh and Young Britt. Johnson entered the Armory during the ninth round and ended up with a seat near Langford. Although the crowd took notice, the two fighters chose to ignore one another.

When the bout ended, the crowd called for Johnson to enter the ring and make a speech. Johnson complied and climbed into the ring. No sooner had he done so than the chant, "Langford! Langford! Langford!" went up among the crowd anxious to see both fighters in the ring together.

Johnson had barely begun to open his mouth to speak when Sam jumped into the ring. Johnson disgustedly turned his back on Sam and walked to the other side of the ring. The crowd called out for Sam to depart the ring and then return after Johnson was finished talking.

Sam left the ring and settled into his seat to listen to what the champion had to say. Johnson raised his hand to silence the crowd and declared that since this was Sam's hometown he'd like him to speak first.

Sam entered the ring again. He proclaimed his willingness to post whatever funds Johnson required for an agreement to fight him. Then he advised he was willing to fight him anytime and anyplace. Johnson shouted that he was interested in making money, and that if Sam could produce it he would take him on. He went on to say that he had attempted to post money for a fight in New York, but Sam and his manager had failed to post their money.

Sam angrily replied that on the day in question he had arrived in New York at 8:00 a.m., that Johnson subsequently departed at 09:00 a.m., and that within three hours after that Joe Woodman had posted the money.

At that point Johnson pulled out a thick roll of bills. Holding it above his head for all to see, he shouted to the crowd, "I'll bet a thousand dollars that Mr. Langford's manager did not post one cent."

Sam's eyes narrowed in anger and, advancing toward Johnson, he shouted, "Gentlemen, I am ready to post $20,000 within three days, or tomorrow morning, and I'll fight Johnson before any club, or I'll go down into a cellar with him and have it out."

Johnson responded saying, "I will meet Mr. Langford tomorrow morning at 11:00 at any newspaper office, and will be ready to post my money. I don't want to indulge in a joint debate, but my money talks."

The crowd yelled for more but the club's manager, Miah Murray, grabbed the two fighters and made them shake hands. The verbal contest was considered a draw. Before departing it was agreed the two fighters would meet the next day.[1]

The following morning the pair met in the office of the *Boston Journal*. Hopes of an agreement quickly dissolved as the two men got into a heated debate. Johnson refused to put up $20,000 for a fight until Sam made the first deposit. Johnson pointed out that it was the challenger's duty to put up the stakes, and that his duty as the champion was to then cover the amount. He offered to hand $1,000 to a stakeholder right then and there and give Sam 24 hours to put up his $20,000—with an agreement that once Sam had done so a failure on Johnson's part to put up an additional $19,000 would result in Johnson's $1,000 going to Sam.

Sam then reminded Johnson of his statement the night before, when he had offered to put up the money. Johnson replied that he had made a mistake in offering to do that.

---

[1] *La Boxe*, 12 October 1910

The debate ended with Johnson telling Sam that he would remain in the city for several days and would cover the money anytime within that timeframe that Sam posted $20,000. He then added that he felt a fight between them would not draw well. Despite the hostilities, the talks ended with the two posing together for pictures.[2]

Ultimately Sam and Joe were either unwilling or unable to post the $20,000 demanded by Johnson. As a result they missed out on what later proved to be the last real opportunity to get the champion back into the ring.

On October 15th, the boxing world was shocked by the news that Stanley Ketchel had been murdered. After a week had passed, Sam and his manager joined a number of others in laying claim to the vacant middleweight title. Sam maintained he was deserving of the title by virtue of his performance against Ketchel. He added that should Billy Papke (the man whom Ketchel reclaimed the title from in 1908) or any other aspirant to the middleweight title desire to dispute his claim, he was willing to meet them in the ring to settle the matter and bet $2,500 on the result.

In Peter Walsh's fine book about the middleweight division, *Men of Steel*, he writes that ten days after Stanley Ketchel's death, *The New York Times* named its four leading middleweight contenders: Billy Papke, Frank Klaus, Eddie McGoorty and Hugo Kelly. There was no mention of Sam.[3]

There was no prospect of Sam gaining an opportunity to fight Papke. Unlike Ketchel, Papke was adamant about drawing the color line and stuck to it. When none of the other men mentioned as serious contenders for the crown responded to Sam's challenge, he was once again left on the outside looking in. Some questioned whether Sam could actually make the middleweight limit and viewed his claim more as an effort, on the part of he and Woodman, to keep his name in print. It would be 1917 before the middleweight division would again have a single champion universally recognized.

On October 31st, Woodman, Sam, and his sparring partners—Big Bob Armstrong and George Byers—arrived in Indianapolis to fulfill

---

[2] *Boston Journal*, 22 September 1910
[3] Peter Walsh, *Men of Steel*. London: Robson Books, 1993

a week's engagement providing boxing exhibitions at the Empire Theater. Sam was billed as "The Man Jack Johnson Is Afraid to Meet." Armstrong, one of Jeffries' trainers for the fight with Johnson, advised *The Indianapolis Star* that Johnson was a marvel on defense:

> "but as sure as the champion meets a strong clever fighter, who bores in and does not try to outbox him, the champion will lose the title. Sam Langford looks to me the boy to turn that trick."[4]

Sam provided exhibitions in the theater twice a day throughout the week, sparring with Armstrong or Byers, or any audience member willing to accept Woodman's offer of $100 to any man who could stay four rounds with Sam.

Once their engagement with the theater was fulfilled the group traveled to Joplin, Missouri where Sam was matched with another middleweight hopeful named Jeff Clarke. Clarke, a.k.a. the "Joplin Ghost," fought out of Philadelphia and boasted that he had lost only one of twenty-five fights. The two men would become very familiar with each other in the years ahead, meeting in the ring a total of twelve times.

Sam and his manager knew that the "Ghost" had a reputation for taking full advantage of the size of the ring to evade his opponent, so they wisely refused to agree to fight Clarke unless it was in a sixteen foot ring.

There is one story that says "Ghost" acquired his nickname from a ring doctor named Sam Grantham. According to Jimmy Bronson, Clarke's manager, earlier that year the doctor took a look at Clarke before a contest and advised that he wouldn't give his authorization for Jeff to fight. When Bronson asked why, Grantham told him that Clarke looked like a ghost. The doctor was convinced his sickly appearance was due to a leaky heart, but Bronson insisted it was only hunger that produced the appearance, and sent him out to fight despite the doctor's objections. But the name stuck: Jeff Clarke, became known as the "Joplin Ghost."[5] Kevin Smith, author of *The Sundowners,* advises that the nickname originated from George Cole in the form of "The Fighting Ghost."

---

[4] *Indianapolis Star,* 1 November 1910
[5] *New York Times,* 20 June 1955

When the two parties met in the ring on November 10th, Clarke, who had been fighting as a professional for just over two years, ran as expected. It didn't do him any good. Sam knocked him to the floor three times in the opening stanza. In the second round, Sam caught him with a left hook that brought the event to an early conclusion.

Sam followed that up with another quick fight, stopping Morris Harris in the second round on December 6th.

After the Harris fight, there was talk of a possible London match between Sam and Tommy Burns. Any chance of that happening fell through when Burns suffered a knee injury during a train accident.

As 1910 drew to a close, it seemed that one disappointment after another was following Sam. Ketchel's death had eliminated the possibility of a large payday on the West Coast, the efforts to put together a second meeting with Jack Johnson had failed again, and now it appeared a potentially lucrative meeting with Tommy Burns might never occur. To top it all off, Sam was thrown in jail on December 19th in Schenectady, New York.

Sam was arrested during a raid on the American Athletic Club, where he was serving as second to "Porky" Flynn in a bout between Flynn and Jack Sullivan. Arrested along with Sam were Flynn, Bob Armstrong, and a matchmaker by the name of Jake Carey. The raid was the result of work by a local church pastor and editor of a socialist newspaper who had caught wind of the bout and arranged warrants for all parties. Sullivan managed a successful escape from the city. The four men were charged with violating Section 1.710 of the penal code regarding "aiding, abetting or encouraging a prize fight or sparring match for which admission is charged directly or indirectly." The club had unsuccessfully tried to skirt the law under the guise of holding the "sparring" event solely for the entertainment of its members ... and providing tickets to non-members in exchange for their signature on a membership application and a fee ranging from $1 to $3 depending upon where the party wanted to sit in order to view the "entertainment."

The four ended up being released on the morning of the 20th after posting bail. Ultimately only Carey, as the event promoter, ended up going to trial. He was found guilty and subsequently required to post a $100 bond promising that he would not violate the penal code over the next year.

Sam started 1911 off on a better foot. On January 3rd, it was announced that Australian promoter, Hugh Mcintosh had arranged for him to fight Australia's heavyweight champion, Bill Lang for a purse of $20,000. They would meet in London on February 16th. Lang had defeated forty-six-year-old Bob Fitzsimmons in 1909, but his resumé also included losses to Jack Johnson four years earlier, and Tommy Burns and Al Kaufmann in 1910.

Then articles were drawn up for Sam to face Joe Jennette in Boston on January 10th at the Armory, to make up for a contest cancelled on December 8th due to Joe's illness.

One of the largest crowds ever to witness a fight in the Armory turned out to see the two men go at it. They were rewarded with one of the greatest boxing matches ever held in the city, according to one unnamed newspaper account.

In addition to producing the only knockdown of the match, Sam broke Joe's nose and loosened several of his teeth on the way to a decisive points victory. Afterward, the Boston writers once again proclaimed Sam the logical challenger to Johnson's title, but the champion replied that after himself, Al Kaufmann was the best heavyweight in the world and would easily defeat such men as Langford, Jennette, or McVea.

Six days later, Sam faced a younger and bigger black fighter named Fred Atwater in Utica, New York. Sam knocked him out with a left hook to the chin in the third round.

Later in life, Sam revealed that it was his left hook that won most of his fights and produced most of his knockouts, but while he was in his prime he saw no advantage in broadcasting that fact. Sam always felt that many of the newspaper men unwittingly assisted him during those years by mistakenly writing that he was doing most of his damage with body punches and right crosses.

Sam was convinced that a number of his opponents read that misinformation and mistakenly focused their training on guarding against his right hand.

Ol' Sam was a pretty cagey fellow, and when the fights with these men began, he did all that he could to convince his opponent that what they'd read was true: he'd keep his left hook under wraps and attempt to land right-hand after right-hand.

Only after enough time had passed and Sam felt his opponent had gotten a little careless about keeping their right hand up would Sam drop the bomb. He would quickly step in and throw a little right, then immediately follow that up with a vicious left hook to the head of his unsuspecting victim. More often than not, that was the beginning of the end for his foe.

Sam learned early on that it was a lot harder for him to land a right hand to the head than a left. This was because his opponent, unless he was a southpaw, had his own left hand held further out in front of his body and could utilize it to brush aside Sam's right hand punches. So Sam spent hour after hour developing his left hook to perfection, until he found that he could put just as much power into his left hand punch as he could his right.

Sam played it smart. He did his best to perpetuate the myth that it was the power of his right hand that the opposition needed to fear. Whenever he had an opponent he felt was a soft touch (one that he could take out with either hand) Sam tried to make sure he ended the fight with a right hand blow. But whenever he had a fight on his hands the left hook was his primary weapon of choice.[6]

During the latter part of 1910, Sam had been hearing reports that Sam McVea was doing great things in Europe. So Sam and Woodman cabled Europe and made it known that if McVea ran out of willing opponents, they would be happy to sail on over and accommodate him. They didn't have to wait long for a reply.

Word was received that McVea would love to meet him in Paris in April. This suited Sam and Joe just fine: he was already scheduled to fight heavyweight Bill Lang in England that February.

Sam and Joe had committed to Hugh McIntosh to meet Australia's heavyweight champion, Bill Lang in England. Lang's real name was William Langfranchi, and he'd captured the Australian heavyweight title by defeating forty-one-year-old Peter Felix on October 3, 1907. British novelist Andrew Soutar described Lang as a six-footer with a pair of big shoulders who was hard as nails. Lang had lasted the full twenty-round distance in an April 7, 1910 decision loss to former heavyweight champion Tommy Burns. He impressed those who

---

[6] *Halifax Herald*, 30 August 1924

observed him working out as being a big and powerful man with considerable speed. After one such viewing, but prior to meeting Sam, Soutar was so impressed by the Australian champion that he later indicated he would have backed Lang to the hilt had he been a betting man.

The day after Sam's win over Atwater, there was a published report stating that Sam and Jack Johnson were going to be matched for a six-round contest at Jack O'Brien's new club in Philadelphia, for a purse of $10,000. The report didn't seem to have much basis, since it would have required Johnson to cancel a number of impending theatrical appearances (lucrative events) and there was another report that Johnson had received a better offer from a club in Paris, France, a much larger purse ($25,000) to meet either Langford or Jennette. Nevertheless, Woodman took the report seriously.

In order that he and Sam might pursue a meeting with Johnson at O'Brien's club, Woodman sought a postponement of the match with Lang. McIntosh refused to delay the Lang contest, indicating that all the arrangements for the fight in England were already in place.

Woodman made it known that after disposing of Lang, he and Sam would be more than happy to rush back home for a match with Johnson, but O'Brien immediately turned his attention to securing Al Kauffmann as an opponent for the champion. Johnson took the opportunity to get in a dig at Sam declaring that Sam had gotten cold feet and decided to run away to England rather than remain in the States and fight.

Before departing for England Sam advised a reporter from the *Police Gazette* that he planned to defeat Lang and then challenge Al Kaufmann. Stated Sam:

> "Nobody believes Kaufmann can whip Johnson at any time, so if Kaufmann wants to prove that he is in line for a match with Johnson he can have a fight with me first. If Kaufmann can beat me then he will be recognized as a first class pugilist. If I beat Kaufmann, Johnson will be compelled to take me on. That's common sense, and I am going to pursue this policy until I have shown the public just what I can do with the man who beat poor old Jeff at Reno last July."[7]

---

[7] *Police Gazette*, 4 February 1911

On January 25, 1911, Sam and Joe set sail for England aboard the steamship *Lusitania* to begin training for the match with the big Australian heavyweight champion.

Sam Langford sparring with young Harry Tracey
prior to his 1911 fight with Bill Lang in England
Newspaper Clipping, Author's Collection

"ONLY ONE FIGHTER I EVER MET REALLY SCARED ME. THAT WAS SAM LANGFORD."

~ BILL LANG

CHAPTER 14

THE RABBIT PUNCH

The English magazine, *Boxing*, ran two stories about Sam in February 1911. One reported that Sam was reiterating his claim to be regarded as middleweight champion of the world:

> Sam is just about as ambitious as he can well be. He wants to be recognized both as heavy and middleweight world's champion, and feels pretty confident that he can mount both thrones, if he is only given the chances. As Sam puts it, "I may be colored, but I've got a white heart. I've gone about beating all these big fellows and have never worried about how big they are. If they will only give me the chance, I'll try to beat them all, but some of them fancy themselves wise guys and just stay aside."

That article also offered the opinion that Sam Langford was an entertaining personality:

> Whenever the boxing business sours on him, or even before it does, he can always feel pretty confident of getting as many music hall engagements as he wants. If he fails to secure all that he asks for, that will only be because the music hall engagements don't know a good thing when they see one. For Sam is a natural born comedian, and his training stunts, for all their earnestness, are always full of humor.

In the same issue, Sam spoke up in an article titled "Why Won't Jack Johnson Meet Me?" In it, Sam continued pressing Jack Johnson for a fight, saying:

"He has given quite a lot of reasons. First of all he said that we shouldn't draw any gate worthy of his attention, but that was all bull as every genuine fan knew.

"I reckon I should stand more than a good chance with Johnson, but I shouldn't like to have to tackle the job under twenty rounds because the longer we went the better chance I reckon to stand. I am figuring on our last and only meeting, and I guess that Mr. Johnson is doing some figuring on it too. That was way back in April, 1906, when I went about 147 pounds and Johnson was all 200. He had it on me during the first ten rounds, and put me down, but I got it on him during the last five, I had him down. Jack has said that he will meet me if some promoter will guarantee him $25,000 for his end, win, lose or draw, besides expenses, and he will, I guess, stick to this figure.

"He will, of course, have to fight someone before long, and he knows it, but I somehow fancy he is praying some big white fellow will come along who will be fancied by the fans. Someone without any great amount of experience, because it keeps looking more and more as though I shall be the proposition he will have to tackle. I guess he's just hoping that Bill Lang will put it across me, but, good fellow as Bill is, I don't think he will. I am getting as fit as I can."[1]

Another British publication, *Boxing World and Athletic Chronicle*, ran an article the same month urgently expressing the need for a man to defeat Johnson before he retire. So great was the dislike for Johnson, the author wrote, that it mattered not whether the man was black, yellow, or white, so long as the current champion was defeated. Sam was specifically named as the party who seemed to be most deserving of a shot at Johnson, especially should he defeat Lang—as most expected he would. It was suggested that readers welcome Sam as a "white man" until another "Fitzsimmons" or "Jeffries" in their prime, could be found to compete with the present black heavyweights.[2]

On one of the evenings leading up to the bout, the promoter, Hugh McIntosh, gave a dinner to the press at the Pillar Hall at Olympia. Lang turned up for the event, but Sam advised McIntosh in advance

---

[1] *Boxing*, 11 February 1911
[2] *Boxing World and Athletic Chronicle*, 9 February 1911

that he would not attend. Sam told the promoter, "I know my place, I wouldn't feel good with all of them white gentlemen, better count me out," Sam said.

A chair was reserved for Sam nonetheless, but, true to his word, he was a no show. His manager attended as the representative for his party. Despite having advised the promoter in advance that he wouldn't attend, Sam apologized to McIntosh later saying simply "I am black."[3]

British author Trevor Wignall recalled Sam once saying that he was conscious of his place. Wignall interpreted this to mean that said "place" was not with whites, who, in any case, would merely have patronized Sam or fawned at his feet. Wignall felt that Sam, like Joe Louis later, was careful to avoid anything that was liable to add to the prejudices against his race.

Comparing Sam with Jack Johnson, Hugh McIntosh said:

> "Sam was far the more likable type. Johnson and I were always at each others' throats. Yet I never had a cross word with Langford. Langford gave me many a laugh, for in place of Johnson's acid wit, he had a droll and whimsical sense of humor."

McIntosh thought Sam one of the easiest fighters to manage that he'd ever met. He found Sam to be a simple happy-go-lucky fellow who loved nothing better than indulging his fondness for long black cigars, loud checkered suits, and bowlers (hats). When it came to fighting, McIntosh said that you were always assured of receiving value for your money if Sam was involved. "Something spectacular was always happening when he set those long arms swinging, and the words 'to quit' had no place in his vocabulary."[4]

Eugene Corri, a well known English boxing referee and the official for the contest between Sam and Lang, viewed Sam as extremely modest and retiring but a man every inch, and one with a great sense of humor. Corri felt that Sam had one curious weakness though—one he never witnessed in any other boxing man. Sam was a terrific worker in the gym at all times, but while athletes generally abstained from

---

[3] Trevor Wignall, *Almost Yesterday*. London: Hutchinson & Co. Ltd., 1949
[4] Hugh Mcintosh, "Laughing Sam Langford, the Black Tornado," *Knockout*, 1936, issue unknown

tobacco when in training, as soon as Sam quit his work and had his bath and rub down, he would enjoy a big fat cigar.

British sportswriters were in hog heaven during the weeks prior to the fight. McIntosh provided a training camp that had an atmosphere to which they were wholly unaccustomed. Many of the training sessions were open to the public. To ensure that attendees had as pleasurable an experience as possible the innovative promoter spent a considerable amount of money providing food, drink, and other amenities for the parties viewing the training. More importantly the sportswriters found that they didn't have to grope for material to fill their articles. In the words of writer Trevor Wignall, "It was brought to us on a cushion."[5]

On one occasion it was arranged for a large crowd to view Sam in training at the Kensington arena. Since the event was attended by a number of ladies, steps were taken to ensure they would not witness anything objectionable. Near the end of the event, American lightweight Jimmy Britt, who was presiding over the event, announced that in order to determine whether Sam was fit his manager, Joe Woodman, had secured the services of one Harry Tracey, who would spar one fast-paced round with Sam.

In came a youngster of no more than six or seven years of age outfitted with fighting togs and gloves. He bounded up the steps to the ring, entered, and he and Sam commenced to spar. After a few seconds the youngster delivered a punch that caused Sam to fall dramatically to the canvas. Time was called and a verdict of "draw" was announced. The act was well received by those in attendance and enthusiastic applause broke out when a revived Sam hoisted the young pugilist atop his shoulders.

This type of lighthearted activity was not uncommon in Sam's training camp. It was noted by many that Sam and his sparring partners were a bunch of first class comedians. This was in high contrast to Lang's camp, where work was reportedly performed in a grim and determined fashion.

It wasn't that Sam didn't take his training seriously, he just believed in having some fun while he was working.

A few weeks prior to the fight McIntosh bribed the stadium

---

[5] Trevor Wignall, *Almost Yesterday*. London: Hutchinson & Co. Ltd., 1949

caretaker to smuggle Lang into an upper gallery at the Olympic Arena, where Sam was training. This would give Lang the opportunity to privately observe Sam in action and get a line on Sam's form. The caretaker had been well cared for by Sam in the way of tips, so he alerted Sam that his opponent was going to be watching. Sam determined he would provide Lang with something to think about.

Speaking of the event many years later in a 1935 interview Lang said:

> "Sam showed me all right! In fact, he took just ten minutes to make me a nervous wreck. At the time, he was sparring with Bob Armstrong, a huge Negro. He knocked Bob cold in about three seconds. He did the same in rapid succession with three other sparring partners, with punches that traveled so fast I didn't even know which hands he used.
>
> "After it all, Sam looked up my way and blew me a kiss!
>
> "That night Mac (McIntosh) asked me what I thought of the 'Tar Baby.'
>
> "'That black imp's not a fighter,' I told him. 'He's a-a-'
>
> "'Threshing machine,' Mac suggested sweetly.
>
> "He had it! After seeing Sam at work, Australia and home seemed very sweet. To make sure I did the journey as a passenger and not as freight I trained twice as hard from that point on. Only one fighter I ever met really scared me. That was Sam Langford."[6]

In the weeks leading up to the fight it became painfully evident that the majority of English fight fans were hoping for a Lang victory. Racial prejudices as strong as those Sam routinely experienced in the States were clearly in evidence. Hundreds of letters from all over England were received by Lang, wishing him luck in his effort to uphold the white race. On the day before the fight a large delegation, mostly women, visited Sam's training camp headquarters and reportedly told him that they hoped Lang would knock off his head.

On the night of the fight an estimated crowd of 8,000 enthusiastic spectators packed the Olympic Arena. The fight promised to be as

---

[6] 1935 interview with Bill Lang from an unknown source

much a spectacular social event as a sporting one. The fans certainly were not disappointed. English sportswriter James Butler wrote that the ringside seats were full of stiff shirts, white ties, and dazzlingly beautiful women.

It was the first time women in England attended a prizefight in any kind of significant numbers. McIntosh added to the evening's atmosphere by providing stewards dressed in short white linen coats with gilt buttons, to show ticket holders to their seats. And at one end of the stadium a full military band was in place, to provide musical accompaniment as the two fighters entered the ring.

Jimmy Britt, former American lightweight champion of the world, had helped promote the fight and acted as Chief Assistant to McIntosh. He was in attendance that night to serve as Master of Ceremonies, and he was attired in an immaculate suit of tails. McIntosh, in full evening dress himself, was in his element as he proudly strolled through the crowd at ringside, nodding and bowing to his friends. As he stopped to talk to Butler he confided that "Lang will eat this colored boy, just eat him."[7]

While preparing in his dressing room, Bill Lang found himself nervous. He reflected upon a morning he had spent in New York with Stanley Ketchel, a.k.a. "The Michigan Assassin." Ketchel had shown Lang around town and included a stop into a saloon, where he proceeded to quickly down three stiff drinks. Knowing that Stanley was in training at the time Lang asked him why he was drinking.

"Bill," Stanley answered, "With a few of these inside, that's when I feel like doing things, and believe me boy, that's when I do em."[8]

As Lang undressed he decided that Ketchel's tonic might be just what he needed himself at that moment. He drank a stiff brandy, and once he got it down his concern lessened a bit.

Meanwhile, Sam had prepared to enter the ring. En route but prior to entering, Sam encountered a Lang supporter who asked Sam whether he had brought a doctor with him, suggestively adding,

> "You're sure to need a medical man before Lang's finished with you."

---

[7] James Butler, *Kings of the Ring*. London: Stanley Paul & Co. Ltd., 1936
[8] 1935 interview with Bill Lang from an unknown source

"Well, if I'm sure to need a doctor, I's surer that Lang will need a coroner," replied Langford.

Sam entered the ring appearing disinterested. He swapped jokes with his seconds and waved to a friend in the audience. This was Sam's method of putting fear into his opponent. The effect on Lang was remarkable. Before he left his corner at the clanging of the gong he appeared to be wondering which of the ring-posts the "Tar Baby" was going to pick up and hit him with.[9]

When Lang got his first look at Sam stripped for battle up close his nerves heightened. Sam couldn't have been more than 5'6" or 5'7" tall, but with arms that seemed to hang below his knees and a pair of shoulders that were the biggest Bill had ever seen, he looked like a gorilla. Sam presented Bill with an impression of even greater strength than Jack Johnson.

Despite Sam's impressive build, to many novices in the crowd it may have appeared a mismatch in Lang's favor as they stood next to each other receiving instructions from Referee Eugene Corri. Sam was some thirty pounds lighter than Lang, who also looked to be a head taller.

Corri, however, was of another mind. He'd never seen a finer specimen of a man of Sam's stature and he couldn't help but be impressed by Sam's physique. There were enough other knowledgeable fight fans—people who knew what Lang was truly up against in Sam—that despite the crowd's obvious preference for him, Lang entered the ring a three-to-one underdog.

As the pair sat in the ring with hands bandaged, the crowd got a very big surprise: an attendant came down an aisle and tossed a pair of white gloves into the ring. Instead of the traditional black-colored mitts, these gloves were as white and shiny as could be. Lang wasn't surprised, as McIntosh had originated the idea and insisted on the white gloves during arrangements for the fight saying they would "show up better against black skin."[10]

When the gong rang to begin round one, Lang led first with a light left and then rushed into a clinch. Sam planted his feet and began

---

[9] Andrew Soutar, *My Sporting Life*. London: Hutchinson & Co. Ltd., 1934
[10] 1935 interview with Bill Lang from an unknown source

winging punches in earnest. He landed a left to Bill's ear and followed it up with two hooks to the body.

The two men exchanged punches liberally throughout the round. Lang appeared to most to be scoring as often as Sam, and his blows were straighter, but Sam's swings clearly were the more powerful of the pair, and they rocked Lang upon finding their mark. Lang attempted to retreat but Sam chased him and continued to rain hooks upon Bill with both hands. When the bell rang to bring the first round to a conclusion, Lang appeared distressed.

Lang came out for round two looking refreshed, but after landing a light left jab to Sam's nose he was forced to go on the defensive once again. Sam followed Bill around the ring, landing several heavy blows, and at one point he cornered the bigger man and laughingly whaled away at him.

Seated near James Butler, McIntosh assured the writer not to take any notice of the blood that was now flowing from Lang's various cuts. "Bill always bleeds as soon as he's touched, just you watch him, he hasn't got going yet!"[11]

As the round neared its conclusion, Sam caught up with Lang again and dropped him with a vicious right hook. Bill took a count of nine before rising to his feet just before the bell. By this time it had to be obvious to all in attendance, including McIntosh, that Bill was badly outclassed.

After round two, Sam's corner was an extremely confident one. His seconds spent the brief interlude swapping stories, seemingly without concern for the proceedings within the ropes.

Lang's corner, on the other hand, appeared completely bewildered. They didn't seem to have the slightest idea how to raise their man out of the stupor in which he was fighting.

In round three, Lang came out to mix it up with Sam. In the midst of one of Lang's attacks, Sam stunned everyone by suddenly dropping his arms to his sides. Even more shocking, he deliberately stuck out his chin, just inviting Lang to give him his best shot.

Lang accepted the generous offer and belted Sam on the point of the chin with four consecutive blows. Sam's seconds were taken aback ... until Sam deliberately turned and winked at them.[12]

---

[11] James Butler, *Kings of the Ring*. London: Stanley Paul & Co. Ltd., 1936

[12] Andrew Soutar, *My Sporting Life*. London: Hutchinson & Co. Ltd., 1934

At that point Lang stepped back as if to assess the result of his blows. Sam stepped forward and in the blink of an eye delivered two crushing blows. Down went Lang. He rose at the count of eight as the bell rang, and he retired to his corner sporting a badly swollen eye and bloodied face. Sam smiled as he walked to his corner.

Despite what he'd endured in the prior round, Lang bravely came out for the fourth round and tried to match Sam's intensity. But Sam quickly assumed command. Sam seemed to ease up on him a bit during the latter part of the round, after which he once again returned to his corner with a big smile.

Lang came out slowly for round five, and Sam looked as if he'd decided it was time to put him out of his misery. He rained punches upon Lang at will. In the latter part of the round, he sent him to the canvas with a hard right to the body. Lang managed to climb to his feet at the count of nine but was quickly dropped again by a grinning Sam who had immediately landed another punishing body blow. Lang was spared a knockout when the bell sounded to end the round, and he struggled to return to his corner.

When Lang came out for round six, he fought desperately to turn the tide, but Sam was too strong for him. Then Sam threw a powerful hook that missed its mark, and he slipped and dropped to one knee. Before he had a chance to rise an excited Lang let loose with a wide swing of his own that struck the top of Sam's head.[13]

"Foul!" cried many in attendance.

At that point the referee had no choice but to stop the fight and award it to Sam on a foul. Sam asked him to let the bout continue, but it was to no avail.

"No, no, Langford," responded the referee, "he has lost."[14]

The fight over, Sam retired to his corner where he promptly lit up a big fat black cigar before departing the ring.

Corri commented afterward that it was a great relief to him that he was able to put an end to the fight in the sixth, as he feared Lang could be seriously hurt before the contest came to an end.

Corri had officiated other Lang fights, and this wasn't the first that had ended on a foul by Lang. Lang had lost in a similar fashion when he fought P.O. Curran, an English heavyweight. In that match, Lang

---

[13] Andrew Soutar, *My Sporting Life*. London: Hutchinson & Co. Ltd., 1934
[14] Eugene Corri, *Gloves and The Man*. London: Hutchinson & Co. Ltd., 1928

lost on a first round foul when (after rushing Curran and causing him to slip to his knees) he delivered a blow that he claimed he'd already started and been unable to stop. Corri—respecting the English boxing rules—had immediately stepped in and awarded the contest to Curran on a foul. He had acted on the same principles that night.

British sportswriter, Trevor Wignall reported from ringside:

> It was as near an approach to mayhem as I ever saw. It was no wonder Johnson sidestepped Langford. What that short-statured, long-armed black boy did to Lang was a sin and a shame. I cannot recall a fight that had more ferocious moments, or in which more blood was spilled. It spouted over me every time Langford connected and at the close Lang looked as if he had been run through a chopping machine.[15]

A number of observers took note of Sam's skill throughout the fight. They noted his ability to thrust his face forward as an inviting target then subsequently shift his head slightly to take the blows on the top of his head, where they had little effect upon him but resulted in some damage to his opponent's hands and wrists.

England's *Boxing* magazine proclaimed Sam "the greatest fighting machine composed of flesh and blood which the human race has ever seen."[16]

After the fight Sam was asked by writers to offer his opinion of Lang.

Sam replied, "Well he's very fast on his feet, but his brain ain't fast. While he was thinking, I was hittin em."[17]

Sam added:

> "I've been fighting for ten years, and I never fouled a man in my life. He hit me low three times, see my protector, that will tell you, but I didn't care about that. I would have won (without the foul) in another two rounds. He could not have stood up against me for very long. That terrible punch of his was a snowflake. It wouldn't hurt a baby. I wasn't knocked down, I just slipped that's all, and I'm sorry a foul ended it. I don't like to express my opinions, but I have them about a man who hits another when he's down."

---

[15] Trevor Wignall, *Almost Yesterday*. London: Hutchinson & Co. Ltd., 1949
[16] *Boxing*, 25 February 1911
[17] Eugene Corri, *Gloves and The Man*. London: Hutchinson & Co. Ltd., 1928.

Responded Lang:

"I was making my own fight, a waiting fight. I wasn't hurt, not a bit. Each time I went down I could have got up sooner, but I wanted to wait. I wanted to use up all Langford's time. I landed a good one when he fell, and then, well, I don't know what's come over me. I was just too anxious, maybe. Yes, I was too anxious. I thought he was getting up. I can't explain it otherwise. In the first round I sprained my right ankle, and it bothered me a lot. I expected Langford to have all the better of the first half of the battle, and then I would come to him. He never hurt me much, although I might have looked damaged. I had him tired and half beaten when I made my awful mistake. It's done, and cannot be repaired."[18]

Sam expressed dissatisfaction with his own performance, chastising himself for not having finished Lang sooner. He also remarked that his punches seemed to lack their usual sting.

Like everyone else in attendance, Sam had immediately taken notice of the fact that the gloves were white. He was sure that McIntosh had ordered the white gloves so that Lang's punches would show up better against his dark body. McIntosh later stated that while making final preparations for the fight he decided it would make for a more attractive spectacle and be easier for the audience to follow if the parties wore white mittens. He added that he'd noticed Sam intently examining the gloves between rounds.

Sam was curious enough about the gloves that he decided to hang on to his, and he took them back to his hotel. Once inside his room he cut them open and discovered that the gloves had been stuffed with rabbit fur instead of hair—a substitution that Sam determined had robbed his punches of their usual effect.

The next time Sam saw McIntosh he walked up to him and said, "I never knew till I licked Lang how many ways there was to work the rabbit punch, Mistah McIntosh!"

"What do you mean, Sam?" replied the promoter, but Sam only grinned and walked away.

McIntosh maintained his innocence and told others that it was only because fighters had a bad habit of working the padding off the

---

[18] *Boxing*, 25 February 1911.

back of their knuckles to make their blows more dangerous, that he had gloves ordered for this fight with a patented stuffing.[19]

When word of the bout results reached champion Jack Johnson, he professed to be unimpressed with Sam's victory, pointing out that he had also defeated Lang, as had others such as Burns, and Al Kaufmann.

Promoter Hugh McIntosh disagreed. Sam's easy victory over Lang convinced him that Sam was formidable enough to come out on top if Johnson would agree to a match.

Opinions varied with respect to a rematch between Sam and the current champion. Former heavyweight champion John L. Sullivan said:

> "Sam is too small to ever expect to cope successfully with a man of Jack Johnson's size and skill. No little man is ever going to whip Johnson. Langford is a wonderfully strong fighter, but there is little question of that in whipping such men as Lang and (Jim) Barry no true line can be secured on him, as far as Johnson is concerned. To my way of thinking it will take a big man, as big as Johnson, and a clever one with a terrific kick in either hand to whip Johnson."[20]

On the other hand, former heavyweight champion James J. Corbett, writing for the *Boston American*, countered, "Sam has proved that he has a chance with any heavyweight in the business, the champion not excluded."[21]

With no major commitments in England, and Johnson continuing to avoid a rematch, Sam and his entourage traveled to Paris. There, he received his first exposure to French culture and began preparing for an April 1st encounter with Sam McVea.

There is some question as to McVea's exact date of birth. It was in the spring of either 1883 or 1884, but there is no question at all but that he grew into a stocky, heavy muscled fighter with a powerful punch. In his prime he stood 5 feet, 10½ inches and his weight ranged from 205 to 215 pounds.

A little known fact is that McVea suffered from bunions on his

---

[19] Trent Frayne. "The Greatest Fighter Who ever Lived," *MacLean's*, 15 Feb 1955
[20] *Halifax Herald*, 25 March 1911
[21] James Corbett, "Weymouth Man Worthy Foe for Johnson," *Boston American*, 14 March 1911

feet. A bunion is a localized area of enlargement of the inner portion of the joint at the base of the big toe. The enlargement is caused by additional bone formation, often in combination with a misalignment of the big toe. The normal position of the big toe (straight forward) becomes outward-directed toward the smaller toes, and the joint at the base of the big toe often becomes inflamed and tender. As a result, McVea had to be fitted with special footwear, both for the street and inside the ring.[22]

McVea began his career in California where he quickly ran off a string of seven early round knockout victories. Then on February 26, 1903 he was matched against future heavyweight champion, Jack Johnson, in Los Angeles. At that point in his career Johnson was just a month short of his 25th birthday and a veteran of over 40 professional fights. McVea put up a valiant effort but was overmatched in the twenty-round bout and suffered a decision loss.

McVea fought Johnson two more times, the last match taking place on April 22, 1904 in San Francisco when he was stopped in the twentieth round. One could accuse Johnson of many things, but being dumb wasn't one of them. He was wise enough to avoid an encounter with either McVea or Langford when they were beyond their 20th or 21st birthday and in their physical primes.

Like Langford, Sam McVea had traveled to Europe the first time in 1907 in search of ring work, but unlike Langford, McVea stayed in Europe, living and boxing in France from June 1907 to mid-1911.

During that time he fought and won a total of 26 out of 27 bouts, 23 by way of knockout. His sole defeat was in an epic forty-nine round battle with Joe Jennette. In that fight he had Joe on the deck twenty-one times in the first nineteen rounds. The fact that Jennette was able to withstand the beating he suffered from McVea during the first half of the fight was a testament to his ability to absorb punishment, as Sam Langford could certainly attest from his experiences with the big heavyweight. Ultimately, Jennette's greater stamina wore McVea down and amazingly he came back to administer his own beating in the later rounds. McVea was unable to come out of his corner for the fiftieth round, and Joe was declared the victor.

McVea decisioned Jennette in two other twenty-round meetings

---

[22] *The Sporting Globe*, 6 November 1937

during his period in Paris. When he faced Langford, the majority of the French sporting crowed looked upon him as a hero and considered him next to invincible. They called him "Le Negre Terrible," and miniature statues of him were sold everywhere in the streets. The idea that the shorter, stocky and much less physically imposing Langford could have a chance against McVea was unfathomable to French boxing enthusiasts.

When Langford arrived in Paris he got a taste of the appeal it must have held for McVea. In Paris there were no color lines, and both men were quite popular. British writer, Trevor Wignall recalled that he often saw them on an individual basis taking in the various Parisian cafés and eateries, and both men received a level of hero worship well above that which they would ever experience in the U.S.

On the evening of the fight, no less than 6,000 fans packed the Cirque de Paris to see their idol, Sam McVea, take on Langford. McVea held an estimated 20-pound weight advantage in addition to his extra three inches in elevation. When the fight got underway Langford quickly realized that McVea was, indeed, a worthy adversary. He also quickly understood that McVea wouldn't be taking the lead in terms of initiating the fighting. McVea was content to let Sam lead and counter off those leads.

Langford started off cautiously, attempting to box McVea until he could get a read on his style. McVea responded in kind. After a while Langford decided that McVea was just a boxer, so he decided to abandon his boxing tactics and he attempted to mix it up instead. Again, McVea responded in similar fashion swapping punch for punch. Langford quit throwing bombs and McVea went back to boxing as well. Initially, everything Langford did McVea followed in kind.

As the fight progressed it became evident that Langford would be both the aggressor and the party delivering the heavier blows. McVea's left jab was quickly established as his primary weapon, and he was able to land it with great regularity.

Despite McVea's popularity it became apparent early in the fight that the vast majority of the crowd was rooting for Langford. He was clearly the smaller man and the aggressor, and the partisan French crowd gained an immediate appreciation for his style of fighting.

The fight was a little disappointing to those who preferred a slugfest. There wasn't a single knockdown throughout the bout, although on three occasions McVea slipped. While Langford showed a desire to turn it into a brawl, McVea assumed a more defensive posture and made excellent use of a left jab to the face while fighting on the retreat throughout most of the contest. That jab landed with enough frequency throughout the evening that it eventually caused a considerable amount of damage to Langford's features, especially his right eye, which was almost completely closed by the time the fight ended.

When the fight concluded, Eugene Corri, who was the sole judge for the bout, ruled it a draw, to the obvious displeasure of the crowd. Questioned about the decision afterward, Corri explained that the attacks by McVea with his left jab had been much more numerous than Langford's. Almost twenty years later, he recalled that after twenty rounds his card showed a difference of only one and a half points in favor of one of the fighters, he couldn't remember which, and he felt that it was close enough to warrant a draw.

A writer from one English publication wrote of the fight:

> It turned out to be as even sided a contest as it is possible to imagine. True, Langford was the most aggressive; he forced the fighting, he kept McVea on the retreat, but he could not get there. As against this McVea's left was continually visiting Langford's face, and in this you have the real story of the fight.

Of the result, English-published *Boxing* magazine reported:

> That it was not a decision popular with the French audience counts for nothing; that it was a decision thoroughly justified and technically accurate we have not the slightest doubt, and the more we have discussed the subject the better we have liked and admired Mr. Corri's decision.

They went on to speculate that Langford had underestimated McVea.[23]

The French viewed the fight much differently. When the draw decision was announced shouts of disapproval filled the arena. Numerous oranges and other such objects flew through the air. A number of major French sporting publications disagreed with the decision. While

---

[23] *Boxing*, 8 April 1911

acknowledging that Langford's face looked the worse of the two, *Le Boxe & Les Boxeurs* reported that Langford was much more the aggressor and landed the heavier blows, while McVea's were generally more of the jab variety.

La Vie Grande Air, one of two parties with exclusive rights to photograph the fight, reported the decision as incomprehensible and expressed the opinion that Langford showed his enormous superiority over McVea. Like *Les Boxeur*, they felt the English preoccupation with the left jab (as opposed to punches that do more damage to the opponent) was to blame for the decision.

Quoted afterward, McVea himself admitted to at least one reporter that Langford should have received the verdict saying, "I was defeated and I am the first to recognize this. Langford is too powerful and too hard. My blows came up against a wall."[24]

Langford was disappointed with the draw. He felt he had done everything he could but McVea was reluctant to mix it up. He credited McVea for his left jab, but suggested that McVea's primary objective seemed to be to stay the course of the fight.

Immediately upon the conclusion of the fight, Langford visited McVea's corner. He was somewhat befuddled as to how McVea had been able to land his left to the face so consistently. Langford claimed to observe that McVea's arms were bent like bow legs. The curved bone made his jab into a hook and Langford found it difficult to defend against.[25]

Years later Joe Woodman would say that he thought this had been one of Sam's toughest fights.

> "The fight went twenty rounds and they called it a draw. My Sam looked a mess. He had lumps as big as hen's eggs on his head. His eyes were slits, all cut up. His nose was as big as your fist. Frankly, I was glad we got a draw. Then McVea came into the dressing room for a few words. When McVea left, Sam turned to me and said, 'Poor McVea, he certainly took a beating, didn't he?'"[26]

---

[24] *Les Boxe & Les Boxeurs*, April 1911

[25] *Halifax Herald*, 4 September 1924

[26] Unknown author. "Sam Langford, Heroic Figure … Tragic Figure," *World Boxing*, July 1973

The two men would get plenty of opportunity to settle the question of who was the superior fighter, as they would go on to meet a total of fifteen times over the next 9½ years.

After the conclusion of the McVea fight, Sam returned to England for a well-earned rest. On or about April 7th, the National Sporting Club held a function to present Sam with an inscribed singlet from the club, as a token of their appreciation for the manner in which Sam had conducted himself while in their country and his performances in the ring.

Shortly after Sam received word that his father had taken ill and was not expected to live, so he immediately made arrangements to return to the States via the steamer Lusitania. Reporters were on hand to greet Sam upon his return to the States, and before continuing his journey to see his ailing father he took the time to express his desire to take on one of the latest white hopes, Oklahoma giant Carl Morris, in the near future.

> "I'll box him any number of rounds, winner take all, or on any other basis he names. He is 9 inches taller and 70 pounds heavier, so he ought to give me a chance. I don't expect to remain in this country long, however, for Mr. Woodman, my manager is trying to arrange several fights for me in London.
>
> "There's big money for the fighters in London and Paris, and it's best for me to go back. McIntosh is ready to hang up a $30,000 purse for Johnson and me, but Jack doesn't seem to be in a hurry to accept."[27]

Sam arrived in Weymouth and found that his father was not dying. While his father recovered from his illness, Sam stayed for a long overdue visit.

In mid-May, Al Kaufmann suffered a knockout loss to "Fireman" Jim Flynn despite a weight advantage of almost thirty pounds. This surprising loss put an end to any thought of a possible match between Johnson and white hope Kaufmann for the heavyweight title, and raised Sam's hopes of getting a chance to fight the champion.

---

[27] *Boxing*, 6 May 1911

SAM LANGFORD UPON HIS ARRIVAL IN AUSTRALIA
NOVEMBER, 1911
BEN HAWES COLLECTION

"Every time the Negro's blows landed, Smith was lifted clean off his feet and deposited in another part of the ring."

~Police Gazette

CHAPTER 15

AUSTRALIA

Sam resumed his ring activity with a quick four-round technical knockout of a badly overmatched Ralph Calloway in Syracuse, New York on May 30, 1911. Calloway was offered up as a last minute substitute for Sandy Ferguson, who claimed illness. Prior to the contest Sam stood before the crowd and stated:

> "If you fellows don't want to see us colored boys box, then pick any two men in town today, heavyweight, paperweight, middleweight or any old weight, white or colored, and I'll stop them both."

> "What about Johnson, Sam?" someone from the crowd replied. Sam grinned.

> "Yes, Johnson can be one of them."[1]

The fans wanted to see Sam in action so the bout went on. Seven days later his nemesis Jack Johnson sailed for England with his wife to witness the ceremonies surrounding the coronation of King George V. Asked if he intended to fight abroad Johnson replied:

> "I'd fight a bear for about $30,000."

> "Will you fight Sam Langford?" he was asked.

> "He ain't no bear, he's a wildcat," replied Johnson.[2]

---
[1] *The Syracuse Herald*, 31 May 1911
[2] *Fort Wayne Sentinel*, 6 June 1911

Sam's next opponent would be Tony Caponi, a rising middleweight contender. Caponi was fresh off a loss to Jim Flynn, but his manager, Larney Litchenstein, felt he was still a legitimate future contender for the middleweight crown and was confident Caponi would make a good showing against Sam.

The fight was originally planned to take place in Kenosha, Wisconsin, but the town's local authorities were not receptive to a mixed-race bout. So, the fight was moved to Winnipeg, Canada.

The pair met on June 16th before 3,000 fans. Although there was no official decision rendered, Sam was considered to have earned a ten-round victory. Midway through the bout, Sam had pushed Caponi through the ropes. The police captain overseeing the event had interrupted it then and advised both parties that he did not want to see a knockout. It was evident that Sam eased up on his opponent thereafter.

Sam placed the cuffs on himself against his next opponent as well, in a fight that took place in New York against a white hope named Jack Fitzgerald. Sam stopped Fitzgerald in the fifth round after the crowd expressed its displeasure for allowing the obviously inferior fighter to stay as long as he did. As the crowd booed, Sam stepped over to the side of the ring and addressed them:

> "Some second or fighter connected with Fitzgerald asked me to let him stay a few rounds to give the members (of the club) a run for their money, and I did, and now that I knocked him out you feel mad just the same."

Reported *Boxing* magazine of the contest and Sam's statement to the crowd afterwards:

> When Negro prizefighters have to lean over the ropes, after slamming their big white opponents to the floor, and explain to the crowd that they could have turned the trick in the first round had they been so disposed, it appears as if it were high time for the white race to get out of the fighting game and turn it over to the blacks for their exclusive use.
>
> When we stop to consider that there are at least four Negro heavyweights in the fighting game at the present time, all Americans too, any one of whom can beat any white man in the world, to say nothing of a number of small Negroes who can do likewise in the lighter divisions among the whites, it's a sad

commentary. Instead of being booed, Langford should have been applauded for his kindness and consideration. Where is the white fighter, may I ask, who would show the same consideration for a Negro that Langford did for Fitzgerald? Where, as a matter of fact, is the white fighter who would not knock the brains out of a Negro opponent as quickly and with as little ceremony as he possibly could?

It is doubtful there are many white heavyweights in this country that could be induced to fight Langford on the level. There are several, it is true, who would be willing to fight him, but they would have to know before they got into the ring that the Negro was tied hand and foot, and that they would get their money regardless of the showing they made.

Langford's position in this fighting game in this country today is similar to the one occupied by Joe Walcott some years ago, when he was in his prime. The only way Walcott could get a fight with a white man was by agreeing to either not hurt him or lie down, or maybe lose on a foul. That's how Langford finds himself at the present time.[3]

Sam stopped his next opponent, "Farmer" Jim Smith, in five rounds before a large New York audience at the Fairmont Athletic Club. Wrote Sam Austin of the *Police Gazette*, "Every time the Negro's blows landed Smith was lifted clean off his feet and deposited in another part of the ring."[4] And whenever Smith did manage to land a significant blow of any kind he had to be disheartened by the fact that Sam would only smile afterwards.

On August 15, 1911—just six days after his match with Smith—Sam faced "Philadelphia" Jack O'Brien at the Twentieth Century Athletic Club in New York. Though highly regarded, the charismatic thirty-three-year-old O'Brien was on the downward side of his career.

Never known as a hard puncher, O'Brien possessed a fine left jab, and was extremely proficient at blocking and countering his opponent's offensive attacks. He was a great admirer of James J. Corbett and, like Corbett, was considered one of the most scientific ring performers of the day. Unlike many of his white counterparts, O'Brien

---

[3] *Boxing*, 22 July 1911
[4] *Police Gazette*, 26 August 1911

met and fared well against many black fighters of the period, including the likes of Joe Walcott, Young Peter Jackson, Jack Blackburn, The Dixie Kid, and even champion Jack Johnson whom he had met in a six-round no-decision fight in May of 1909.

In 1905, O'Brien had won the light heavyweight championship of the world by stopping forty-four-year-old Bob Fitzsimmons in the thirteenth round. At that time the light heavyweight class was relatively new, and it didn't yet hold much interest in boxing circles. As a result, O'Brien had never officially defended the title.

In March of 1909, O'Brien fought Stanley Ketchel. For the majority of their fight, O'Brien relied upon his footwork and brilliant counterattack to make Ketchel look like an amateur, but in the tenth and final round he tired badly and Ketchel was finally able to overpower him. Just prior to the bell Jack absorbed a knockout blow, but the bell rang before a count of ten could be completed. The pair met again three months later, and Ketchel knocked the older fighter out in the third round.

O'Brien was in fine condition when he met Sam. He had trained in earnest for five weeks to ensure he would be at his best for the encounter. Never more than 170 pounds, even when fighting larger opponents, it was expected that Jack would give up at least 10-20 pounds to Sam. The fact that O'Brien had not remained very active in the past year was also held to be in Sam's favor.

Sam and Jack fought before an estimated crowd of 7,500 fans, including such boxing greats as Bob Fitzsimmons, Tom Sharkey, Billy Papke, Kid McCoy, and Peter Maher. In fact, McCoy, a fighter whom O'Brien admired almost as much as Corbett, served as one of O'Brien's advisors for the event. It was rumored that each fighter would receive approximately $5,000 for their efforts, and the betting odds established Sam as a three-to-one favorite.

O'Brien appeared somewhat timid as he waited for the bell to open the fight. Sam, on the other hand, looked like he hadn't a care in the world. When the proceedings commenced, O'Brien quickly demonstrated a bit of his old-time form in the way of nifty footwork and boxing skills. That didn't last long. Sam waded in and immediately began to land heavy blows that considerably slowed his opponent. At one point in the opening session Sam floored O'Brien with a left to the head.

Many in attendance felt that Sam was pulling his punches. It was clear from the start that he possessed the stronger punch and was simply too strong for O'Brien. At one point, Sam left Jack gasping for air with a hard right to the stomach, and in the second round Sam bloodied Jack's nose. He also sent O'Brien to the canvas in the third stanza with a left hook. The bout was decidedly one-sided. In the fourth round, Sam floored Jack for the third time with a right to the head and a left to the stomach, but the bell rang before a count could be completed.

O'Brien tried to keep his distance in the fifth round, but Sam landed a light jab, and when O'Brien attempted to counter with a right, Sam stepped in and landed a vicious left hook to the jaw that sent Jack crashing to the boards. He bravely regained his footing at the count of nine, but referee Charlie White, seeing no sense in letting him continue to take a beating, stepped in and stopped it. Many believed that Sam could have ended the fight in the first round but had decided to give the large crowd a little run for their money.

O'Brien was helped to his corner where he removed his gloves and rubbed his jaw as if in great pain. Sam departed for his dressing room with a big grin on his face.

After the fight a friend of Sam's congratulated him and excitedly told him he was now a champion.

"What am I champion of?" Sam asked.

"You're champion of the world, yes indeed, world's champion light heavyweight."

Sam looked at him and asked for an explanation.

The friend explained that the light heavyweight championship had originated in 1903. Jack Root had become the division's first champion when he decisioned Kid McCoy in April of that year. He subsequently lost the title, less than two months later, when he was knocked out by George Gardner. Fitzsimmons then took the title from Gardner in November of 1905 and remained the champion until 1905, when he was knocked out by O'Brien.

"So you see, beating O'Brien makes you the champ doesn't it?" said Sam's friend.[5]

---

[5] *Halifax Herald*, 6 September 1924

In truth, while it can be argued that O'Brien never really officially defended the title he won from Fitzsimmons, he had been defeated previously when Ketchel knocked him out in their second meeting, which took place in 1909. In any case, there was little interest in the light heavyweight title in 1911, and the matter was not pressed.

Eventually, in 1912, Jack Dillon claimed the vacant light heavyweight title when he defeated Hugo Kelly, but he wasn't fully recognized as the champion of that division until 1914 when he defeated a couple of more contenders for the crown.

Having faced both Langford and Ketchel, O'Brien had more respect for Sam. In *A Neutral Corner* A.J. Liebling wrote that O'Brien considered Ketchel "a bum distinguished only by the tumultuous but ill-directed ferocity of his assault." Langford on the other hand he felt had a "mystic-quality and when he appeared upon the scene of combat you knew you were cooked."[6]

Nine days after defeating O'Brien, Sam met rugged Italian heavyweight Tony Ross again. Ross was fresh off an impressive performance against Joe Jennette, and some folks believed he might be able to reverse his previous loss to Sam. Sam put an end to his aspirations with a left hook to the jaw in the sixth round.

An agreement was then made for Sam to face Joe Jennette again, this time in a ten-round contest that would be held in New York. Jennette had tried to get Sam to agree to a longer distance but Sam declined saying, "You ain't human, I won't fight you over ten rounds because I intend to fight for a long time yet."[7]

Sam knew that Jennette could withstand a tremendous amount of punishment and that he would suffer the same if he agreed to a longer match. Despite the failure to secure a longer contest, Jennette succeeded in gaining agreement to one point strongly in his favor, the match would be held in a 24-foot ring.

As August came to a close, Joe Woodman announced that, Jennette not withstanding, Sam was running out of willing opponents in the States but that Australian promoter, Hugh Mcintosh, had planned a

---

[6] A.J. Liebling, *A Neutral Corner*. San Francisco: North Point Press, 1990
[7] *Boxing*, 16 September 1911

series of fights for him down under. McIntosh was also still trying to find a way to put a match together between Sam and Jack Johnson.

In fact, McIntosh had been making arrangements to entice six American fighters to come to Australia to perform over the coming winter and into the early part of the next year. In addition to Sam, he wanted to bring over Al Kaufmann, Jim Flynn, Jimmy Clabby, Billy Papke, and Packy McFarland. His plan was to guarantee each fighter a specified number of matches and have them engage in an elimination tournament of sorts, with the ultimate victor obtaining an opportunity to fight Jack Johnson for the world's title.

Sam and Joe advised the press that before making the trip to Australia they would like to fight both Joe Jennette and Jim Flynn to clear up any doubt as to the legitimacy of Sam's claim as the primary contender for Johnson's crown. They reasoned that while Flynn was not highly rated, the fact that he'd defeated Al Kaufmann (whom Johnson himself had said was the man with the best chance to defeat him) would only further strengthen their case. Speaking of Johnson, Sam said:

> "I am goin' to Australia to make him fight me or show him up as a rank coward. If Johnson can get Hugh McIntosh to agree to give him $30,000 he'll probably agree to meet me, which means that I'll come back here with the championship of the world. But I'll not be satisfied that Johnson really wants to take a chance until I see him in the ring pullin' on the gloves.
>
> "I've got an old score to settle with this colored gentleman. We met in Chelsea five years ago in a fifteen-round bout. I weighed 140 pounds then, while Johnson weighed 190. He was as much of an unknown as I was and nobody outside of the Boston sporting men paid any attention to us. It was just after the fight started that I caught Johnson on the point of the jaw with a right hook and flattened him on the floor like a flapjack. His eyes were rollin', and he almost turned white. When he got up he looked scared to death, and hung on until the gong ended the round. After that he wouldn't mix with me, and just stuck out his left hand, jabbing me in the face the rest of the way. The referee said he won on points, but you can bet that Johnson was glad when it was over."

Speaking of Johnson's victory over James Jeffries the previous year, Sam added:

> "I could have stopped Jeffries myself in Reno in quicker time than Johnson did the trick. I stopped Bill Lang in six rounds, while Lang stayed nine with the champion. Johnson knocked out Jim Flynn in eleven rounds while I did it in one."[8]

Meanwhile, one by one the men Mcintosh had hoped to convince to come to Australia began to turn him down. First Al Kaufmann decided not to go, and then Jim Flynn. Ultimately, Jack Johnson, who had given McIntosh a verbal commitment, also indicated that he preferred retirement to making the trip across the ocean. Did the fact that Sam was going to be there have anything to do with their decisions? New York boxing writer, Bob Edgren, wrote that Johnson was a wise champ, ducking Sam, and that it was a pity Sam wasn't a "white hope," or the whole sporting world would insistently demand that Johnson meet him.[9]

On September 5th, Sam met Joe Jennette before a large crowd in New York's Madison Square Garden. The fight followed a familiar pattern for the pairings between these two. Sam immediately established himself as the aggressor, landing the heavier blows, while Joe relied on his jab and spent the majority of the fight taking every advantage afforded him by the large 24-foot ring.

> "It was no shame to him (Joe) that he stuck and ran. You would get out of the way of Sam's short, man-killing counters as naturally as you would get off a railroad track in the face of an onrushing train," wrote one reporter.[10]

Sam knocked Joe down in the first, fourth, and tenth rounds on his way to a victory on points.

On October 6th, Sam met Tony Caponi in New York, their second match within the space of four months. Caponi was unable to break through Sam's defense and Sam showed him no respect whatsoever. At one point in the first round, Sam went so far as to push his jaw toward Tony and then laughingly receive Tony's responding blow. In fact, Sam

---

[8] *Washington Post* 27 August 1911

[9] *Syracuse Herald*, 28 August 1911

[10] unknown source, newspaper clipping, 6 Sep 1911

smiled throughout most of the fight. Caponi tasted the canvas three times—twice in the second session, and the last time in the third—after which the referee stepped in and put an end to the lopsided fight.

The ease with which Sam handled his outclassed opponent in this bout raised questions in the minds of many boxing fans. Had Sam simply carried his foe when they met in a ten-round no-decision contest only four months earlier?

Sam was making relatively good money at this point in his career and was not afraid to spend it. He liked to have a good time and he had developed quite a reputation for his flashy wardrobe, as evidenced by the following excerpts from a newspaper article that October:

> Merchant tailors of the world are apt to become the globe's most affluent men if we continue to have a few more black pugilists among the top-liners of the heavyweight division.
>
> Naturally, you read all about the wonderful effects in sartorial art that Jack Johnson, champion of them all took abroad with him to dazzle the throngs at King George's coronation. Jack set out to be a fashion leader in his set, but we have just discovered that he has a close rival in the person of Sam Langford.
>
> Sam is able to dress well and at the same time look well, but there is a difference between the two big blacks. Johnson with his frame of 240 odd pounds and Sam with his of something in the vicinity of 170 or so. Johnson likes to mingle with the whites, while Langford is for sticking in the main with people of his own color.
>
> But this difference in the inclination of the two men doesn't make any difference with Sam's passion for the good things and the latest in the line of hats, shoes, and clothing. He was asked about a new and rare-looking hat, that covered his close cropped head the other day.
>
> "Nice bonnet, isn't it?" Sam asked as he took it off and smoothed it affectionately. It was a pearl gray lid of the finest of fuzzy felt, really a creation. "That's my hobby right now," Sam continued as he replaced the hat on his powerful head.
>
> "Ah just can't keep out of the hat stores. What do you think of a fighter like me paying $15 for a lid?" and the famous fighter threw his head back and let loose of a hearty guffaw.

Sam, as already stated, displays his toggery for the edification, and perhaps sincere jealousy, of his own people, but he knows how to dress and dress well. I asked him if all of his clothes were Boston-made and he laughed again.

'No, some ah got in Paris and some in London, some in New York, some in Baltimore, and if I stayed a week in any other place ah'd just have to have some new suits made up," and again he guffawed.

"Guess nobody in the world can lick me, but certainly those tailors do get my goat. Ah fall for them any time I see anything new on their shelves."[11]

In mid-October, Hugh McIntosh—desperate to bring some American pugilistic talent to Australia for the coming winter—improved upon his original offers to Sam, "Porky" Flynn, "Cyclone" Johnny Thompson, and one or two others who subsequently agreed to make the trip to Australia. Sam was promised at least six fights while there.

Sam considered having his wife and four-year-old daughter accompany him on the trip, but it didn't pan out.

The schedule McIntosh set up required the group catch a November 1st departure aboard the steamer *Zealandia*, which would be sailing from British Columbia (B.C.); Canada's westernmost province. Sam and his party traveled west through Canada, arriving in Vancouver, B.C., just in time to catch the departing ship, which the captain had kindly delayed by a couple of hours for their benefit.

In addition to the boxing talent aboard her, the *Zealandia* was carrying a contingent of sporting men making the trip to Australia. These included Irving H. Wheatcroft, a millionaire horseman, members of the American tennis team challenging Australia for the Davis Cup, and Ivoy Larsen, a champion cyclist. The ship was being referred to as "the sporting ship."

The *Daily Province*, a Vancouver newspaper raised an interesting question when reporting on Sam's departure. They asked where Sam's six guaranteed matches were to come from unless he fought Sam McVea six times.[12]

---

[11] *Winnipeg Tribune*, 21 October 1911
[12] *The Daily Province*, 24 November 1911

On November 11, Hugh McIntosh announced that instead of a match between Langford and Bill Lang he had matched Langford and McVea for a twenty-round go in Sydney, on December 26th. He hoped to have the winner face Jack Lester, a large Polish-American heavyweight, and he still held out hope of enticing Jack Johnson to come to Sydney a few months afterward to face the winner of that match.

Sam and his party arrived in Sydney on November 25th and were immediately ushered off to a hearty reception at the Bateman Hotel. Awaiting them were leading members of the local boxing community, as well as ex-heavyweight champion Tommy Burns, all of whom turned out and enthusiastically welcomed the fighters to Australia. McIntosh addressed the crowd, telling them that Sam had fought for him in England and in France, and he could affirm that Sam was both a gentleman and a clean and fair fighter. He laughingly told the crowd that he'd had a hard time convincing Sam to come to Australia once Sam heard that the continent was a land of snakes.

Tommy Burns was given an opportunity to say a few words. He expressed his confidence that Sam would enjoy his visit because, in his own experience with Australia, he'd found they always treated a boxer well, no matter what color he was—so long as he behaved like a gentleman, and he knew Langford would do that.

When it was Sam's turn to address the gathering, he said he was pleasantly surprised and pleased with the reception they had received, both at the boat and the hotel, and that he was sure their stay was going to be a pleasurable one.

One of Woodman's first acts was to seek out the Australian trainer, Duke Mullins, whom they had met in England to present him with an offer to train Sam during his stay in the country. An agreement that was suitable to both parties was quickly reached. Mullins immediately discovered that his new charge had some funny little habits. For instance, for breakfast Sam insisted upon six raw eggs in either sherry or milk, and it was Sam's custom to enter a ring for training or fights with either a pinch of tobacco in his cheek or an unlit cigar. As soon as a round was over he would look for his chew. If he was in a fight, Mullins had to put it into his mouth or take it out behind the cover of a towel. Sam called for his unlit cigar the moment a fight was finished, regardless of the outcome. He would stroll to his dressing room with it dangling from the corner of his mouth.[13]

Mullins found Sam to be one of the most likeable men he ever met in a lifetime among fighters. He said he was as good natured, good tempered, and carefree as any of the other fighters he trained, and that outside of the ring he was one of the nicest fellows you could ever meet.[14]

McIntosh, intent on generating as much interest as possible in Sam's upcoming match with McVea, invited a large number of sportswriters to watch him work out. The writers assembled around the ring in great interest, admiring Sam's performance and laughing at his jokes.

Jack Lester was also working out in the same gym. When nobody paid him any attention he walked over to see what all the fuss was about. After watching Sam shadow box for a while, Lester remarked, "There's nobody in the world, not even a nigger, can knock me out with a punch on the jaw."

"Is that so, Mr. Lester? Maybe I couldn't knock you out, but if I ever does hit you on the jaw, I sure will give you a mighty bad headache," Sam replied.

Lester was in a nasty mood and very persistent.

Sam became angered and said, "Say Lester, I've finished my trainin' for today, but I'se not too tired to fight you, jes' step into de ring and I'll attend to you."[15]

Lester departed, but not before Sam voiced his opinion to him about how ungentlemanly it was for one fighter to come to another's training quarters to throw out a challenge.

Sam tried in vain to get McIntosh to match him with Lester while in Australia, offering to fight him for next to nothing simply for the pleasure of administering a beating. He had to wait, though, and didn't get an opportunity to test Lester's jaw until October of 1913.

A boxing exhibition for the relief of the dependents of a number of Australian men who had recently lost their lives at sea off the North Coast took place on November 27th. As planned, Sam went through

---

[13] *The Sporting Globe*, 23 October 1937

[14] *The Sporting Globe*, 30 October 1937

[15] Hugh McIntosh, "Laughing Sam Langford. The Black Tornado," *Knockout*, 1936

his paces during a four-round exhibition with Dave Smith and made a big hit with the crowd. In fact, Australia took to Sam almost immediately for his fighting qualities and good nature.

Not everyone was receptive to professional prizefighting, however. On November 29th the *Sydney Daily Telegraph* published a long letter to the editor from E.A. Blow, State President of the W.C.T.U., protesting the inclusion of professional boxers in a festival to raise money on behalf of their principal hospital. The writer declared that prizefighting was brutal, demoralizing, and infectious, and altogether unworthy of being associated with the high ideals of charity.

Despite the objection of Mr. Blow and his supporters, the professional boxers did appear at the Nellie Stewart carnival held at the Stadium on December 19th, where McIntosh had arranged for an exhibition between ex-heavyweight champion Tommy Burns and Sam.

It was estimated that the crowd numbered approximately 15,000 for the event that included a beauty contest in addition to the boxing. Burns was reportedly fat as butter. Even so, the two men were introduced as "the greatest fighting machines in the world."

Burns, breathing heavily, and in an exaggerated crouch, followed Sam around the ring, leading for the face, and Sam made playful swipes in the direction of Burns' body. Finally, after an innocent swing over Burns' head, Sam fell clean over and acted as if he'd lost consciousness, to the delight and laughter of the crowd. The lighthearted performance between the two fighters left protesters with nothing to complain about.

McVea and Langford met in the ring for the second time before 20,000 fans, including key Australian ministers and clergy. It was an extremely hot sunny day on December 26, 1911 at the open air Stadium in Sydney. The bout was scheduled for twenty rounds and was billed as being for the championship of the British Empire.

Langford entered the ring first, his hair closely cropped. He was dressed in a loud robe. McVea joined him shortly after attired in a robe every bit as garish as Langford's, his handlers shielding him from the hot sun under a very large red and blue umbrella.

As was the case in their first meeting, the two appeared unequally matched. McVea looked much bigger, and weighed approximately 196 pounds compared to Langford's estimated weight of 170. Only in the chest and shoulders department did Langford appear to measure up to his larger opponent. Despite this, Langford entered the ring a slight 5 to 4 favorite. As usual, Langford carried a pleasant expression on his face looking every bit like a man without a care in the world. McVea on the other hand wore a look of determination.

Well-known Australian sportsman Snowy Baker was on hand to officiate the match. He called the pair to the middle of the ring for instructions and informed them that both must break fair from clinches. When Baker had finished with his instructions, Langford looked up at McVea's face, and, thinking of the key he'd bestowed upon him two years earlier remarked, "By de holy Lord, Sambo, I ain't made no mistake with that key."[16]

Upon returning to his corner and being advised by Duke to keep his guard up against McVea's dangerous left hook, Langford replied, "It's a pity they don't allow anyone to help you in this business, once you crawl through the ropes you am all alone."

Langford's laugh could be heard throughout the nearby seats when Duke answered, "Oh, you won't be lonely, McVea will keep you company for the next hour or so."[17]

The bell sounded to open round one and both men advanced slowly towards the center of the ring. Langford feinted and McVea retreated, quickly establishing a pattern that would last throughout the fight. Langford attempted to force the fight, while McVea was content to box on the retreat, sticking and moving to avoid Langford's punishing blows. The advantage in round one was Langford's, and round two was more of the same.

Langford opened round three effectively, landing blows with both hands to the head and body. To his detriment, at one point he just missed landing a hard right hook to McVea's jaw. McVea was able to land his own left hook in reply, knocking the "Tar Baby" to the canvas. Langford immediately bounced back up to his feet, but he was somewhat shaken. He boxed defensively for the balance of the round. That round belonged to McVea.

McVea also took rounds four and five, boxing cleverly on the retreat and bloodying Langford's mouth in the fifth session.

---

[16] *The Sporting Globe*, 23 October 1937
[17] *The Sporting Globe*, 30 October 1937

Early on in the fight it became clear that Langford's manager had done him a great disservice by agreeing to the stipulation calling for a clean break at all times during the contest. The reason for the stipulation was that the fight was going to be filmed and previously filmed bouts had been spoiled by too much "hugging and clinching," so called "infighting." This stipulation might not have mattered so much except that the referee interpreted this to mean that infighting of any kind would not be allowed. Snowy Baker repeatedly stepped in and broke the fighters whenever Langford appeared ready to deliver heavy punishment at close range.

Infighting was a skill that Langford had mastered, and it was especially important to him when facing larger foes. McVea on the other hand was more effective when relying upon his left jab and boxing skills from the outside.

McVea wasn't slow in realizing the importance of the referee's interpretation of this rule. Whenever Langford succeeded in working his way in close to position himself to deliver heavy body blows, McVea quickly fell into a clinch and waited the inevitable separation by Baker so he could resume boxing at long range.

Though Langford exhibited few signs of outward frustration, there were a number of occasions where he employed the use of his forearms to attempt to escape the embrace of McVea, only to be warned by Baker time and again for doing so.

Rounds six through nine were fairly evenly contested, the edge likely going to one or the other depending upon how much weight one placed upon aggressiveness as opposed to skill exhibited while boxing on the retreat. At all times Langford was the aggressor, while McVea scored effectively catching the smaller man coming in. Most in attendance felt these rounds belonged to Langford.

As early as round eight, the effects of McVea's left jab upon Langford's right eye began to show. By round ten, Langford's left eye was nearly closed and McVea was bleeding at the mouth, but neither fighter appeared at all concerned.

Rounds ten through twelve belonged to Langford as he continued to force the action, but while McVea seemed to be tiring, Langford wasn't feeling much better.

"Duke, de old boat am rocking bad," he remarked to Mullins as he returned to his corner.[18]

The canvas was burning hot and Langford's feet blistering badly. McVea was catching him with his left hook, and Sam's sore feet were inhibiting his ability to get out of the way of those punches.

Somewhere about the thirteenth through fifteenth rounds Langford's left eye was closed completely. He continued to pursue his larger opponent and while the fighting was relatively even, the general consensus was that McVea held a slight edge in rounds fifteen through seventeen.

Langford went all out in round eighteen, but although he appeared to win the round McVea was able to avoid suffering any serious punishment.

When round nineteen commenced, both fighters were spent. Langford looked all in, and McVea, tired as well, looked uncertain as to whether or not Langford was playing possum and trying to lure him into opening up. Not willing to take a chance, McVea boxed cautiously and the paced slowed.

The twentieth and final round opened to loud applause. The fighters partook of a mutually respectful handshake in the center of the ring. The crowd had cheered the participants equally throughout the contest and anticipated a rip roaring finale; however, there was little left in the tanks of either fighter. When the bell rang ending the event, the crowd roared its approval of the performance exhibited by the participants. An exhausted Langford sat heavily upon his stool as he waited for the verdict. He'd spent twenty rounds chasing McVea about the ring and wrestling the bigger man in clinches.

There were hoots and whistles of dissatisfaction throughout the Stadium when Snowy Baker rendered a decision victory in McVea's favor. The majority in attendance, favoring Langford's attacking style, felt that he deserved the decision and that, at worst, he should have received a draw. As he had done when a decision (draw) was announced in their first meeting in Paris, McVea leapt in the air upon the announcement of a decision in his favor.

The Sydney Referee, a publication considered by many to be the leading authority on boxing in Australia at the time, expressed the following opinion of the verdict:

---

[18] *The Sporting Globe*, 30 October 1937

The pity of it was that so great and generously waged a contest should have been marred by such a glaringly wrong decision as the verdict in Sam McVea's favor. I cannot recall more than a few cases where a ring ruling had so little justification.

Former heavyweight champion Tommy Burns, in attendance for the fight, was even blunter in his assessment of the decision:

"The decision was awful. Believe me, and I mean it too, it was absolutely the worst decision that it's been my lot to witness.

"Why, Langford won all the way. He was streets in front, and gee he should have certainly got it. I had a good opinion of Snowy Baker's refereeing once, but it's all gone. He certainly won't referee a fight that I have got anything to do with."[19]

Sam and Joe were flabbergasted by the decision, but Sam figured he'd get another crack at McVea before he left Australia, and he promised himself he'd leave no room for any doubt the next time they met.

The unsatisfactory result of Langford's fight with McVea on Boxing Day prompted Australian sportsmen to clamor for another meeting between the pair. On January 10th, McIntosh announced that he had arranged for a rematch on January 26th, but McVea's manager, Billy McClain, disputed that. He advised that McVea had injured his arm and would not be right for some time. McIntosh refuted the legitimacy of McVea's claim and two weeks later used the Australian publication *The Referee*, to try to force McVea to agree to another match. In a story headlined, "Big Sam Wants No More of Little Sam, so Says McIntosh," McIntosh challenged McVea:

"I cannot say with any great degree of definitiveness when a return match may take place between Sam Langford and Sam McVea. For some reason or other McVea appears to regard the smaller man as a proposition to be avoided, and evinces a strong desire to side-step him, which it seems improbable to lead his attention away from, no matter how well the argument against may be put.

"I have tried and tried again to convince McVea and his manager, Billy McClain of the mistake they were making, but

---

[19] *The Referee*, 26 December 1911

to no purpose, they have plainly made up their minds that another match shall not be if there is any possibility of getting out of it; consequently I determined on Monday to become busy in another direction and put the leverage of the law into motion.

"I may not be able to force McVea to face Langford, but I certainly am in a position to make him pay heavily for refusing to do so. My solicitors advise me that there is no doubt about the strong hand I hold.

"Fighting Langford has been a good deal of a gold mine for McVea. He netted no less than 2,500 pounds out of the two battles, which was more than the whole of the rest of his fights brought him. Plainly, Sam McVea knows who won that match on Boxing Day, and by exactly how much it was won, too. He would take a chance had the margin been narrow, and he would jump at the offer of another go did he think the verdict was really earned by him."[20]

The fight fans of Australia eagerly awaited McVea's reply.

---

[20] *The Referee*, 24 January 1912

FRENCH POSTCARD OF SAM MCVEA

CA. 1909 - 1911

BEN HAWES COLLECTION

> "SAM LANGFORD? NO SIR! NOT FOR ME. I AIN'T GOING TO FIGHT THAT BABY ANY MORE."
>
> ~SAM MCVEA

CHAPTER 16

MASTERING MCVEA

As the year 1911 came to a close, nobody seemed to know whether Jack Johnson would ever defend his title again. One report had him signing with Hugh McIntosh for a fight in Australia, either versus McVea or Langford sometime in February. Another report indicated he would face "Fireman" Jim Flynn in New York in June or July.

While efforts to sort out Johnson's plans continued, Sam settled in for a lengthy stay down under. He got Mullins to send a cable to America on his behalf, arranging for his car to be shipped to Sydney.

This car, a Chalmers, had been won from another party by Sam one night while playing dice in a poolroom. Mullins said he would never forget the way Sam sat at the wheel of that car, his cap on his head at a rakish angle, with an unlit cigar dangling out of the corner of his mouth.[1]

On February 7th, the *Sydney Daily Telegraph* reported that on the 19th Sam would be participating in a benefit being held in the town of Wyalong. The event would raise funds for the many families in that town which had lost husbands and fathers in a recent mining disaster.

A day later, the *Daily Telegraph* reported on how Sam would be spending his time before the Wyalong benefit. Jim Barry, who had failed in nine previous attempts, would be making a tenth try to defeat Sam that coming Saturday, February 12th. The report speculated that

---

[1] *The Sporting Globe*, 30 October 1937

the use of heavier gloves and the application of Australia's "clean-break" rule might play in Barry's favor. The advertisement for the bout billed Sam as the "Champion Light Heavyweight of the World."

On February 12th, 3,000 partisan fans in favor of Barry were quickly disappointed. It immediately became apparent that Barry was no match for Sam. Midway through the opening round, Sam landed a number of heavy blows and sent the heavier man to his knees for a count of four. The pair talked to each other throughout the fight. In the fourth round Sam pointedly urged Barry to fight rather than hold onto him. It was a rough fight. At one point a frustrated Barry threw Sam over his hip and sent him crashing to the floor. Despite his action, Barry reached down and assisted Sam to his feet, and the two men shook hands before resuming their battle. Later, in the fifteenth round, Barry complained to the referee that Sam was infighting. The referee didn't agree, and the fight continued. Although outmatched, Barry proved his gameness and the contest went the full 20 rounds. There was little argument when Sam was awarded the verdict.

On March 2nd, Australian fight fans were excited to learn that Langford had been matched to meet McVea again on Easter. The much anticipated rematch was expected to draw a good crowd in light of the controversy that surrounded their previous bout.

McIntosh claimed he encountered a little resistance in making the match, as neither of the men particularly relished the idea of facing one other again. Though Langford feared no man, he'd begun to wonder if McVea might be just too big for him. McVea on the other hand, wasn't anxious to absorb any more of Langford's thunderous blows regardless of the size of the purse. He initially sought a delay, claiming that he'd injured his right hand in the previous fight with Langford. But the legal action McIntosh had threatened convinced McVea that it was in his best interest to accept the match. This was the fight the fans wanted to see, and McIntosh was going to make sure they got it.

Prior to the match with Langford, McVea fought his own bout with Barry on March 16th. When that fight took place, Langford made sure to secure a ringside seat so he'd be able to study McVea's every move. He was determined to gain any advantage he could.

Like Langford, McVea defeated Barry via a decision, giving Langford an opportunity to witness a full twenty rounds of action.

Sam later revealed that he learned more about McVea from watching him box Barry that evening than he had from their first two fights put together.

The issue of who would serve as the official for the Langford-McVea contest was still in debate as late as April 4th. Langford and his manager were dead set against having Snowy Baker officiate again. Baker usually served as the official referee for bouts at the stadium, but Sam and Joe felt they hadn't received a fair shake in the previous meeting and strongly opposed the use of his services for another go with McVea. Woodman maintained that he and Sam had the right to say who would serve, and McIntosh claimed they were incorrect while acknowledging the provision in Langford's agreement that the referee should be acceptable to Langford.

Someone proposed that McIntosh referee the bout and render a decision with the assistance of two judges, but McVea's manager (concerned about McIntosh's ability to remain impartial given the recent legal proceedings he'd initiated against McVea) suggested they find another party. Arthur Scott was ultimately agreed upon. Scott had officiated a number of important matches at the Sydney Sports Ground, and his honesty was considered beyond reproach.

Baker was extremely upset when it came out that he'd been replaced as the stadium official for the event at the request of a fighter. He vehemently protested participants having a say in the appointment of a referee, and he announced his resolve not to serve as referee for any future stadium contests until the management took a similar stance. Baker was later convinced by McIntosh to reconsider and continue to referee future stadium contests, though he would never again have an opportunity to officiate any matches involving Langford.

As expected, the third meeting between the pair aroused much interest. A crowd of approximately 15,000 filled the Sydney Stadium on April 8th. The two fighters encountered one another on their way to their respective dressing rooms as they arrived for the event.

"How's you tonight, Big Sam?" Langford greeted McVea.

"All right Tar Baby, an this is mah night for steppin'" replied McVea.

Slapping McVea between the shoulders, Langford replied, "Good on you, Beau, and it am my night for hittin'."[2]

When the men entered the ring and stripped for action they both appeared fit. McVea rippled with muscles over his large frame, and Langford, while not showing the same definition, also appeared well trained. One reporter writing for the Melbourne Argus newspaper wrote that McVea appeared noticeably uneasy entering the ring.

As usual, Langford assumed the role of aggressor, attacking with a vengeance from the opening bell. Sam had learned from his first two fights with McVea that it was difficult to reach him with a solid blow because he was constantly on the retreat. To counter this, he'd trained to increase his speed, to improve his ability to get in range and deliver his punches. As in their previous meetings, McVea relied mainly on the use of his left and holding whenever Langford was able to get inside.

The prevailing opinion among those attending was that Langford appeared much quicker than he had previously. He stayed on top of McVea in the opening round and rained thunderous blows upon his body. McVea sought refuge in the form of clinches throughout the round, only to have Langford rough him up and attempt to lift his head with one hand so that he could attempt to knock it off with the other. Unlike their previous encounter, and much to McVea's dismay, Langford found that he was frequently able to utilize his considerable infighting skills in this meeting.

Midway through the second round it appeared that Langford might be in trouble as his right eye began to swell from the impact of McVea's left jabs, but he devised an effective defense. When McVea tried to deliver a left, Langford was often able to block it with his right glove and subsequently deliver his own left to McVea's jaw. He then immediately showered McVea with a series of quick left jabs.

When the second round ended the police officer in charge of the event sent notice to Langford through the referee that he must cease his close-quarter fighting. Langford simply smiled in response, but it was observed that the warning had an obvious impact, as the employment of any infighting tactics on his part in rounds three and four

---

[2] *The Sporting Globe*, 30 October 1937

diminished considerably, much to McVea's advantage. Langford received no further warning from the police officer.

It wasn't all Langford during the early rounds. McVea impressed onlookers with his boxing skills, but Langford was able to land his punches and effectively block more of McVea's jabs than he had in their previous bout. Sam frequently employed the use of a crouch, and when he unleashed his heavy right hand swings to McVea's body the crowd often let out a loud gasp in unison, expressing their sympathy for McVea. Langford launched a right with deadly intentions in the sixth round with such force that when it missed its mark he found himself on all fours upon the mat. The 7th round was pivotal. Midway through the round McVea backed himself too close to the ropes and, upon coming out of another of many clinches, he rebounded off the ropes at the same time that Langford delivered a wicked left hook. The blow exploded against McVea's jaw and he dropped heavily to the canvas.

Though he was clearly hurt, McVea managed to climb back to his feet and was able to grab Langford in a hug that neither Langford nor the referee could get him to release. One reporter compared it to an octopus clinging to a rock. Round and round the two whirled, Langford frantically trying to release McVea's grip, while the bigger man held on for dear life. When the bell rang to end the round McVea trudged groggily to his corner. Up until that point the general opinion was that despite Langford's greatly improved performance, McVea had still managed to outbox him.

For the next three rounds McVea appeared to suffer from the effects of the knockdown blow, and he wrapped Sam up in a clinch at every possible opportunity. It finally appeared that the cobwebs might be clearing for him in the latter part of the eleventh round, but Langford found the mark with two powerful blows.

From that point on and through the eighteenth round it was all Langford, though McVea staged periodic rallies in each round and continued to work on Langford's eyes.

In the nineteenth round, McVea, realizing that a knockout was his only chance, fought desperately, and in the eyes of many he won that session. But Langford came out with more determination in the twentieth and final round and tipped the balance back in his favor.

Langford suffered his share of punishment throughout the bout. His right eye was almost closed by the finish, but it was clear the fight belonged to him. He had forced the fighting throughout the contest, never allowing McVea a moment's rest. It was no surprise to anyone in attendance when Scott raised the smaller man's hand in victory, and they wildly cheered the result.

McVea, while badly disappointed, offered no excuses for the loss. Langford was extremely pleased with his victory and felt that he had proved himself McVea's master.

When McIntosh approached Sam the next day and suggested another fight between the two, Sam replied, "I don't want to fight him, get me somebody tough, I beat him too easily."

"Oh, you didn't beat him, there were extenuating circumstances," replied McIntosh.

McIntosh went on to explain that on the night before the fight he had driven to Sydney to take care of some personal matters. He returned the next day at daybreak and around 5:00 a.m., as he neared McVea's training camp, he saw a man sitting dejectedly under a tree. It was McVea.

McIntosh immediately pulled over in his automobile and inquired as to the reason McVea was up so early on the morning of the fight. McVea initially told the promoter that he couldn't sleep and had come outside to get some fresh air, but when pressed further explained that he and his woman had had a heated argument, and he'd decided to come outside where it was cooler.

"How long have you been out here?" asked McIntosh.

"Well, I'd guess about six hours" replied McVea.

McIntosh tried to convince McVea to go home and get some sleep, but the fighter would have none of it.

"You don't know that woman. There's just no sleep when she's in a mood like she is now," said McVea. McIntosh left McVea sitting under the tree.

McIntosh's meaning was clear. He was implying that McVea had not been at his best as a result. Langford listened closely, and once McIntosh had finished his story responded, "Chief, you know what I'd a done if I was McVea?"

"No," replied McIntosh.

"Well, after our fight last night, I would have gone straight home to that woman and said, 'Woman I've done lost one fight tonight, but now I'm gonna win one.' And then I would have grabbed the back of her neck with one hand and shoved her chin forward and I would have hit her plumb on the chin and said, 'I wins'. Yes, indeed, that's what I would have done and that's what every man ought to do with an obnoxious-dispositioned wife who wants to fight these here nasty world battlers."[3]

The Australian paper *The Referee* applauded the performance of Arthur Scott as the third man in the ring and took an additional shot at Snowy Baker's decision in the previous encounter between the two. Will Lawless wrote:

The white-haired referee made a mistake, as I said at the time, and have stated on many occasions since, which I could not understand until he explained later that a good deal of Langford's work at close quarters—'his uppercuts and right chops,' etc.—was not allowed because it occurred in "clinches." Never was such an untenable defense of a decision heard before. Just the same amount of Langford's scoring in this most recent bout and perhaps a little more, was done in so called "clinches," and Arthur Scott very properly allowed for it in the reckoning because it was legal and in conformity with the rules of the game. The "clinches" were no clinches at all. McVea was the only man holding on both occasions, but it takes two to provide a clinch; each must be embracing the other. That Snowy Baker should have fallen into such an error was certainly a surprise to me.

Referee Scott, for his part expressed his admiration of Langford's performance saying, "He did some very clever things, most of which only one placed as I was could see."[4]

The next month there were reports that Langford and McVea would

---

[3] *Winnipeg Tribune*, 30 October 1926
[4] *The Referee*, 10 April 1912

meet again very soon, but with nothing yet in place arrangements were made for Langford to face Jim Barry again on May 13th, in Melbourne.

Two days prior to Langford's match with Barry a number of prominent individuals and their lady friends were invited to witness Sam in training at Fred Porter's gymnasium. Besides the typical work on the heavy and speed bags and two-round sessions with his four sparring partners, Sam astounded the visitors by frequently standing almost motionless before his partners in the ring and allowing them to rain blows upon his head, which he received indiscriminately on his chin, nose, and forehead, smiling all the while.

When Sam and Barry met for the eleventh time of their careers two days later, Sam had little trouble with Barry, garnering another victory before a packed house. The end came in the 11th round when Sam floored Barry with a crushing left hook. Although Barry managed to stagger back to his feet with a silly grin, it was clear he was helpless, so the referee stepped in and awarded the fight to Sam.

Next up for Sam was a former stable mate, a fighter named Dan "Porky" Flynn. Like Sam, "Porky" had been managed by Joe Woodman, but a couple of months before, the fighter and manager had had a disagreement of some kind and Flynn had decided to end the relationship. One report indicated that the row was between Sam and Flynn, and Flynn himself confirmed this some months later during an interview given in the States upon his return home. He didn't provide the specifics, saying only that there were good and sufficient grounds for the falling out between he and Sam. In any case, arrangements were made for a match to take place between the pair at the Melbourne Athletic Pavilion on May 27th. That would mark Sam's last appearance in Melbourne.

Despite the nickname "Porky," Flynn was not an overweight fighter. In fact he stood 6'1" tall and possessed a muscular physique. The nickname was acquired as a result of his fondness for pork.

"Porky's" résumé included four victories over Jim Barry, as well as additional wins over the likes of John "Sandy" Ferguson, "Gunner" Moir, The Dixie Kid (Aaron Brown), and Jack "Twin" Sullivan. He was considered a clever fighter, and he believed the experience he'd gained from sparring with Sam would give him an edge. He was confident he could defeat Sam.

When the two men met in the ring that evening Flynn stood almost a head taller than Sam and, at a weight of approximately 188 pounds, outweighed Sam by eleven pounds. Sam looked a little beefy, while Flynn looked trained to the minute.

The fight was generally well-contested throughout, though at no point did it appear that Flynn could hurt Sam. In fact, so confident of this was Sam that at one point in the opening session he dropped his hands and allowed Flynn to land blows with both fists, smiling upon their receipt. A hook, followed by two lefts to Sam's face in round two only succeeded in producing another big grin from Sam, who then proceeded to deliver a combination to Flynn's head, causing the latter to cover up.

By round seven, Sam began to pick up the pace. He also began to taunt Flynn. "Porky" had been trying to land blows to Sam's stomach throughout the bout with minimal success, and during this round Sam walked up to him laughing, with his head back and stomach extended, to the delight of the crowd. Flynn's blows seemed to carry little effect. However, when Sam struck it was as if he put his whole body behind the blows, and it was obvious they hurt. By the time the bell rang to end that session, Flynn was beginning to display signs of the punishment he'd received.

The end came suddenly in the fourteenth round, Sam landing with both fists at will and battering Flynn about the ring while the latter bled profusely from the mouth. An uppercut sent Flynn staggering against the ropes, obviously helpless, and Sam looked appealingly at the referee who then stepped in and halted the fight.

Observed *The Melbourne Truth* afterwards:

> It seems to us that there is no "real white hope" in view just at present. Every bloomin "hope" we know in a world's championship connection happens to have skin as black as printer's ink.[5]

On June 3rd, it was reported that Sam had signed a new agreement with McIntosh to remain in Australia for another six months based on plans to match him with Joe Jennette and Jack Johnson. The news came as some surprise since Sam had been booked to depart for

---

[5] *Melbourne Truth*, 1 June 1912

Vancouver aboard the steamship Zealandia the following week. Since he was going to remain in Australia for at least another six months, Sam immediately cabled his wife and requested that she and their daughter come and join him in Australia. It was also reported that McIntosh had cabled a good offer to Tommy Burns along with Johnson and Jennette.

On June 6th, Johnson compared himself to Alexander the Great when he told a reporter:

> "Alexander the Great had nothing on me. I'm too good for any other man in the world. There is not anyone left for me to lick. After July 4, I will meet the rest of these white, black, and blue hopes at the rate of one a week. This means Sam Langford, too, but Sam must post a side bet. I'm feeling fine, and believe me, I could put Palzer, McCarty, Flynn and Langford in a ring and whip the bunch without exerting myself."[6]

Six days later, Hugh McIntosh confirmed that he had signed Sam to a new six-month agreement and announced that he expected to stage a series of matches in Sydney over the next six months: Sam Langford, Joe Jennette, and Jack Johnson would be the principals.

Extensive renovations were underway at the Sydney Stadium, including the addition of a roof. McIntosh was making every effort to line up a series of heavyweight bouts that would take place in the revamped Stadium and ultimately culminate in a world's heavyweight title contest there. It was hoped that Jennette could be matched to fight Langford on the night of the improved stadium's opening, which was set for July 22nd. Should Jennette fail to arrive in time it was reported that McVea and Langford would be matched instead.

Two days later, on June 14th, it was announced that Mr. T.V. Coyle, proprietor of Royal Pictures, had secured the moving pictures of the recent fight between Langford and McVea. Furthermore, he had signed Langford to appear at screenings of the film over twelve nights. Sam would describe the action to the audience, demonstrate his training methods, and spar with friend and sparring partner, John "Liver" Davis. The vaudeville tour, which included appearances by a ju-jitsu expert known as "Professor" Stevenson and films of additional fights

---

[6] newspaper clipping, source unknown, 6 June 1912

(Bill Lang vs. Bob Fitzsimmons, and "Gunner" Moir vs. "Bombadier" Wells, among other acts) was well received and provided Sam with lucrative employment while awaiting his next bout.

A number of rumors circulated as to why Sam had to remain in Australia, including one that he and Joe Woodman had severed their relationship. Eventually it was learned Sam had been unable to leave because he and his entourage had spent money faster than it had come in. Sam had spent money freely on cars, clothes, tobacco and gambling and gotten himself in a position where he was unable to afford to pay both his debts and the return fare to the States.

Income from the two Melbourne matches wasn't enough to overcome the result of Sam's spending. So they were forced to stay longer than they had planned in order to line up some more bouts, pay off their debts and build up their bankroll.

On July 10th, Sam met the arriving Canadian/Australian liner R.M.S. Makura in the Sydney harbor to greet his wife and four-year-old daughter. Witnesses said that Sam jumped for joy when he saw his wife and daughter at the rails of the vessel straining to locate him amongst the crowd. Sam said he couldn't be happier at that moment than if he'd defeated Jack Johnson and won himself a fortune.

Sam's wife, Martha, was described as a bright, cheery, intelligent little lady, as darkly colored as her famous husband. Asked by a reporter for a statement, Martha replied, "I know I shall like Australia very much, because Sam does."

After numerous goodbyes the family left for their temporary home in the town of Sutherland.[7]

Duke Mullins recalled that both mother and child kept strictly away from the party's training quarters. He felt sure that there was a good chance that Mrs. Langford never saw her husband with a glove on. He remembered Sam's daughter, Charlotte, as a pretty little child who displayed many of the playful characteristics evident in her father.

During the month of July, a report surfaced that T.S. Andrews (a Wisconsin newspaper man acting on behalf of Hugh McIntosh) had signed the champion, Jack Johnson, to a contract to fight both Langford and McVea in Sydney, Australia. The report was that Johnson would

---

[7] *The Referee*, 10 July 1912

receive $45,000 plus $5,000 for expenses, along with first class round trip tickets for the two fights, which would take place within the next six months.

In the meantime, it had become clear that even if Jennette were to agree to come to Australia it would not be in time to participate in the Stadium opening, which had been pushed back to August 3rd. The plan to instead match McVea and Langford was carried forward.

The *Sydney Daily Telegraph* ran an article on July 24th reporting that it seemed the outcome of the McVea-Langford bout would depend on the referee's interpretation of the rules. Under the rules, a certain amount of boxing at close quarters (though not enough to be called infighting) was allowed, and Langford would be able to pile up the greater number of points. There would be little doubt as to his victory. If the boxers were kept strictly at arm's length, McVea would be the victor as a result of his superior jab. One report stated that while McVea was a boxer of wonderful ability and strength, he seemed to lack the true fighting spirit, whereas Langford was a born fighter.[8] Regardless, the general opinion was that the outcome of this match would decide which of the two men would have the right to challenge Johnson for the heavyweight title.

Later in July, it was reported that Johnson had announced his retirement. Citing a failure on the part of promoters to pay him what he felt he was worth, the amount of money he already had, and a reluctance to let as much as a year go by before he might receive an offer worth fighting for again, Johnson announced that he was through with the ring.

Four days afterward, Johnson reversed himself, saying that he would meet Joe Jennette for $25,000, and if he could get $30,000 he would also face Langford. Nobody knew what the champion's real plans were at this point. McIntosh still appeared to believe that he would be successful in bringing Johnson to Australia, and whether or not that was true, that is what he was feeding the public through the press.

On August 3rd, Langford faced McVea before a crowd of approximately 8,000 fans. This was their third meeting in Sydney and their

---

[8] *Sydney Daily Telegraph*, 24 July 1912

fourth meeting overall. Unfortunately, Superintendent Goulder—the police officer in charge of the affair—interfered in ways that made this fight less exciting than their previous match. The Superintendent was not very experienced in the boxing game. One observer claimed that Goulder laid down so many new instructions that the fighters became almost afraid to hit one another. The same observer noted that the officer forbade infighting and seemed to regard anything closer than eighteen inches as such.

Goulder's orders, under rules laid down by the New South Wales Police Department, were not to allow any kidney punches. It quickly became apparent, however, that the inexperienced Superintendent didn't know exactly what a kidney punch was.

Midway through the second round, Langford got inside McVea's guard and with both hands free, landed two heavy body blows.

"If you do it again I'll stop it," bellowed the Superintendent, prompting the two fighters to momentarily cease all action.

Those at ringside looked questioningly at one another, wondering if they had missed seeing an infraction of some kind.

In the fourth round, in the middle of a flurry between the pair, Langford landed a right hand blow to McVea's stomach, and the Superintendent leaped to his feet and stopped the contest, mistakenly believing that an illegal blow had been landed. Nobody had the slightest idea as to the reason for the interruption. Before it could be sorted out, the bell rang, ending the round. Referee Scott held a private conversation with the Superintendent during the break, and the fight was allowed to continue.

The whole complexion of the fight changed thereafter, as both fighters seemed unsure as to what was allowed and what was not. Often Langford would get inside his bigger opponent's guard, apparently having an excellent opportunity to deliver punishment, only to apparently let the moment pass rather than risk disqualification for infighting.

This should have been to McVea's advantage, but it wasn't. Langford had developed an ability to block McVea's vaunted left hand, and without the ability to consistently score with his left, McVea was almost helpless. He was unable to keep Langford at bay, and Langford bore in throughout the contest, piling up a substantial lead on points.

Neither fighter suffered a knockdown during the twenty-round affair. Langford got the better of things by a significant margin though. The verdict in his favor was thoroughly deserved and met with the all around approval of the crowd.[9]

By mid-August, boxing fans were speculating as to who would become the new champion if Johnson carried out his threat of retirement. The general consensus at the time was that Langford and Joe Jennette were the most worthy among the current crop of contenders. Jennette's manager, Dan McKettrick, issued a statement saying that he had refused an offer of $15,000 from Hugh McIntosh for Jennette to fight in Australia. McKettrick wanted his man to fight Langford in Los Angeles and indicated Jennette was ready to meet Tommy Burns or any other white hope.

Burns was extended an offer of 10,000 pounds and a percentage of the gate by McIntosh to come to Australia to face Langford, but he wasn't biting either.

On August 21st, stories of possible matches involving Johnson in Australia were revived when American newspaperman T.S. Andrews (continuing to act on behalf of Hugh McIntosh) reported that since Johnson had been using the excuse of the promoter failing to post a forfeit before he would sign articles, McIntosh had agreed to put up a forfeit of $15,000 to bind the matches with McVea and Langford. Andrews maintained that since Johnson's demands had been agreed to it was now up to him to either sign articles or be called a "quitter."

In early September, Langford and McVea traveled to Perth, Australia to prepare to fight again. On September 11th, McIntosh's hopes of luring Johnson to Australia suffered another serious blow when Johnson's white wife, Etta—despondent over her husband's philandering ways and her lack of social acceptance—committed suicide in their apartment above the champion's recently opened *Café de Champion*.

Shortly afterward, on September 14th, a newspaper story attributed to Jim Barry declared that Langford and McVea were virtual hostages in Australia. Barry, who had expressed his dissatisfaction with the amount of money he'd been paid for bouts arranged by

---

[9] *The Australian*, 10 August 1912

McIntosh, claimed that the only man making any money in Australia was McIntosh.

"He gets both ends and the middle. They regard him as a king there, and anything he does or says is law with the natives," said Barry.

Barry went on to say that McIntosh had Langford and McVea tied up so that it was impossible for them to leave the country. He advised that in order for a colored man to enter Australia McIntosh had to put up a bond of $1,000 for six months, and as long as he cared to renew the bond the boxer must remain there. Barry said McIntosh told him that if he ever got (Jack) Johnson back to Australia he would keep him there as long as he was able to draw a gate.

> "I have advised Johnson of his intentions. There is not a chance of his going there unless McIntosh posts his money in an American bank and also signs a contract that he can leave as soon as his three fights are over," said Barry.[10]

On September 19th, a reporter from *The Chicago Defender* interviewed Jack Johnson and reported that the champion looked tired but was reconsidering the possibility of going to Australia. Five days later, the *Reno Evening Gazette* ran the headline "Johnson-Langford Sign Today for a Battle," and reported that final arrangements for a proposed championship bout between Johnson and Langford to be staged in Australia on December 26th were underway, and Johnson said that he expected to sign up with McIntosh's representative, W.C.J. Kelly, the next day. Kelly was authorized to offer Johnson $50,000 for two fights with Langford and McVea, that amount to include his training expenses.

Langford and McVea met for a fifth time on October 9th. If there had been doubts as to Langford's superiority over McVea beforehand, they were surely extinguished by the result of his victory in this contest.

The fight was held at the Perth Exhibition Rink before a crowd of over 3,000. As in their previous meeting, the police instructions were that there should be a clean break and no kidney punches. Langford was the aggressor throughout, doing all the forcing, consistently

---

[10] *Winnipeg Tribune*, 14 September 1912

following McVea around the ring and forcing him into the ropes and corners.

The scheduled twenty-round contest was cut short suddenly in the eleventh round when, following a heated exchange during which Langford pounded upon McVea's body, McVea fell into a clinch. The referee cried for the pair to break, and while the men were trying to loosen from one another Langford landed a hard left to the stomach followed by a left to the jaw.

McVea immediately dropped his hands and appealed to the referee that he'd been fouled, as the referee stepped between them. When referee Harrison disagreed, McVea retired to his corner and quit. Harrison implored him to fight on, but McVea refused and Langford was subsequently named the winner. Sam walked to the center of the ring and raised his right hand. The crowd appealed to them to fight on, but when Langford turned to McVea the latter said nothing and made no move to rise from his stool.

On October 12th, *The New York Times* reported that Johnson had accepted McIntosh's offer to fight in Australia, and would leave on the 25th to begin training for a December 26th fight against Langford. The formal contract was to be signed within a few days. Two days later Johnson confirmed that he had accepted the offer of $50,000 to fight Langford and McVea in Australia.

On October 15th, a possible hitch in the signing was reported, when it was announced that Johnson had insisted that, before he would depart to Australia, a $15,000 forfeit had to be posted in the U.S. by the Australian promoter instead of with a newspaper in Sydney, Australia. McIntosh's representative, Kelly, confidently advised that the dispute over the forfeit would be resolved within the next few days.

On October 17th, Johnson was arrested in Chicago and charged with violating the Mann Act for transporting Lucille Cameron, another white woman, across state lines from Milwaukee, Wisconsin to Chicago, Illinois. The Mann Act had been passed into legislation in 1910 in an attempt to prevent the use of recreational drugs and alcohol and to try to stop the prostitution trade, more specifically known as "the white slave trade" at the time. Over time, the interpretation of the bill was broadened to forbid the transportation of women in interstate or foreign commerce for the purpose of prostitution or any other immoral purpose.

In his book *Papa Jack, Jack Johnson and the Era of White Hopes*, author Randy Roberts writes that in theory it meant that any man who took a woman other than his wife across interstate lines and then had sexual intercourse with her was in grave danger.[11] In truth, it wasn't strictly enforced along those lines, but worded that way to prevent those prosecuted for trafficking in prostitution from being able to escape.

In 1912, a group of men determined that the Mann Act could be used against Jack Johnson. Johnson was subsequently arrested for transporting Cameron across states lines. Cameron subsequently (less than two months later) married Johnson and refused to cooperate with authorities, and the case fell apart.

Meanwhile, what with all of Johnson's troubles in the States, the dispute regarding the $15,000 forfeit that he insisted upon being posted by McIntosh did not get resolved. On October 22nd, it was announced that the planned fights had been called off. McIntosh indicated that Johnson's negotiations had angered the sporting men and public of Australia so much that the matches were no longer desirable. He added that Johnson wasn't very popular down under to begin with, and that the recent news of his troubles with the law over a white woman had further decreased interest in bringing him to the country. Already aggravated by his dealings with Johnson, McIntosh decided he would be inviting trouble if he brought Johnson to Australia so he quickly put an end to the negotiations.

Johnson's troubles continued to mount. Chicago authorities shut down his café on October 30th, declaring Johnson an undesirable person of bad character. Only eight days later, he was arrested again for violating the Mann Act, this time based on charges of having transported a known prostitute by the name of Belle Schreiber across state lines in the past. Belle (unlike Cameron) was very willing to cooperate with the authorities, and the case would go to trial the following year.

Any possibility of a Johnson-Langford bout extinguished, McIntosh scheduled yet another meeting between Langford and McVea to take

---

[11] Randy Roberts, *Papa Jack, Jack Johnson and the Era of White Hopes*. London: Robson Books, 1983

place on December 26th in Sydney. Many years later, the promoter shared that it became increasingly difficult to get them into the ring together. In his words McVea was frightened of a licking from Langford, and Langford was too lazy to train.

On one occasion McIntosh summoned McVea to his office to advise him of a match he was planning.

"Well Sam," he greeted him, "I've got some good news for you. I've fixed up a nice match for you."

"A nice match, boss?" McVea replied. "Who am it with?"

"Sam Langford," McIntosh replied.

McVea rolled his eyes and shook his head. "Sam Langford? No sir! Not for me. I ain't going to fight that baby any more."

But McIntosh knew how to handle McVea. He knew it would do no good to argue with him at that time. He would give him some time to think it over, and then a day later gently persuade him to accept the match.

Once McVea had departed his office, McIntosh summoned Langford. Shortly afterward a long black cigar appeared around the door followed by Langford in another of his loud suits.

"Morning big chief," said Langford, "you wanna see me about something?"

"Yes, Sam," replied McIntosh, "I've got a good fight fixed for you."

"With who, Mister Mac?" Langford asked grinning.

"You're old pal, McVea," said McIntosh, as Langford's grin disappeared.

"For the Lord's sake," Langford said, "Ain't there nobody in Australia I can fight except that big smoke?"

But where McIntosh would coddle McVea, he knew that wasn't the way to deal with Langford.

"What are you talking about!" he bellowed. "You're a prizefighter aren't you? I pay you to fight, don't I? What is the difference who you fight?"

Langford immediately attempted to calm the promoter.

"Easy, Mister Mac, easy. That's right enough. You are the boss around here. I'll fight one of them hairy fellers in the zoo if you pay me enough!"

McIntosh said that was typical of Langford. You couldn't rile him in or out of the ring, and he was always quick to respond in a manner that would bring a smile to the promoter's face.[12]

Langford may not have feared McVea, but in addition to snakes there was one other thing he was deathly afraid of: sharks. Sam's Australian trainer, Duke Mullins, said that while training at a beach for a fight the camp members often went for a swim in the baths, which were filled with water from the local bay. Sam would never go in the water above his ankles for fear of sharks. Australian sportswriter W.F. Corbett showed Sam the openings where the water entered the baths, to demonstrate that they were too small to allow a decent-size shark through. But Sam could not be appeased, and replied, "Oh, you jes' never know Mr. Corbett, a little baby shark might have got in and growed."

Mullins said that Sam was serious as a judge when it came to sharks.[13]

At the end of October and into November, McIntosh put forth serious efforts to lure Joe Jennette to Australia. Believing that Johnson would soon be out of the picture and forced to vacate his title, McIntosh hoped to hold a heavyweight elimination title contest involving McVea, Langford, and Jennette. Despite an offer of $25,000 and 25% of the gate, he ultimately failed to convince Jennette and his manager, Dan McKetrick, to come to Australia. Their refusal effectively put an end to McIntosh's hopes of staging a heavyweight elimination contest that would produce a victor whom he could proclaim heavyweight champion of the world.

McIntosh wasn't the only promoter who attempted to create a new heavyweight champion. Men such as James Coffroth and "Uncle" Tom McCarey immediately set about making plans to match the leading "white hopes" of the day against one another, with the winner

---

[12] Hugh McIntosh. "Laughing Sam Langford. The Black Tornado." *Knockout*, 1936
[13] *The Sporting Globe*, 23 October 1937

ultimately being named the new heavyweight champion of the world. The *Los Angeles Times* had contacted Tom McCarthy upon news of Johnson's troubles with the law and suggested the heavyweight title be declared vacant, and that McCarthy offer a diamond belt for a new heavyweight champion of the world but that no Negro fighter be permitted to participate nor ever fight for the title again.

Of course, as Harry Carr of the *Los Angeles Times,* wrote, this had nothing to do with prejudice. In Carr's words:

> **Any intelligent man will tell you that prize fights between black men and white men have been a curse to the Negro race. They have roused racial feeling to a fiercer heat of hatred than did the southern lynchings.**

To be fair to Carr, he went on to explain that it was his feeling that the race riots and killings that had occurred around the world after the Johnson-Jeffries bout had done a great deal of damage to boxing, and he claimed it was his fear that the boxing game might be ultimately "snuffed out" as a matter of political practicality by government officials in order to ensure peace and safety. And so it was that the white heavyweight championship came about.[11]

In early November, Sam accompanied one of his sparring partners, a lightweight named Dave Depena, to Newcastle in order to work in his corner for his bout with an exciting young fighter named Les Darcy.

Looking to rattle Darcy, Sam reportedly sidled up to the young man before the match and warned him of Depena's hitting power, going so far as to say Les would be better off facing him than the dangerous Depena.

To Sam's great surprise, Darcy enthusiastically responded that he'd love to go a few rounds with him. Sam stared at Darcy with a puzzled expression for a moment and then simply walked away without any further comment.

Darcy then went out, dropped Depena for a count of nine in the sixth round of their November eleventh contest. Darcy continued punishing Sam's protégé into the ninth round, when the referee intervened and stopped the fight to prevent Depena from suffering any further punishment.

---

[11] *Los Angeles Times*, 1 January 1913

Sam then traveled to Tamworth, where he could witness Colin Bell, another sparring partner, fight. While promoting the appearance, the *Tamworth Daily Observer* noted that Sam—while training in Perth—had recently provided an exhibition that raised a sum of 60 pounds, donated to the Perth hospital. Tamworth marked the occasion by providing a reception in Sam's honor.[15]

On Boxing Day, December 26, 1912, Langford and McVea fought for the fourth time that year, once again in Sydney and before a crowd estimated at 8,000.

Throughout the bout, there were a number of fierce exchanges between the pair. Langford dropped McVea for a count of nine in the fourth round, and from that point on McVea bled profusely from the mouth. The tenth round found McVea looking a mess. He staggered around, blood dripping continually from his mouth. Langford, tiring badly, substantially decreased his punch count and basically pushed McVea around the ring. The eleventh and twelfth rounds provided even less action, though the general consensus was that they belonged to Langford.

The thirteenth round was McVea's last. According to Langford, when the round opened McVea caught him on the point of the jaw with a left hook and for a moment he thought he might be done for. He said everything went black and he saw "stars, eight McVea's, angels, undertakers, and the pearly gates. But then, for only a moment the fog lifted and he saw only one McVea standing directly in front of him."[16] McVea was swaying back and forth on unstable legs, but he was preparing to deliver a right hand punch.

Before he could deliver it, Langford delivered his own right hand blow to McVea's jaw. It landed, and down went McVea. He tried to rise at the count of nine, but his legs wouldn't respond and he was counted out.

Langford was so exhausted at that point he would have fallen himself had his seconds not rushed forward to gather him in their arms.

Langford's victory was immensely popular with the crowd. The *Tamworth Daily Observer* reported that the contest clearly

---

[15] *Tamworth Daily Observer*, 4 November 1912
[16] *Halifax Herald*, 8 September 1924

demonstrated Langford's superiority at all points.[17] In the meantime, back in the United States the search continued for a "white hope" who might be able to wrest the heavyweight crown away from Jack Johnson. One such hope was a promising young bruiser by the name of Luther McCarty. Former heavyweight champion Jim Jeffries was interviewed on January 4, 1913 and asked if he would have any interest in facing McCarty inside the ropes.

"Me fight McCarty? Well I should say not. I'm done with fighting. But how long do you suppose these fellows would last with Sam Langford? Why, he would just name the round he would knock them out in," said Jim.[18]

---

[17] *Tamworth Daily Observer*, 28 December 1912
[18] *Ft. Wayne Sentinel*, 4 January 1913

SAM LANGFORD

AUSTRALIA 1912

BEN HAWES COLLECTION

"IF EVER YOU HEAR OF A MAN DRAWING THE COLOR LINE YOU CAN BET YOUR LIFE THERE IS SOME NEGRO HE IS MIGHTY AFRAID OF."

~JOHN L. SULLIVAN

CHAPTER 17

TROUBLES DOWN UNDER

In January of 1913, Sam and Joe were not in a financial position to leave Australia. They had not only blown most of the money that they'd earned, but had built up some debt and were involved in a lawsuit.

McIntosh admitted that he had Langford and Woodman tied up in a lawsuit, and indicated that was one of the reasons why Langford hadn't been able to return to America. Commenting on their position, McIntosh said:

> "The black men—Langford, McVea, and Johnson—drove me out of business. You see these blacks have absolutely no sense of business and they have an idea that money flows in Australia like water does in America.
>
> And they play a peculiar system, the black boys. They always wait until they think they have a promoter in the hole, and then they come along with outrageous demands for more money at the eleventh hour. McVea is one of the worst in this respect, but they are all bad. It's nothing at all for one of these black fellows to make a demand for $2,000 or $3,000 a few days before the match, and that, too, after they have signed to fight for a certain amount.
>
> Langford is a regular baby when it comes to financial matters. One day he came into my offices in Sydney and borrowed

$1,500 off me. Before the night was over he was around for another $500. Naturally enough I would not give him all the money he wanted and we had a falling out.

Despite that, I will always say this for Langford, he is far and away the best heavyweight in the world now. I have tried time and again to get Jack Johnson to meet Langford but Jack would never accept terms or sign for a meeting with the little black fellow.

When I would get Johnson near the point of a match with Langford he would stall me off with some excuse. Finally I made things so hot for Johnson that he admitted to me that Langford was too tough a game to tackle, and he passed the little fellow up.

A match between Langford and Johnson would have drawn no end of money in Australia. A good man can make a lot of money in my country, and had Johnson boxed Langford in Australia he could easily have carried off $50,000 for his end."

McIntosh went on to say that Joe Woodman was the most natural spendthrift he had ever met:

"That man does not know the value of money. He got himself involved with a money lender and he needed to settle up before he could leave the country. I took over some his debts and was interested in being repaid, Woodman is a fiend for the horse racing game. He played the races like a millionaire, and though he took vast sums of money out of the boxing game he put it all back in the racing sport, and when he didn't have money of his own he borrowed money to play the races. He is flat broke now."[1]

Langford confirmed the truth of the promoter's comments about Woodman when he spoke with Igoe Hype, who wrote an article that appeared in an April 25, 1935 newspaper:

"Joe was betting a thousand a race in Australia and I wound up fighting and knocking out Porky Flynn in fourteen rounds (May 27, 1912) because Joe had to pay off. I didn't get a quarter (from that fight)."

---

[1] *Winnipeg Tribune, 26 July 1913*

Duke Mullins estimated Sam made approximately 3,000 pounds during his stay in Australia, yet left its shores almost broke. He spent his money as fast as it came in. Duke tried to encourage Sam to save some of his earnings for his old age, but Sam told him that he didn't believe it was in the cards for him to live to a ripe old age.

Langford countersued McIntosh for about 1,200 pounds which he claimed was the balance of 2,500 pounds that McIntosh had agreed to pay him for five boxing matches in Australia. When only three of the five matches occurred, Sam and his manager went after the promoter in court to obtain the additional funds. McIntosh countered that Langford had sabotaged his efforts by advising certain American boxers (who the promoter had counted on luring to Australia for matches) that it wasn't in their best interests to come to the country. He advised that he would willingly offset his own losses incurred as a result of Langford's actions against Langford's claim. Langford and Woodman vehemently denied the accusation.

Tackling the white promoter in a court of law in his hometown proved futile, and on March 7th the court found no basis for Langford's complaint and ruled in favor of McIntosh. He was not required to pay Sam the additional monies. The *Melbourne Argus* reported that during the proceedings Sam had been forced to admit that he was virtually illiterate: his writing was limited to his name, and he could barely read the print in his contract. It's hard to imagine this having much bearing on the case though because, as his manager, Woodman would have been responsible for handling the negotiations and ironing out the details of the contract with McIntosh.

With the decision, Sam and Joe had no choice but to immediately get back to work and build up their bankroll. They didn't have the funds to leave the country so on the same day the ruling came down, *The Brisbane Courier* announced a March 15th bout between Sam and Jim Barry.

Sam continued to demonstrate his generosity to others even though his lack of funds prevented him from returning to the States. A day after his match with Barry was announced, *The Referee* published a letter from a reader who had been a passenger on the same boat that Sam had traveled to Brisbane on for the fight with Barry, in which he praised Sam. The passenger's letter read as follows:

On behalf of the second-class passengers I have been asked to drop you a line re: the following: When a day out from Sydney a stowaway was discovered, some chap down on his luck and the authorities threatened to 'send him along,' when Sam Langford came to light with his fare, without a murmur, or putting it to music, and I reckon he deserves a word. He is no friend of mine, or any of the other passengers, but he must be a "white man."[2]

Duke Mullins recalled the event. Sam had learned of the stowaway from a ship's steward with whom he'd been talking. Afterward, Sam asked Duke what they did with stowaways. Duke told him that when they arrived in Brisbane the man would be put in jail. The next morning Sam asked the ship's Chief Officer if he could have a word with the stowaway. When he met him and learned that he was sick and just trying to get home to his family in Queensland, Sam paid the stowaway's fare.

This type of behavior wasn't atypical of Sam by any means. Throughout his career there are examples of his generosity, coming to the aid of individuals who were down on their luck.

Sam and Jim Barry fought on March 15th before a large Brisbane audience. Barry expressed confidence in his ability to defeat Sam even though he had lost all of their previous meetings. He told *The Brisbane Courier*, "I put Langford down for nine seconds the last time we met, and I think we can get him down for the ten this time."[3] However, after what had been a long string of competitive battles between the two men, this last meeting proved to be something of a farce.

The contest lasted less than twenty seconds, and Sam was as surprised as the crowd.

The Brisbane Courier's report of the fight ran under the headline, "A Heavyweight Fiasco. Jim Barry Quits in Less Than a Round." The article reported that Barry had made barely any attempt to box. Before a half-minute had gone by he went down from a blow to the neck but quickly rose. Then when Sam tried to land a right to the body, Barry went down from a right hand that appeared to land below the shoulder blade. At that point, Barry dropped to one knee and remained in that

---

[2] *The Referee*, 12 March 1913
[3] *Brisbane Courier*, 11 March 1913

position until counted out, at which point he sprang to his feet and ran from the ring amidst an angry demonstration from the crowd.

Given time to reflect, the referee, Frank Craig, admitted it might have been more appropriate to declare the bout "No contest," but by way of explanation said simply, "a man cannot think of everything on the spur of the moment."

There was great dissatisfaction on the part of those who had attended the bout, enough so that Sam and Woodman conceded that it would affect the size of the crowd expected for their next scheduled match: with McVea on March 24th. A unique set of articles for the match was published in *The Courier* on March 19th to reassure fans that what transpired in the Barry-Langford match would not be repeated. It said that if in the opinion of the officials for the fight either man failed to do his best, the fighters would receive no payment and everyone in attendance would receive a full refund. Both fighters were required to sign the document.

The actions proved successful as, once again, a large crowd was on hand on March 24th to witness the match between Langford and McVea. It wasn't until two days after the Langford-McVea fight that Jim Barry defended himself He said his hip and side had been injured prior to the bout, and that he had tried to have the contest postponed but the promoter had refused.

The Langford-McVea contest went the full twenty rounds and was officially ruled a draw by Referee Craig, but the crowd clearly judged Langford the winner. It was reported by *The Lone Hand* that the first ten rounds with the exception of the fifth were won by Langford. McVea was judged to be the winner of the eleventh and twelfth rounds: he landed a powerful hook to Langford's jaw in the latter of those two rounds, dropping Langford for a count of two. Langford recovered quickly however, and in the estimation of that periodical's reporter, he had McVea hanging on during the rest of the fight in order to avoid punishment.

Sam and Joe continued to be at odds with Hugh McIntosh, and in mid-April it was reported that McIntosh had accused Woodman of advising Joe Jennette not to accept a $15,000 guarantee to visit the Antipodes because of the alleged unfair methods practiced by McIntosh. A commission was appointed by the court in Sydney to investigate the charges. Jennette's manager, Dan McKetrick, declared that he received no such advice from Woodman and that he would be willing to testify to that should he be asked to do so.

Meanwhile, Sam appeared in Rockhampton before large theater crowds, giving sparring exhibitions with "Liver" Davis, Jack Read and Dave Depena under the management of Messrs. Birch and Carroll.

Finally, in May, Woodman announced that he and Sam would be returning to America in late June, after one last fight. That would be against Colin Bell on June 19th.

The announcement of Sam's upcoming return produced little excitement on the part of fight fans back home in the States. The reason: it was well known that it would be difficult, if not impossible, for Sam to get many matches with the leading white heavyweights in the United States. Most of them had drawn the color line, and there was very little interest in seeing Sam battle Joe Jennette and other fighters whom he had already faced so many times.

Regarding the issue of the color line, former heavyweight champion John L. Sullivan himself was credited with saying that if you ever hear a man drawing the color line you can bet your life there is some Negro he is mighty afraid of facing.

On May 28th, *The New York Times* reported that Hugh McIntosh, recently retired Australian fight promoter, had arrived from Australia with news that Sam was expected to follow on the next steamer. Regarding the current heavyweight picture, McIntosh said:

> "Langford, McVea, and Jennette, stand as a black barrier against all the white heavies in sight. The only hope of a white champion is to pick out the likeliest candidate in sight and train him for a couple of years. Experience counts for a great deal in the ring, and the three Negroes I have named have been in the game for from ten to fifteen years. They know too much for any of the inexperienced white men.
>
> As for Jack Johnson, he is definitely out of it, whatever the outcome of his legal difficulties.
>
> Very likely by the time a dangerous white man is developed, Langford, McVea, and Jennette will have outlived their

fighting days. As things look now that seems the likeliest path by which a true champion of the world will arrive."[4]

The time that Sam spent in Australia left a huge impression on McIntosh. Asked on another occasion to comment on Langford the famous Australian promoter said:

> "Boxing will never see another Sam Langford. There will never be another like the Boston Tar Baby, with his incredibly long gorilla like arms, his grotesque, top-heavy body, coal-black and squat his wide, engaging smile perpetually splitting his broad countenance, and his inevitable cigar. And more's the pity. For Langford, beyond all shadow of doubt was one of the miracle men of boxing. Something of a fistic freak, if you like, but a fighter nevertheless, and a remarkable personality.
>
> What an amazing glove fighter Langford was. No more than a light-heavyweight, and so short that the majority of his opponents towered over him by six inches or more. Yet he was invincible. His physique was astounding. He was so hugely proportioned above the waist that, at first glance, he appeared almost as broad as he was long. His colossal shoulders and back, smooth and shining, suggested a wall of coal. His chest was so deep and barrel-like. And the length of his arms was something to marvel at. His speed and punching powers were alike phenomenal, and so it was small wonder that even the great Jack Johnson, having once fought fifteen anxious rounds with the Tar Baby, carefully side-stepped another encounter with him.
>
> Johnson was not afraid of a hiding, but he did not want to risk his title. I spent months trying to persuade Johnson to agree to a match with Langford, but he obstinately refused and one day he frankly told me the reason.
>
> 'Say, Mister Mac,' he drawled, 'you're only wasting your time talking to me. I don't want to fight that little smoke. He's got a chance against anyone in the world. I'm the first black champion and I'm going to be the last.'"[5]

Duke Mullins, the man who'd trained and befriended both Johnson

---

[4] *New York Times,* 28 Mary 1913
[5] Hugh McIntosh. "Laughing Sam Langford. The Black Tornado." *Knockout,* 1936

and Langford during their respective stays in Australia, substantiated what McIntosh said about Johnson's reluctance to face Sam a second time. In his memoirs, Mullins said that Johnson was never anxious to talk about Langford and normally changed the subject quickly whenever Sam's name was brought up. However, one day when dismissing Langford from a conversation, Johnson said there were dozens of easy money white men for him to meet without having to fight a tough guy like Langford. While Johnson told Duke that he felt Joe Jennette was the toughest man he ever saw, he admitted to him that Langford was the most dangerous. Duke's own opinion was that Sam had an even-money chance with Johnson before Jack became champion, but that as Sam's weight increased and he lost some of his speed, he would have had a tough time dethroning Johnson. By Mullins way of thinking, Johnson was the greatest fighter the world had ever known.

In a series of newspaper articles that Jack Johnson produced in 1929 he said that Sam had the greatest right cross the ring ever saw, past or present, and when he laid it in, the party was over. "I can still hear the wind whistling as his right hand passed by my face," Jack said.[6]

On June 19th, Sam faced off with the big Australian heavyweight, Colin Bell. Bell, known as the "Moree Mountain" was an impressive twenty-nine-year-old physical specimen with an enormous chest and set of shoulders. He was considered one of Australia's greatest athletes of all time and once won the professional jumping championship of Australia. Some of his performances included a standing high jump of 5'7," a standing broad jump of 12'4", and a standing back jump of 10'1". He was also considered an accomplished sprinter. He stood 5'10" tall, weighed approximately 190 pounds, and had only taken up fighting two years earlier.

Bell had learned to box under the tutelage of Larry Foley, a renowned Australian fighter who retired undefeated at the age of 32 in 1879 and eventually opened up a very successful gymnasium known as the White Horse. Foley had tutored such giants of the ring as Peter Jackson "The Black Prince," Young Griffo, Bob Fitzsimmons and

---

[6] *Saskatoon Star-Pheonix*, April 16, 1929

Frank Slavin to name a few—so although Bell got a late start in the game he couldn't have picked a finer trainer.

Sam and Bell fought a fifteen-round draw on a sweltering summer day in Rockhampton, Australia in an event promoted by George Lawrence. The bout turned out to be very poorly attended, and the blame for this was affixed to ticket prices that were set too high.

Neither party was pleased with a draw, and a story that has often been repeated is that Sam, knowing Bell's reputation as an accomplished sprinter, immediately challenged Colin to a 75-yard footrace—with the understanding that the winner would then be awarded the decision. Sam reportedly jumped out to the early lead, but Colin caught him at the wire and the footrace—like their bout—ended without a winner. The two men would go on to meet again a little over a year later in Boston to determine who was the better man.

Sam and his entourage departed Sydney for San Francisco by way of Pago Pago and Honolulu on June 28th aboard the *S.S. Sonoma*.

Reporting on Sam's departure from Australia a few days afterward, *The Referee* noted that as proof of Sam's great popularity, in spite of the great number of sporting events going on at the time, a very large number of sporting men were present at the docks to wish him well and see him off.[7]

Sam's wife and daughter enjoyed their time in Australia immensely. Sam's daughter Charlotte absolutely loved it there. Many years later, anytime she spoke to her young granddaughter about traveling with her parents it was always about Australia. She would bring up that period of time often when sharing stories of the past. It was obviously a very happy time for the young family. Sam's wife, Martha, also shared with her family numerous stories and photographs concerning their time together in that country.[8]

While Sam and his entourage enjoyed a layover in Pago Pago, his father, Robert, quietly passed away on the 4th of July, at his home in Weymouth Falls. He was 68 years old. He hadn't been well for some time and, unfortunately, Sam was unable to get home in time to see him before his death. Although his return to the States after such a

---

[7] *The Referee*, 2 July 1913

[8] Carol Doyle. Phone interview. October 21, 2007

long absence was an eagerly anticipated event for Sam, his enthusiasm was dampened by the death of a father with whom he had reconciled.

Meanwhile, Jack Johnson had troubles of his own. His trial for violating the Mann Act had gone to court in Chicago on May 17th. He was ultimately found guilty by the all-white jury. He was convicted and sentenced to a year in jail and a fine of $1,000 by Judge Kenesaw Landis, the future commissioner of baseball. Johnson remained free pending an appeal of the decision.

In mid-June, rather than carry out his sentence, Johnson fled the country with his new wife by way of Canada, and the couple ultimately made their way to Paris, France.

When Sam arrived in San Francisco, he found that little had changed in terms of the difficulty in lining up any fights with the leading white heavyweight contenders. Arthur Pelkey, the latest white hope, announced before Sam's ship arrived that he would not fight a black man. It was well known that Jess Willard, another top contender, was of a similar disposition.

Carl Morris and "Gunboat" Smith were mentioned as two possible opponents, but most felt it would take some doing to convince them to face Sam. The lack of willing opponents posed a serious problem for Sam, especially since the public was growing tired of seeing him fight men he'd already been matched with a number of times. Some suggested he might do better to give Paris a try, but after being in Australia for the past year and a half Sam was in no hurry to go overseas again.

As it became clearer that there would be a limited number of qualified opponents in the States—let alone fights that would generate much in the way of a good sized purse—the idea of traveling to Paris for a few fights began to gain more appeal. The possibility of facing Jack Johnson, who was living in exile in France, was being discussed.

It was believed that Johnson would now be more receptive to fighting Sam because he needed the money. Rumor was that Woodman had received cables from a French promoter saying that he had already signed Johnson to a contract for a fight that was to take place in October or November. Johnson would receive a $30,000 guarantee, while Sam would receive 25% of the gross of the gate. The report speculated the fight could attract a gate of as much as $100,000.

In early August it was announced that, before departing for Paris, Sam would be matched with "Porky" Flynn and Joe Jennette. Before leaving San Francisco Sam gave an interview to William Slattery of *The San Francisco Call*. That city's Board of Supervisors had passed a resolution that effectively prevented Sam from fighting a local white heavyweight named Charlie Miller upon his return to the city. In his interview with Slattery, Sam reiterated his strong desire to fight Johnson for the title, voiced his gratitude for the treatment they'd received in Australia (outside of that of Hugh McIntosh, whom Sam felt treated them unfairly) and expressed his wish to fight in San Francisco if they would let him. Sam also told Slattery that— although he'd sometimes gone easy on some of his foes—he'd never faked a fight in his life and would always be on the level in the future, whomever he fought.

Sam and his wife were very happy to get back home to Boston, and one correspondent to the Australian publication *The Referee* indicated that their arrival back home was the sensation of the week for that part of the country.

His first fight back in Boston was on August 26th against former stable mate, Dan "Porky" Flynn. It was their second match, and they met at the Atlas Athletic Club in Boston for a scheduled twelve-round contest.

Flynn had been bragging that Sam was not the boxer he'd been a few years prior and that if he obtained another match with Sam he felt sure he would defeat him. Flynn felt that he'd learned Sam's style to perfection by sparring so much with him and knew how to beat him as a result. He planned to keep Sam at bay with a long left jab and whenever Sam left him an opening he'd shoot his right to the jaw or body. He predicted a victory for himself by decision.

Sam did not take Flynn's comments seriously. As far as Sam was concerned, he had never shown Flynn what he was fully capable of inside the ropes. He spent the week leading up to the fight making daily public appearances at the Howard Theater in an athletic sketch entitled "The Training Camp" (in which he was assisted by his sparring partners and Joe Woodman).

On the day of the fight, Sam appeared, in the words of at least one reporter, "as fat as a hog"[9] Regardless, for the most part Sam had

---
[9] *Boxing*, 20 September 1913

his way with Flynn. "Porky" gave his fans hope approximately two minutes into the first round when he caught Sam with a short right to the jaw that dropped Sam to the mat for a count of four. Sam was somewhat dazed when he climbed back to his feet, but he backed into a corner, smiled and stalled off Flynn until he could recover from the blow. Sam had taken Flynn's best shot, and Flynn lost his confidence. Sam gave Flynn a boxing lesson in the second and third rounds, and in the fourth round Sam delivered his own short right hand blow to the jaw, which knocked Flynn to the canvas for the full count.

The next day it was announced that Sam had been matched with John Lester Johnson for a ten-round bout at the Atlantic Garden Athletic Club in New York on September 9th.

Upon entering the arena that evening Sam encountered Johnson stretched out on a rubbing table with a handler fanning him. Sam inquired:

"What are you doing, boy?"

"Just taking a little nap," replied Johnson.

"Why now? You're gonna' be taking one in that ring," replied Sam.[10]

It turned out Johnson was badly mismatched. Sam had a good fifteen pounds on him. As the pair waited for the opening bell Johnson had the look of a man about to face the hangman's noose. As soon as the round began Johnson hopped on his bicycle and pedaled away from Sam as quickly as he could. Anytime Sam was able to corner him, Johnson immediately fell into a clinch. Since Johnson was intent on running from him, Sam gave chase. He hit him with a powerful right hand swing in the only part of his anatomy that he could reach. Those who witnessed the blow were mixed in their opinion of where it landed. Some said it was in the left kidney, some said it was the base of the spine, and still others said it landed squarely on Johnson's buttock, in which case the punch really should have been ruled a foul.

In any case, regardless of where the punch landed, there was no question of the result. Johnson pitched forward, landed head first on the canvas and remained there until the count of nine. When he arose

---

[10] Ted Perkins. "Back in New York, Where he Started 40 Years Ago, Lew, Old Ring Impresario, Just Lives for Laughs." *The Ring*, issue unknown.

he started another sprint, but Sam soon cornered him and dropped him again with the same blow. Once again Johnson rose at the count of nine, but when Sam began to throw another blow at him he fell to the canvas before it was half way there. The referee, deciding the contest was a joke, immediately stopped it and awarded Langford the victory.[11]

Johnson gained some measure of notoriety later in his career for a ten-round decision victory over Jack Dempsey in 1916 while the future champion was still learning his trade and badly over-matched by his then manager, John "The Barber" Reisler. Johnson broke three of Dempsey's ribs in the second round of that fight, and only a courageous performance on the part of the twenty-one-year-old "Manassa Mauler" enabled him to finish the ten-round bout on his feet. At the time the victory didn't do much for his reputation: Dempsey was still three years away from clubbing his way to the heavyweight crown over big Jess Willard.

A couple of days after Sam's match with J.L. Johnson, it was reported that a proposed bout between he and "Gunboat" Smith in New York's Madison Square Garden would definitely not take place: the New York State Commission refused to budge from their stance of not allowing bouts between black and white fighters. At a special meeting with the commission, Woodman and Smith's manager, Jim Buckley, requested that the rule preventing bouts between a white and black fighter be rescinded. The commissioners turned down their request, saying it would not be in the best interests of the sport to hold mixed bouts in the state of New York.

Since there was no problem with staging a fight between two black men in New York, arrangements were made for Sam to face his old adversary, Joe Jennette in the Garden on October 3rd. The contest was billed as an elimination bout to see which of the parties would fight Jack Johnson in Paris that December.

Sam and Joe met in Madison Square Garden before an estimated crowd of 2,500 and a gate of $16,000. To the surprise of most, and disappointment of Sam, Jennette emerged with a ten-round decision victory.

---

[11] 1913 newspaper clipping from unknown source

As usual, Joe's best weapon against Sam was a stiff left jab, which he utilized to good effect throughout most of the evening to score points and keep Sam at bay. Sam's best round of the fight came in the fourth when he hurt Joe with heavy combinations to the head, often causing Joe to fall into a clinch. The tide began to turn Joe's way in the fifth, though Sam was effective with his attacks to the body.

In the sixth round it became clear to all that Sam was tiring. It was in this round that the fears of those who were behind Sam but worried about his condition were fully realized.

While Joe had entered the fight looking extremely fit and weighing what for him was a nice fighting weight of 195 pounds, Sam came in at just over 199 pounds with rolls of fat around his midsection. He was clearly not in peak condition, and the extra weight began to take its toll in this round. Joe easily out-boxed him.

By the time the fight reached the seventh round, the majority in attendance knew that Joe would simply need to keep utilizing that left jab and stay out of harm's way to cruise to a victory. There were periods of relative inactivity throughout the final four rounds—and the crowd hollered its obvious displeasure. But there were also spurts of fast and furious action with Sam doing everything he could to land a hard right on Joe's noggin. Joe boxed brilliantly, and when Sam was able to land a hard right Joe was able to turn his head before impact and ride with the punch rather than absorb its full impact.

The fight was poorly received by the New York crowd, which had been expecting an epic battle. Sam had failed to train properly, and it was obvious that he was not in top condition. The fight certainly didn't help his case for a fight with the champion.

Sam followed the Jennette fight with another lackluster performance twenty-four days later when he was awarded a fifth round technical knockout victory over Jack Lester, the "white hope" who had taunted him during a training session upon his arrival in Australia. The two men fought before an estimated crowd of 1,500 in Taft, California. Included in that crowd was respected San Francisco boxing writer, W.W. Naughton.

Naughton wrote that the Langford he witnessed against Lester bore little resemblance to the compact, active fighter of a couple of years before, and that he looked fat and badly out of shape. He felt that Langford had given his best during the fight, but that he was simply unable to perform to the level that he had in the past.

There is, however, some question as to whether Sam did truly give his best that day. James Kilty, a writer who was in attendance that day maintained that the "Tar Baby" was known for being a little lenient with some of his foes. While noting that Lester was a bruising fighter and a protégé of Tommy Burns, Kilty implied that Sam's original intention was, very likely, to take it easy on him. Burns was in Lester's corner for the fight which was officiated by George Blake, a well known and respected boxing man in Southern California. The fight was scheduled for twenty rounds, and there was a lot of pre-fight speculation as to how far it would go. Woodman told Kilty that he expected Lester, "a tough customer," to last at least ten rounds. There was a fair amount of wagering placed on the issue. Kilty said that up until the fourth round Lester was giving a good account of himself, and Langford was boxing beautifully. Then Lester, "who had an acid tongue," began to insult and taunt Sam.[12]

This differs from Naughton's account, which indicates that Lester was in all kinds of trouble in the third round serving as a punching bag for Sam and ending the round cringing, after suffering a brutal shot to the ribs.

In any case, Lester may have succeeded in making Sam mad during that round because he certainly paid a heavy price during the fourth round, when he was floored no less than five times. These encounters with the mat resulted primarily from crushing blows to the body. Lester was on the verge of being counted out when the bell rang.

Sam was awarded the victory when Lester's seconds tossed in the sponge before the fifth round began. And with that move, several gamblers who had bet on Lester lasting for ten rounds, lost their wagers.

Asked to comment regarding his apparent poor condition afterward, Sam excused his lack of conditioning by saying that he had been idle the last six months in Australia and was now finding it difficult to remove the excess weight.

Naughton, commenting on promoters' efforts to arrange a fight between Sam and "Gunboat" Smith later that month, offered his opinion

---

[12] James Kilty, *Leonis of Vernon*. New York: Canton Press, 1963

that Sam was in no shape at the time for a hard battle. Proving prophetic, Naughton wrote:

> There are reasons for arguing that a Smith-Langford match is a matter that should be allowed to hang for a while.
>
> Just at present Langford's condition is such that he is far from being a fit subject for a championship contest. He is so gross in fact that after he has exerted himself for a few rounds on a boxing platform he seems to puff out like a frog in the fable and he cuts a ridiculous figure. There comes a time in the experience of all athletes when the flesh which accumulates is there to stay and it is beginning to look as though Langford has reached that stage.

Naughton went on to say that while he didn't feel it would be impossible for Sam to rid himself of the surplus weight, it was his belief that it would take at least three months of hard work to get into proper condition. He questioned whether Sam was still motivated enough to forego his habits of easy living and train religiously enough to achieve that level of condition. Concluded Naughton:

> As he is at present he is not fit to be sent against any man who approaches him in class. Many of the matches he signs to may be justified on the basis that his superiority to his opponents will manifest itself even if his condition is faulty, but displays of that kind can scarcely be described as sterling sport. He is in no shape to do himself justice.[13]

---

[13] *San Francisco Examiner*, 9 November 1913

"Gunboat" Smith
ca. 1915
Beagles Postcard
Author's Collection

"LANGFORD, YOU SEE, COULD PUNCH WITH EITHER HAND AND HAD A WALLOP EVERY TIME HE LANDED, NO MATTER WHERE HE STARTED THE BLOW."

~ "GUNBOAT" SMITH

CHAPTER 18

"GUNBOAT"

Despite the concern expressed regarding Sam's condition, a fight was arranged between he and "Gunboat" Smith, and it was set to take place only a week after Naughton's comments.

Smith's first name was Edward. His nickname "Gunboat" was given to him by a sailor because of his size twelve feet. Smith stood 6'1" and weighed in the neighborhood of 170-175 pounds. He possessed a good right hand and had defeated big Jess Willard, future heavyweight champion, over twenty rounds in May of 1913. Smith was the man who convinced Babe Ruth that baseball was more to his liking, with a sock on the jaw during a sparring session between the two men. "Gunboat" was a leading contender in 1913 and in early 1914 he briefly held the title of White Hope Champion after knocking out Arthur Pelky.

Smith had also sparred separately with both Stanley Ketchel and Jack Johnson as they prepared for their fight in October of 1909. Years later, he revealed that during a training session with the champion he'd landed a punch on Johnson's jaw that sent him through the ropes and left him with a lasting impression of his power.

There was some question as to whether or not the fight with Sam would actually take place. Accusations were swirling that a fix was in: Sam was going to allow Smith to go the full scheduled twelve rounds if not win the contest. It was rumored in boxing circles that this was why Smith was willing to face Sam. A sporting man of some notoriety, B.H. Benton, tried to have the contest prevented by the authorities.

Sam and his manager strongly denied all rumors of a fix. As far as Smith's willingness to face Langford was concerned, Sam's fights were not at the level of performance they had been prior to his departure for Australia and Smith's confidence was high because he hadn't suffered an official loss in his previous twenty-nine bouts.

They met on November 17th at the Atlas Athletic Club in Boston before a record crowd of 6,000. When Sam entered the ring that night he was greeted with a tremendous ovation by the hometown fans. Still, when he disrobed it was apparent that he was out of shape. In a story authored by Smith in a Winter 1942 issue of *Fight Stories* magazine, Smith said that the moment Sam disrobed he knew he was going to win. "Langford was fat, hog fat."

As the two men awaited the opening bell, though, Smith's manager, Jim Buckley, warned his man to avoid mixing it up with Sam.

Sam admitted later that he didn't do much training for the fight. He started off slowly, taking it easy for a couple of rounds while "Gunboat" piled up an early lead. By the time Sam decided he'd better open up and show some of his skill, he found that he'd badly underestimated Smith. "Gunboat" had a guard that Sam found difficult to break through, especially with punches to the body.

While many at ringside seemed to think that Sam could have taken Smith any time he wanted to and that he was pulling his punches, the truth was that Naughton had been correct: Sam was in no condition to perform at a level his fans had come to expect from him. Smith clearly out-boxed him in the early rounds.

Sam began to fight more desperately with each passing round, but even though he was able to land an occasional blow, Smith effectively utilized his left jab to keep Sam at bay while rocking him with right hands. Round after round the pattern continued, Sam fighting more wildly as Smith continued to increase his lead. Upon the conclusion of the twelfth and final round it was clear the decision belonged to Smith. Neither fighter had visited the canvas during the entire fight and "Gunboat" had won the majority of rounds.

The Boston Herald had Smith winning ten of the twelve rounds.[1]

---

[1] 1*Boston Herald*, 18 November 1913

Not all reports of the fight were as one-sided, but it was clear Smith had won. Smith had fought a careful tactical fight. He'd utilized his left jab effectively and by keeping on the move he'd minimized Sam's opportunities to fight inside. Sam, responding to accusations that the fight was fixed, said:

> "That's the problem for a fighter who gets the rep of being a 'knock-em-dead boy'. If he puts a tough cookie to sleep, the customers simply say, well, he should have, and, if that tough cookie goes the distance, or wins, the customers usually have got it figured out that the fight was a phony. That boy was just about as tough and rough as any white man I ever tackled in my life. And, lawdy me, couldn't he hit with that right hand."[2]

Smith reported that every time Sam hit him, "He'd break my shoelaces, and I was tickled to death to get the hell out of there."[3]

But that wasn't the message Sam heard after the fight. Word reached Sam that Smith was so good he could lick Sam anytime. That aggravated Sam to no end, and he was determined to get another crack at Smith.

Sam would have to wait for another meeting with Smith. He was booked to fight in Paris the next month.

On December 2nd, Sam and Joe Woodman set sail for Paris aboard the steamer *Kronprinzessin Cecillie*. Sam would face Joe Jennette, this time at Luna Park on December 20th.

As the bout neared, Joe Woodman felt compelled to reply to reporters commenting on Sam's weight:

> "Tell everybody to cut that out about Sam having run to fat. As you know, Sam is tremendously big-chested, and while he has certainly grown heavier, he is all muscle. His legs, too, have become larger, but they are as firm as a tree. To show that I am not shooting any hot air, I am willing to make the light heavyweight limit for any man in the world. As for the saying that Sam has gone back, that is all bunk."[4]

Meanwhile, Sam went about the business of preparing for the fight. In typical fashion his training was not without some lighthearted

---

[2] *Halifax Herald*, 10 September 1924
[3] Glenn Stout, "Fighting Blind," *Boston*, February 1987
[4] *Boxing*, 20 December 1913

moments. It was reported that he made time to spar daily with famous writer George Bernard Shaw, who was a decent boxer as well as a huge boxing fan.

Jennette believed that he would repeat his previous performance and emerge victorious. His confidence was buoyed by the fact that he and his manager had successfully lobbied for the scheduling of a full twenty-round contest. Joe was well known for his endurance, and the longer match would greatly increase the odds in his favor.

The fight turned out to be a corker. The two men wasted no time feeling one another out, and the action was fast and furious from the opening bell. *Boxing* reporter F. Hurdman-Lucas wrote that the pair put on the most entertaining heavyweight contest in French history.

Lucas reported that Jennette appeared nervous in the first five rounds, a trait that the writer had not witnessed in Joe before, but he went on to say that now, having seen Langford in all his glory, it was understandable that Joe would be apprehensive. "I would sooner face a battery of cannon than the Boston Tar Baby," wrote Lucas.[5]

Jennette, as shown in their previous encounters, was the more effective at long range where he effectively utilized his left jab to land with great frequency to the face and body. At close quarters Sam was Joe's master. Throughout the first twelve rounds the battle seesawed back and forth as the two men sought to exert their will upon the other.

In round thirteen, Sam set himself apart from his foe as he floored Jennette three times. The first knockdown occurred when Sam worked himself inside and suddenly got home with a quick right hand, immediately followed up with a well placed left hook to the head. Jennette went down for a count of nine before slowly rising with glassy eyes. As he regained his footing, his corner showered him with a partial bucket of water, raising cries of protest from the crowd. The cries died as Sam quickly advanced and landed another combination that sent Joe crashing to the canvas for the second time in the round. Once more, the durable big man climbed to his feet, but he discovered his legs were unstable and he fell to the floor for a third time. Somehow he managed to rise again, and as Sam prepared to deliver the *coup de grace* the bell rang ending the round.

---

[5] *Boxing*, 27 December 1913

Miraculously, but certainly not to the surprise of anyone who knew much about Joe and his recuperative powers, Jennette managed to come out strong for the fourteenth and held his own during the round. He also won round fifteen, and the crowd vigorously applauded his courageous performance. The two men split rounds sixteen through nineteen.

Joe came out in the twentieth and final round throwing caution to the wind. Leaving himself uncovered he immediately began a two-fisted attack. Sam slowed him up with a vicious left hand swing that landed full on the mouth and produced a flow of blood. Another left and right sent the big man reeling backwards into the ropes where he swayed about unsteadily. It looked like the end was near, but Joe dodged the powerful blows aimed at his jaw and by generous use of clinching managed to finish the bout on his feet.

The crowd roared its approval for the performance exhibited by both fighters. Sam was awarded the decision. Based upon his performance the press once more held him up as the next logical opponent for the champion, while Jennette was praised for his courageous performance.

Sam received a visit in his dressing room afterward from a few bearded Frenchman who were intent on examining him. They closely examined his physique and took great care in measuring his arms.

"Who are these fellows?" Sam inquired.

He discovered that they were museum curators and officials from the Paris Zoo, sent by a wiseguy American press correspondent. The officials had been told that Sam was some sort of prehistoric specimen, who had been found living in a tree by some explorers.[6]

Sam was immensely popular with the French, and he took advantage of that to mix with various members of its society. He'd made a number of friends among the French during his previous visit to Paris a couple of years before, so he took the opportunity to renew some of those friendships. It's clear from a letter reprinted in a book titled *Confessions of a Literary Archeologist*, that Sam even developed a friendship with the famous painter Picasso, who was living in France at the time.

Sam traveled to London for the holidays where he received an offer to fight Matthew, a.k.a. P.O. (Petty Officer) Curran, an English

---

[6] John B. Kennedy, "Tar Baby. An Interview with Sam Langford," *Colliers, The National Weekly*, 21 May 1927

heavyweight, in Paris before another Luna Park Arena crowd on January 24, 1914. Curran was an Irishman known for letting his temper get the better of him at times when the action in the ring got a little hot, which explained the high number of disqualification losses on his record.

When Sam returned to Paris for the fight, he found himself crossing the channel on the same boat as Curran, or rather Curran found Sam leaning over a railing taking in the view. Curran, a stocky man, approached Sam from behind and inquired:

"Are you Langford?"

"Yes," replied Sam.

"Stand off," said Curran requesting Sam to step away from the railing.

Sam did as he was asked and Curran slowly walked around him looking him up and down. Finally he said to Sam:

"I heard you were tough. You don't look tough."

"That's right mister," Sam replied, "I sure don't look tough, and I ain't tough on boats."[7]

Curran continued on his way and Sam silently resolved that he'd show Curran just how tough he was once they were in the ring together.[8]

On the night of January 24th, Curran lasted less than twenty seconds against Sam. At the sound of the opening bell Sam rushed forward and immediately stunned Curran with a powerful blow that landed flush on the jaw. Before Curran cleared his head, Sam followed up with another smash to the jaw, ending the short fight. The crowd, barely settled into their seats, were greatly disappointed and loudly voiced their displeasure toward Curran as he was guided from the hall.

Sam returned to London where he boxed a short three-round exhibition with sparring mate Bob Armstrong on January 26th, then took a short vacation. On February 15th, after a large send off from friends at Easton Station, he sailed back to the United States accompanied by Woodman, Bob Armstrong, George Byers, and "Liver" Davis.

---

[7] *Halifax Herald*, 9 September 1924

[8] *Halifax Herald*, 9 September 1924

Once he was back home, Sam defeated a black heavyweight named Bill Watkins in a first-round technical knockout in the National Sporting Club in New York. Watkins was advertised by the press as being good enough to make Sam extend himself, but the fight lasted barely half a round.

Sam fought again only four days later in the Empire Athletic Club in New York, meeting Jim Johnson for the second time in his career. Thirty-one-year-old "Battling" Jim was only three months removed from having fought Jack Johnson to a ten-round draw in Paris after the champion fractured his left forearm during a third-round exchange and had been forced to fight the rest of that bout with a relatively useless left appendage. Although Sam appeared chubby and out of shape, he was clearly the superior boxer. With the exception of the third and eighth rounds, Sam dominated the action and was able to emerge with a relatively easy ten-round decision victory.

During the early part of April, Joe worked feverishly to line up another big money fight in Paris for Sam with either Georges Carpentier or Jack Johnson. Sam was hopeful, but there was nothing imminent.

On April 15th, he defeated George "Kid" Cotton, a former sparring partner of Jack Johnson's, in Chattanooga in an eight-round decision. George, whose real name was Sylvester, was dubbed "George" by Jack Johnson, who felt the name Sylvester was unsuitable for a fighter.[9] The match with the "Kid" was supposed to be easy money for Sam, but the "Kid" surprised him in the first round with a right hand as they came out of a clinch that put Sam upon his seat on the canvas. Embarrassed and angry, Sam went after the "Kid" with a vengeance but failed to put him away.

Sam followed his victory over Cotton with a technical knockout victory, five days later, over "Roughhouse" Ware in Memphis, Tennessee.

"Roughhouse," whose real name was William Ware, was born in Cairo, Illinois on August 26, 1892. He was a rough character who acquired his nickname because of his inclination for getting into trouble in the local taverns. He carried a long scar on the left side of his

---

[9] Kevin Smith, *The Sundowners: The History of the Black Prizefighter Volume II Part 1 1870-1930*. CCK Publications, 2006

face from a street brawl in which he used a coal shovel to knock his opponent senseless.

Sam knocked "Roughhouse" down three times in the opening round and spent the next three rounds knocking him all over the ring. He came out for the fifth intent on ending the bout and sent Ware into the ropes with a hard right to the jaw. As Ware began to fall, Sam landed a left hook to speed up the process. Ware managed to climb back to his feet, but he was glassy eyed and Sam immediately sent him to the mat again with a left to the jaw. When he rose once more, Sam knocked him into the ropes and was about to deliver the final blow when the referee stepped in and saved Ware from a sure knockout.

Joe Woodman was unsuccessful in making matches in France with either Carpentier or Johnson, or with any of the leading white hope contenders in the States. Sam was growing increasingly tired and frustrated at having to fight the likes of black fighters such as Jennette, McVea, Jim Johnson, John Lester Johnson, and Kid Norfolk many times over. He'd lost track of how often he'd fought some of these men, winning and losing the so-called World Colored Heavyweight title a number of times. Like Sam, these fighters had the same difficulty finding white fighters willing to meet them in the ring; there was little choice but to continually fight one another. The paying public eventually tired of seeing the same old match-ups over and over, and the size of the gates dwindled.

So when it was suggested to Sam that he face Harry Wills, a relatively unknown, big, black heavyweight nearing his 25th birthday, Sam agreed. They would meet in New Orleans on May 1, 1914. While he didn't know it at the time, Sam would go on to fight Wills more times than any other single opponent in his entire career.

When Sam disrobed in the ring that evening he wore the mantle of World Colored Heavyweight Champion. The reports were that he appeared fat, and when the two men were brought to the center of the ring to receive instructions the crowd shouted with amusement regarding the height differential between the two. But it was nothing new to Sam; he'd fought this kind before. He just looked up at Wills and smiled confidently.

If anything Sam was too confident. He felt he was facing just another in a long string of local favorites whom he'd polished off so easily in the past. He didn't realize the seriousness of the challenge before him until he'd given the first four rounds away, and it wasn't until the sixth that he clearly won a round.

Sam opened a cut above Wills' eye with a right hand cross in the second round, but Wills staggered him with a powerful right cross just prior to the sound of the bell ending the third session. The fighting intensified in the fourth round with both men landing a number of significant blows. The pattern in this fight was similar to Sam's matches with Joe Jennette. Like Jennette, Wills, as the bigger man, had the better of the exchanges at long range while Sam clearly benefited from exchanges that took place between the pair on the inside. Though Sam staggered Wills with a left hook to the jaw it was generally conceded that the fourth round belonged to Wills by a small margin.

In the sixth, Wills appeared to tire and Sam landed a number of hard blows, including a right hook to the jaw that staggered the big man.

The trend continued in round seven as Wills was caught, not once, but twice more with powerful left hooks to the jaw by Sam. The youngster was cleverly baited into the latter of those two hooks when Sam dropped his hands to his sides and Wills—apparently thinking Sam was tiring—foolishly advanced with his own guard down. The left hook that greeted him on the jaw nearly sent him to the canvas, and Sam won his second round in a row.

Wills came out strong in round eight and exchanged punch for punch with Sam in a round considered even by most. The ferocity of the fighting picked up even more in round nine. At one point Sam landed a powerful left to the mouth, knocking out two of Wills' teeth. Wills landed some heavy right crosses of his own during the session, though, and was generally considered to have earned the round by a slim margin despite his missing ivory.

An appreciative crowd was on its feet for the tenth and final session. There were many shouts of encouragement for Wills from the partisan crowd as Sam tried desperately for a knockout. He couldn't do it. Both men landed some big blows during the round and they were fighting furiously at the bell. The round could have been awarded to either party without too much argument on either side.

Wills was awarded the decision on points as a result of the

significant lead he'd built up during the early rounds. Sam was disappointed with the loss, but he had no complaint with the decision. Wills impressed him as a powerful fighter who would only get better, and Sam anticipated evening the score with him in the future.

There is at least one unconfirmed report that after his victory Wills asked Sam to relinquish the belt that he'd been awarded for winning the colored heavyweight title. The belt was studded with a diamond, ruby, an emerald, and a pearl. Sam told him to go get it and handed over a pawn ticket. The gold had been dug out before the belt was pawned.[10]

Sam rebounded from the loss to Wills with a four-round knockout victory over Bill Watkins in Rochester, New York on May 25th. Then, in mid-June, a newspaper report surfaced that made Sam's blood boil. The article stated that since "Gunboat" Smith's impressive May performance against Jack Blackburn the boxing fans had become more willing to believe that his decision victory over Sam the previous November had not been a fluke.

The writer said that while Sam had long been the bane of the so called white hopes—knocking them out or cutting them to pieces as he wished—in "Gunboat" he had met his match and was clearly outfought in the majority of the rounds. The writer raved about Smith's training methods and conditioning. Smith was reportedly looking for a shot at Jack Johnson's title. Sam pressed Joe to make arrangements for another match with Smith as soon as possible.

A couple of days later the British boxing publication *The Mirror of Life and Boxing World* reported that a record amount of 6,000 pounds had been deposited at the *Sportsman* office by co-promoters Gerard Austin and Herbert Harris for a proposed Johnson-Langford match, and as late as mid-July they were still saying that Johnson would box Sam in London that autumn. As many as three different promoters were making claims that they would be promoting the match.[11]

Sam didn't fight again until August 12th when he defeated "Battling" Jim Johnson in a tough ten-round no-decision bout held in New York's Empire Athletic Club.

---

[10] *Nevada State Journal,* 20 April 1924
[11] *The Mirror of Life and Boxing World,* 13 June 1913

On August 22nd, *The Mirror of Life and Boxing World* reported that a fight between Jack Johnson and Langford no longer appeared imminent. The champion was in Paris and the latest word was that he would wait until the war was over before giving serious consideration to any more boxing matches. Three days later, Sam knocked out George "Kid" Cotton in the fourth round before a Boston crowd in an uneventful contest.

Without any promising opportunities on the horizon, Sam settled for return engagements with "Battling" Jim Johnson, Joe Jennette, and Colin Bell over the next six weeks. He was unimpressive in his bouts with Johnson and Jennette, earning a draw and a decision victory but appearing out of shape. He fared much better against Bell, knocking the Australian heavyweight to the canvas seven times en route to a fourth-round knockout victory. The ease with which he dispatched Bell caused those who witnessed this performance to call into question how on earth Bell had managed to achieve a fifteen-round draw in their prior meeting.

Bell was no slouch though. He fought "Battling" Levinsky to a ten-round draw in August of 1915, in a contest that a local newspaper felt he had the better of. He went on to defeat future heavyweight championship contender Tom Heeney twice in 1922, after winning the Australian heavyweight title in 1921 at age thirty-seven.

Two weeks later, Sam finally received his wish for an opportunity to avenge his loss to "Gunboat" Smith. The two men met before a Boston crowd on October 20th. Since his victory over Sam the previous November, "Gunboat" had performed impressively against Arthur Pelkey, Jack Blackburn, Georges Carpentier, and "Cyclone" Johnny Thompson. The only real setback suffered from those contests was a loss to Carpentier in a fight held in London when "Gunboat" struck the lighter man while he was on his knees in the sixth round and was subsequently disqualified. That loss did little to diminish his reputation though, as the majority of fans felt he had been well on his way to a victory before the foul. It should be noted, however, that many felt he'd lost a ten-round bout with "Battling" Levinsky the previous month, though no official verdict had been rendered.

Based on the results of the previous meeting between Sam and "Gunboat," there were a number of gamblers more than willing to place bets on a repeat victory by Smith. Sam didn't see it that way. He thought he'd learned a few things about how to penetrate Smith's defense in their last meeting, and he knew he was in better condition for this fight. He gathered up all the cash he could lay his hands on and bet it on himself to win.

When the pair met in the ring that evening, Sam looked extremely confident. One witness later claimed that when the two men shook hands and "Gunboat" saw what condition Sam was in for this contest, he exhibited demonstrable fear. That may be true, because in the 1942 Fight Stories article referred to earlier in this chapter Smith said that while he sat in his training room having his hands bandaged he thought about how sick he had been for three or four days after their previous meeting from the force of Sam's punches. And when he came face to face with Sam in the center of the ring to receive the referee's instructions, Sam grinned and remarked, "Gunnah, ah'm in puffect shape t'night," and Smith could see that he was.

Sam assumed command from the opening bell and before the round was over he dropped his larger opponent for a count of seven with a sweeping right hook. By the time the round ended it was clear that the "Gunboat" was sinking.

Sam came out for the second session just as aggressively and floored Smith two more times. He put Smith down early in round three and Smith stayed down. A number of sportswriters in attendance felt that "Gunboat" chose to let himself be counted out to avoid suffering any more punishment from Sam.

Some fans felt that the results of this fight proved that the first meeting between the two had been staged, but Sam said there was no truth to that at all. He claimed he'd been beaten fair and square by Smith in their first encounter.

One newspaper source questioned the judgment of Smith and his manager risking a second meeting with Sam when they had been in line for a possible shot at Jack Johnson's title. The decisiveness of Smith's loss effectively put an end to those aspirations.

Boxing writer Frank Menke wrote that Smith's victory on points over Sam in their first meeting falsely gave many the impression that he was a real fighter, when the fact of the matter was that Sam had been badly out of shape and as much as thirty pounds overweight.

Menke also felt that Smith's loss effectively cleared the way for Jess Willard, a man he felt lacked a fighting spirit, to become the leading white hope contender for the heavyweight title.

Smith continued to fight until 1921, but many boxing followers believed he was never the same. Smith always felt that he'd peaked in his first fight with Sam. Asked during an interview sometime in the 1920s who the best heavyweight he ever saw was, Smith—who had faced heavyweights Jess Willard, Frank Moran, Jack Dempsey, Fred Fulton, and Harry Wills—responded:

> "That's an easy one. Sam Langford, and nobody ever came close to being as good as he was at his peak. Why, old Sam could do everything. He could punch from any position and hit hard, too. He was a master boxer, difficult to hit, but if you did land you might just as well try to make an impression upon the floor of the Garden. He would take all the heart out of you and then give you a fine pasting. He ruined me. I was all through after that last fight with Langford in Boston.
>
> Other colored heavyweights have cleaned up on Langford's reputation. Langford you see, could punch with either hand and had a wallop every time he landed, no matter where he started the blow. That's where he was different from those who have tried to follow in his trail.[12]

Fighting again only six days later, Sam dropped a disappointing ten-round decision to Jeff Clarke. Clarke had improved since their meeting four years earlier and Sam's condition was not as good as it had been. Clarke, after getting knocked to the canvas in the second round, stayed away from Sam. Sam was forced to chase him, and he was in no condition for that kind of fight. Eventually, Sam stopped in the middle of the ring, and exclaimed breathlessly, "For the lord's sake man, stop long enough to do some fighting! You are the scariest ghost I ever seen."[13]

For the last five rounds, "The Ghost" danced in and out of range, piling up a few points while remaining out of harm's way. It wasn't an enjoyable fight for the fans, but it was the only kind of fight that Clarke had any hope of winning.

---

[12] Alfred Dayton, newspaper article, unknown source and date, 18 May 1930

[13] *St. Louis Post-Dispatch*, 30 March 1916

After that disappointing performance, Sam continued west to Los Angeles where promoter, James Coffroth, promised to set him up in a rematch with Harry Wills.

When Sam arrived in Los Angeles at the end of October, word leaked from Juarez, Mexico that promoters from that city had revealed they had backing for a contest between Langford and Jack Johnson. When told of this, Sam just laughed and said, "That nigger will never get into a ring with me."[14]

While awaiting another opportunity to fight Wills, a match was made for Sam to face Tom "Bearcat" McMahon on November 10th in Vernon, California. The twenty-four-year-old "Bearcat" came into the contest with a fairly impressive résumè, including (over the previous two years) wins over Jim Barry, Al Kubiak, Al Kaufmann, and future world heavyweight champion Jess Willard. But Sam put a six-round technical knockout over on the "Bearcat" when the referee, George Blake, stepped in and stopped it after Sam dropped McMahon for a count of nine and it was apparent to all that he was on the verge of being knocked out.

Despite the victory, some of the more astute observers in attendance were less than impressed by Sam's performance. West Coast boxing instructor, DeWitt Van Court, covering the bout for the *Los Angeles Times*, wrote that Sam appeared "hog fat" and didn't take control of the contest until the fifth round. In Van Court's opinion, Sam misjudged his distance by many inches throughout the contest, a sign that his ring skills had deteriorated. Sam was still fast on his feet and his defense looked as good as ever, but he was no longer the same fighter of old.[15]

Sam's second fight was in San Diego, where he secured another six-round technical knockout win on November 16th against a badly overmatched big, black fighter named Jim Cameron. Once again, fans were far from impressed with Sam's performance. He appeared out of shape, with a significant amount of flesh hanging over his belt. The crowd booed him as he left the ring.

On November 21st, noted boxing writer Bob Edgren of *The New York World* suggested that Jess Willard challenge Sam in order to help

---

[14] *Los Angeles Times*, 30 October 1914
[15] *Los Angeles Times*, 11 November 1914

improve his case for a fight with Jack Johnson. Edgren had a much higher opinion of Willard than many of his counterparts. Though acknowledging that Jess was too good natured and even tempered to make a great fighter, Edgren felt him to be fairly clever, a heavy hitter, and faster than most credited him. He was convinced that Willard would fare better against Langford than had "Gunboat" Smith. It seemed highly unlikely, though, that Willard and his manager would make Smith's mistake, risking a match with Langford.

On November 26th, Sam met big Harry Wills for a second time. Instead of San Francisco with Coffroth promoting the match, the pair ultimately fought before a Vernon crowd in a scheduled twenty-round match promoted by Tom McCarey. It was reportedly the first time in seven years that two black fighters would entertain the local public in a main event. The last time had been in 1907, when Sam defeated Young Peter Jackson.

Former featherweight title holder, Johnny Dundee, was in town to attend the fight and said he thought Wills had a good chance of defeating Sam again:

> "I never saw such a hitter," said Dundee of Wills, "the trouble with most of the fighters who get into the ring with Sam is cold feet. When old Sambo spits on his hands and rubs his knees they begin to look for the way out. Whichever wins today, I expect it to be by knockout. Both of them are too strong and hit too hard for the fight to end any other way."[16]

Sam and Wills wasted no time feeling one another out when the bell rang. Both fighters advanced rapidly toward one another and let loose with respective haymakers. Sam's missed, but Will's blow landed flush on Sam's chin, and down he went. He climbed to his feet and was soon knocked down again. He rose and commenced action effectively enough that he managed to drop Harry for a count of four. The way Sam remembered it, though, he found himself on the canvas no less than six times during that opening round.

In his book *The Making of Champions in California*, noted boxing instructor DeWitt Van Court indicates that when the round concluded

---

[16] *Los Angeles Times,* 26 November 1914

Sam was so groggy that he started for Wills' corner.[17] George Blake, the referee, took him by the arm and said, "Come Sam, you are going to the wrong corner."

"Steady mate, steady mate," Van Court says that Sam repeated as he staggered unsteadily back to his own corner.

Round two didn't go much better for Sam. Wills sent him to the canvas again, but Sam hadn't fought in the ring for twelve years without learning a little bit about how to take care of himself when he was in trouble. He stalled and kept out of harm's way as much as possible to gain the time needed to clear his head and regain the full use of his legs. Still, Wills was much bigger and stronger. Even in the clinches, he bullied Sam about and pounded on him something fierce.

When Sam returned to his corner with some difficulty after the second round he kicked away the stool his seconds had placed there for him, preferring to stand and lean with his back to the ropes instead. Asked by a reporter after the fight why he had elected not to use his stool between rounds, Sam replied, "I figured if I ever sat on that stool, I'd never get up again."[18]

For the next eleven rounds, the two men waged their war, Sam on the receiving end of the greater amount of punishment. When the thirteenth round ended, Wills had a big lead on points and Sam appeared all in.

When the fourteenth round opened, it looked like Wills was going to end the battle. He threw a number of haymakers that failed to find their mark while Sam desperately tried to find the strength to fight back. After a minute of the round had gone by the pair fell into a clinch. When they separated Sam spotted an opening and—gathering all the energy he could muster—launched a booming left hook that landed flush on Harry's jaw.

At first it didn't appear that Wills had suffered much damage from the blow, but then his eyes glazed over and he stumbled backwards against the ropes, where he sagged helplessly with his arms dangling at his sides.

Sam quickly advanced before his prey could recover and delivered

---

[17] DeWitt Van Court, "The Making of Champions in California," Los Angeles, Premier Printing Co., 1926

[18] *Chicago Tribune,* January 1956

another powerful left hook to Wills' exposed jaw. Wills toppled to the floor. Sam immediately turned, retired to his corner, and Referee George Blake counted Wills out. A stunned crowd watched as Harry's seconds came out and helped him to his stool. Some at ringside felt that Wills had decided the action too rough and despite his big lead on points allowed himself to be counted out rather than accept any more punishment from Sam. The vacant look in Will's eyes, though, told the real story.

After his victory, Sam stopped at Vernon's famous bar, Jack Doyle's, and purchased a round of drinks for a packed house of patrons to kick off his celebration as he had two weeks earlier after his win over McMahon.[19]

He followed his knockout of Wills with a six-round exhibition in Bakersfield against a fighter named Charley Short, and then he and Joe Woodman headed for San Francisco where Joe had made arrangements for Sam to fight two white hopes in four rounds on the same day.

Arriving in Frisco on November 30th, Sam and Joe were disappointed to discover that the Police Committee of the Board of Supervisors scuttled the scheduled stunt.

While the pair were in town the *San Francisco Chronicle* interviewed Woodman, who indicated they would head east next but also went on to say that 1915 would be Sam's last year in the ring. Joe said it had nothing to do with Sam slipping, but rather Sam's desire to settle down and become a farmer on a piece of land he'd purchased in Milford, Massachusetts. Joe said:

> "In my opinion Sam is good for four or five more years of hard campaigning, but he and his wife, who is a colored woman, are anxious to settle down to the quiet life of the farm. Sam has made enough money to take care of himself for the rest of his days, if he behaves himself."[20]

Joe went on to say that Sam still desired a shot at Jack Johnson's title before retiring. He hoped to secure a fight with him during the coming year. Sam, he said, was not fat, but had a build that gave that impression, especially his expansive chest and shoulders. Joe claimed that Sam weighed 185 pounds and sported a mere 32" waist.

---

[19] *Double Kayo,* August 1956
[20] *San Francisco Chronicle,* 1 December 1914

Sam supported Woodman, issuing the following statement:

> "You see I'm now twenty-eight and dis fightin am one tough game. I like to fight alright, cause I like the money. But now I'se got about enough coin salted down to quit and settle down on a little farm I'se got back near Boston. I'se got a wife and baby and I done just started the youngster to school and now I want to quit kickin around and go back home to be with my wife and baby."

When asked how much money the fight game had netted him, Sam replied:

> "My wife looks after the coin and I does the fightin. Whenever I gets my share of the receipts after a fight I always make tracks for my ole friend the Western Union and every cent of that money goes direct to Mrs. Langford in Boston. And what does she do with it? Why, she banks it, of course. You didn't think she totes it around in her stocking did you?"[21]

Sam ended the year with another tough fight against "Battling" Jim Johnson, in New York on December 10th. He managed to escape with a ten-round no decision victory. One newspaper questioned who he would find to fight next:

> He appears to have all the heavyweights in the country buffaloed to such an extent as to destroy any interest in any fight in which he is a principal.[22]

Later that month, Charley Cutler, a one-time sparring partner of Jack Johnson and a man who had boxed with Sam a number of times, offered his opinion that Sam was the greatest heavyweight in the ring. "He is the hardest hitter and, in my opinion would defeat the champion in a finish fight."[23]

The question on many fight fans minds though, was whether he'd ever get the chance.

---

[21] *Reno Evening Gazette*, 25 November 1914

[22] unknown source, newspaper clipping

[23] *Winnipeg Tribune*, 26 December 1914

JESS WILLARD

HEAVYWEIGHT CHAMPION, 1915-1919

AUTHOR'S COLLECTION

"Sam would have been champion anytime Johnson had given him a second opportunity. Man! How that baby could hit."

~Joe Jennette

CHAPTER 19

AN END TO HEAVYWEIGHT TITLE HOPES

On April 5th, 1915, Jess Willard knocked out Jack Johnson in the twenty-sixth round in Havana, Cuba and ended any hope Sam had of ever fighting for the heavyweight crown. Johnson had held the title for seven years. It would be twenty-two years before a white title holder would give a black fighter an opportunity to fight for the prestigious title again.

The International Boxing Union in Paris refused to recognize Willard as the champion until he met and defeated Sam. The union's position was that since Jack Johnson had failed to fight Langford the previous November, after Langford defeated Joe Jennette, Sam had become the champion by default. This was of little consolation to Sam. He and Joe Woodman realized the union's stance would have very little impact.

If Sam was going to keep fighting it looked like he would have to fight many of the men he'd faced a number of times already, and in most of the towns they'd already fought in.

The day after Johnson lost the title, Sam defeated "Battling" Jim Johnson by a slight margin in a dull, ten-round contest held in the 135th Street Athletic Club in New York City. He followed that up a week later with a twelve-round decision loss to Joe Jennette in Boston, in a match in which he was clearly out-pointed. The press blamed the loss on an apparent lack of condition on Sam's part.[1]

Reduced to fighting the same men over and over for smaller purses, Sam kept up his hectic pace and traveled to Montreal where he faced "Porky" Dan Flynn six days later on April 19th in a match that was stopped in the sixth round and ruled no-contest due to inactivity on the part of both men.

Sam took a little time off before tackling Jim Johnson again on June 8th at Brooklyn's Broadway Sporting Club.

Still heavy at 192 pounds, he had little trouble with his larger 220 pound opponent. Johnson was in trouble a number of times throughout the fight and was knocked to the canvas in the sixth round by a left to the jaw. Sam punished the big man throughout the bout and was awarded a ten-round decision victory.

On June 29th, he suffered a surprising twelve-round decision loss before a hometown crowd to Sam McVea. The general opinion of most in attendance was that McVea clearly won the majority of the rounds, possibly as many as nine or ten of the twelve. Although Langford appeared to be in good condition his judgment of distance and ability to land blows no longer seemed to be what they had once been.

Finding it increasingly difficult to make a match locally, Sam and Joe Woodman turned their attention westward and discovered an eager and willing host in Denver, Colorado. It was Sam's first appearance in the city, and he received a hearty welcome at the train depot on July 12th from a large crowd anxious to catch a glimpse of the famous "Boston Tar Baby."

Sam had come to Denver to face a local black fighter named Jack Thompson. Thompson was a big, tough man standing 6'2" and weighing approximately 200 pounds. He was considered quick on his feet for his size, and was also known for possessing a decent punch and a liberal use of the rabbit punch, a downward chopping blow to his opponent's neck. He'd relocated to Denver from St. Joseph, Missouri the previous year and had gained a certain amount of notoriety by defeating eight of the toughest local men that promoters had been able to

---

[1] *The Indianapolis Star*, 14 April 1915

find for him. It had become difficult to make a match for him locally, so Sam was persuaded to fight him.

During a lengthy interview with Sam, local boxing referee and fight reporter for the *Rocky Mountain News* Abe Pollock indicated that Sam had nothing but good to say for such fighters as Sam McVea, Joe Jennette, Jim Barry, Jim Flynn, Jess Willard, and in fact every man he was asked to comment about.[2] It was anticipated that though Sam was somewhat past his prime, the first meeting between the two men would provide a true measure of just how good Thompson really was, and whether or not he should be considered a serious contender in the heavyweight ranks.

For the next few days the local papers were full of lengthy accounts of the training sessions in the old Baker Theater, which were observed by crowds numbering 500-600 daily. Favorably impressed by Thompson's performances over the previous year, many of the local fight fans anticipated a strong performance on his part against the famed "Tar Baby."

Despite the buildup, the scheduled fifteen-rounder turned out to be a major disappointment for the 2,000 who witnessed the event. The match lasted only thirty-two seconds!

By the estimation of Gene Fowler, fight reporter for *The Denver Post*, there was only nine seconds of actual fighting when one took into account that the two men used two seconds advancing to the center of the ring, and after receiving blows from Sam, Thompson lay on the canvas for nine seconds and the ropes for another ten, before a towel from his seconds came sailing into the ring from his corner.[3]

Asked by one reporter what punch he'd used on Thompson, Sam replied, "Well Chief, that was my pump-handle punch. I uses it on tough niggers, and Jim Flynn."[4]

Sam proved so popular in Denver that Jack Kanner, the promoter for the National Athletic Club, convinced him to meet Sam McVea in the city's Stockyard Stadium on September 30th.

The fight was highly anticipated by the local fight fans. As they

---

[2] *Rocky Mountain News*, 13 July 1915

[3] *Denver Post*, 17 July 1915

[4] *Denver Post*, 17 July 1915

had prior to Sam's encounter with Jack Thompson, 500-600 fans showed up daily at the National Athletic Club gym to observe the training routines. This would be McVea's first western U.S. appearance in eight years.

Local veteran boxing scribe Otto Floto of *The Denver Post* hailed the match as an opportunity to witness the last of the great "colored fighters," believing—as did some others at the time—that with the doors closed against mixed matches (and the accompanying title shots and greater gates) men of color would disappear from the fight game altogether.

The twenty-round contest was fought before a crowd estimated between 5,000 to 7,000. It was ruled a draw by referee Eddie Pitts. Neither fighter was ever in serious trouble during the contest. There were no knockdowns but the action was steady, and the fans were treated (on behalf of both fighters) to a fine exhibition of fighting science and ring generalship.

The fighters received 55% of the gross receipts for their efforts; approximately $4,000 to be split between the two of them. Langford received 30% of the receipts, while McVea drew 25%.

Having made a number of fans in Denver and still having difficulty finding new opponents, Langford lined up another fight there for October 18th against "Battling" Jim Johnson in the National Athletic Club. It was their eighth meeting.

The Denver press devoted a significant amount of pre-fight coverage to the contest, playing up the fact that the new boxing commission in New York had announced that they were going to allow mixed matches in the near future, and this could mean that the winner of this contest would have significant opportunities against leading white contenders. It was also noted that "Battling" Jim had never been knocked out. It was anticipated that this match would be a real slugfest, unlike the previous bout between Langford and McVea.

Approximately 2,000 fans were treated to a full fifteen rounds of savage fighting. When the fifteenth and final round came to a close with both men on their feet, the decision was awarded to Sam by referee George English.

With no other immediate prospects Sam agreed to tackle Sam McVea for the third time within a five month period. They were scheduled to meet in New York's Harlem Athletic Club over ten rounds.

Wrote one reporter of yet another meeting between the two men:

> Everybody laughs when, every few weeks, Sam McVea and Sam Langford are matched, but there is good reason why these two Negro fighters keep pummeling one another.
>
> There is nobody else for them to fight.

The same reporter wrote that Langford and McVea were slowly fading, and that when they were gone, the day of the Negro fighter of prominence would be over.[5] Like Otto Floto of *The Denver Post*, that writer felt a lack of opportunity would prevent black men from pursuing boxing as a career.

The two men fought to a twenty-round draw on November 23rd. Afterward *The Afro-American Ledger* reported that Langford's performance indicated he had gone to seed and was far from the fighting demon of yore.

Langford's last fight in 1915, or at least his last fight that occurred inside the ropes, took place on December 3rd when he was matched with Harry Wills for a third time, before a New York crowd in the Harlem Athletic Club. The fight proved entertaining, with plenty of action, and Wills was awarded the decision on points upon conclusion of the tenth session.

Sam had tried to land a big blow throughout the fight, but for the most part Wills was able to prevent him from doing so through the effective use of his long left jab. Whenever Sam succeeded in landing one of his big swings, Wills came back for more without the slightest indication of suffering any damage.

Sam appeared discouraged and afterward expressed his dismay at his inability to hurt the bigger man. He left the club in a foul mood, having (in the estimation of most fight fans) won as little as two of the ten rounds.

Five days later he found himself in a Roxbury, Massachusetts court brought up on charges of domestic abuse by his wife, Martha, who claimed she'd been badly beaten by Sam when they met on Tremont Street in Roxbury. It was a very frustrating time for Sam. He

---

[5] *Beloit Daily News*, 11 December 1915

and his wife were living apart, he realized that he would never have an opportunity to fight for the heavyweight crown due to Johnson's loss to Willard, and he was having difficulty finding opponents.

Sam had been raised in a violent childhood environment. He also was a drinking man. It seems plausible that with the deterioration of his relationship with Martha and the difficulties he was encountering career wise, he may have taken out his frustrations on his wife while under the influence of alcohol. It's also known that Martha enjoyed a cocktail or more on occasion herself, so perhaps she played some part in the altercation.[6] The charges were subsequently dismissed less than two weeks later, when Martha failed to appear in court.

Looking back upon this time period many years later Sam said:

> "It was along about then that I became sure that no matter how good I became I'd never be a world's heavyweight champion because the doors were closed. Up to that time I had trained rather seriously for practically all my fights. But I got disgusted and said 'what's the use of training, I ain't going anywhere in particular,' and I wasn't.
>
> "I wanted to go all right, but those white boys wouldn't let me. I had reached thirty (years of age), and when a fellow is thirty, he isn't willing to train as when he is younger. So I just didn't take care of my figure any longer and I began to get nice and fat, and I never did get my figure back."[7]

The year 1916 arrived, and Sam resumed a hectic schedule against many of the same black men he'd fought over and over. He fought Harry Wills on January 3rd and lost the twenty-round verdict before a large New Orleans crowd that was treated to one of the hardest fought contests seen in that city in some time. Although Sam had a slight edge over the first six rounds, the bigger man gradually wore him down as the fight went on. Wills appeared to have Sam's number.

Seventeen days later, Sam was back in action in Savannah, Georgia, where he knocked out the much heavier Andrew Johnson with a fourth round blow to the solar plexus.[8]

---

[6] Carol Doyle. Phone interview, October 21, 2007

[7] *Halifax Herald*, 9 September 1924

[8] *Savannah Tribune*, January 22, 1916

Sam fought Harry Wills again in New Orleans on February 11th in another bout scheduled for twenty rounds. But this time, Sam surprised the big fellow and his hometown fans when he capitalized on an opening in the nineteenth round, landing a hard left hook that knocked Wills out. It had been a hard fought contest, and speaking of the knockout in a magazine interview years later Wills said:

> "In the eighteenth I had Sam in a lot of trouble. But he weathered that round. With the banging of the nineteenth gong I sailed in, figuring that if I could crowd Sam into a corner I could stop him. That was about all I did, sail. For Sam caught me going in, and I went down and out. I don't know how long I was out, but there's no mistaking the fact.

Wills always maintained that Sam was the best fighter he ever fought.

> "He was a real professional, the kind of fighter you'd like to be but know that no matter how hard you try you'll never make it. Sam never made a mistake, he always held command and when he knocked me out in New Orleans in 1916, I thought I had been killed."[9]

Wills thought Langford was without equal when it came to punching power.

> "Talk about hitting! Well, I've met some hard punchers in my time, and all I can say is that the hardest blows any of them ever landed on me were like a slap in the face from a woman compared with those bone-crushing wallops of Langford. They seemed to go right through you.

> "When Sam hit you in the body you'd kind of look around half expecting to see his glove sticking out of your back. When he hit you on the chin—well, when that happened you didn't think at all until they brought you back to life again."

Wills suffered a much greater tragedy as a result of the outcome of the fight. His fiancée, Miss Edna Jones, was to become his bride the day after the fight, but she committed suicide after becoming despondent over the defeat and the crimp it put in Wills' title aspirations.

Sam would go on to fight Harry thirteen more times over the next

---

[9] *The News Sentinel*, 2 September 1922

five years, but he never defeated him again. The young heavyweight was on his way up the ladder, while Sam was heading downward. Three weeks after the knockout he lost a ten-round decision to Harry, and then another on April 25th. Of his showing in the latter fight, a reporter for the *St. Louis Dispatch* wrote of Sam's performance:

> According to his performance against twenty-four-year-old Harry Wills last night Sam is an obsolete battleship. His artillery lacks range, though of heavy caliber, his tonnage is too gross for his altitude, and his old engine is unable to develop the speed and endurance of former years.

The same reporter pointed out that Sam's footwork no longer kept up with his head. Whereas in the past, his footwork was one of his chief assets, he had reached a point where he had to rely more on his ring craft and his punch. Afterward, Sam commented on Wills:

"He's tough, he's awful tough."

"Did he hurt you much, Sam, when he knocked you down in that second round?" he was asked.

"Yes, sir, he hurt me. That right hand of his got me on the point of the jaw. It wouldn't do to get many of those. You know iron breaks now and then, and my jaw ain't iron."[10]

Sam fought others during this period of time, including McVea, Dave Mills, Cleve Hawkins, and Jeff Clarke. Jess Willard was in the audience the night Sam defeated Hawkins in New York on February 28th. Cleve called himself the "Canadian Wolf." After chasing the bigger man all around the ring for the full ten rounds, Sam reportedly called the matchmaker over and breathlessly requested, "The next time I fight here match me with a fighter, not a runner."

After later recovering his wind, Sam said of the Wolf, "I do hear them wolves don't do no fighting, except when in the pack."[11]

A March 31st match between Sam and Jeff Clarke in St. Louis was significant from the standpoint that it was Sam's first ring appearance in the city, where only recently had the way been paved for a bout between two blacks to take place. Sam knocked Clarke out in the fifth round to take a 2-1 lead in their series.

---

[10] "Sam Langford, the Ali of His Generation," *Boxing*, March 1997
[11] *St. Louis Dispatch*, 26 April 1916

Many years later, a St. Louis native and well-known boxing referee named Harry Kessler recalled Sam's 1916 visits to the city. In his autobiography Kessler wrote:

> As a young fellow, about fourteen or fifteen years of age, I remember well the times when Sam Langford came to town. The "Boston Tar Baby" would enlist us kids in his training routine at Tommy Sullivan's Old Future City Athletic Club on Pine Street. For free, we got to take turns heaving a very large medicine ball into Sam's abdomen to toughen up his stomach muscles. Why, I did not fathom. His stomach was like steel to begin with! But while Jess Willard was fighting the black heavyweight champion for expense money, the only way Sam Langford would get near a title fight was to buy a ticket ... to watch someone else![12]

On May 5th, a story was released that said Sam was all but broke despite the money he'd earned in the ring over the previous fourteen years. According to Joe Woodman, the primary reason for this was that Sam had turned over all of his life savings ($35,000) to his wife Martha, from whom he'd separated. But that wasn't the only reason. In 1956, Joe said:

> "Nobody ever wanted for anything if Sam knew about it and it was in his power to get. People say he squandered most of the money he made. I say much of it went to friends and acquaintances who were down on their luck at a time when it wasn't hard to be down."[13]

The long series of bouts between Sam and Joe Jennette resumed on May 12, 1916, in Rochester, New York. Jennette started out impressively, winning the first three rounds, but in the fourth round Sam landed a heavy blow to Joe's stomach, doubling him over. Future *The Ring* magazine editor, Nat Fleischer, was in attendance that night and believed the blow effectively took all of the steam out of Joe, and he was never able to recover from it.

In the seventh round, Sam threw a hard left hook that landed on the point of Joe's chin and sent him crashing to the boards face first.

---

[12] "The Amazing Sam Langford," *Sports Novels*, September 1952
[13] Harry Kessler, *The Millionaire Referee*. St. Louis: Harkess Publishing, 1982

While Joe managed to roll over and attempted vainly to regain his feet, his manager, Dan McKettrick, attempted to revive him by throwing water on him from his corner, but Joe was counted out before he was able to regain his senses.[14] After so many battles between the two, Sam had finally knocked him out.

Reminiscing about this fight a number of years later, Sam said the knockout was an accident. There was some discussion of another fight between the pair shortly thereafter, so Sam had no desire to knock he and Joe out of a little money. So on that night, when he and Joe got into action, Sam threw a lot of punches around, but they were wild. He wanted to make it look as if he was trying to knock Joe's brains loose. The crowd enjoyed the show, and Joe had no idea Sam wasn't trying to hurt him so he was doing his best to punish Sam until the knockout occurred. Said Sam:

> "I sort of put my right on the floor, wound it up nicely and threw it at Joe. I didn't mean to hit him, just fan his head. But that fool Joe stumbled, or something, and shoved his chin right in the way. That punch hit him where he grows whiskers. I saw Joe stagger, I saw his knees bend. I thought there was some trick in it, and that Joe was trying to fake me into a trap and then maybe knock me dead. But no! Joe crumbled to the floor and was counted out, and out of all the surprised people in the place, I was the most surprised of all. Joe had gone out, so dead, cold out, that it was about ten minutes before he really came back to life."[15]

It was a feat that neither Jack Johnson nor Sam McVea had ever accomplished in any of their many battles with Jennette.

Over the years there were various allegations of Sam having participated in a number of fixed contests. After discussing the accidental knockout of Jennette, Sam took the opportunity to comment:

> "In all the years that little Sammy was out there strutting his stuff, there was not one time when Sammy had an agreement with the other boy. Little Sammy did do some agreeing about fights, but he did all of it himself."[16]

---

[14] *The Afro-American Ledger*, 17 January 1956
[15] *The Syracuse Herald*, 13 May 1916
[16] *Halifax Herald*, 11 August 1924 & 11 September 1924

While it might be true that Sam never had an agreement with another fighter, there are a number of examples of instances where he complied with a promoter's request to take it easy on a foe in order to give the crowd a little run for their money.

Jennette maintained a healthy respect for Sam for the rest of his life. In a September 1958 issue of *The Ring* titled "Last of the Big 4," Joe stated:

"Jack (Johnson) was powerful and a wonderful defensive boxer, but he didn't believe in overworking or taking chances. If you didn't hurt him, he didn't hurt you. I boxed him nine times and we could have made it nine more times with nobody getting hurt. Jack was afraid of Langford though. He beat Sam once, when Sam was only a middleweight, but he wouldn't have anything to do with him when Sam got bigger and better."

Two months later, another article concerning Jennette appeared in the November 1958 issue of *Boxing Illustrated* in which Joe voiced his opinion that Langford was the greatest fighter who ever lived.

"Sam would have been champion any time Johnson had given him a fight. And Johnson knew it better than anybody. Man! How that baby could hit, nobody else could hit like that. Well, maybe Joe Louis could, but don't forget that Sam only weighed about 160 pounds. Louis was about 195," said Joe.

In June of 1916, it was reported that Langford and Sam McVea had booked passage to sail south for a twenty-round match in Buenos Aires, Argentina, scheduled for August. The two men were among a number of boxers who ventured to that country that summer, hoping to find an opportunity to make some good money. Unfortunately, it was a financial disappointment for most of the boxers, including Langford and McVea, who had only one fight while there. Most of the boxers found themselves fighting for a number of very small purses in order to earn enough money to return to the States.

The fighters' visit to Argentina did have one notable impact though. A young Argentine college student by the name of Luis Firpo attended most of the bouts involving the American fighters and later said that he became so enthusiastic about the sport that he decided to become a boxer himself. Firpo came within one second of defeating Jack Dempsey for the heavyweight title on September 14, 1923 when he knocked the champion out of the ring near the end of the first round.

Around the time of the Argentine adventure, another interesting event involving future heavyweight champion Jack Dempsey almost took place, this one involving Sam. At the time, twenty-one-year-old Dempsey was under contract to a man by the name of John Reisler, a.k.a., "John the Barber." Reisler had no interest in nursing Dempsey along in his young professional career and had presented him with an opportunity to fight a couple of seasoned professionals in "Gunboat" Smith and Sam, men Dempsey felt he had no business facing at that stage of his career. After refusing to fight either man, Dempsey felt obligated to accept when Reisler subsequently proposed John Lester Johnson as an opponent.

He received a brutal beating at the hands of Johnson on July 14th, suffering cracked ribs from a punishing body attack. Afterward, when he insisted on some time to recover before accepting any additional fights, Reisler—fed up with him—told him to go ahead and beat it, but to remember to come back when he was ready to fight again.

Dempsey, of course would ultimately go on to be discovered by Doc Kearns, and wrest the heavyweight championship from Jess Willard in 1919. Kearns eventually had to pay off Reisler when the latter laid claim to the fighter based upon their previous agreement, but that's another story.

Many years later, Dempsey, reflecting on this period of time in his autobiography titled *Dempsey* (co-authored by Bob Considine and Bill Slocum), was quoted as saying, "The hell I feared no man. There was one man, he was even smaller than I, I wouldn't fight him because I knew he would flatten me. I was afraid of Sam Langford."

Dempsey, comparing opportunities to fight both Sam and "Gunboat" Smith at that stage in his career, said that although he knew Smith would defeat him at the time, he felt he'd eventually be able to take him. Sam, on the other hand he could never envision defeating.[17]

Sam's manager, Joe Woodman, agreed with Dempsey. During an interview with New York newspaperman Joe Williams in May of 1925,

---

[17] *Halifax Herald*, 11 August 1924

Woodman said that it was his opinion that the Langford he managed at his best would have beaten any man in the ring of that day.

"You mean his size?" Williams asked.

"I'm including Dempsey (the current heavyweight champion), if that's what you are leading to," replied Woodman. "Langford was at his best against the rushing type of fighter. His great power and his ability to drop a man with a short blow made him very dangerous.

Dempsey just happens to be the type that would be easiest for Langford."[18]

"Gunboat" Smith, who fought both men during his career said in the 1942 *Fight Stories* article:

"Langford versus Dempsey, both in their prime would have been bad news for Dempsey. He could be hit easily with a right hand and if anybody had a right hand it was the 'Tar Baby'. I'll go further and declare that Langford would have waded through every heavy champ we've had including the current soldier boy, Joe Louis. Louis is a great champ, I grant, but he's inclined to get hot and bothered when the going gets rough. Langford was as cool as an iceberg every minute he was in there. He never lost his head."

And, Jack Johnson also believed Sam would have knocked Dempsey out.

"Yes, the Dempsey who beat Willard at Toledo," Jack said. "Langford's right cross would have reached Dempsey's jaw a split fraction of a second before Dempsey's left hook could reach old Tham. Everything in the ring is style, or rather a comparison of styles. Had any one ever taught Dempsey how to get away from a left hand, or if anyone had ever taught him to use a right cross, he would have been twice the fighter he was. As it was he was never more than a left hooker and you can't pin greatness on a left hook and get away with it."[19]

After returning to the States Sam was matched for a November 30th meeting with Jim Barry, but Barry had to pull out of the fight

---

[18] Jack Dempsey. *Dempsey, by The Man Himself.* NY: Simon and Schuster, 1959
[19] *Saskatoon Star-Phoenix,* April 16, 1929

when he carelessly burned his right hand over a gas stove a couple of days prior to the event. So "Big" Bill Tate, a 6'6" black fighter who tipped the scales at 226 pounds, was brought in to take his place ... and Sam suddenly had another new playmate to go along with Harry Wills. Sam and "Big" Bill would go on to face each other a total of eleven times over the next six years. Their first meeting resulted in a no-decision verdict.

The Syracuse Herald's report of the contest the next day ran with the headline, "Bill Tate Makes Good Showing In Go With Langford—Sam Discovers New Battler for the Pork Chops League." That was a term many in the press were using to describe the group of black fighters including men such as Langford, McVea, Wills, Jennette, (Jim) Johnson, and Bill Tate who had to fight one another time and again to earn a living.

Over the next seven months Sam fought, with mixed results, a number of his fellow league members including "Battling" Jim Johnson, Tate, Jack Thompson, and Wills. The lone exception was a Kansas City white hope named Bob Devere whom Sam decisioned twice. But men such as Devere were generally few and far between. Sam was no longer able to take Wills' measure, and his days of displaying a chiseled physique were long past—trained or not—but he still carried a dangerous punch and was very capable of putting an opponent to sleep.

He demonstrated this again on May 2nd in his fight with Bill Tate. That morning a St. Louis newspaper reported that, according to his manager Sam had not trained for the previous two matches, but that, "For tonight, Sam is O.K." Continuing, the reporter said:

When Sam pays an opponent the compliment of even slight preparation it can be taken for granted that he has a score to settle. It was so with all other black boys. Sam lets them drift along until they get comfortably settled in the conviction that the old man is done. Then he lays them up for repairs. Tate is Sam's latest meal ticket, and it looks like he has picked tonight to do a little punching.[20]

Sam left no doubt from the beginning that this match was going to be different than the pair's previous two meetings. He crowded

---

[20] *Appleton Post*, 30 May 1925

Tate around the ring in every round, continually breaking through his left jab to bang away at the bigger man's body and hammer him with occasional hooks upstairs. The finishing blow came in the sixth round. It was a short punch, but it had all of Sam's weight behind it and completely laid the big fellow out.

Sam also followed the lead of a number of other pugilists in the early part of 1917 and took up residence in Chicago, Illinois. Sam had many friends on the south side of Chicago, where he made his new home; but the primary reason given for the move was that it was expected a boxing bill would pass into law during an upcoming legislative session. That would put Chicago on the pugilistic map and make it a lucrative part of the country to operate out of for professional boxers.

Boxing had been banned in Chicago since a fight between Joe Gans and Terry McGovern in 1900. Gans had reportedly taken a dive, and the city had banned boxing. In December of 1916, a petition was circulated by the Second Regiment Athletic Association to repeal the law prohibiting boxing.

In early June, it was announced that Sam would face another heavyweight, big Fred Fulton, in Boston on June 19th. Fulton stood 6'4½ and hailed from Rochester, N.Y. He hoped to use the fight with Sam and a subsequent match with Frank Moran to lend credibility to his efforts to obtain a title bout with heavyweight champion, Jess Willard—assuming he could defeat both Langford and Moran.

Fulton is said to have sought the advice of Harry Wills prior to the match, asking him the best way to defeat Sam. Wills, with a straight face, said:

> "The best way, Mister Fulton, is to take a club and when he ain't looking just bust him on the head, and when he turns around with ever so much surprise, just bust him again and knock him dead."
>
> "And then?" asked Fulton.
>
> "Nothing, only don't miss the second shot, that's all," said Wills.[21]

The twenty-six-year-old Fulton was a legitimate title contender

---

[21] *St. Louis Dispatch*, 1 May 1917

when he faced Sam. Although he was coming off a loss to Carl Morris on a foul, Fulton entered the ring against Sam carrying an impressive record of 29-2. Twenty-six of those wins had come via knockout. He was known for possessing a rapier like left jab and carrying a good punch in both hands. The fact that he stood over 6'4" tall with a long reach was also certainly to his advantage.

That didn't do much to ease the concerns of his manager, Mike Collins. Collins said he warned Fulton that it was vital that he keep away from Langford's deadly left hook, and in the days prior to the match he told Fulton again and again never to use his right, because if he did he'd leave himself open for Langford's left.

The night before the fight Sam maintained he was visited by a man late at night who told him that he was to carry Fulton for the full fifteen rounds or he wouldn't receive his share of the purse. Sam claimed that he needed the money and agreed to do so.

As it turned out, there was no need for any such agreement. Fulton was more than capable of handling Sam. He was in the peak of his career, while Sam was clearly on the decline.

Sam looked slow from the very beginning and was never really in the contest. The *Boston Herald* reported that he looked as "slow as a truck horse, with layers of extra weight draping his massive frame, and appeared far from the fighter of old." The few punches Sam landed showed no effect upon Fulton according to the *Herald*.[22]

That wasn't entirely true, according to Fulton's manager. Collins said that when Fulton first laid eyes upon Langford in the ring he found it hard to believe this short pudgy fighter was the same man his manager feared. For the first two minutes of the opening round he jabbed Sam in the face at will. When Sam tried to return fire, Fulton easily held him off with his extended left. As his confidence grew Fred began to smile.

"Stop that you crazy fool," Collins yelled.

But Fulton continued to grin. Collins knew what was coming. He concluded that Fred was going to try and land a right hand despite the instruction he'd received. Sure enough, after landing a few more lefts to get Sam off balance, Fred threw a big right hand, but quick as a flash Sam slipped the punch and landed a hard left behind Fulton's

---

[22] Fred Dartnell, *Seconds Out! Chats About Boxers, Their Trainers and Patrons.* London: T. Werner Laurie Ltd., 1920

ear, sending him reeling backward and buckling his knees. But Fulton recovered and resumed his reliance upon the left jab.

When the round ended, Collins berated him for attempting to land the big right hand. Fulton grinned at him and replied, "I know better now, look here," and he directed Collins' attention to a large lump that had risen just behind his ear.

Had the blow landed two inches forward, Collins was sure Fulton would have paid a steep penalty for his failure to follow instructions. Instead, his lesson learned, Fulton stuck to the game plan for the balance of the fight.[23]

Fred's height and long arms made it difficult for Sam to get inside. He tried to reach Fulton with overhand rights, but they continually fell short. When he tried to attack the body, Fulton was able to hold him off with his long arms. But Sam was confident that eventually he'd be able to work himself in close enough to do some damage.

In the fourth round Sam edged in closer so he could launch an attack, but before he could do so Fulton threw a heavy right aimed for his chin. Sam ducked and the punch exploded upon his temple. Sam immediately experienced intense pain. He later described it like a thousand needles shoved into his skull. He managed to stay on his feet and finish the round, but he was badly shaken.

When he returned to his corner he realized he couldn't see at all out of his left eye. He thought it had swollen shut, but when his corner didn't pay any attention to the eye he said, "Say, try to get my left eye open quick I can't see out of it at all."

They looked at the eye and one of his corner men replied, "Nothing wrong with it, Sam. It ain't swollen."

Sam thought that was strange, but when the bell rang to open the fifth round, he rose from his stool and went back out to resume the fight with one eye. He continued to receive further punishment, the pain in his head worsening as the round went on, and then just before the round concluded everything went black. He managed to find his way back to the corner, but he was now almost completely helpless.

Blind, or close to it, Sam went back out for round six. He was hoping that Fulton would get close enough to him that he could grab him and land some blows during the ensuing infighting. But that wasn't

---

[23] *Boston Herald*, 19 June 1917

Fulton's game. He preferred to fight at long range, and he pelted Sam with long lefts and rights throughout the round.

When Sam returned to his corner after the disastrous round his corner man excitedly inquired:

"What's the matter, what's the matter? You never hit him once and he hit you a hundred times."

"I can't see out of either eye and I couldn't grab him because he wouldn't come close enough to me," Sam replied.

"Then this fight is over now, Sam" his corner man said, "I'm not going to let a blind man go out there and get murdered."

When the bell rang to begin the seventh session, Sam remained on his stool. Once the referee realized Sam was not going to continue he pronounced Fulton the winner.

Sam was very unhappy when some of the newspapermen wrote afterward that he just quit, without giving him the benefit of the doubt. He was more than willing to admit that Fulton was a good, tough fighter, but it rankled him that anyone would think he'd quit against anyone unless he was completely blind. Years later Sam said,

"Yes, boys, I quit to Fulton, but I didn't quit until I couldn't see out of either eye and I couldn't even feel him anymore. That's why I quit. I never did think much about fellows that went around and made excuses for themselves. So, after the fight, I didn't tell the people why I quit."[24]

Sam never recovered the sight in his left eye. The sight in the right eye was restored a week later, but the left eye, the one nearest to the blow suffered to the temple, had been put out of business for good.

Regardless of the eyesight problems that Sam experienced against Fulton, a number of men felt the fight was the first real sign that Sam had slipped, performance wise. Joe Woodman, for one, was convinced of it, and he urged Sam to quit the ring. He feared Sam would go completely blind if he continued to fight. He pleaded with Sam to call it a career, but Sam stubbornly refused. This was how he made his living. What else would he do if not fight?

---

[24] *Lincoln Daily Star*, 21 January 1918

Joe realized the futility of trying to convince Sam to retire, but he also knew that he couldn't in good conscience continue to arrange fights for him. Their friendship would continue, but the long partnership between the two as fighter and manager wouldn't last much longer.

Although Sam was on the downhill side of his career, Fulton benefited quite a bit from the win in the press. He'd go on to continue his quest for a match with the champion, Jess Willard, and fight another fourteen times without a loss until suffering a one-round knockout to a rising contender by the name of Jack Dempsey on July 27, 1918. He never did get a chance to fight for the title, though he remained a top contender through the end of 1922.

Sam took a little time off to recover from the beating he suffered against Fulton, and returned to the ring just shy of two months later on August 17th against Andre Anderson in Buffalo, New York. Twenty minutes before the pair entered the ring, Sam called Howard Carr, Anderson's promoter, over for a private conversation. Leaning in so that nobody else would hear what he shared, Sam smiled and said, "I likes you Mr. Carr, and for that reason I am tipping this off to you. Tell your man not to lead with his chin when we get into the ring."

Howard laughed and returned to his fighter.[25]

Despite reportedly "carrying tons of fat"[26] Sam earned a second round technical knockout against the badly outclassed Anderson. When declared the winner, Sam turned toward Carr and shouted, "Your man failed to follow instructions."[27]

A month later, Sam concluded his long series of bouts with Joe Jennette with a twelve-round decision in Toledo, Ohio. While Sam appeared to be carrying some excess baggage, he was the aggressor throughout the contest, and appeared fresh and strong at the finish. When his hand was raised in victory upon the conclusion of the twelfth round there was little argument. It was generally attributed to

---

[25] *Halifax Herald,* September 12, 1924
[26] *Denver Post,* 17 December 1917
[27] *Milwaukee Free Press,* 18 August 1919

his aggressiveness and to, in the words of one newspaper report, the "steam behind each and every punch started by Sam Langford."[28]

Joe continued to fight regularly until November of 1919, after which time he retired from the ring, only to come back for a final fight on June 1, 1922 when he fought a six-round draw against Harry Gibson. After retiring from the ring for good he purchased a two story building in Union City, New Jersey where he ran a limousine shop, Jennette's Auto Service out of the main floor, while living on the second floor. He passed away on July 2, 1958, just shy of what would have been his seventy-ninth birthday.

Remarkably, Sam was back in action less than a week after his fight with Jennette, losing a twelve-round decision to Harry Wills in Brooklyn, New York on September 20th. He lost again to Wills in Toledo three weeks later. The outcome of the latter contest left some speculating whether Wills had adopted Sam's habit of saving future meal tickets. One reporter thought Wills worked only hard enough to outpoint Langford. Another said Wills should have beaten Langford early in the game, but that had he done so he would have been cutting into his future meal ticket. More likely, Wills had learned his lesson and knew better than to take any unnecessary chances with Sam.

The Toledo Boxing Commission agreed with those that thought Wills had carried Sam, and at a special meeting on November 20th, ruled that the contest had not been legitimate. They issued a ruling that Sam and Harry Wills were to be barred from any further bouts in Toledo.

Sam signed on with Denver-based promoter Jimmy Hamill, to fight Kid Norfolk, a tall light heavyweight fighter out of Panama on December 17th in Denver's Stockyard Stadium. The Kid, whose real name was William Ward, was being billed as the heavyweight champion of Panama at the time and was considered by some to be the best new "colored" fighter to enter the game in some time. He had excellent footwork, was fast and smooth, and some described him as a thing of beauty in the ring. The Kid had been touring the country with quite a bit of success and impressed a Boston crowd by the ease with which he had trimmed Billy Miske only two months earlier. Confident in his chances with the "Tar Baby," Norfolk was quoted as saying that while

---

[28] *Denver Post*, 17, December 1917

Sam "may be playing the major league game now, he'll only be a bush leaguer after I get through with him."[29]

One afternoon, while still in Chicago and preparing for the upcoming bout Sam sat on a rubbing table apparently contemplating one thing or another. The physique that had once looked so impressive now had rolls of flesh around the middle.

An onlooker approached Sam, and while staring at his protruding stomach, proceeded to tell Sam in vivid detail how Kid Norfolk had hit his last opponent so hard in the belly he all but killed the poor fellow. Receiving no reaction from Sam, he repeated the story, this time with a different victim. Still receiving no reaction, he shared a similar story about a third victim. Listening to the one-sided conversation, the gym's owner, Kid Howard, turned to another onlooker and remarked that this guy might not know it, but he was fixing poor Norfolk up good talking like that to Sam. Just about then, Sam looked up at the first man, and, after studying him for a moment said, "Look buddy, tell that little so and so that if he hits me in the belly, that this belly will bounce back at him and break his wrist."[30]

As the press covered the training during the week leading up to the fight they raved about Norfolk's marvelous physique, along with his cleverness and swiftness of foot. He was described by different writers as a whirlwind and a cyclone. Some wondered whether Sam would be able to lay a glove on him.

On December 17th, Sam entered the ring shortly before 10:00 p.m. wearing his famous old green kimono around his bulk. He entered to huge applause from a crowd of 2,000. Kid Norfolk came out next, and when he tossed off his robe a murmur of appreciation swept the stadium: he was splendidly conditioned and had a finely chiseled physique.

Once the preliminaries were out of the way, the bell rang and the Kid danced around lightly, shooting out two straight lefts that landed successfully on Sam's noggin without receiving a blow in return. He came in again and tried to land a body blow, but missed and received a hard right to the body from Sam, which he partially blocked. He

---

[29] unknown source, newspaper clipping, 15 September 1917
[30] *Denver Post,* December 1917

reverted to attacking from a distance and managed to bloody Sam's mouth when two more straight left jabs landed. When the pair fell into a clinch shortly thereafter, the Kid also showed that he knew a little bit about infighting as well, landing a right to the head and a left to the body on the break. Sam's face flashed with anger while the Kid danced confidently out of reach.

The two men stalled for the next minute, looking for an opening. Then Sam let loose a long swing that caught the Kid high on the side of the head and sent him spinning. Sam rushed in, but the Kid had enough presence of mind to fall into a clinch. Sam landed some heavy kidney punches while the Kid cleared the cobwebs. The two men separated and sparred for openings from a distance. Sam apparently found what he was looking for first and landed two more bombs to the head just before the bell rang to end the first session. Suddenly all of the confidence that the Kid had demonstrated early in the round completely disappeared as he retired to his corner.

The second round began with the Kid on his bicycle, pedaling fast and furious in reverse with Sam in hot pursuit.

When Sam caught up to him, the Kid fell into a clinch and paid heavily for it when Sam sent in kidney blows that could be heard throughout the arena.

After the second clinch of the round, Sam feinted with his left and then landed a hard right hook to the body that dropped the Kid to the canvas for a count of seven. As soon as he rose to his feet he rushed into a clinch from which Sam tried desperately to escape. When the referee stepped in to pry the pair apart, Sam found another opening and managed to loosen his right arm and land an uppercut on the Kid's chin that sent him crashing to the mat for the second time in the round. For a time it looked like the Kid wouldn't beat the count, but he managed to woozily climb to his feet. He came forward and fell into a clinch. Sam pushed him away, shot a left jab to the face, followed it with a right to the body, and then a big left hook to the jaw that sent the Kid sprawling across the canvas and under the ropes for the full count.

Feeling his oats afterward, Sam sat in his dressing room and told his audience that he was still the king, and indicated a desire to meet Jess Willard. When asked later why he knocked the Kid out so quickly as opposed to saving him for more future fights, Sam, surely remembering the Kid's promise to send him to the bush leagues, replied:

"Well I'll tell you, that fellow wasn't in my league at all, so I had to remove him from the scene as quickly as possible. He belongs in the minor league and I am in the majors."

When asked about his success with bigger fighters, Sam explained as follows:

"You see, I've got these big folks all figured out. If I cannot reach their heads I can plunk em in the body and beat them that way. You know they can duck with the head, but they can't duck with the body. There's an old saying that if you want to kill a tree you just need to take an ax and chop at the stump. You might kill the tree quicker by chopping it off at the top, but you'll find it just as sure by chopping at the bottom, but it may take longer. It's the same way with a fighter. If you can't hit him in the head the way to do it is to chip him in the body, just as you would a tree. And if you do that they will die just like the tree. That's what I do to them."[31]

The victory over Norfolk ended Sam's year on a high note.

---

[31] 30 Jim McNamara, "A Stroll Through Memorable Fistic Lane," letter to *Veteran Boxer* magazine, October 13, 1952.

HARRY GREG AND "TIGER" FLOWERS

Author's collection

"WHAT THEY (WOMEN) TAKE AWAY, NOTHING CAN PUT BACK!"
~SAM LANGFORD

CHAPTER 20

PASSING OF THE TORCH

Sam fought about eighty-six times between 1918 to 1922, and one-third of the contests were with four men: Jeff Clarke (8-9), Harry Wills (6), Jack Thompson (7), and "Big" Bill Tate (7).

Harry Wills, more than any other man during this period, ensured Sam's slide from the top continued, defeating him in all of their matches during these years. Sam's first two fights in 1918 took place against Wills in Panama, the first on April 14th. Wills was confident he would knock out Sam, but he was also respectful of Sam's punch. Sam trained hard for this contest. One sportswriter who watched him workout reported he looked to be in good shape and had shed some weight, coming in at 187 pounds. Wills knocked Sam out in the sixth round.

Reflecting upon the defeat, Sam said he saw the punch coming and tried to duck it, but the next thing he knew he was on a cot in his dressing room with Joe standing over him.

"When do we fight? Ain't it almost time for us to get in the ring?" asked Sam.

"You've done all the fighting you're going to do today," replied Joe.

Thinking Joe was joking, Sam asked, "What do you mean?"

"The fight is over," said Joe.

"What happened?" Sam asked Joe.

"Oh, nothing, except you forgot to duck," replied Joe.

After a minute, Sam asked, "How long ago was that?"

Joe took out his watch, looked at it, and replied, "One hour and twenty-five minutes ago."[1]

Sam briefly considered retirement. There was no question that Wills had his number. Even so, the thought of retirement was quickly cast aside.

Wills believed he was unbeatable at this time, and he wanted a fight with Jess Willard or Fred Fulton. The reality was that neither he nor Sam had a chance of a bout with the champion, regardless of their performances in the ring.

His choices limited, Sam agreed to meet Harry Wills again in Panama on May 19th. Wills boasted that Sam wouldn't last more than ten rounds. Sam went down in the seventh, the victim of a technical knockout. He was saved by the bell, but it was a grueling fight and he was a beaten man. His seconds wisely tossed in the sponge.

Sam displayed gameness and sportsmanship, but the papers reported that he'd been badly outclassed by Wills, whom the *Panama Star & Herald* called the world's greatest heavyweight.[2]

Sam returned to the States and a frenzied schedule, fighting and winning five times in August. The last bout was on August 22nd, an eight-round decision victory over "Battling" Jim Johnson. It was the twelfth fight and final pairing between the two men.

It was, in fact, Johnson's final ring appearance: he died just two months later, at age thirty-five, of influenza. Johnson was one of an estimated 675,000 Americans who died in an epidemic that became known as The Spanish Flu. Between 1918-1919 the deadly disease killed approximately one-fifth of the world's population. In September of 1918, it arrived in the Boston area and quickly spread through the busy seaport. The disease struck with amazing speed, often killing within hours of the first sign of infection. Death was usually the result of uncontrollable hemorrhaging that would fill a patient's lungs and drown them in their own body fluids.

On August 28th, the press reported that Sam had been offered a

---

[1] *Halifax Herald*, 15 September 1924
[2] *Panama Star & Herald*, 20 May 1918

position as boxing instructor to "colored" troops in the St. Louis area. It was said the offer suited Sam because he was over the draft age, married, and had little chance of serving overseas. On September 12th, another report said Sam had been offered the position twice before but had turned it down to pursue his prizefighting career. Although the report stated Sam was now ready to accept the position, Sam did not. He resumed his ring career instead.

He met Jeff Clarke on October 31st. The referee, Martin Flaherty, ruled the bout a draw, but both *The Boston Globe* and *The Lowell Sun* reported that Clarke had performed best. *The Sun* also reported that prior to the match Sam was served a warrant for non-support of his wife. The police had taken Sam into the station, but he had been immediately released on bail.

On December 28, 1918, Sam had the opportunity for a rematch with Fred Fulton. The pair was booked to meet in San Francisco's Civic Auditorium. The day before the scheduled four-round event, Harry Smith of the *San Francisco Chronicle*, wrote that he'd attended Sam's workout the previous day and found it to be a lazy one. Smith said Sam appeared fat and seemed content to let his sparring partners whale away at him.[3]

Fulton was established as the pre-fight favorite. Sam maintained that he'd learned his lesson in their last fight and wouldn't repeat the mistake of fighting Fulton from the outside. He'd fight on the inside, and he told anyone who would listen not to be surprised if he knocked Fulton out.

It wasn't to be. Sam was no longer the fighter of old. Now he just was old, at least in boxing terms. Fulton proved too big and strong for Sam and earned an easy decision victory. He kept Sam at arm's length most of the contest, peppering him with left jabs and dropping in the occasional right hand. Boxing writer Harry Smith was sure that the Langford of ten years before would have easily won, but this version wasn't up to the task. Fulton tried to land a knockout blow and had a number of chances but was unable to accomplish the mission. In the last round he managed to land a right hand bomb to Sam's jaw, but

---

[3] *San Francisco Chronicle*, 27 December 1918

Sam seemed to catch himself just before falling, and managed to carry on.

Sam's first fight in 1919 also took place in San Francisco. He met another pudgy fighter, Willie Meehan, on March 4th in a short four-round contest in the Coliseum Rink. The *San Francisco Chronicle*'s report of the fight ran under the headline, "Meehan Wins Fight Between Two Fat Men, Sam Langford Has Eaten Too Many Greasy Pork Chops to Scrap Any More." Harry Smith, reporting for the *Chronicle* wrote that Willie kicked the pudgy Langford around the ring, punching him as you would thump a bass drum. He said that no bear that ever went into winter quarters was as fat as Sam Langford, and that there was nothing resembling speed in his movements. It was Smith's opinion that "all that he ever had in the way of fighting machinery, even the cleverness, the ring generalship, was missing."[4]

That September, *The Register* in Sandusky, Ohio published an article that included an interview with Sam. When asked who he thought was the greatest fighter, Sam picked Jack Johnson. He said that no man could lick Willard because Willard had licked the greatest man that ever lived.

> "Didn't you say that Jeffries would lick Johnson?" we kidded Sam.
>
> "Yes. Yes I did say that but I was sore at Johnson then. You know he gave me quite a licking a long time ago in Boston, and when he got to be champion he never would talk about me again. I was sore at him but all the time, way down in my heart, I knew that he was a great man. The day I saw him beat Jeffries made me surer. Jeffries was in good shape that day. He never could have taken the licking he did if he wasn't in good form. You know he was just as fast as ever, but he was like a baby when he boxed Johnson. I tell you that Johnson was so big, so strong, so clever. He had everything. He was never hurt, never had a black eye or a cut, and never broke a hand, and he beat the best in the world. I call that considerable doing. He was never even tired in the fight. He just fought his own way, went about it in a business like way, and made the other fellow look foolish. Hit? Yes sir! I never hit the floor

---

[4] *San Francisco Chronicle*, 29 December 1918

harder in my life than the night he hit me. I thought I'd go right through the floor of the ring."[5]

Sam fought Jack Thompson at the Tulsa Athletic Club on October, 20, 1919. The winner was to receive a diamond studded belt valued at $1,500, on the condition that they agree to meet Harry Wills at the club at a later date. Upon the bout's conclusion it was ruled a draw by the referee, Lem Wallace. According to reporter Larry Dailey of the *Tulsa Daily World* the verdict of a draw did Sam a great disservice. Dailey had Sam clearly winning eight rounds, Thompson winning two close rounds, and the other five rounds even. By the last round, Thompson's left eye was closed and he was bleeding from both the mouth and nose. Sam was relatively unmarked.

A day later, the *Tulsa Daily World* announced that the club's promoter, Walker Machen, had gone ahead and presented the diamond studded belt to Sam, which they deemed symbolic of the world's Negro Heavyweight Boxing Championship. Sam in return agreed to meet Harry Wills before the club in November.[6]

The pair met on November 5th in a fifteen-round contest that was dominated by Wills.

Joe Woodman was no longer managing Sam. The pair had parted company earlier in the year, when Sam refused to follow Joe's advice to retire from the ring before he got hurt. Joe knew Sam's best days were behind him and Joe worried that Sam was risking his health, especially his eyesight. He urged Sam to quit, but Joe's words had fallen upon deaf ears. Although they remained lifelong friends, their partnership came to an end.

When Joe left him, Sam simply found other parties willing to fulfill the manager's role. After Sam's loss to Wills, his new manager, Howard Carr of Chicago, issued a statement saying that he was taking Sam to England in a few weeks for several bouts. Carr claimed that they would attend the Joe Beckett-Georges Carpentier fight in London on December 4th, where Sam would challenge the winner. It never transpired. Neither did a possible trip to France that Carr spoke of in early January, for a series of bouts to culminate in a meeting with

---

[5] *The Register*, 6 September 1919
[6] *Tulsa Daily World*, 22 October 1919

French boxing idol Georges Carpentier. Sam's visits to the European continent were all behind him now.

By the time 1920 rolled around, there was no question that Sam was no longer the feared fighter he once had been. He did, however, discover to his pleasure that willing opponents in the States were no longer as difficult to find as they had been in the past. All of a sudden there were a number of men hoping to build their reputation at his expense. In Sam's words, "After successive losses to Wills, lots of folks began to say, 'Poor Sammy. He's all done now.'"

But Sam wasn't so sure about that. Maybe Wills had his number, but he believed he was good enough to beat most of those in the game. In his own view, his performance during 1920 represented something of a "comeback."[7] Overall he had enjoyed a very good year, winning twenty of twenty-five contests.

He began by easily defeating Jeff Clarke over ten rounds in Kalamazoo on January 16th. That was followed by a February 23rd meeting with "Battling" Gahee in Memphis at the Southern Athletic Club. Gahee no doubt got his nickname as a result of having fought in France during World War I, where he saw heavy action against the Germans. He was honorably discharged in 1918 after being shot and severely wounded in a battle near Frappelle.[8] Gahee, whose real first name was William, was a youngster with a powerful physique and was considered something of a "comer" while Sam was well past his prime.

In 1920, the fights in Memphis were promoted by Billy Haack. Haack was a one-man show and a tough customer. He made the matches, put up the money, and usually did the refereeing. He didn't take any guff from any manager or fighter. If any was given he wouldn't hesitate to slug the offending party. New York sports writer Joe Williams witnessed Haack knock one young fighter cold when the man tried to hold him up for more money just prior to a scheduled bout. Just before leveling the boom on the surprised fighter, Haack told him that instead of getting more money he was going to fight for nothing. Sam wasn't a problem fighter for Haack. He fought for Haack four times,

---
[7] *Halifax Herald,* 16 September 1924
[8] Kevin Smith, *The Sundowners: The History of the Black Prizefighter 1879-1930.* CCK Publications, 2006

and in Haack's book Sam was aces. In 1944, when he heard Sam was down on his luck he sent some funds to Sam. In Billy's opinion Sam was one of the greatest fighters of all time and would have defeated Joe Louis easily.

Recalling Sam's 1920 contest with "Battling" Gahee, Billy said that before entering the ring that evening Sam sauntered into his office and said, "Chief, I see you got a sellout tonight. What do you want me to do with this Gahee boy. You want me to whip him quick or give the crowd a show?"

Billy told Sam that he wasn't the one doing the fighting: Sam was ... but he added that the crowd was more interested in action than in how long the fight lasted.

"Ok, Chief," Sam replied and exited the office.[9]

Early in the first round, Gahee managed to land a right to Sam's jaw and stagger him. Instead of gaining confidence from the blow, Gahee seemed to become frightened of Sam: he spent the remainder of the round running from the old veteran.

Sam dropped the youngster four times in the second session, the last time for a full count from Haack, who was serving as the referee. A local reporter for the *Memphis Commercial Appeal* reported that Gahee ultimately acquiesced more out of fear of what Sam might do than from what he'd actually done.

Sam then knocked out the Jamaica Kid in seven rounds on March 29th and thrashed Jack Thompson over fifteen rounds on April 5th. The victory over Thompson was followed by a third-round knockout of Canada's reigning heavyweight champion, Silas Green, before tackling Harry Wills in Denver on April 19th.

The Wills meeting produced another loss on Sam's record. The big fellow dominated him over the course of their fifteen-round encounter. Wills sent Sam to the mat no less than four times in the first round, but he was panned by the press for his inability to prevent Sam from lasting the distance.

The Denver Post reported that Sam appeared dazed and helpless from the first round through the sixth, but Wills' lack of aggressiveness prevented him from achieving a knockout. While acknowledging

---

[9] *Syracuse Herald-Journal*, 31 January 1944

that Wills administered a "terrific beating" to Sam, *The Post* felt he failed to live up to his advance notices, and he wouldn't match up against Dempsey or (Fred) Fulton. In Wills' defense, it was noted that Sam employed every trick in the trade to last the distance: he stayed in close, clinched when in trouble, and made no attempt to lead.[10]

The bout with Wills proved to be the low point of the year for Sam. He resumed his winning ways less than a month later with a third-round technical knockout over Marty Cutler in Windsor, Ontario, Canada. He followed that with wins over Jeff Clarke, "Roughhouse" Ware, Pinky Lewis, Jack Mitchell, Jack Thompson, and Pinky Lewis again.

Joe Woodman was no longer managing Sam, but he issued a statement on July 6, 1920 indicating that he was still keeping tabs on Sam and that the "Tar Baby" had lost about thirty pounds since the advent of Prohibition.

The Eighteenth Amendment, the National Prohibition Act (also referred to as the Volstead Act after its author, Andrew Volstead) took effect January 16, 1920. It made illegal the import, export, transport, sales and manufacture of liquor. The objective of the Act was to decrease drunkenness and lead to a reduction in crime. It worked at first, but only until effective illegal means of manufacturing, transporting, and distributing liquor had been established. A year later, Americans' alcohol consumption had actually increased.

Langford faced Sam McVea on August 14th in Chicago for the fifteenth and final meeting between the pair. Their last fight didn't turn out to be one of their better performances. According to the *Chicago Tribune,* "fans began filing out as early as the seventh round when it was clear the bout wasn't going to live up to their expectations in terms of action."[11]

McVea went on to fight just six more times before his untimely death on December 23rd of the following year, as a result of pneumonia. McVea died penniless.

Sam made his acting debut on the big screen in the latter part of 1920, when he played a role in a film titled *The Brute*. The film was

---

[10] *Denver Post*, 20 April 1920

[11] *Chicago Tribune*, 15 August 1920

advertised "as the greatest colored picture ever made." It was the story of a gambler named Bull Magee who poses as a gentleman and wins over the girl he desires by giving money to her aunt, who believes him true. He later proves a brute, beating the girl who he ends up marrying. Ultimately the girl's first husband returns and defeats the brute. A secondary plot in the movie focused on a black boxer who struggles against a group that tries to lynch him. The ad for the film read "See how brutes are handled. See the great gambling den where a fight is framed for the championship of the world. Does Sam Langford fake the fight? Come and see."[12]

At the time, a number of blacks voiced their displeasure over the scenes of gambling, wife beating, and poor behavior. They wanted a more positive portrayal of the black community. They weren't alone in harboring concerns about the film, as many white men heading local censorship boards feared the aggressive portrayal of blacks in the film might encourage rioting. The film was banned in Chicago on that very basis: a July 1919 race riot in that city was still fresh on the minds of censorship board members. Despite concerns and objections, the film was generally well received by its black audiences.

Sam met big George Godfrey in Hot Springs, Arkansas on November 17, 1920. During World War I, George (whose real name was Feab S. Williams) had worked as a boxing instructor based in Alabama. One day, as Sam came through, he saw Godfrey and was impressed with the big twenty-four-year-old. He introduced himself, encouraged George to look him up in Chicago after the war, and promised to "make a fighter of him." When the war ended, George did that, and he worked out with Sam for a time in his gym.[13]

Godfrey shared an amusing story about one of those training sessions with sportswriter Damon Runyon a few years later. Sam was passing on a number of tricks to George, and one day, while the two were sparring, the thought of dropping a big right hand on Sam's chin crossed his mind:

> "I just wanted to see if I could hit some with that right hand. But doggonit if he ain't seen the evil look in my eyes.

---

[12] *The Afro-American Ledger*, 1 October 1920
[13] Robert Jones. "What About George Godfrey," *Knockout* c. 1926-1934

No more did I get that big paw of mine in position to experiment, then I detect a change in Sam's face. Next thing I know, some charitable soul was pushing water on my face. Seems like I done been knocked cold. I was kind of ashamed to look at old Sam. He done seen that evil light in my eyes when I was gonna let go of that right. But Sam didn't say much. All he told me was, 'George, don't never forget, the wages of sin am death and damnation.' I guess he was right. Sam was a powerful sharp man."[14]

Sam knocked his former pupil out in the second round of their November 17th meeting. A Langford left to the mouth drove George's lower lip into his upper teeth and cut him severely. Sam inflicted enough damage in this contest that Godfrey claimed it was the worst trimming he ever received and that for a week afterward he was forced to live only on such food as could be taken through a straw. In later years, Godfrey was quoted as saying that Sam did more damage to him with one punch than any other fighter he ever faced.[15]

Sam closed out the year on the West Coast by winning four more fights: a seventh round technical knockout over "Tiny" Jim Herman (in Portland, Oregon), and then three decisions. The first victory by decision was in six rounds over Terry Keller in Aberdeen, Washington on December 9th; the second in six rounds over Clem Johnson in Mansfield, Oregon on December 23rd; and the third was in ten rounds against Jim Barry of San Francisco, in Portland, Oregon on December 29th.

By the year 1921, most of Sam's customers had grown old and decided that they didn't want to do business in the ring with him anymore. As Sam remembers it, there were plenty of promoters more than happy to put him on their card, but it was more difficult for him to find willing opponents. Despite the fact that he fought eighteen times that year, 1921 was not very profitable for Sam.

Sam avoided a loss over the first eight months, either defeating or drawing with the likes of Brad Simmons, Jeff Clarke, Jack Thompson, Bill Tate, "Tiny" Jim Herman, Alfred Johnson, Bill Watkins, "Bearcat" Wright, George Godfrey, and "Topeka" Jack Johnson. The August

---

[14] *Afro-American Ledger*, 21 July 1928

[15] Robert Jones. "What About George Godfrey," *Knockout* c. 1926-1934

17th victory over George Godfrey in Covington, Kentucky was by way of a first-round knockout. George came out early in the opening session, determined to try and put Sam to sleep right away. As soon as Sam realized what George was up to, he knocked the big fellow out in a hurry. When he saw him afterward, he informed him he'd done so, "Just to show you not to get smart with your betters."[16]

Sam fought to a six-round draw just two days later against "Topeka" Jack Johnson in Topeka, Kansas. According to *The Topeka Daily Capital*, when Sam entered the ring he greeted the referee with, "Hello big chief, how are you?" and when someone at Sam's side asked him if he wanted some lemonade he smiled and said, "Thanks, I've got some corn whiskey."[17]

The streak came to an end on September 5th in Ft. Worth, Texas, when Sam dropped a twelve-round decision to Lee Anderson, whom he'd defeated only three weeks earlier.

He rebounded from that loss with a second-round knockout of Young Peter Jackson in Toronto, Ontario on October 18th. At the time, Jackson was generally considered the Canadian heavyweight title holder by many, on the basis of his performance against former white hope contender Arthur Pelkey in a controversial bout that was ruled a draw. Sam received a tremendous reception upon his arrival in Toronto. He was hailed as the "King of Smokey Swat" by the *Toronto Star*, and Toronto's black community organized a special reception and downtown parade to celebrate his visit.[18]

Prior to the contest, Jackson spoke almost reverently of Langford and his punching ability. Still, he stated that he planned to dance around the ring and in and out of range so fast that Sam and his one good eye wouldn't get a bead on him.

Sam was complimentary of Jackson's speed, but expressed the opinion that he lacked a good punch and that it would be a short contest.

A large crowd of approximately 6,000 attended the well-publicized event. They were greatly disappointed that it didn't last longer.

---

[16] Robert Jones. "What About George Godfrey," *Knockout* c. 1926-1934

[17] *Topeka Daily Capital*, 20 August 1921

[18] *Toronto Star*, 14 October 1921

Sam weighed a reported 198 pounds and was described as "rolling in fat," and carrying a large "front porch," while Jackson carried only 171 pounds into the ring.[19]

Jackson was badly outclassed, hitting the deck three times before the contest was halted in the second round. He appeared frightened from the beginning, and *The Toronto Daily Star* observed that Sam tossed him around like one would a toy balloon.

Reporting on Sam's win over Jackson the next day, *The Star* wrote:

> A pickaninny has as much chance in a rassling match with a gorilla as Young Peter Jackson had with Sam Langford. They say Langford trained on pork chops. Well, if he did he done gobbled up Mistah Y.P. Jackson in two bites like any other pork chop.[20]

Larry Gains, a heavyweight good enough to go on to capture the titles of Canadian Heavyweight Champion in 1927 and the British Empire Heavyweight Champion in 1931, tells an amusing story of meeting Sam while the latter was training in Toronto in the early 1920s.

According to Larry, a trainer by the name of Tom Goodman took him and another young man named Doug up to meet Sam at the Allington Hotel, where he was staying while in training. Larry said that when they entered Sam's room they found him sitting up in bed wearing his pajamas, smoking one of his big black cigars. On the table next to him was a half-filled glass next to a bottle of whiskey. His sparring partners sat playing cards at a nearby table.

> The trainer introduced the two young men and Sam kindly offered to answer a few questions. Doug was the first to speak, saying that he'd always heard fighters weren't supposed to smoke.
>
> Sam said that was right, but if the fighter went for a good long run the next morning he'd be alright.
>
> Doug then asked about the consumption of liquor, and once again Sam replied that it would be better if a fighter

---

[19] *The Evening Telegram Toronto*, 19 October 1921
[20] 20 *Toronto Daily Star*, 19 October 1921

avoided it altogether but that as long as it was followed by a good long run the next morning the fighter would be alright.

At that point, Larry said that Sam turned to him and asked him if he didn't have a question he'd like to ask. Larry had been glancing at a light blue nighty draped across the other side of the bed. It obviously belonged to a woman, so he began to ask, "Mr. Langford, I thought that fighters ..."

But Sam quickly cut him off and said, "I know what you're going to say, but with women a good run won't help you at all. What they take away, nothing can put back!"[21]

Larry ran into Sam again in the late 1920s, while training in a Boston gymnasium. According to Larry, Sam would sit on a bench along the wall of the gymnasium, with a brown derby atop his head and a white cane in his hand, listening to the fighters go about their paces. A friend would bring Sam to the gym each day and take him home at night.

One day, Larry walked up to Sam and slipped ten dollars into his top pocket.

"What's that?" Sam asked.

"That's just something with which to buy a drink tonight, Sam ..." said Larry.

"I don't take anything for nothing. If you want to give me money, let me earn it," said Sam.

"All right Sam, how do you want to earn it?" said Larry.

"Tell me who you're gonna fight and I'll tell you how to beat him," replied Sam.

Larry told him he was going to fight "Big Boy" Peterson. Sam considered this with some care, pursing his lips and nodding his head, clearly in deep thought.

Finally, Sam said, "Larry, I'll tell you the best way to beat this fellow. Hit him, but don't let him hit you."[22]

Sam turned thirty-six in 1922. By then it had been known for some time that he was fighting with only one good eye. His lack of training

---

[21] Larry Gains, *The Impossible Dream*. London: Leisure Publications, 1976
[22] Larry Gains, *The Impossible Dream*. London: Leisure Publications, 1976

and additional weight had robbed him of his quickness. The loss of speed was magnified by the fact that he was now fighting younger and quicker opponents, since so many of his former contemporaries had fallen by the wayside. His "good eye" was a primary target for his opponents. Sam didn't blame them in the least:

> "Boxing is one of those sports where you can be too sportish after the old gong rings," he said. "The main idea is to win. You go out and beat or get beaten. And that means you've got to find the weak spot of the other fellow and keep on banging away at it."

In 1922, banging away at Sam's good eye was an excellent strategy. It had reached the point where after a fight Sam couldn't see at all for a couple of days. Then, according to Sam, "the right would do some flickering and after a while I could see a little bit with it." But he was noticing that something was growing over that eye. Finally a doctor informed him it was a cataract, a clouding of the normally clear lens of the eye. Surgery is the only way a cataract can be removed.

The doctor advised Sam to quit fighting. Sam considered it, but he wondered who would hire a man who didn't know much about anything other than fighting, was blind in one eye, and going blind in the other. He wrote letters to some of the men he had lent money, but when he didn't hear back from any of them he decided he had no choice but to keep fighting. He rationalized this by telling himself that he'd probably lose sight in that eye even if he didn't fight. He might as well go down swinging.[23]

Sam fought approximately twenty times in 1922. Again, it's difficult to say this with certainty, because it is believed that he may have participated in a number of unrecorded contests. Sam's highlight of that year was his June 5th match with Theodore "Tiger" Flowers in Atlanta, Georgia. The future middleweight champion was just two months shy of his 27th birthday and had captured the Mexican middleweight title two months earlier. He was a 5'10" southpaw weighing in the neighborhood of 159-169 pounds. He was known as the "Georgia Deacon" for his religious devotion. He was very fast and elusive, but known to possess a "weak chin." While in Mexico, he'd

---

[23] *Halifax Herald,* 17 September 1924

fought seven to ten fights, losing only once, against heavyweight Lee Anderson.

The local press billed the event as a match-up of youth, conditioning, and speed (on the part of Flowers) versus the experience and punching power of the older and slower Langford. "Tiger" was expected to have a fighting chance as long as he was able to stay away from Sam and box, but if he tried to slug it out or do any infighting with Sam, it was feared that Sam would make short work of him.

When "Tiger" climbed into the ring with Sam he'd been fighting professionally since 1918 and had only suffered three setbacks: to "Panama" Joe Gans, Kid Norfolk, and Lee Anderson, respectively.

When the opening session began, Flowers quickly gained the favor of the Atlanta crowd as he dazzled them with his speed and volume of punches. They shouted with joy as "Tiger" landed what seemed to one writer to be as many as one hundred slaps to Sam's head during the round. Sam reportedly appeared puzzled by "Tiger's" offensive tactics, and it appeared clear he had no defense for Flower's attack.

There was, however, one brief period during that first round that should have cast an ominous shadow over Flower's chances, at least in the eyes of the more experienced observers. At one point during the round "Tiger" appeared to put everything he had into a series of blows upon Sam's face. That would have proved disheartening to most fighters, but Sam simply laughed and stuck out his jaw for more. "Tiger" couldn't hurt him. Although Sam was bloodied and came out of that opening round with a discolored eye, he knew he still had a puncher's chance and just needed an opening to deliver the finishing blow.

He found the opening during the second round. Sam pursued "Tiger" and accepted nearly twenty blows to the face as he searched for his opportunity. Finally he managed to tie "Tiger" up in a clinch that allowed him to deliver a lot of punishment to the younger man's body. Then, as they were coming out of the clinch, quick as a cat, Sam delivered a short right hand blow to the jaw. It traveled no more than six inches.

Many of the fans didn't even see the short blow. But they witnessed "Tiger" fall flat on his back, hitting the floor with a thud. As Referee Glynn counted, "Tiger" writhed on the floor, regaining enough of his senses to attempt to beat it. He only managed to get up to all fours when the last number was reached. The "Tiger" had been knocked out.

Afterward, *The Atlanta Constitution* reported that doctors warned Sam the optic nerve in his good eye was badly damaged. If he didn't stop fighting he would lose the sight in that eye.

Flowers would continue boxing and go on to a distinguished career. Ultimately he would capture the middleweight championship of the world with a fifteen-round decision victory over the great Harry Greb on February 26, 1926. Tragically, after losing the title to Mickey Walker in December of that same year, Flowers would lose his life the following year on November 16th of 1927, following an operation for sinus trouble. According to his biography, written by Henry Grady Edney in 1928, Flowers was operated on for a sinus growth over the right eye. He collapsed as he came out of the anesthetic and never recovered consciousness. He was only thirty-two.

Sam fought "Bearcat" Wright next, in Galveston, Texas on June 19th. Wright stood 6'1", had very large arms and shoulders, and (over the course of his career) weighed anywhere from 205 to 230 pounds. During the Mexican Civil War he had fought under General Pershing as a member of the 24th Infantry, a unit primarily responsible for guarding the U.S./Mexico border to ensure the war didn't spill over onto U.S. soil. Once that did happen, the 24th entered Mexico and engaged Pancho Villa's forces. Wright began his boxing career as "Hard Hitting" Wright, in bouts promoted in various locations along the border. Ultimately he chose Omaha, Nebraska as a home base.[24]

Sam came away from this fight with a twelve-round draw. At least one source indicates that Sam could have ended the fight against the younger man early had he been so inclined. Asked afterward why he hadn't, Sam laughed and replied, "What's the use of putting Wright in wrong? He's comin and I'm goin."[25]

That didn't prevent Sam from knocking out Wright in five rounds when they met a month later in Tulsa, Oklahoma on July 17th.

In addition to Langford, Wright fought an impressive group of men over his sixteen-year career, including the likes of Fred Fulton,

---

[24] Kevin Smith, *The Sundowners: The History of the Black Prizefighter 1879- 1930 Vol. 3*, (unpublished manuscript)

[25] unknown author, "The Amazing Sam Langford," *Sports Novels*, Sep 1952

Primo Carnera, Mickey Walker, George Godfrey, Max Baer, and Jack Johnson very late in Johnson's career. Interviewed shortly before his death in 1975 by a young black reporter, Wright said that Langford was the greatest fighter he ever fought: "Lord how that man could punch. Every time he hit you, it hurt," said Wright.[26]

Sam's August 11th meeting with Brad Simmons was the second pairing between the two, their first meeting in Cincinnati the previous year having ended in a draw that neither party agreed was right. This match took place in Wichita, and gave the fight fans of that city their first opportunity to see the "Tar Baby" in action.

Simmons was no match for Sam. He hit the canvas a total of twelve times over ten rounds. After one knockdown—when it appeared Simmons had no intention of rising—Sam implored him to get up, saying, "Come on nigger, get up. Is you black or is you yellow? We gotta put on a show for the folks."[27]

Simmons got up. He fought gamely at times, but he was badly outclassed, and Sam toyed with him in the final round. It was a humiliation that Simmons would remember when he faced Sam again in 1926.

Sam finished the remainder of 1922 without a loss, in a string of ten fights against "Battling" Owens, "Cyclone" Smith, Jack Taylor (three times), Jim Barry (not the Chicago heavyweight), James "Tut" Jackson, Bill Tate, Kid Roscoe, and Sonny Goodrich.

---

[26] Letter from boxing historian Tim Leone

[27] Tim Leone, *Blind, Broke, and Black*. Privately published. No date.

1911-1922 341

SAM MCVEA, PARIS, FRANCE CA. 1909 - 1910
BEN HAWES COLLECTION

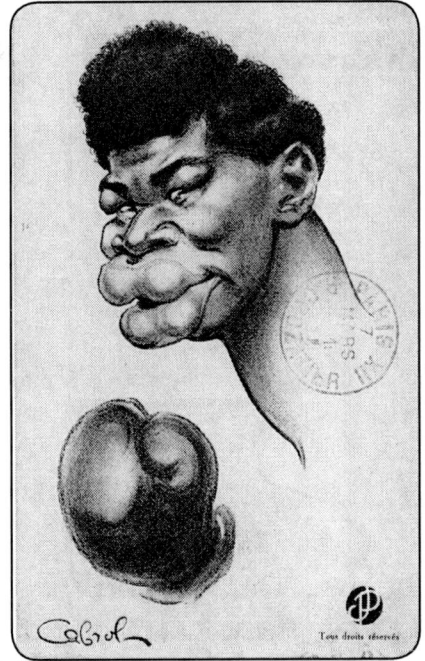

FRENCH POSTCARDS OF SAM MCVEA CA. 1909 - 1911
BEN HAWES COLLECTION

JIMMY WALSH, JEM MACE, BOB FITZSIMMONS, SAM LANGFORD

MAY 1911

BEN HAWES COLLECTION

LANGFORD-McVEA FIGHT PROGRAM

THE FOLLIES CABARET, DENVER, COLORADO

SEPTEMBER 30, 1915

BEN HAWES COLLECTION

ENGLAND'S
SPORTING BUDGET'S
PERIODICAL
DEPICTION OF
SAM LANGFORD
1911
AUTHOR'S COLLECTION

LOWER LEFT
SAM LANGFORD
PARIS, FRANCE 1911
BEN HAWES COLLECTION

LOWER RIGHT
BILL LANG POSTCARD
CA. 1911
AUTHOR'S COLLECTION

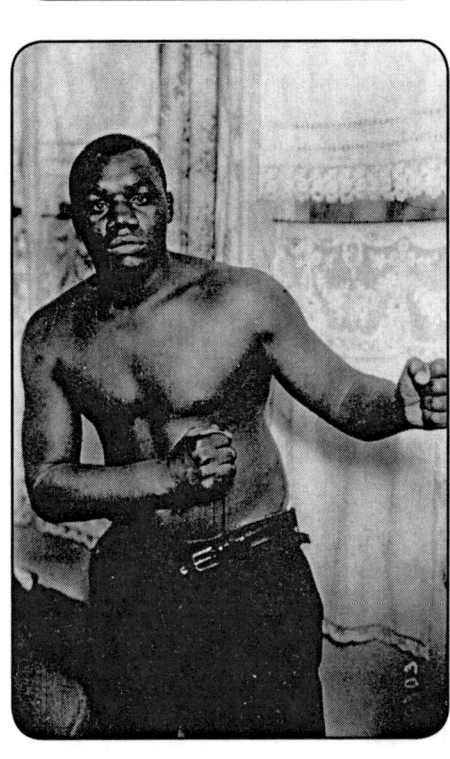

344 SAM LANGFORD: BOXING'S GREATEST UNCROWNED CHAMPION

SAM LANGFORD LANDS LEFT HOOK TO BACK OF BILL LANG'S HEAD
ENGLAND'S OLYMPIA STADIUM
FEBRUARY 21, 1911

LANGFORD KNOCKS LANG THROUGH THE ROPES
FEBRUARY 21, 1911
BEN HAWES COLLECTION

**SAM LANGFORD AND REFEREE EUGENE CORRI
WATCH BILL LANG TAKE A COUNT OF NINE**
ENGLAND'S OLYMPIA STADIUM FEBRUARY 21, 1911
AUTHOR'S COLLECTION

SAM LANGFORD AFTER HIS VICTORY OVER BILL LANG
PHOTO TAKEN BY SPORT & GENERAL ILLUSTRATIONS, LONDON
BEN HAWES COLLECTION

346 SAM LANGFORD: BOXING'S GREATEST UNCROWNED CHAMPION

DUKE MULLINS AND SAM
CA. 1912

DEPARTURE FROM VANCOUVER B.C. CANADA FOR AUSTRALIA VIA THE ZEALANDIA
NOVEMBER OF 1911
TOP L-R: DAN "PORKY" FLYNN, UNKNOWN, SAM LANGFORD AND TERRY KELLER
MIDDLE L-R: TWO UNKNOWNS, JOHNNY "CYCLONE" THOMPSON, & JOE WOODMAN.
FRONT L TO R: JAMES "LIVER" DAVIS, TWO UNKNOWNS, AND JOHNNY THOMPSON JR.
AUTHOR'S COLLECTION

Photo taken upon Sam's arrival in Australia

November 1911

It was tradition for all foreign boxers to have their pictures taken with Australian fighters, sports writers, etc. on these rocks upon arrival. To Langford's right is Jim Barry. Over Langford's left shoulder is his trainer, Duke Mullins. Sam's frequent sparring partner "Liver" Davis is pictured in the lower left corner.

Ben Hawes Collection

Sam Langford and Dan "Porky" Flynn

Promotional photo prior to May 27, 1912 match

Melbourne, Australia

Ben Hawes Collection

SAM LANGFORD
UNDATED
BEN HAWES COLLECTION

SUTHERLAND, SYDNEY, AUSTRALIA
CA. 1913
L TO R: DAVE DEPENA, "LIVER" DAVIS, FRED DAVIS,
ARTHUR COBB, MICK SMITH, SAM LANGFORD AND JACK READ
AUTHOR'S COLLECTION

COLIN BELL
CA. 1912-1913
BEN HAWES COLLECTION

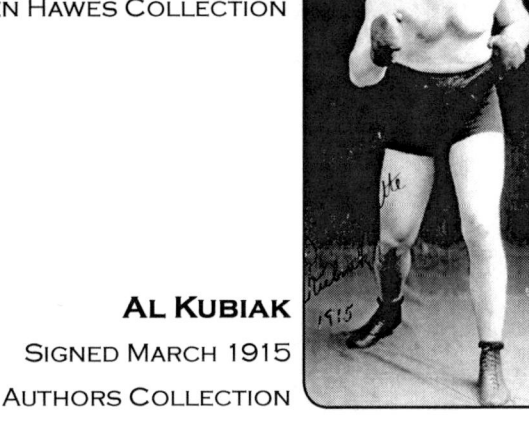

AL KUBIAK
SIGNED MARCH 1915
AUTHORS COLLECTION

SAM LANGFORD

CA. 1913

AUTHOR'S COLLECTION

AD FOR LANGFORD-JENNETTE 12/20/1913 BOUT
TO BE HELD AT LUNA PARK IN PARIS
AUTHOR'S COLLECTION

LANGFORD KNOCKS DOWN JOE JENNETTE IN THEIR 12/20/1913 MATCH IN PARIS AT LUNA PARK.
LANGFORD WON THE 20-ROUND DECISION
RICHARD SELF COLLECTION

**SAM AND MARTHA LANGFORD WITH THEIR
DAUGHTER, CHARLOTTE**

ARRIVAL IN SAN FRANCISCO UPON RETURN FROM AUSTRALIA
JULY 19, 1913

DON SCOTT COLLECTION

"Roughhouse" Ware

ca. 1914 - 1915

Ben Hawes Collection

Sam Langford

ca. 1915-1917

Ben Hawes Collection

Jack Lester

1913

Training for October 27 fight with Sam Langford (Taft, California)

Ben Hawes Collection

354 SAM LANGFORD: BOXING'S GREATEST UNCROWNED CHAMPION

FRED FULTON

APRIL 1914

BEN HAWES COLLECTION

HARRY WILLS
BEN HAWES COLLECTION

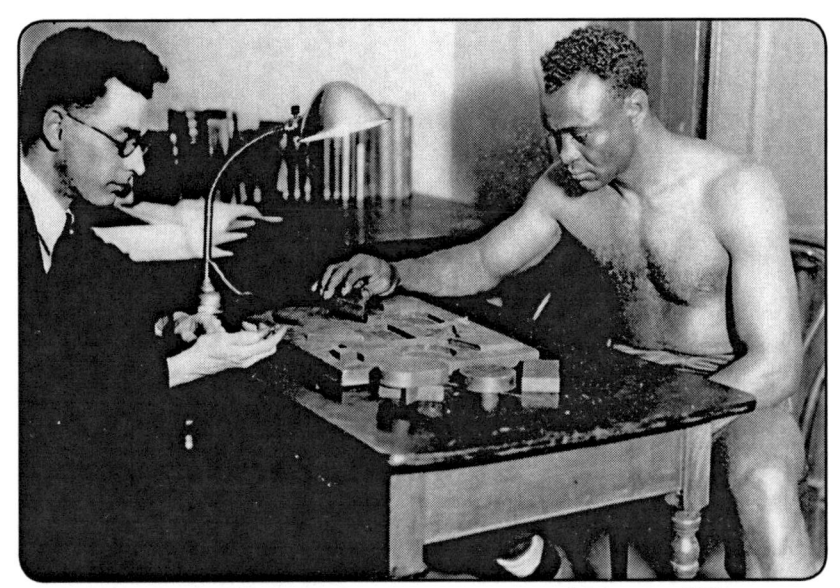

HARRY WILLS
CA. 1918
AUTHOR'S COLLECTION

356 SAM LANGFORD: BOXING'S GREATEST UNCROWNED CHAMPION

SAM DOWN IN ROUND 2 VS. HARRY WILLS
VERNON, CALIFORNIA NOVEMBER 26, 1914
LANGFORD CAME BACK TO KNOCKOUT WILLS IN THE 14TH
BEN HAWES COLLECTION

HOMER SMITH'S TRAINING CAMP
KALAMAZOO, MICHIGAN 1920
FRONT ROW, L TO R: UNKNOWN, "SHADOW" MORRIS,
JACK HERRICK, UNKNOWN, HOMER SMITH, AND SAM LANGFORD
AUTHOR'S COLLECTION

"I'M PLENTY OLD, BUT NOT TOO OLD TO BE CHAMPION OF MEXICO."
~SAM LANGFORD

CHAPTER 21

"HEAVYWEIGHT CHAMPION OF MEXICO!"

Sam estimated he made between $2,000-$3,000 fighting in 1922, but it was all gone by the end of the year. As he said:

"A fighter must have seconds and things like that and he's got to pay them and he's got to pay his living expenses, and $2,000 or $3,000 doesn't go as far with a fighter as $750 goes with anybody else who isn't in the fight game."[1]

So in early 1923, when he learned about an elimination tournament in Mexico City promoted by Baldomero Romero for the heavyweight championship of Mexico, Sam decided it might not be a bad way to make some money and pick up a title at the same time. He signed on as a participant.

Sam's first opponent in the tournament was Jim Tracey. The fight received a lot of attention in Mexico City, as the local press described Tracey as the Australian and New Zealand heavyweight champion. The twenty-six-year-old Tracey weighed 210 pounds, stood 6'3" and had a reach of 81½" Despite Tracey's advantage in size and youth, and the fact that Sam was struggling with his eyesight, Sam put the "champion" to sleep in the sixth round of their fight on March 2nd.

Sam knocked out his second opponent in the tournament, Chihuahua Brown, in the first round on March 17th. That set the stage

---
[1] *Halifax Herald*, 17 September 1924

for a match with a young twenty-four-year-old Californian fighter and the current Mexican title holder, Jim Savage, for the championship on March 31st. The fight generated very little excitement in the States, but it created great interest and a considerable amount of betting in Mexico. The Chapultepec bull ring was set up to accommodate 6,000 spectators, and the advance ticket sales indicated it wouldn't be enough to meet demand.

Sam had trained seriously for several weeks leading up to the match. Some Americans in town for the tournament expressed pleasant surprise at how well conditioned he appeared. Asked by one party how old he was, Sam laughed and replied, "I'm plenty old, but not too old to be the champion of Mexico."[2]

Sam was the early betting favorite. That quickly changed, however, when one of Kid Savage's handlers observed Sam walk across the gymnasium and attempt to take a step up where there was no step. His failing eyesight was evident. Once word of that problem spread, the betting quickly flipped in favor of the Kid.[3]

When Sam climbed into the ring to face Savage, he was experiencing great difficulty seeing out of his "good" eye. His handlers, whom he had to rely upon for guidance into the ring and to his corner, were so concerned about his eyesight that they wanted to call the fight off, but Sam wouldn't hear of it. He needed the money too badly.

"Don't worry about little Sammy, I don't need to see that boy, I just got to feel him," said Sam.[4]

A report after the fight indicated that Savage was so afraid of Sam that he was noticeably trembling as he waited in his corner.

Savage was extremely cautious as the fight began, running around the ring and making sure to keep his distance. Sam struggled to follow his movements around the ring.

Periodically, Sam would get a bearing on Savage's location then rush him in an attempt to corner him. He failed miserably for a time, but eventually he managed to catch Savage near the ropes and successfully measure him for a right uppercut that landed on his chin.

---

[2] *Beloit Daily News,* 31 March 1923

[3] *The Nova Scotia Historical Quarterly,* Vol. 4 No. 3, September 1974

[4] *Halifax Herald,* 18 September 1924

That punch knocked out Savage, one minute and forty-five seconds into the round.

And just like that, Sam was the heavyweight champion of Mexico. A number of fans climbed into the ring and lifted the obviously pleased and smiling new champion on their shoulders. The crowd roared its approval. Sam was widely praised for his performance by both the crowd and the promoter, who promised to line up a match between him and the champion of Spain.

In his dressing room, a very happy Langford exclaimed, "This is a great place. I'm gonna stay here where's I's the champion."[5]

Sam didn't get to rest on his laurels for long. He defended his new crown eight days later, April 8th, against a 220-pound Spanish champion and ex-bullfighter, named Andres Balsas. Balsas, born in Barcelona in 1896, had fought in thirty-one fights and scored nineteen knockouts. One reporter told his readers that in appearance Balsas looked more like a strongman than a fighter. George Lawrence, an American promoter who first spotted Balsas, said that the big man had a chest like the one that Tom Sharkey used to display: 45" expanded. Balsas stood 6'0" tall and had a reach of 74".

Sam suffered a knockdown in the fifth round, but Balsas quit in the next round, claiming he was unable to continue due to a broken wrist.

The new champion of Mexico was a fighting champion. Within two months, he fought five bouts, knocking out, in rapid succession: Chihuahua Brown, third round, on April 13th; Andres Balsas, third round, on May 6th; Art Surans, third round, on May 16th; Jack Voigt, eleventh round, on May 19th; and Jim Tracey, fourth round, on June 15th.

Sam's winning streak and Mexican heavyweight title reign came to an abrupt end on July 27th in Juarez, Mexico. He was matched against a younger, taller, and heavier opponent named Clem Johnson. Sam had defeated Johnson 2½years earlier, in December 1920, in a six-round decision. Clem was then twenty-three years old. Johnson was now riding an eight-match losing streak, and Sam's fighting abilities and eyesight had significantly deteriorated since their last match.

---

[5] *Boxing Blade*, 14 April 1923

Clem was the aggressor with his left almost immediately after the opening bell, and he won the vast majority, if not all, of the first twelve rounds. By the start of the thirteenth round, Johnson's left hand had landed often enough that even Sam's "good" eye was of no use to him. One minute and twenty-five seconds into the round, unable to see his young foe anymore, Sam admitted the futility of the task before him. Turning his back on Clem, he headed to his corner while motioning to the referee that he was through. His four month reign as Mexico's heavyweight champion was over.

Still he was back in the ring six days later against "Fireman" Jim Flynn in Mexico City. Three months earlier, Flynn—speaking to a newspaperman about the game's hardest hitters—had said:

> "If you ask me, I'll say that the hardest hitter I ever went up against was Sam Langford. I fought most of the heavyweights of the last twenty years, Jack Johnson among them, and I think Langford could knock a fellow colder than any of them. It was like being hit with a baseball bat. He hit you so hard you didn't feel it. It was like taking ether—you just went to sleep and you didn't know anything about it until you woke up."[6]

But the Langford who Flynn glowingly described was from the past. When the two aged ring warriors faced one another in August of 1923, Sam defeated the forty-three-year-old "Fireman" in a dull ten-round contest.

It was a full two months before Sam climbed back into the ring to tackle Jim Flynn on October 19th, again before a Mexico City crowd. Sam made quick work of Flynn this time, knocking him out in the third round.

It was becoming more frequent at this point in his career for people to ask Sam when he planned to hang up his mitts. One newspaperman bluntly asked whether he didn't have any plans to retire from the ring, since it must be clear to Sam that he wasn't as good a fighter as he once was. Replied Sam:

> "Say, does a tennis player retire cause he's beaten? No sir! Do they send a horse out to pasture cause he loses two or three

---

[6] *Washington Post*, 6 May 1923

races? Do you quit playing billiards cause you is beaten once in a while? Why should I retire when I can whip so many more men than can whip me?

"To stop a punch once in a while doesn't hurt me. When everybody's whipping me, I'll retire. But I'm not going to quit so long as there's so many dubs that think they're good."[7]

Sam concluded the year with another knockout of Andres Balsas on November 14th, and a ten-round decision loss against Sam Goodrich in San Antonio, Texas on December 21st. There is also an unconfirmed report that he knocked out Kid Roscoe in Mexico City on December 11th.

As 1924 began, Sam found that he was still in demand in Mexico so he agreed to meet Jim Flynn again, this time in Juarez on January 6th. He earned an eight round decision. He returned to Juarez two weeks later to knock out Tom Riley in two rounds.

At this point in Sam's career it's difficult to confirm all of his fights. There is reason to believe that he fought a number of fights that never found their way into the record books. He served as the referee for a fight card held at the Ventura Athletic Club in California on April 2nd, and then his next two officially recorded fights took place in San Fernando, California against a fighter named Jim "Jam" Barry—not the Chicago heavyweight—whom he defeated by four round decision on April 4th and fought a no-contest bout against on April 16th. He fought again two days later against Sam Olson in Bakersfield, California and was awarded a four-round decision by the ringside judges. Around this time, Sam's former manager, George Lawrence, was quoted as saying that Sam was destitute and threatened with total blindness. *The Halifax Chronicle* reported that when the contest with Olson ended, Sam groped his way to his corner, feeling along the ropes.

Summarizing the bout, *The Vancouver Sun* reported:

> Sam Langford, hero of many ring engagements was awarded the decision over Sammy Olson of Los Bancos, here last night after four rounds of mediocre fighting. Langford was fat

---

[7] *Halifax Chronicle*, 5 December 1923

and slow on his feet and was utterly lacking in ability to land his onetime famous knockout punch.[8]

The day after the fight, *The Halifax Herald* said:

> Sam Langford, Negro boxer, is blind in one eye and will lose sight of the other unless he is able to raise money for an operation, it was learned today. Efforts are being made to arrange a benefit. "Sam made a fortune and actually gave it away to fellows who were down and out," a friend declared, "and now he is broke and going blind."[9]

On April 28th, the *Nevada State Journal* reported that Sam was going to be taken to New York City where Dr. James Smith, one of the nation's noted eye specialists, was going to perform an operation to attempt to save the sight of Sam's good eye. Smith had volunteered to pay all expenses.

Sam's manager during part of 1920-1922, Frank Tessin, confirmed what was becoming common knowledge regarding Sam's poor eyesight: he said that they had kept silent about Sam's blind eye. "It would never do to let his opponents know that weakness," Tessin said.

Commenting on Sam's financial situation, the *Journal* added:

> Sam is broke. He fights anybody, anywhere, just to exist. The money he had, said to be as much as $30,000 at one time, is gone. Sam gave much of it to other down and out fighters, like he himself is now.

Said Tessin, "The rest, Sam squandered. Most of it he lost because there were too many aces and sixes on the dice."[10]

Sam obviously should have called it a career long before, but he wasn't ready to hang 'em up. He agreed to another fight, this time in Los Angeles, where they tried to help him out by giving him someone soft in another four-rounder, but as Sam would say later:

> "Nobody is soft if you're trying to fight without hardly any sight because you can't see where the punches are coming from or where to throw yours. By that time my right eye was so bad

---

[8] *Vancouver Sun,* 19 April 1924
[9] *Halifax Herald,* 19April 1924
[10] *Nevada State Journal,* 28 April 1924

I knew that it was crazy for me to keep on fighting, even if I starved by not fighting. So I decided I'd fight just one more."

They matched Sam with a younger fighter out of Bangor, Maine named Eddie Trembley. It looked hopeless for Sam, as he was peppered throughout the first round without being able to mount a significant counterattack. In Sam's words, "I couldn't find that Trembley, and he hit me a hundred punches."[11]

In the second round, Sam managed to get the younger man into a clinch and let loose a wallop that landed on Trembley's chin, lifting him off his feet and sending him sprawling across the ropes. Sam knew he'd hurt him. One more solid blow and he was sure he would finish him. But once he knocked him into the ropes, he lost sight of him. A sportswriter who knew of Sam's failing eyesight was sitting at ringside and recalled that when Sam knocked Trembley into the ropes it was obvious he couldn't see him. He watched Sam turn slowly around trying to find Trembley and wildly swinging his arms. He continued to flail about with furious left and right swings, but it was no use. He couldn't find him, and in a few moments the opportunity was lost. Trembley recovered and stayed out of harm's way for the remainder of the round.

Trembley came out fresh for the third round and landed upon Sam at will, while Sam tried desperately to get in range to tie him up. But Sam could no longer move as he had in his youth, and the problem with his eyesight only compounded the problem. When the round ended, his cornerman, Danny Goodman, urged Sam to let him put a stop to it.

"Sam, this is murder. It's got to stop. I'm going to throw in the sponge," said Danny.

"No, I'll get through this fourth (and last) round alright," said Sam.

And he did. But Sam figured he had received as many punches in that final round as he ever took in an entire fight, his whole career.[12]

The Chicago Defender reported that the only time Sam could really defend himself was when he was in a clinch.[13] Trembley was awarded the decision. When Sam removed his gloves he figured his fighting

---

[11] *Halifax Herald*, 18 September 1924

[12] *Halifax Herald*, 18 September 1924

[13] *Chicago Defender*, 3 May 1924

days were over, and for awhile it looked as if they were. He didn't fight again in 1924 (although there are some unconfirmed reports of bouts in Mexico City between July and October, as well as during the first five months of the following year).

On May 1st, *The New York Times* reported that James J. Johnston (boxing promoter and manager, as well as National Sports Alliance President) had announced his intention of petitioning the State Athletic Commission to sanction a boxing show benefit for Sam, who was reportedly destitute. Johnston announced that if the show was approved, proceeds would be placed in a trust for Sam in order to insure him a steady future income.

After his career had ended, Sam offered his own perspective on the issue:

> "In my day I earned a lot of money. I don't know just how much. Maybe it was $500,000. When you first see that you think it an awful lot and figure I ought to have a pile of it left. But, boys, I haven't any of it left and I don't think I was what folks can call extravagant with it, either.
>
> "My manager got his share of that $500,000. Let's say his cut was 25%, about $125,000, which sounds like much but it's little as regards what other managers got. Through the years I had to pay trainers and handlers and also their expenses, training camp bills. I guess I spent $100,000 that way, which isn't big when you remember it was spread over twenty-three years. Any top notch fighter who can operate on $4,500 a year for trainers, etc. is mighty economical.
>
> "Sometimes my traveling expenses were paid. Most of the time they weren't. I guess I spent about $25,000 that way and I had friends who were 'broke' and they needed money and another $50,000 went to them.
>
> "Those expenses or gifts took away $300,000 and left me $200,000. Divide that by twenty-three years and you find that in all my fighting lifetime I didn't average much more than $9,000 a year, and I had to spend some of that treating friends.
>
> "Yes, I earned about $500,000 but all I got out of it was $9,000 a year, and I was in a profession where a man had to be a fairly liberal spender to get along and where he was nearly

always the boy who had to grab the dinner checks and pay them."[14]

When he had money, Sam knew how to spend it, but not all of his earnings were spent for pleasure. He invested but lost considerable sums in bad real estate investments in Boston. Altogether, he bought three homes in Boston. He turned them all over to his wife under a separation agreement in late 1915.

"The biggest money I ever got for a fight was about $10,000 for meeting 'Iron' Hague in London. The next biggest was $7,500 when Hugh McIntosh paid me in Australia for one of the festivals there. I just don't remember top money in this country (United States), but it was around $3,000, and I think that came through fighting 'Gunboat' Smith the second time in Boston.

"I once fought Joe Jennette on percentage in a house where the gate was only a few hundred dollars. I boxed in New Orleans on percentage for a Negro promoter and it drew only $75.00 and I got one fourth of that. Very often I got no more than $150 or $200 for my fights. And that wasn't only at the beginning, but also in the last few years of my career.

"From 1916 to 1924, I fought about 120 battles and my total earnings for those fights were around $110,000, which is about $900 a fight. And that's less than a lot of bum preliminary fighters got although during that time I was fighting, or willing to fight, the greatest ring men in the world.

"Yes, little Sammy is broke. And little Sammy is more than half blind. But I'm not complaining about it. That's the way things go. You either win or you lose. I've lost in fights and nobody heard me doing an awful lot of crying about it. If I lose now in the fight to save the last bit of sight, well, I just lose, that's all.

"Whatever does happen, I still can do a lot of laughing even if I can't see and my pockets are flapping around in the wind. I can laugh about some of those funny things that happened to me in my fighting days."[15]

---

[14] *Halifax Herald,* 20 September 1924
[15] *Halifax Herald,* 20 September 1924

Sam had a reputation for helping out any fighter who was down on his luck. His complete disregard for money was a source of amazement to those around him. Sam would collect a $5,000 purse one night and the next morning be out scrounging for another fight, in all probability broke.

A writer for the Sydney, Australia paper *The Referee* recalled that when Sam was in town he thought nothing of buying a round for the patrons of his favorite bar time after time:

> His favorite haunt was the Tivoli Hotel. There he would entertain all who laughed at his quips and drank his booze as fast as he liked to buy it. The muster was always so big around where Sam was that one required the Bank of England to follow the pace. Still "Little Tham" liked company and kept on buying.[16]

Sam was also a man who paid his debts. A west coast ring announcer known as "Megaphone" Cook attested to this in a July 19, 1925 issue of the *Los Angeles Times*. Prior to departing for Australia in November, 1911, Sam had accumulated a debt of $7.00 to "Megaphone." While in Australia, he informed Woodman of the monies owed and sent payment to the announcer in San Francisco, but the funds were returned when they went undelivered. When Sam returned to San Francisco in the summer of 1913, "Megaphone" was one of the first men he looked up, specifically for the purpose of paying off his debt.[17]

On May 10th, George E. Bower, chairman of the boxing board, responded to Jimmy Johnston's proposal and countered with one of his own based upon an idea from William Muldoon. Muldoon had suggested that the proceeds from an upcoming Langford boxing show (June 19th at Henderson's Bowl in Brooklyn, New York) be used to form the basis of a trust fund that would serve a broader need: he proposed a portion of proceeds go to pay for Langford's needs and that the remainder be placed in a trust for broken boxers, their widows and dependents, and other unfortunates who had been left destitute as a result of the passing of some great fighter.

On May 23rd, Sam arrived in New York City to undergo the eye

---

[16] *The Referee*, Sydney, Australia 11 December 1924
[17] *Los Angeles Times*, 19 July 1925

operation by Dr. James W. Smith. Dr. Smith would remove a cataract and preserve the sight of his right eye. The next day, Leach Cross, former contender for the lightweight championship of the world, offered to meet any 133 to 135 pound boxer on the Pacific Coast in a match for the benefit of Sam. Other boxers also volunteered their services.

Sam visited the eye specialist on May 26th for an examination and some preliminary treatment. After Sam had been under examination for almost three hours, the specialist placed a liquid in Sam's right eye. Sam was then walked from the dark room to the operating room. For a time Sam blinked in the light that poured through a window.

"Sam, can you see anything?" asked the doctor.

"I can and I can't, because I see a blur of light," answered Sam.

"Well, you're facing a strong light. I'd expect the blur. Turn your back on that window and see what you can see," said the doctor.

Sam turned as directed. Facing a large glass cabinet fourteen feet away he looked wonderingly, and gradually his face lighted up into a wondrous smile.

"What do you see Sam?" asked the doctor.

"I see a big bookcase full of bandages," said Langford. "Golly, boys, I can see!"

Object after object was pointed out and Langford identified them.

"Sam," said the doctor, slapping Langford on the back, "we've got along pretty well for the first examination. You come back here Tuesday. This fluid is making you see for the first time. You'll not be able to see at all in a day or so, but that is to be expected under the circumstances. Tuesday I will know whether we can help your eye without an operation. It may take a double operation to remove the cataract. I may have to go in above the eye and remove it. Again, it may respond to the treatment I have just given it, in which case we won't have to cut."

"I'd love that last though I'm not a coward, doctor," replied Sam with a laugh.

"Now we're going out in the street, Sam," the doctor told him.

The doctor followed Sam down to the sidewalk. He seemed as happy about the good start at restoring Sam's vision as the old warrior was himself. Then Woodman and Sam started to walk to Broadway. Sam would not be led. "I can see, Joe. I can see boy. Don't lead me, I can see."

The two walked to the corner where Sam turned and went into a cigar store. He purchased a long cigar. Then he got into a cab with Woodman. On the way downtown to Woodman's office Sam laughed like a schoolboy: "Goodness me! I can write my girl in Los Angeles now and tell her that I saw the doctor, saw him for sure, saw the yellow cab and ..."

Here Woodman still wondering about Sam's sight, pointed out of the cab window and asked, "What's that in front of us Sam?"

"That's a big oil truck and it's painted red!" replied Sam, and he lay back and laughed till he fairly shook.

Joe Woodman said afterwards that he had never known Langford to be so happy:

"I knew the doctor had worked wonders in this first treatment," said Woodman, "but I was certain of it when Sam pointed out the big red oil truck. It was good to hear the old fellow laugh with joy. Say, he had me swallowing a dozen Adam's apples. It's all just fine. I didn't believe that you would bring as much happiness into a man's life. It was well worthwhile."[18]

On June 5th, the press reported that Sam's recent surgery, performed for free at New York's French Hospital by Dr. James Smith—an admirer of Sam's when he was in his prime—had proved a success. Sam had checked into the hospital under the name of "Joseph Price" to try and prevent drawing attention to himself.

A few days later Sam left the hospital on his own and said:

"It's wonderful to be able to take a man out of the darkness. There must be some satisfaction for the Doc in that. He's a marvelous man. You've all made me the happiest man in the

---

[18] *Halifax Chronicle*, 27 May 1924

world. Only a man who has lost his sight and had it brought back to him can understand how I feel. Just bless you all."[19]

A 1935 reference to this 1924 operation indicates that the surgery may have involved more than the removal of a cataract. That later article says that Dr. Smith operated to draw together a muscular fold in the retina of the eye.

There are a number of conditions that can increase the chance of a detached retina, including severe trauma, which can easily be experienced from blows to the head like those Sam was subjected to throughout his career. It is a serious problem that almost always leads to blindness unless it is treated, and it's quite likely that this is what Sam suffered in his bout with Fred Fulton in 1917.

Sam was back in Chicago three weeks later. He announced that he could see perfectly with the right eye. *The Chicago Defender* reported that Sam was going to be a boxing instructor, but there was some confusion as to exactly where he'd be providing this instruction. One day the press reported that he'd be providing instruction out of a billiard parlor on Cottage Grove Avenue co-owned by a man named George Wilson. A few days later, they were reporting that Sam would be given a lifetime position as boxing instructor by Kid Howard, the owner of Howard's Gym—better known as the Arcade.[20] The latter proved to be true.

There had been talk of putting on a local benefit on Sam's behalf for a number of months. Finally, a man named Percy Brown stepped forward to promote the event. He went so far as to offer to pay for all acts and expenses if necessary. As it turned out, the performers joined together and provided their services for free at the Lafayette Theater on August 23rd.

On September 6th, Sam left for the West Coast, while another benefit was being planned. On September 13th, *The Chicago Defender* reported that a huge benefit and testimonial for Sam was planned by Col. Patton of the Eighth Illinois infantry, Grant Frazier, and "Roughhouse" Wilson. It would be held the night of September 23rd at the local armory, which had been donated for the event. Members

---

[19] *Davenport Democrat and Leader*, 10 June 1924
[20] *Chicago Defender*, 28 June 1924

of the theatrical profession as well as a number in the field of sport agreed to perform for free. Sam's former adversary, Jack Johnson was reportedly trying to arrange his schedule so he could participate. Many of Chicago's white citizens came forward to help insure the show's success, including Kid Howard, owner of Howard's Gym, and Jim Mullen, owner of Mullen's Gym. The paper urged fans to attend and show their appreciation to:

> a man who has carried the race's color to all parts of the globe, a man who in the boxing ring was feared by all and a man who has won the race many friends in all parts of the globe.[21]

It was claimed that every dollar above the actual expenses to put on the show would be turned over to Sam.

The event went off as planned, though not without some controversy. An article written by Frank Young appeared in *The Defender* four days afterward complaining that the public had been intentionally led to believe that Harry Wills was going to make an appearance, and that the handbills advertising the event listed a number of men in the community as event officials, when they had only promised to aid a good cause. Young claimed that Sam had played a part in the deception.[22]

In June of 1925, Sam made it known that he was short on funds and more than happy to sell his memories to anyone willing to pay $100-$200. It is unknown whether he had any takers on this offer.

While visiting family and friends over the holidays in Weymouth Falls at the end of 1925, Sam provided an interview to *The Halifax Herald*. During the interview he spoke of a planned comeback in the ring. The reporter wrote:

> Sam Langford, the Boston Tar Baby, whose career in the prize ring was brilliant, promises a comeback. Langford's title is now professor, for he is a professor of boxing and "the manly art," as he says, in Kid Howard's gymnasium on West Madison Street in Chicago, where he may be seen daily. If the title does not cling to him it will not be his fault, for he has consistently refused to go the easiest way, the panhandling mooching way of Kid Broad and many others.

---

[21] *Chicago Defender*, 20 September 1924
[22] *Chicago Defender*, 27 September 1924

But Sam won't do it. Easily as he might frequent Chicago's dark belt, taking dimes and drinks from the men in all walks of life who frequent it and who know him personally or by reputation, he won't do it. But he still has the old Langford spirit and the Tar Baby pride and he won't beg nor mooch nor panhandle, and so he's on the comeback.[23]

There are unconfirmed reports of Sam participating in a number of bouts in Mexico during 1925, fighting the likes of Wolf Larsen, Jack Taylor, Frolin Gonzales, and Jim Briggs. The only official bout in the record books is a December 7th contest in Fort Bliss, Texas, in which he and a fighter by the name of Tim Sullivan fought to a six-round draw.

---

[23] *Halifax Herald*, 9 January 1926

Sam Langford greeting Italian heavyweight Erminio Spallo

December 17, 1925

Author's Collection

"HE'S THE MOST ENTERTAINING TALKER OF ANY RING MAN I'VE EVER MET, AND I'VE ENCOUNTERED A FEW."

~SAM HUGHES

CHAPTER 22

RETIREMENT

In 1926, at age forty, Sam attempted a comeback. On July 1st in Shawnee, Oklahoma he knocked out Young Jack Johnson in two rounds. His comeback ended a month later on August 2nd in Drumright, Oklahoma when he suffered a technical knockout to Brad Simmons. Simmons was a mediocre black fighter whom Sam had easily beaten only a few years earlier. The fight was stopped after Sam received a blow that injured his good eye and made it impossible for him to see.

Simmons' brother was quoted as saying that Brad had been resentful of the treatment he'd received by Sam in their fight in 1922, so he poked him in his good eye shortly after this fight started.[1] Once Sam couldn't see, the referee stepped in and stopped the fight, awarding it to Simmons on a technical knockout. It turned out to be Sam's last official ring appearance. He was finally finished as a professional pugilist.

With his own career over, Sam returned to Chicago where he resumed working with younger fighters in Kid Howard's gym.

In August, he traveled to Buffalo, New York with a couple of his protégés: a heavyweight named Joe Boykin, and "Bad" Jeff Baulknight, a light heavyweight. They were slated to fight in Bison Stadium for the Queensberry Club. Sam was asked by a reporter from the *Buffalo*

---

[1] Glenn Stout. "Fighting Blind." *Boston*, February 1987

Courier Express for his thoughts on the upcoming heavyweight title match between the current champion, Jack Dempsey, and the challenger, Gene Tunney. Sam replied:

> "I do not care to predict the outcome of this match, for I have never seen Gene Tunney in my life, let alone do any boxing. Dempsey, I have seen up on more than one occasion. I cannot say whether the long layoff will have harmed Dempsey sufficiently enough to make him a victim to Tunney, for as I say, I really don't know how good Tunney is.
>
> "What I do think, however, is that Jack Dempsey ought to give Harry Wills a chance at the title. By not doing so, I believe he shows he is somewhat afraid of Wills. It proves it to me by the fooling around he has done with Harry. First, he goes West and signs up with Floyd Fitzsimmons to box Wills and then he comes back East and signs up with Rickard for a bout with Tunney. I guess he doesn't care for any of Harry's game, else he would give the man who has been chosen as the logical contender for his title a chance with him."

The gathering pressed Sam to share stories about some of his most important fights, but he declined. One man—excitedly telling others about Sam at the same time Sam was being interviewed—was making it difficult for Sam and the reporter to hear each other. Sam put a stop to that by turning towards the man and saying, "Hyah friend, we can all sing together, but we can't all talk together."[2]

Sam had high hopes for his two fighters, and they received considerable press in the weeks leading up to their contests. It was noted that "Bad" Jeff had boxed the great middleweight "Tiger" Flowers four times, along with Tommy Loughran and Chuck Wiggins, and also claimed a victory over Jock Malone. He was reportedly battering his sparring partners all over the ring. Boykin, it was said, could claim victories over such noted men as George Godfrey and Luis Firpo.

However, there is no evidence whatsoever in any record books to back up these claims. One can only assume they were made with the intent of building up the gate. Sam accepted several bets at odds of 1:2 that both his men would score knockouts.

The fights proved disappointing on the whole. Boykin emerged

---

[2] *Buffalo Courier Express*, 9 August 1926

victorious with a third round technical knockout over Art Fairbanks, but Baulknight was far from impressive and suffered a ten-round decision loss against a local Italian light heavyweight by the name of Lou Scozza. Baulknight's performance was especially poor, the local headline reading "Black Hides As Italian Seeks Fight," that reporter theorizing that "Bad" Jeff must have left all of his badness down in Memphis.

The crowd (which wasn't anything to write home about) was apparently drawn in to see the celebrated Boston Tar Baby more than anything else. That was the opinion of the *Buffalo Evening News,* based on the tremendous response Sam received when introduced in the ring before the evening's entertainment.[3] It was clear to all that Sam was not going to benefit much in the future from either of his fighters.

Sam made the news again when he was found drunk and disoriented in Boston and was arrested on September 13th. He was released the next day on probation because of his "good name."[4]

A month later, Sam was credited with helping a young twenty-four-year-old future heavyweight champion, Jack Sharkey, defeat thirty-seven-year-old Harry Wills. To most, it may have appeared that it was simply a matter of youth being served—Wills was certainly past his prime—but those in the know were aware that wasn't the whole story.

Sharkey's handlers felt it was important that nothing be overlooked in the preparation of their man. They thought about how to help ensure a victory that would advance his career and, knowing that Sam had faced Wills many times, they thought he might be of use. When the match between the pair was set, they contacted Langford. It was a wise decision on their part. While Wills had ultimately been able to conquer the aging Langford, Sam always knew what it took to defeat Wills. For weeks prior to the October 12th contest, Sam schooled Sharkey in Wills' weaknesses and helped him develop a plan to defeat the older man.

By the date of the fight, Sam was convinced that Sharkey would win. He rounded up what little money he could place his hands on

---

[3] *Buffalo Evening News,* 26 August 1926

[4] Tim Leone. *Blind, Broke, and Black.* Privately published, no date.

and bet it all on the younger fighter.[5] He was in Sharkey's corner in Ebbett's Field in Brooklyn, New York that night, and Jack didn't let him down, winning in the thirteenth round when Wills was disqualified for excessive holding.

Two months later, it was reported that Sam was trying to scrape up $500 in order to open a shoeshine stand. In his words, he would then "be fixed for the rest of [his] life."[6] He appealed to the National Sports Alliance, requesting the funds be provided from money that had been raised during the 1924 benefit show in Brooklyn. He didn't have much luck initially, and it was suggested that his situation would need to be reviewed by the boxing commission. As Sam was led away from the office of an individual connected with the 1924 promotion by a friend, Sam remarked, "I'm not much good around gymnasiums anymore. One eye is gone, the other is going and about the only time I make any money is when some of the boys pass me a handout."

That December it was announced that a number of New England's "Negro" boxers had expressed their willingness to participate in the bouts the athletic commission sanctioned for the benefit of Sam Langford, "in order to help him raise the necessary funds for a shoe-shining business."[7] A New York based columnist, Joe Williams, came out shortly thereafter and disputed the notion that Sam would use the funds from a benefit to open a shoe shining business, saying simply that "It was too late for Sam to learn any new footwork."[8]

Sam continued to work with fighters to earn a living. At that time he was acting as a trainer and advisor to Homer Robertson, a Boston middleweight champion. Robertson was reportedly one among a number of black boxers who had volunteered to take part in the benefit show. Others included Chick Suggs, a featherweight out of New Bedford; George Robinson and Jack Townsend.

A few weeks later, newspaper columnist Ed Hughes, wrote a tribute in the paper about Sam and the benefit being staged on the 19th. When he interviewed Sam the day before the benefit, Sam told him,

---

[5] *The Morning Chronicle*, 16 October 1926
[6] *Beloit Daily News*, 17 December 1926
[7] *Daily Kennebec Journal*, 20 December 1926
[8] *The Post Frederick*, 5 January 1927

"I've always smiled when things were coming my way, and I make it a rule to keep smilin' when they forget me. That's the way I take life."

Hughes found Sam to be an enjoyable sort to pass the time with and wrote of him, "He's the most entertaining talker of any ring man I've ever met, and I've encountered a few."[9]

The benefit for Sam was held at New York's Walker Athletic Club. It raised between $5,000-$6,000 and was proclaimed the most successful benefit for a fighter since one given for "Terrible" Terry McGovern at Madison Square Garden, when the former champion was down on his luck. Sam, wearing darkened glasses, was led into the ring to rousing cheers on the arm of Joe Jennette, who wept openly once the cheers had died. Ring announcer Joe Humphreys addressed the crowd saying, "Sam's skin is black, but I defy anyone to find a man with a whiter heart." He then offered Sam an opportunity to speak. Sam, overcome with emotion, was unable to do so and whispered to Humphrey, who then advised the gathering that Sam wished to express his appreciation to everyone in attendance. A number of fighters—including Eddie Anderson (known as the Wyoming Cowboy), Izzy Grove, and "Canada" Lee—provided their services for free, as did the club's ushers, officials, and the club's owner, Eddie Koven.[10]

Sam appealed to the commission to turn over the entire proceeds of the benefit to him in a lump sum. In late February, the word was that he wanted the money to open a training camp in New England, but the commission refused—thinking it would be unwise for Sam in his present physical condition, with his failing eyesight. His needs would be better served by the establishment of a trust fund from which he could receive a monthly income. They set aside the funds with a $75.00 per month payment going to Sam. Sam accused the commission of "holding out" on him.

Sam persisted. By late March of 1927, the New York Boxing Commission announced that they had been so pestered by Sam that they had voted to turn it all over to him.

On June 9th, an article appeared in the paper in which George W. Harris, treasurer of the Langford Benefit Committee, stated that

---

[9] Ed Hughes. "Ed Hughes Tribute to Sam Langford," unknown newspaper source, 19 January 1927
[10] *Beloit Daily News*, 20 January 1927

he and William Muldoon had issued Sam a check in the amount of $4,724.22. Harris added:

> "Those who know Sam think the money won't last a year with him. Two years ago, a benefit was given for him at the Lafayette Theatre, and two years later it was necessary to give another benefit."[11]

In mid-June, Sam defended himself in a letter to the editor of *The Pittsburgh Courier.* It read as follows:

> I wish to state the naming of George W. Harris as treasurer and William Muldoon as trustee was not in accordance with my wishes. Muldoon ran a benefit for me in New York in 1924, which netted $8,900. I never received any of this amount. So why should I let him act as trustee for the last benefit?
>
> George Harris, self-elected treasurer, was paid off the day after the fight. I asked him how much his expenses were and he told me they were fifty dollars. I paid him there and then. They decided to pay me seventy-five dollars a month; until the amount of the benefit was used up. I am forty-one years old and am not a native of Oklahoma and do not need a guardian. Would you ask Mr. Harris where I could live on $75 a month and would he be willing to go there?
>
> Yes, P.A. Brown did run a benefit for me in Lafayette theatre in 1924. I received $445. Percy Brown did give me that. I guess George Harris wanted a percentage of that money.
>
> Concerning the money realized at the last benefit (in 1924), I received $4,724.22. I was entitled to it. The benefit was for me. However, I didn't receive it until I had taken the matter to court, costing me $300. That in all probability is what Mr. Harris didn't like.
>
> At the present time, I have at Cambridge, MA, 550 Mass Avenue, the Air Castle Gymnasium which represents some of the money I received in New York. I am giving boxing lessons and physical culture exercises to seventy-five members. This gives me sufficient income to care for my everyday needs. As a matter of fact it looks very promising for the future. You will please note in your paper that there remains at all times a

---

[11] *Pittsburgh Courier,* 9 June 1927

standing invitation for Mr. William Muldoon and Mr. George Harris to take a course in physical culture or boxing lessons (mostly boxing lessons) absolutely free at my gymnasium. They announced at the ring side that the benefit netted $6,000, and when I went to New York for the money it had decreased to $5,000, when I got it was $4,724.22. All this depreciation in three months. If I had left it another three months I would no doubt have received what Paddy shot at—nothing. Well nevertheless old friend, sporting writer, I am here living the life of Reilly, and as happy as sand flies in June. This is not George Byers' gym, but is mine.[12]

Shortly thereafter, Mr. Percy Brown responded to Sam's letter with one of his own, sent to the editor of *The Pittsburgh Courier.*

In justice to Mr. Harris and also to give, the true facts which Mr. Langford's letter does not mention, allow me to say the following:

It was due largely to my request and urging that Mr. Harris interested himself in the matter, bringing it to the attention of the white daily papers and ensuring publicity it received.

As is known, Mr. Muldoon is the commissioner and has charge of all such affairs and it was within his power to appoint whom he chose as treasurer. He naturally considered Mr. Harris as being the best man for the position, he being a prime mover in the affair.

In regards to the amount of money the benefit netted and the amount Langford received, I have this to say. Six of the fighters appearing on the bill received amounts varying from $250 to $400, making a total of $2,062. For the printing of the tickets and other printing, $125; for the state tax $307.30. Sam himself received an initial payment of $328.50 and for sums I advanced him, I received $160. All these monies were paid by check, signed by Mr. Muldoon and countersigned by Mr. Harris and deducted from the funds. As for the $50 Mr. Harris received, it was no tin payment for his service, as he made no charge for that, but in payment of expenses he incurred in Langford's behalf.

---

[12] *Pittsburgh Courier,* June 1927

> I hope I have stated the facts clearly and deeply regret that Langford would be so unsportsmanlike as to make unjust insinuations against one who helped to make it possible for him to receive what he did.[13]

In May of 1928, Sam made a number of boxing exhibition appearances in Halifax, Nova Scotia. He appeared in the Halifax Hippodrome on May 22nd with a boxer named Joseph Hartnett and received a presentation at ringside. *The Halifax Chronicle's* account of the event the next day indicated that Sam looked like a huge rubber ball, and that while he exhibited many tricks, he paid close attention to the timer in order to ensure that he didn't exceed the allotted time of two minutes per round.

Once he and Hartnett finished sparring, Sam entertained the crowd with short summaries of some of his best fights. *The Chronicle* reporter wrote that Sam had a humorous way of storytelling, which had to be heard to be fully appreciated.[14]

On May 29th, *The Chronicle's* sports editor, W.J. Foley, stated that he had interviewed Sam the previous day. Foley said Sam was still active in the ring and that any night that week could be seen at the Lynch shows at the North Commons providing sparring exhibitions. The Lynch Shows included joy rides, a merry-go-round, and other popular attractions. Sam continued to provide these exhibitions in connection with the Lynch Shows through the months of July and August, while also occasionally serving as a referee for small town boxing contests.

On July 26th, *The Moncton Daily* shared Sam's views about the upcoming heavyweight title bout between the champion, Gene Tunney, and challenger Tom Heeney of New Zealand, as well as his opinion of the champion as a fighter:

> "Don't look for a knockout, I expect Tunney to win on points, with the fight going to the limit. This is the day of the big money fighters, or what I would call running boxers. In the old days it was stand up and fight, but the old order has changed. Today, it seems to be, how much can I get out of a fight. Take back in the days of Corbett, Fitzsimmons, Sullivan, Johnson,

---

[13] *Pittsburgh Courier,* June 1927

[14] *Halifax Chronicle,* 24 May 1928

although Johnson is the man I chased over half the American continent, but all of these fighters stood up and fought, instead of running around the ring or falling into clinches.

"If Tunney had been in the ring in the years gone by, he would not have had a chance against the fighters we had in those days. Dempsey to my mind is still the champion of the world. He is my idea of a fighter, as he carried the battle to his opponent and never did back away.

"These fighters we have today are mere boxers, with the leading boxers getting the decision. It was not like that in the old days. A man had to be a fighter, and he had to be a good fighter to get up among the top notchers. I pick Tunney to win on points, as I do not consider that Heeney can reach him to administer the knockout punch. Tunney cannot administer a knockout to such a man as Heeney, but he can outbox him."[15]

On July 26th, Gene Tunney retained his heavyweight title with a twelfth-round technical knockout of Heeney. Tunney subsequently announced his retirement from the ring.

Prior to the fight, a writer named Ed Sullivan wrote a piece that *The Afro-American Ledger* ran about Gene Tunney's magnificent training headquarters for the bout. Sullivan said that (former lightweight champion) Johnny Dundee took a long look at Tunney's training facilities and remarked, "If they turned Sam Langford loose in a camp like this and let him train for three months he could have licked every heavyweight that ever came up the pike, in one night."[16]

Dundee gave Sullivan the impression that Sam never trained very strenuously, and took it a step further saying that Sam's training diet typically included a fair amount of gin.

George Godfrey backed that up, sharing a story about catching hell from his manager Jimmy Dougherty one day for breaking training rules. After waiting for Dougherty to conclude his tirade, Godfrey said that he replied, "Yes sir, sure am heap of sense in what you say. Only an exceptional man like Sam Langford could break the training rules and win. Sam was an exceptional man."[17]

---

[15] *Moncton Daily*, 26 July 1928

[16] *Afro-American Ledger*, 21 July 1928

[17] *Afro-American Ledger*, 21 July 1928

Sullivan wrote that it wasn't unusual for Sam to knock down as much as a quart of gin in his dressing room before he went into the ring to tackle an opponent. And that while he didn't require a lot of attention from his seconds in the corner during a contest, one thing he did require of them was that they not forget to tote his gin back to the dressing room once the fight had concluded.

Once the summer carnival shows came to an end, Sam returned to Boston to spend another winter scrounging out a living as best he could. Every once in a while Sam's name would appear in various sports pages around the country, but as his public appearances lessened so did his name in print.

In February of 1929, a heavyweight championship trophy referred to as the "Tunney-Muldoon heavyweight trophy" (after the retired champion and William Muldoon, the Chairman of the New York State Athletic Commission) was produced to award to future heavyweight champions. A committee in charge of the engraving of the trophy initially prompted a minor controversy when they openly debated the merit of including Tommy Burns' name on the trophy, because some parties felt that he hadn't won the title within the ring.

Burns' supporters rushed to his defense, and the committee ultimately decided to include his name on the trophy. The debate spurred one New York writer to voice his opinion that the real injustice concerning the trophy was the fact that Sam Langford's name would not be among that list of champions, having never receiving an opportunity to fight for the title.

W.O. McGeehan, the noted sports columnist for the *New York Herald Tribune* couldn't have agreed more. McGeehan was a huge fan of Gene Tunney's, and considered him the greatest fighter America ever had, except for possibly one man, and that man was Sam Langford.

Later that year, McGeehan wrote that it was his belief that, when in his prime, Sam could have defeated any human being, black or white. He went on to say, however, that the reason for this was because Sam had inherited something from the jungles of his ancestors, the power and coordination of one of the higher apes. Despite his obvious admiration for Sam's fighting abilities, it was fairly easy to read between the lines and recognize that McGeehan must have viewed

Sam as relatively simple minded, but a physical freak of nature with a superior fighting instinct.[18]

Sam made the news again in May of 1931, when he appeared in a Boston courtroom before Judge Michael J. Murray and a large audience as a result of having filed a complaint against a West End taxi driver by the name of Joseph Ziskin. Sam had been struck and knocked down from behind by Ziskin's automobile while attempting to cross a street. Though badly shaken, Sam was not seriously hurt.

Sam said to the judge, "I was struck when my back was turned and I can feel the pain yet. The auto knockout was the second in my career."

Sam went on to explain to the judge that he was almost blind, but that the good people of the West End watched out for him when he crossed the streets. Once Sam was finished, Judge Murray responded that a man was not bound to stay in bed just because his eyesight was poor.

"Pedestrians have rights on the streets which motorists are bound to respect," said the judge.

He went on to say that a man driving an automobile in city traffic had a duty to take into consideration that not every pedestrian was capable of making a ten-foot leap to safety and to drive accordingly.[19]

By June 2nd, Sam was well enough to appear in a ring at the old Howard Theatre in Boston with fifty-eight-year-old Joe Walcott for a boxing exhibition under the management of Jim Toland. Sam would be led into the ring where he and Joe would provide a very tame demonstration of the manly art, while a gentleman regaled the fans over a loudspeaker with tales of their respective past glories. Toland had made arrangements for the two men to give a number of exhibitions throughout the New England area. Afterward, Sam and Joe would often go somewhere where they had some privacy to visit and talk about old times. These appearances continued into the following year.

The 1930s were hard on Sam, just as they were for many others. In 1932, Sam was living in a Harlem tenement, spending much of his time sitting out front (weather permitting) where he would accept

---

[18] *Oakland Tribune*, 4 December 1928
[19] *Digby Courier*, 29 May 1931

handouts from people who wanted to shake his hand or listen to his stories. By April 1933, Sam could often be seen "puttering around half blind, in a hot-foot joint in Harlem."[20]

A year later, a newspaper article briefly mentioned that Sam had fallen into a pattern of touring the eastern provinces of Canada with a tent show during the summers and then returning to the States, where he would survive the winter months with the assistance of handouts and relief payments, like a number of other men at the time as the country suffered through the Depression.

In January of 1935, an article written by Jack Cuddy, titled "Boston Tar Baby Helpless Broke" appeared in various newspapers:

> The blind "Boston Tar Baby" who smashed his way through the rings of the world for twenty-two years like a berserk jungle gorilla, is down, and out, facing eviction from a wretched tenement hotel one week hence.
>
> Forgotten by millions who roared his name across 300 arenas, old "Ho Ho" shuffles about the icy streets of darktown, where he can get a boy to lead him, and pick up bits of food or clothing. Gone are the thousands of dollars he won with his crushing fists.
>
> He was sitting tonight in an old rocking chair in Harlem's municipal food distribution station, a fat old fellow in a tattered overcoat and decadent shoes, with a black cap pulled down over his curly gray wool. His face was that of an ancient chimpanzee, pancaked nose, hammered down brows, and lips punched into permanent blubber. Both ears are cauliflowers and he can scarcely open his eyes.
>
> It wouldn't do any good to open the left one anyhow because Fred Fulton hit Sam on the forehead and severed a cord to the optic nerve back in 1917. Sam fought for seven years with one eye. Now cataracts prevent him from seeing anything more than "shapes and shadows" in daylight.
>
> The food distributing station allows the old battler just enough rations to keep him half alive. "They help's a lot," he explained, "but I has to keep hustling around."
>
> Although existing in abject poverty, the battered Tar Baby,

---

[20] *Frederick Post*, 28 April 1934

at 49, has a wealth of memories. And he has an amazing ability to recall names, places, and dates as he relives his career.

Now for amusement, the old warrior sits in his squalid room and dreams of the good old days. "Sometimes I listen to the radio. No, I don't have one, but all the neighbors has. Don't know what I'll do if they take my room away next week," the old Negro said. "Ain't much heat here, but it's better than freezing in the doorways."[21]

That March, Sam underwent another operation at the Neurological Hospital, Welfare Island. This procedure corrected a detached retina in the right eye. It was performed by Dr. James Smith, the directing ophthalmologist at the hospital and the man who had performed Sam's operation in 1924. Sam, who was living on relief at the time, was described as cheerful and mentally alert, and the report was that he would be remaining in the hospital for a month or more.

On April 24th, *The New York Times* reported that the bandages had been removed from Sam's right eye and the operation had been a success.

Sam couldn't have been happier and had a difficult time finding words to express his feelings. According to reports he just lay on a cot in the hospital and repeated over and over again, "It's wonderful, just wonderful."

Around the same time, it was announced that plans were afoot for Joe Louis to stage a benefit for Sam, to be held in New York that summer. Sam and Joe had become friends. The young heavyweight had helped fund Sam's operation by donating all the proceeds from sparring sessions before his fight with Primo Carnera.

Additionally, it was reported that on April 25th Sam planned to see his first boxing match in more than five years: Louis vs. Carnera on June 25th. Louis defeated the ex-champion Carnera on that date by a technical knockout in the sixth round, and Sam was there to witness it from a front row seat. *The New York Times* wrote that Joe was "a reminder of the one and only Sam Langford.[22]

Joe was a great admirer of Sam's. His trainer, Jack Blackburn, told

---

[21] *Nevada State Journal*, 25 January 1935
[22] *New York Times*, 26 April 1935

him that Sam Langford was the best of those old timers, and Jack had seen them all. Further demonstrating his generosity, Joe also boxed a pair of short sparring exhibitions at the Pioneer Sporting Club in New York during the month of May to benefit Sam.

Sam took advantage of his rediscovered eyesight to observe Joe in training for a match with former heavyweight champion Max Baer, in September of 1935, and correctly forecast the outcome of their September 24th match when he said, "He's just too much for Mr. Baer."[23] Joe knocked Baer out in the fourth round of the contest.

Approximately one week later, the "Barbados Demon," Joe Walcott, met his fate along a quiet road near Massillon, Ohio. He was en route to Los Angeles at the time, accompanied by two young men who had convinced him that he should go there to see if anyone would be interested in making a movie about his life.

When the three men stopped in Massillon to spend the night Joe was refused a room because of his color. The two young men suggested he sleep in the car and gave Joe fifty cents to buy razor blades. It was the last they ever saw of Joe.

After leaving the men, Joe made his way to Dalton, Ohio, approximately ten miles away, where he spent some time in a bar. Very early in the morning, a musician driving home from a job in Massilon failed to see Joe shuffling along the road and struck and killed him.

An undertaker from the town of Dalton was summoned to collect the body. He tried, but could find no one to identify and claim the body. Joe didn't have any identification with him on that last walk. He was buried unidentified.

Some years later, the undertaker remembered only that the deceased had been about 5'0" feet tall, with a very thick neck, long arms, a smashed nose, and a lot of scar tissue around the eyes. In his pockets were found two packages of razor blades and thirty-seven cents.

After the mystery of Joe's disappearance was solved, the funeral home helped locate Joe's gravesite. A collection was taken up to erect a stone marking his final resting place. It read simply, "Joe Walcott, Boxing Champion."

---

[23] *The Daily Times-News*, 16 September 1935

Two months later, Sam lost another bout with an automobile, when he was struck by a taxi on November 18th while crossing a Harlem street not far from where he was living. With his improved sight, Sam had been able to pick up a few odd jobs: he was on his way to work when he attempted to cross against the traffic light. The driver of the oncoming taxi saw him and sounded his horn, but Sam became confused and was unable to avoid being hit.

The driver, one Eustace Eaves, recognized Sam, and immediately picked him up and raced him to the hospital, where it was discovered that he had suffered some internal injuries.

The next day, *The New York Times* published a letter Sam had received from the city's Mayor LaGuardia. The letter read:

> **My Dear Sam, I am counting on you to keep that fighting chin of yours up, and to win another sure victory up there in Harlem Hospital with a clean-cut knockout. I know what it means for a man of your energy to be cooped up. I just got out of a hospital myself a few days ago.**[24]

The mayor also added an invitation for Sam to visit him in City Hall as soon as he was able to leave the hospital.

After his release from the hospital on November 24th, Sam took the mayor up on his invitation and paid him a visit. Sam showed up wearing the same overcoat he'd had on when hit by the taxi, now badly ripped. The mayor inquired after his health, and Sam announced with a big smile that while he was healed, the doctors couldn't do much for the coat. He then confided to the mayor that he was flat broke. LaGuardia instructed him to report to the 369th Infantry Armory at Lenox Avenue and 143rd Street, near his home, where a job would await him.

Sam reported to the Armory on December 5th, but nobody there knew anything about a job for him. After a few phone calls to City Hall it was discovered that Sam had misunderstood the start date of the job. He was ten days too early.

Sam was told to report to the 23rd Street municipal lodging house for a job interviewing men applying for shelter at a salary of $25.00 per week, to be paid from private sources. After December 15th, he

---

[24] *New York Times,* 22 November 1935

would be put on the payroll of the Department of Public Welfare. In a book later written about Mayor LaGuardia, *The Great Mayor Fiorello LaGuardia and the Making of the City of New York*, author Alyn Brodsky wrote that when the mayor learned that Sam would have to wait before the job began, he quietly paid Sam two weeks' salary out of his own pocket.

The following year, a baseball double header was staged at the Polo Grounds on September 20, 1936, by four teams from the Negro National League, with a share of the proceeds to be donated for Sam's benefit. The Pittsburgh Crawfords were matched against the Black Yankees, and the Nashville Elite Giants opposed the Philadelphia Stars before an estimated crowd of 18,000 fans. Former heavyweight champion Jack Dempsey was there along with Olympic gold medalist Jesse Owens, who threw out the ball at the beginning of the second game.

In early 1937, it was reported that Sam was spotted walking slowly along a street in Harlem, New York, hawking pictures of Joe Louis.

After Louis retained his heavyweight title with a tough fifteen-round decision over Wales' Tommy Farr that August, Joe's trainer, Jack Blackburn, told reporters he thought that Negro fighters never really find themselves until they are past age twenty-five. He figured that Louis was at least two years away from his peak. By that time, he said, "he would have Joe," (who was already the word's heavyweight champion mind you) "in Langford's class."

SAM LANGFORD

LISTENING TO HIS RADIO IN A PRIVATE NURSING HOME

NOT LONG BEFORE HIS DEATH.

BEN HAWES COLLECTION

"WHAT YOU WANT TO WRITE ABOUT OLD SAM FOR? HE AIN'T NO GOOD ANY MORE."

~SAM LANGFORD

CHAPTER 23

THE FORGOTTEN MAN

While being interviewed about the prospects of his latest fighter, Ike Williams, in March of 1943, Joe Woodman was asked about Sam. Joe told the questioner that Sam, nearly blind, was working as a night watchman at a New York municipal lodging house.

In early January of 1944, Al Laney, a sportswriter for the *New York Herald Tribune*, wanted to write a story about Sam Langford, a great boxer who had seemingly fallen off the face of the earth. Knowing that Sam's last known residence was in Harlem, Laney began his search for Sam among the various businesses lining Lenox and Seventh Avenues.

To Laney's great astonishment, many people he questioned about Sam's whereabouts were not aware of Langford's history. At least a dozen who knew Sam claimed that he was dead. The search seemed futile, but Laney continued his quest and eventually learned that Sam was alive and residing in the city on 139th Street, in a rundown hotel. A woman at the front desk confirmed that Mr. Langford was, indeed, living there. She led Laney to a tiny, dirty bedroom at the end of a dark, third-floor hallway. It was there that Laney finally found Sam, just one month shy of his fifty-eighth birthday: he was sitting on the edge of his bed listening to an old radio.

Sam was very surprised to learn he had a visitor, but he quickly rose to his feet and searched for a string attached to a single bulb hanging from the ceiling, to illuminate the dark room. Successfully accomplishing the mission, Sam turned to Laney in surprise and asked, "You come to see me?"

"That's right Sam, I'd like to write a story in the newspaper about you, if you don't mind," replied Laney.

Later, Laney told others that it took some work to convince Sam that he really wanted to interview him for a story.

"What you want to write about old Sam for? He ain't no good any more," Sam said, and he asked Laney if he'd ever seen him fight.

Laney lied to him and said that he had, and that Sam was the greatest he'd ever seen. That pleased Sam and he laughed.[1]

Laney, like so many others, was surprised at how short the old fighter was. He wondered how such a short man could have fought such giants as Fred Fulton, Harry Wills, and Jack Johnson.

Laney learned that Sam had all of twenty cents in his pocket and that he was getting by on a few dollars he received each month from a foundation for the blind. Twice a day, two young boys would take Sam to a restaurant for a meal; other than that, Sam said he spent all of his time sitting alone, listening to the radio.

He impressed Laney as an intelligent man with a good memory, and he was a fine storyteller. Despite living under such dreary circumstances, Sam portrayed himself as cheerful. Laney noted that all the stories Sam told were of an amusing variety. When Sam was asked about any of the mistreatment he'd received during his career, he simply laughed and went on to tell another humorous story.

Sam asked the reporter about old sportswriters he counted among his friends, and requested that Laney convey his regards to each of them.

When he'd gathered the information he needed, Laney went back to the office and banged out the story on his typewriter. But he didn't stop there. He was so moved by Sam's situation that—in conjunction with a group of New York businessmen and women—he initiated a drive on Sam's behalf. That ultimately resulted in setting up a trust fund worth $10,892. Among the 705 individuals who contributed to the fund were men such as Jack Dempsey, Beau Jack, Fritzie Zivic, boxing promoter Mike Jacobs, Joe Louis, and famed New York nightclub owner Toots Shore.

---

[1] *Digby Courier*, 3 February 1944

Newspapers in cities such as Denver and New Orleans, where Sam had entertained so many fight fans, appealed to their local boxing fans. Many responded, sending in their contributions.

The fund was administered by the Guaranty Trust Company. Sam was provided an initial payment of $125.00, followed by $75.00 per month until April of 1945. After that, the balance of $9,000 was invested in an insurance company so Sam would be provided an annuity guaranteeing him $49.18 a month for life.

Some were not so generous. An unnamed heavyweight who had fought Sam a number of times and had saved a million dollars worth of winnings refused to contribute a dime. Laney told Langford about it and Sam thought it over a minute. Then he said, "You want to make me rich, Mr. Laney? ... Just ask that man to give a dollar for every round I carried him."[2]

On Christmas Day of that year, Laney wrote a follow-up story based upon a Christmas Eve visit with Sam. "Chief," said Sam, "this is going to be the best Christmas I ever had. Maybe you could put that in the paper."

Sam asked Laney to let everyone know that he was happy, and to thank everyone for their contributions to his well being. He asked him to thank everyone for their letters and the many fine gifts he'd received, including a guitar, three boxes of cigars, a pair of gloves, several neckties, candy, a bottle of gin, and $5.00 for a Christmas dinner.

The man Laney had found sitting alone only eleven months earlier in a dark bedroom was found this time surrounded by friends, in a room that had been decorated for the holidays. Laney was pleased to learn Sam would be among friends on Christmas Day as well. As usual Sam was in good spirits, laughing often throughout the visit. He compared Sam to a child in his obvious enjoyment of the gifts and remembrances of his friends.

> "You see that bottle, Chief," said Sam, "if you come back here on the 4th of July there'll still be some in it. But tomorrow I'm gonna have myself a couple of good belts. Oil myself up some for a little guitar playing. Boy! Listen to that thing talk. She sure talk sweet, don't she?"

---

[2] *Oakland Tribune*, 23 December 1952

When Laney was ready to depart, Sam asked him to be sure to tell all his friends that he was the happiest man in New York City. He had his guitar, a bottle of gin, and money in his pocket to buy Christmas dinner. Sam said, "No millionaire in the world got more than that, or at least they can't use any more. Tell my friends all about it and tell 'em I said God bless 'em."[3]

A similar article, written by United Press correspondent Jack Cuddy, appeared in July 1945, and reported that Sam's dingy little room in a Harlem location had become "a bit of heaven" for him since Laney's article had been written some eighteen months earlier.[4]

When the fund had been set up for Sam the previous year, some of the committee members suggested to Sam that he move to better surroundings, but Sam told them he was comfortable where he was, and that he was already accustomed to his current environment. Though sightless, he was able to find his way around with the use of his cane. Now that he had enough money to purchase tobacco for his pipe, plenty of food to fill his belly, his own radio, and "friends" coming to visit him and talk about old times, he was perfectly happy. He passed the time puffing away contentedly on his pipe, listening to fights on his radio, and recalling his many fights with old-timers who had begun to drop in on him with greater frequency.

The pages on the calendar turned to 1946 and Sam was still living quietly in Harlem, existing on the monthly annuity he received from his trust fund and whatever other monies he could garner from anyone willing to pay him to share his stories of past ring glory.

There wasn't much news about Sam in those days, other than the occasional reference to him in connection with a historical boxing match or a humorous story related to the ring.

That June, his long time nemesis, Jack Johnson, died of internal injuries suffered in an auto accident twenty miles north of Raleigh, North Carolina. For several years, Johnson's sole source of income had come from personal appearances, and he was on his way from Texas, where his most recent appearance tour had ended, to New York to see the second Joe Louis-Billy Conn fight. He'd been accompanied

---

[3] *New York Herald Tribune*, 25 December 1944
[4] *Daily Register*, 13 July 1945

by a Mr. Fred L. Scott, whom he'd hired to assist him with driving whenever he became tired.

Scott, who suffered only minor injuries when he was thrown from the car, later explained that the pair had pulled into a diner just outside of Raleigh late in the day on June 9th. When they entered the diner, they were told they'd have to eat in the back or not at all. Since they were so hungry, Johnson reluctantly agreed. After they finished their meal and Johnson was back behind the wheel of his automobile he reflected upon the treatment they'd just received, became very angry, and tore off along Highway 1 at an alarmingly high rate of speed.

As the pair roared into a corner highway nearing a small town called Franklinton, Johnson found himself heading straight for an oncoming truck. He swerved to avoid the collision, and the vehicle jumped off the road, smashing into a telephone pole. Johnson, badly hurt, was rushed to nearby St. Agnes Hospital where he was subsequently pronounced dead at 6:10 p.m., the result of internal injuries and shock. He was sixty-eight years old.

His wife, Irene, was notified of his death and made arrangements to have the body transported to Chicago, where a large funeral was held for him at the Pilgrim Baptist Church. Afterward, he was buried in the Graceland Cemetery next to his previous wife, Etta Duryea Johnson, who had committed suicide in 1912.

Two years later, in June of 1948, word came out of Nova Scotia that Sam's hometown of Weymouth Falls wanted to add onto its existing school and rename it after him. The community had outgrown its little one-room school, and by 1947 it had become so overcrowded that half of the students would attend in the morning and the other half in the afternoon. The community needed to raise at least 10% of the cost of a new school in order to obtain government aid for the construction.

In November 1948, it was announced that a campaign had been launched to raise $10,000 for building of the school. As part of that effort, 3,000 letters were to be sent out, along with small pamphlets on Sam's life.

The fundraising was successful, and by early 1949 construction was underway. The Sam Langford School became the public school for local children from elementary grades through grade twelve. In 1957, the Weymouth Consolidated School was built in Weymouth for high school students, and the Sam Langford School was then used solely for the purpose of educating elementary students. The school closed in 1967, and for a number of years thereafter it was used primarily for the purpose of housing community meetings. In 1979, the name of the building was changed to the Sam Langford Community Centre. A plaque commemorating Sam's memory was erected on the site in June of 1992 and remains to this day. In April of 1996, the first black multi-cultural library in northwest Nova Scotia was opened inside the Centre. Although still in place, the building is no longer open, due to its poor condition and lack of funding.

In 1949, a young college student named Marvin Gilmore was working his way through school as a night shift orderly at the Boston State Hospital. Interviewed in October of 2007, the long-time President and CEO of Community Development Corp. of Boston, Inc., said that it was in that hospital that he met and cared for Sam Langford.

Marvin didn't know how Sam ended up in Boston State Hospital, which was a mental institution, but clearly remembers thinking that Sam didn't belong there:

> "He wasn't crazy, he should not have been in that hospital, he deserved better," said Marvin. "His mind would wander occasionally when he spoke, but I enjoyed spending time talking to him. He was kind and gentle and very proud of his boxing career."[5]

Marvin quit the hospital job sometime in 1951, after he graduated from school. By that time Sam was no longer there. In all likelihood, Sam ended up in the hospital as a result of blindness, lack of funds, and an inability to care for himself.

Although his daughter, Charlotte Wade, was extremely fond of her father and loved him very much, her mother, Martha, (from whom Sam had separated many years before) was already living with her. Charlotte's daughter, Carol Doyle (Sam's great-granddaughter), thinks that providing care for Sam would have been very difficult for her mother, but she does remember Charlotte going to visit Sam often.[6]

---

[5] Marvin Gilmore. Telephone interview, October 2007

[6] Carol Doyle. Telephone interview, October 21, 2007

In late June 1950, Sam's former manager, Joe Woodman, was sought out by a fight reporter and asked if the former great heavyweight champion Joe Louis would have stood a chance against Langford. "Yes," replied Joe, "A chance of getting killed!"[7]

By this time it was really only through comments in the news such as these that Sam's name was being kept alive. Often he would be mentioned in connection with the deaths of some of his former opponents, such as Willie Lewis and Tom McMahon, as a particularly formidable opponent these men had faced in the ring during their boxing careers. Sam's public appearances had become few and far between.

Further illustrating just how many had forgotten his greatness, it was announced in December of 1950 that a large group of Canada's sportswriters and broadcasters had overwhelmingly selected the former welterweight champion of the early 1930s, "Babyface" Jimmy McLarnin, as Canada's outstanding boxer of the half century. McLarnin received thirty-two of the forty-three total votes. Others receiving the remaining votes were Sam, Tommy Burns, Larry Gains, Lionel Conacher, and Arthur King, the British Empire lightweight champion at the time.

Certainly, McLarnin, was a great fighter, but it would seem a grave injustice to place his accomplishments in the ring above those of Sam. But time marches on, and the light of even the greatest dims with each new generation.

Almost two years later, in the summer of 1952, Sam wanted to move back to Boston. He contacted his former manager and friend, Joe Woodman, to let him know of his desires, and with Joe's assistance, arrangements were made for him to travel by train to his old stomping grounds.

A couple of days later, on August 8th, a United Press story came out of Boston advising that Sam was back in the city where he'd begun his pugilistic career, living on $1.65 per day at a cheap hotel named the Argonne on Bullfinch Street, in an area known as Bowdoin Square. That figure essentially represented the daily amount Sam derived from the monthly interest he received on the trust fund that had been established for him back in 1944.

---

[7] *The Zanesville Signal*, 26 June 1959

Jack Conway Jr., a writer for a local Boston paper, visited Sam at the hotel. Sam told the writer that he had become lonesome for Boston and decided it was time for him to return to the city of his youth. Tapping a chipped white cane on his bedpost for emphasis while he spoke, Sam said the Argonne was a nice little hotel and that he was thankful that it only cost him $8.75 a week to live there since his monthly income from the trust fund was only $49.50.[8]

Despite his blindness and meager existence, Sam maintained a jovial demeanor. He always chose to maintain a positive outlook on life, and when asked how he could keep such a rosy outlook under his current conditions, Sam consistently replied that he'd had plenty of good times during his life, and he still had his memories of those periods.

The stories of Sam's circumstances prompted the Veteran's Boxers Association to sponsor a benefit on October 28, 1952, at the site of many of his fights in Boston, the old Mechanic's Hall. The event, possibly Sam's last public appearance, was attended by approximately 1,000 boxing enthusiasts and netted $2,000. Former heavyweight champion Gene Tunney was one of several contributors who added another sixty dollars a month toward this additional fund set up for Sam.

By early 1953, Sam was living at the William Tell Hotel, a gloomy establishment inhabited primarily by persons with little means. Located across the street from the hotel was Bill's Lunch, a small bar on Cambridge Street, which served as Sam's last place of employment and hangout for nearly two years. The bar's owner, Phil Barbanti, an ex-pug himself, idolized Sam. Each day, Barbanti would send a man over to Sam's hotel to pick him up and bring him over for lunch. Afterward, Sam would be taken for a short walk and returned to the bar where he would sit in a booth drinking beer and spinning tales of his boxing career to the customers. Barbanti had a sign outside the bar advertising Sam as an attraction from four o'clock in the afternoon until ten o'clock in the evening. In return Sam received his meals, all he cared to drink, and a fee of ten dollars per week.[9]

Sam didn't think much of the modern crop of fighters, outside of

---

[8] *Digby Courier,* 14 August 1952
[9] *The Nova Scotia Historical Quarterly,* Vol. 4. No. 3, September 1974

Joe Louis, whom he declared was the greatest counter puncher he'd ever seen other than Joe Gans. As for the rest, Sam said, "These fellows today don't know how to feint a man. Only a few of them know how to hook. They dance around. They run sideways, but they don't fight."[10]

During this period of time, Sam visited the home of his daughter Charlotte on Howard Street regularly. His great-granddaughter, Carol, remembers that she would spend every Saturday at her Grandmother Charlotte's home, and to the best of her recollection she believes that Sam would visit at least once a month. Carol referred to her Grandmother Charlotte as "Big Granny" (because she was a "normal" sized woman approximately 5'7" or 5'8", with large hands like her father) and her Great Grandmother Martha as "Little Granny" because she was barely 5' tall, if that.

Carol was born in 1948 and would have been no more than five or six years old at the time of these visits.

> "As soon as I arrived and opened the door I could smell that cigar, and I would say, 'Ok, that's it, where is he? I know he's here somewhere!' There was two windows in my grandmothers kitchen, and he sat in the window on the right hand side by the sink. That is where he would sit, and after they would kind of coax me to go over and say hello, I would say 'Hi.' He had very large hands, a very wide nose, and his voice was very low and very gentle. He wore dark glasses, was always in a suit, and always with a bow tie."

Carol remembers that Charlotte had large hands like her father, and that she was always afraid that her nose would widen like her father's, so she would continually pinch it in the hopes of avoiding that fate. Throughout the day she continually reminded her young granddaughter to do the same.

Carol also recalls that whenever this man was in her grandmother's home there were always a lot of knocks on the door and people coming in and talking and "a lot of ruffles and flourishes." She never recalled any unpleasantness between Sam and Martha, and says Martha never said anything bad about him. In fact, Carol remembers that she spent

---

[10] Jan Morrison. "Amazing Career of Sam Langford." *Ebony*, April 1956

much of her time visiting her great-grandmother in her bedroom, rummaging through Martha's three large suitcases full of newspaper clippings concerning Sam's boxing career and looking at the many photographs of their travels together. Martha would also proudly show her the jewelry that Sam had given her, which was kept tucked under the mattress of her large, four-poster mahogany bed.[11]

By 1954, it had been determined that Sam could no longer care for himself. His daughter, Charlotte, had been named his legal guardian and arranged for him to be cared for in the Upland Nursing Home, run by a widow named Grace Wilkins. Mrs. Wilkins typically charged $35.00 per week to care for older persons, but agreed to accept less than that to accommodate Sam's meager allowance.

It was in this nursing home that Sam lived out the rest of his life in a simply furnished room on the second floor. He never left that floor. He slept on a double bed and spent the bulk of his time resting on his bed or sitting in a chair smoking a cigar or chewing tobacco and listening to his radio. Every once in a while, a visitor would come to see him, and he'd enthusiastically talk about his past.

One of those visitors was a chaplain named Kenneth Sullivan who had spent his boyhood in Weymouth, Nova Scotia hearing countless stories of the legendary "Boston Tar Baby." In 1955, Sullivan traveled to Boston specifically to meet his boyhood hero. Later, in 1992, he wrote a wonderful account of that visit in *Growin' Up on the Back Road*. Kenneth discovered Sam to be a contented old man, "fiercely proud of what he'd accomplished during his life, and genuinely grateful for the experiences that had come his way." Later that same year, Sam told another visitor, "Don't nobody need to feel sorry for old Sam. I had plenty of good times. I been all over the world. I fought maybe 600 fights, and every one was a pleasure!"[12]

Charlotte visited Sam regularly, taking various foods that she knew he'd enjoy, such as fruit and different types of cookies. His great-granddaughter, Carol, also remembers visiting Sam with her father (Sam's oldest grandson Joseph) on at least one occasion. Joseph was very proud of his grandfather, and in fact gave boxing a try while he

---

[11] Carol Doyle. Telephone interview, October 21, 2007
[12] *The Nova Scotia Historical Quarterly*, Vol. 4 No. 3, September 1974

was in the Navy, but Carol believes he gave it up when he found out you got hit![13]

Mrs. Wilkins found Sam to be a good natured guest. She treated him well, sometimes buying him pajamas, underwear, and tobacco. Sam in turn expressed his desire that he not become too much of a burden upon her.

One day, Mrs. Wilkins asked him what he would do if he could do anything in the world that he wanted. Sam replied:

> "Missus, I've been everywhere I wanted to go, I've seen everything I wanted to see, and I guess I've eaten just about everything there is to eat. Now I just want to sit here in my room and not cause you any trouble."[14]

And that's just what he did.

---

[13] Carol Doyle. Telephone interview, October 21, 2007

[14] Trent Frayne. "The Greatest Fighter Who Ever Lived." *MacLean's*, 15 Feb 1955

SAM LANGFORD'S GRAVESITE
Photo courtesy of Carol Doyle

EPILOGUE

Sam died on January 12, 1956, less than two months shy of his seventieth birthday and only ten weeks after being enshrined in Boxing's Hall of Fame. The official cause of his death was listed as malnutrition and cerebral arterial sclerosis. He was survived in death by his estranged wife, Martha; his daughter, Charlotte, and her second husband, Cecil Wade; his two grandsons, Joseph Roberts, age twenty-nine, and William Roberts, age twenty-four; and three great-grandchildren.

He was buried in the Cambridge, Massachusetts Cemetery. The specific interment location is listed as #348 Amaranth Patch. Originally buried without a headstone because his daughter did not believe in them, a proper granite headstone was later paid for and placed at the gravesite on January 15, 1986 by St. Louis boxing historian, Tim Leone, after receiving permission from the family.

Martha Langford died on March 2, 1964, at the age of seventy-seven, in the Cambridge City Hospital. Joe Woodman lived to ninety-six. He died in a New York nursing home in May, 1969, after an extended illness.

At the time of Sam's induction into Boxing's Hall of Fame in October of 1955, he was the only non-champion accorded the honor. He was inducted along with nine other ring greats including Gene Tunney, Mickey Walker, Benny Leonard, and Harry Greb. Many ring experts considered Sam the greatest pound-for-pound fighter in the history of boxing. Under different circumstances, he might have been a champion at five different weights: lightweight, welterweight, middleweight, light heavyweight, and heavyweight.

Sam was most likely in his prime from 1907 through 1912. During that stretch of time, he lost only two bouts out of fifty-three recorded contests. One of those was a surprising loss to "Fireman" Jim Flynn in 1908, when Sam was badly out of shape. He avenged that loss with an eighth round knockout of Flynn, slightly more than two months later. The other loss between 1907-1912 was a greatly disputed decision loss to Sam McVea on December 26, 1911 in Australia. Sam also avenged that, by defeating McVea in their next four matches on that continent.

The great featherweight champion of the early 20th century, Abe Attell, was asked in 1951 if Sugar Ray Robinson was the best of all time, either as a welterweight or middleweight. He named Ketchel as the greatest welterweight he'd ever seen and said that, "As for the middleweights, I'll take Sam Langford—the greatest of them all at that poundage."[1]

Attell is also credited with the following statement, made while commenting on photographs of great boxers that lined the walls of Jack Dempsey's former restaurant on Broadway, in New York City:

> "Now there was a fighter for you. Sam Langford! Yes, sir, in my book he was just about the greatest of them all. Sam was born about twenty-five years too soon. In his day, the Negro fighter didn't get much of a break. He had to fight the way he was told. Nobody will ever know how many fighters Sam had to carry. If he didn't agree to carry them he wouldn't get any work."

That quote appears in an article written by Joe Williams for *The Knockout* magazine. Williams went on to say that off the record, Attell named a number of fighters Langford had carried, and that you'd be surprised at the dignity and importance of those fighters' positions in ring history.

When Williams asked Attell what he thought Langford would do against Joe Louis, Abe reportedly smiled and replied:

> "Just too much fighter. There wasn't anything Sam couldn't do and if he had a weakness nobody ever found out what it was. I have plenty of respect for Louis as a hitter, but I can't see him hitting Sam hard enough to make him mad."[2]

Nat Fleischer, founding editor of *The Ring* magazine, called Sam

---

[1] *Washington Post*, 22 March 1951
[2] Joe Williams. "All Fighters Know When They're Slipping Old Time Says." *The Knockout*, 22 July 1939

one of the hardest punchers of all time, and ranked the little man seventh among his personal list of all-time great heavyweights. Said Fleischer:

> "Sam was endowed with everything. He possessed strength, agility, cleverness, hitting power, a good thinking cap and an abundance of courage. He feared no one. But he had the fatal gift of being too good and that's why he often had to give away weight in early days and make agreements with opponents. Many of those who agreed to fight him, especially of his own race, wanted an assurance that he would be merciful or insisted on a bout of not more than six rounds."[3]

Gentleman Jim Corbett, the great John L. Sullivan's conqueror, placed Sam fifth on his personal heavyweight list.

Other leading sportswriters of that era had even higher opinions of Sam. Hype Igoe, well known boxing writer of the *New York Journal*, proclaimed Sam the greatest fighter, pound-for-pound, who ever lived. The aforementioned Joe Williams, respected sports columnist of the *New York World Telegram*, wrote that Langford was probably the best the ring ever saw, and the great Grantland Rice described Sam as "about the best fighting man I've ever watched."

In 1999 Sam was voted Nova Scotia's top male athlete of the twentieth century.[4]

---

[3] Nat Fleischer. "The Langford Legend." *The Ring*, March 1956
[4] *The Nova Scotia Historical Quarterly*, Vol. 4, No. 3, September 1974

AFTER 1922 407

SAM LANGFORD
AND JOE WALCOTT
1931
IN JIM TOLAND'S GYM
BOSTON

LANGFORD SPARRING
WITH
JOSEPH HARNETT
BILLY LYNCH TRAVELING
CARNIVAL SHOW
CA.1930S
COURTESY OF
NOVA SCOTIA TOURISM,
CULTURE & HERITAGE

JOE WALCOTT AND COMEDIAN BILLY B. VAN

IMPERIAL THEATRE,
CA. 1930
AUTHOR'S COLLECTION

UNKNOWN AND JOE WOODMAN

CA. 1950S
AUTHOR'S COLLECTION

AFTER 1922 409

JOE LOUIS AND SAM LANGFORD
CA.1935
AUTHOR'S COLLECTION

JOE LOUIS HEAVYWEIGHT CHAMPION 1937-1949
AND (ON LEFT) HIS TRAINER **JACK BLACKBURN** SITTING RINGSIDE
AUTHOR'S COLLECTION

410 Sam Langford: Boxing's Greatest Uncrowned Champion

JESSE OWENS, SAM LANGFORD AND JACK DEMPSEY

JESSE OWENS THROWING OUT THE BALL FOR A NEGRO LEAGUE DOUBLEHEADER STAGED FOR LANGFORD'S BENEFIT AT THE POLO GROUNDS IN NEW YORK

SEPTEMBER 20, 1936

RAY MCCORMICK-BOB SHEPARD COLLECTION

(EARLIER ERA PHOTO)
JACK DEMPSEY DEFEATS JESS WILLARD

TOLEDO, OH JULY 4, 1919

DEMPSEY CAPTURES THE HEAVYWEIGHT CROWN

AUTHOR'S COLLECTION

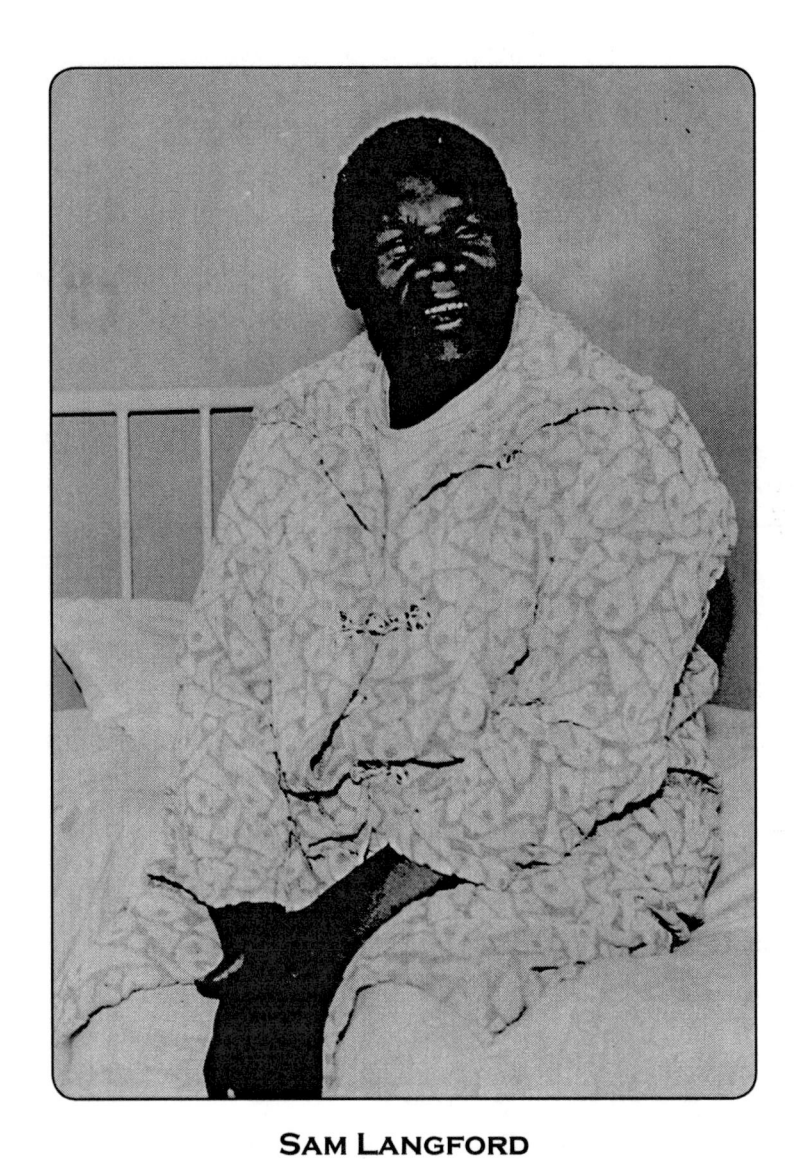

SAM LANGFORD
AFTER 1935 EYE OPERATION
NEW YORK APRIL 26, 1935
BEN HAWES COLLECTION

New York's Mayor LaGuardia and Langford

November 24, 1935

Sam is showing the Mayor his coat, torn when he was struck by a taxi.

Ray McCormick-Bob Shepard Collection

Sam signs a contract with Charles Schwartz

(Burlesque King of Brooklyn)

December 12, 1935

(Contract to appear in show at the Oxford Theatre)

Ray McCormick-Bob Shepard Collection

AFTER 1922 413

SAM LANGFORD HISTORIC SITE MEMORIAL AND COMMUNITY CENTER
WEYMOUTH FALLS, NOVA SCOTIA
COURTESY WEYMOUTH CULTURAL HERITAGE CENTER

SAM'S EXTENDED FAMILY
CAMBRIDGE, MA 1948

SEATED (L TO R) : **BIG GRANNY CHARLOTTE WADE** (SAM'S DAUGHTER), UNKNOWN, **GREAT-GRANDMOTHER LOTTIE** HOLDING SAM'S GREAT-GRANDDAUGHTER **CAROL DOYLE, ELEANOR ROBERTS** (CAROL DOYLE'S MOTHER), **JOSEPH ROBERTS** (SAM'S GRANDSON, ELEANOR'S HUSBAND, AND CAROL DOYLE'S FATHER)
BACK ROW: 2ND FROM LEFT IS BIG GRANNY'S HUSBAND, **CECIL WADE** (SAM'S SON-IN-LAW) (ALL OTHER UNIDENTIFIED)

Appendix

SAM LANGFORD'S PROFESSIONAL RECORD

1902

Apr 11	Jack McVicker	Boston, MA	WKO	6 ARB

1903

Jan 15	Arthur Pratt	Boston, MA	W KO	2 BH
Jan 22	Billy Chisholm	Lawrence, MA	W NWS	6 TL
Jan 23	Luther Manuel	Boston, MA	D	4 BMJ
Feb 6	Luther Manuel	Boston, MA	D	5 BG
Feb 27	Luther Manuel	Boston, MA	W PTS	10 BG
Mar 4	Sadler Jennings	Chelsea, MA	W KO	2 TL
Mar 5	John Johnson	Boston, MA	D NWS	6 BG
Mar 6	Luther Manuel	Boston, MA	D NWS	6 BG
Mar 26	John Butler	Boston, MA	W PTS	6 BG
Apr 3	Bob Allen	Boston, MA	W NWS	BG
Apr 16	Bob Allen	Boston, MA	W PTS	6 BG
Apr 20	Andy Watson	Lawrence, MA	L NWS	12 BG
May 8	Andy Watson	Boston, MA	D NWS	10 BG
May 25	Billy Jordan	Cambridge, MA	W NWS	6 BMJ
May 26	Chick Monahan	Boston, MA	W KO	1 BG
May 29	Andy Watson	Boston, MA	D NWS	10 BG
Jun 5	Tim Kearns	Boston, MA	W TKO	2 BG
Jun 15	Andy Watson	Gloucester, MA	D PTS	12 BG
Jun 19	Walter Burgo	Boston, MA	W TKO	8 BG
Jun 26	Danny Duane	Boston, MA	L PTS	12 BG

Jul 16	Belfield Walcott	Scituate, RI	W PTS	20 BG
Aug 28	Kid Griffo	Boston, MA	W PTS	12 BG
Sep 15	Shadow Morris	Boston, MA	W PTS	12 BG
Oct 5	Arthur Cote	Boston, MA	W TKO	5 BG
Nov 20	Patsy Sweeney	Boston, MA	W KO	12 BG
Nov 28	Joe Reed	Boston, MA	W TKO	4 BG
Dec 8	Joe Gans	Boston, MA	W PTS	15 BG
Dec 23	Jack Blackburn	Boston, MA	L NWS	12 BG

1904

Jan 6	Andy Watson	Salem, MA	D PTS	12 BH
Jan 11	Jack Blackburn	Philadelphia, PA	D NWS	6 PI
Jan 27	Belfield Walcott	Boston, MA	W NWS	6 BH
Feb 13	Charlie Johnson	Boston, MA	EXH	5 BH
Feb 22	Bill Lewis	New Bedford, MA	W TKO	2 BH
Apr 11	Dave Holly	Cambridge, MA	L PTS	10 BH
Jul 29	George McFadden	Manchester, NH	W TKO	2 BH
Sep 5	Joe Walcott	Manchester, NH	D PTS	15 BH
Sep 30	Dave Holly	Baltimore, MD	D PTS	15 PI
Nov 4	Dave Holly	Philadelphia, PA	D NWS	6 PI
Nov 24	Andy Watson	Webster, MA	W NWS	12 BH
Nov 25	Tommy Sullivan	Marlboro, MA	W NWS	12 BH
Dec 9	Jack Blackburn	Marlboro, MA	D PTS	15 BH
Dec 22	Joe Reed	Berlin, NH	W KO	9 PI

1905

Jan 16	Joe Reed	Webster, MA	W TKO	5 BH
Jan 20	George Gunther	Chelsea, MA	W PTS	15 BG
Jan 27	Belfield Walcott	Boston, MA	W NWS	6 ARB

Feb 13	Dave Holly	Salem, MA	W NWS	15 BH
Mar 3	George Cole	Chelsea, MA	NC	9 BH
Mar 13	George Gunther	Portland, ME	W PTS	12 BG
May 16	Bogardus Hyde	Webster, MA	W TKO	12 BG
May 26	Yng. Peter Jackson	Marlboro, MA	W PTS	15 BG
Jun 16	Yng. Peter Jackson	Chelsea, MA	W PTS	15 BG
Jul 4	Larry Temple	Marlboro, MA	L PTS	10 BG
Aug 18	Jack Blackburn	Leiperville, PA	W NWS	15 PI
Sep 7	Larry Temple	Marlboro, MA	D PTS	15 BG
Sep 20	Jack Blackburn	Allentown, PA	D PTS	10 PI
Sep 29	Yng. Peter Jackson	Baltimore, MD	D PTS	15 BG
Oct 7	Jack Blackburn	Philadelphia, PA	NC	4 PI
Dec 25	Joe Jennette	Lawrence, MA	L TKO	8 BG

1906

Feb 28	Larry Temple	Chelsea, MA	W KO	15 BG
Mar 19	Black Fitzsimmons	Webster, MA	W TKO	11 BG
Apr 5	Joe Jennette	Chelsea, MA	W PTS	15 BG
Apr 26	Jack Johnson	Chelsea, MA	L PTS	15 BG
Jun 13	Yng. Peter Jackson	Southbridge, MA	L TKO	5 BG
Nov 12	George Gunther	Val. Falls, RI	W PTS	12 BG
Nov 21	Yng. Peter Jackson	Rochester, NY	W PTS	15 BG
Nov 29	George Gunther	Haverhill, MA	W TKO	3 BG

1907

Jan 11	Joe Jennette	Lawrence, MA	D PTS	12 BG
Jan 31	Kid Williams	Rochester, NY	W KO	6 PI
Apr 22	James "Tiger" Smith	London, England	W KO	4 BG
Jun 3	Geoff Thorne	London, England	W KO	1 BG

Aug 27	Larry Temple	Chelsea, MA	W PTS	10 BG
Sep 25	Jim Barry	New York, NY	W NWS	6 PI
Oct 15	Jim Barry	Chelsea, MA	W NWS	10 BG
Nov 12	Yng. Peter Jackson	Los Angeles, CA	W PTS	20 MFP
Dec 17	Jim Barry	Los Angeles, CA	W PTS	10 BG

1908

Jan 14	Jim Barry	Los Angeles, CA	W NWS	10 BG
Feb 10	Black Fitzsimmons	Boston, MA	W TKO	4 BG
Mar 3	Joe Jennette	Boston, MA	D PTS	12 BG
Mar 11	Larry Temple	Boston, MA	W NWS	8 BG
Apr 7	Jim Barry	Boston, MA	W TKO	2 BG
May 19	"Sandy" Ferguson	Boston, MA	W PTS	12 BG
Jun 19	Jim Barry	Bronx, NY	W KO	3 PI
Jul 21	John Wille	Brooklyn, NY	W KO	2 PI
Aug 7	Tony Ross	Bronx, NY	W TKO	5 PI
Sep 1	Joe Jennette	New York, NY	W NWS	6 PI
Dec 21	"Fireman" Jim Flynn	San Francisco, CA	W KO	1 PI

1909

Mar 17	Jim Barry	Philadelphia, PA	W NWS	6 PI
Mar 29	Morris Harris	Brooklyn, NY	W TKO	7 PI
Apr 3	John Wille	Philadelphia, PA	W KO	2 PI
Apr 14	Jim Barry	Albany, NY	D NWS	10 PI
Apr 17	Al Kubiak	Philadelphia, PA	W NWS	6 PI
Apr 27	"Sandy" Ferguson	Boston, MA	D PTS	12 BG
May 24	William "Iron" Hague	London, England	W KO	4 PI
Jul 13	John "Klondyke" Haines	Pittsburgh, PA	W NWS	6 PP
Sep 28	Dixie Kid (A. Brown)	Boston, MA	W TKO	5 BG

Nov 2	John "Klondyke" Haines	Boston, MA	W KO	7 BG
Nov 23	Mike Schreck	Pittsburgh, PA	W TKO	1 PP

1910

Jan 10	Dixie Kid (A. Brown)	Memphis, TN	W KO	3 BG
Feb 8	"Fireman" Jim Flynn	Los Angeles, CA	L NWS	10 BG
Feb 22	Nat Dewey	Cheyenne, WY	W KO	1 BG
Mar 17	"Fireman" Jim Flynn	Los Angeles, CA	W KO	8 PI
Apr 14	Jim Barry	Los Angeles, CA	W KO	16 PI
Apr 27	Stanley Ketchel	Philadelphia, PA	D NWS	6 BG
May 14	"Battling" J. Johnson	Philadelphia, PA	W NWS	6 PI
May 17	Al Kubiak	New York, NY	W TKO	2 NYT
Sep 6	Joe Jennette	Boston, MA	W PTS	15 BG
Nov 10	Jeff Clarke	Joplin, MO	W TKO	2 PI
Dec 6	Morris Harris	Boston, MA	W KO	2 BG

1911

Jan 10	Joe Jennette	Boston, MA	W PTS	12 BG
Jan 16	Fred Atwater	Utica, NY	W TKO	3 BG
Feb 21	Bill Lang	London, England	W DQ	6 Boxing
Apr 1	Sam McVea	Paris, France	D PTS	20 Boxing
May 30	Ralph Calloway	Syracuse, NY	W TKO	4 BG
Jun 16	Tony Caponi	Winnipeg, Canada	W NWS	10 MFP
Jun 29	Jack Fitzgerald	New York, NY	W KO	5 NYT
Aug 9	"Farmer" Jim Smith	New York, NY	W TKO	5 NYT
Aug 15	Jack O'Brien	New York, NY	W TKO	5 NYT
Aug 24	Tony Ross	New York, NY	W KO	6 NYT
Sep 5	Joe Jennette	New York, NY	W NWS	10 NYT
Oct 6	Tony Caponi	New York, NY	W KO	3 NYT
Dec 26	Sam McVea	Sydney, Australia	L PTS	20 JH

1912

Feb 12	Jim Barry	Sydney, Australia	W PTS	20	JH
Apr 8	Sam McVea	Sydney, Australia	W PTS	20	JH
May 13	Jim Barry	Melbourne, Aust.	W TKO	11	JH
May 24	Dan "Porky" Flynn	Melbourne, Aust.	W TKO	14	JH
Aug 3	Sam McVea	Sydney, Australia	W PTS	20	JH
Oct 9	Sam McVea	Perth, Australia	W TKO	11	JH
Dec 26	Sam McVea	Sydney, Australia	W KO	13	JH

1913

Mar 16	Jim Barry	Brisbane, Australis	W KO	1	JH
Mar 24	Sam McVea	Brisbane, Australis	D PTS	20	JH
Apr 2	Jerry Jerome	Brisbane, Australis	EXH	10	BC
Jun 19	Colin Bell	Rockhampton, Aust.	D PTS	15	REF
Aug 26	Dan "Porky" Flynn	Boston, MA	W KO	4	BG
Sep 9	John Lester Johnson	New York, NY	W KO	1	NYT
Oct 3	Joe Jennette	New York, NY	D NWS	10	NYT
Oct 27	Jack Lester	Taft, CA	W TKO	5	ARB
Nov 17	Ed "Gunboat" Smith	Boston, MA	L PTS	12	BG
Dec 20	Joe Jennette	Paris, France	W PTS	20	PR

1914

Jan 24	Matthew "P.O." Curran	Paris, France	W KO	1	Boxing
Mar 23	Bill Watkins	New York, NY	W TKO	1	NYET
Mar 27	"Battling" J. Johnson	New York, NY	W NWS	10	PR
Apr 15	George "Kid" Cotton	Chattanooga, TN	W NWS	8	MFP
Apr 20	"Roughhouse" Ware	Memphis, TN	W TKO	5	PGRB
May 1	Harry Wills	New Orleans, LA	D NWS	10	PP

May 25	Bill Watkins	Rochester, NY	W KO	4	PP
Aug 12	"Battling" J. Johnson	New York, NY	W NWS	10	NYT
Aug 25	George "Kid" Cotton	Boston, MA	W KO	4	BG
Sep 15	"Battling" J. Johnson	Boston, MA	D PTS	12	BG
Oct 1	Joe Jennette	New York, NY	D NWS	10	PR
Oct 6	Colin Bell	Boston, MA	W KO	4	BG
Oct 20	Ed "Gunboat" Smith	Boston, MA	W KO	3	BG
Oct 26	Jeff Clarke	Joplin, MO	L NWS	10	PR
Nov 10	Tom McMahon	Vernon, CA	W TKO	6	PR
Nov 16	Jim Cameron	San Diego, CA	W TKO	6	PR
Nov 26	Harry Wills	Vernon, CA	W KO	14	PR

1915

Apr 6	"Battling" J. Johnson	New York, NY	W NWS	10	NYT
Apr 13	Joe Jennette	Boston, MA	L PTS	12	BG
Apr 19	Dan "Porky" Flynn	Montreal, Canada	NC	8	BG
Jun 8	"Battling" J. Johnson	Brooklyn, NY	W NWS	10	NYT
Jun 29	Sam McVea	Boston, MA	L PTS	12	BG
Jul 16	Jack Thompson	Denver, CO	D PTS	20	PGRB
Sep 30	Sam McVea	Denver, CO	D PTS	20	PR
Oct 18	"Battling" J. Johnson	Denver, CO	W PTS	15	RMN
Nov 23	Sam McVea	New York, NY	D NWS	10	NYT
Dec 3	Harry Wills	New York, NY	L NWS	10	NYT

1916

Jan 3	Harry Wills	New Orleans, LA	L PTS	20	PP
Jan 20	Andrew Johnson	Savannah, GA	W KO	4	ST
Feb 11	Harry Wills	New Orleans, LA	W KO	19	PP
Feb 17	Sam McVea	New York, NY	W NWS	10	NYT

Feb 28	Cleve Hawkins	New York, NY	W NWS	10 NYT
Mar 7	Harry Wills	Brooklyn, NY	L NWS	10 NYT
Mar 22	Dave Mills	Syracuse, NY	W TKO	2 SH
Mar 31	Jeff Clarke	St. Louis, MO	W KO	5 PP
Apr 7	Sam McVea	Philadelphia, PA	W NWS	10 SH
Apr 25	Harry Wills	St. Louis, MO	L NWS	8 PP
May 2	Sam McVea	Akron, OH	D NWS	12 MFP
May 12	Joe Jennette	Syracuse, NY	W KO	7 SH
Aug 12	Sam McVea	Buenos Aires, Argentina	D PTS	20 PGRB
Nov 30	"Big" Bill Tate	Syracuse, NY	W NWS	10 SH
Dec 12	"Battling" J. Johnson	St. Louis, MO	W KO	12 PR
Dec 29	Bob Devere	Montreal, Canada	W NWS	10 IBRO

1917

Jan 1	"Battling" J. Johnson	Kansas City, MO	W PTS	12 BG
Jan 25	"Big" Bill Tate	Kansas City, MO	L PTS	12 PP
Apr 10	Jack Thompson	Brooklyn, NY	W NWS	10 PR
Apr 19	Bob Devere	New York, NY	W NWS	10 PR
May 1	"Big" Bill Tate	St. Louis, MO	W KO	6 PP
May 11	Harry Wills	Philadelphia, PA	L NWS	6 PR
Jun 19	Fred Fulton	Boston, MA	L TKO	7 BG
Aug 17	Andre Anderson	Buffalo, NY	W TKO	2 BG
Sep 14	Joe Jennette	Toledo, OH	W NWS	12 PR
Sep 20	Harry Wills	Brooklyn, NY	L NWS	10 PR
Nov 12	Harry Wills	Toledo, OH	L NWS	12 PR
Dec 17	Kid Norfolk	Denver, CO	W KO	2 PR

1918

Apr 14	Harry Wills	Panama	L KO	6 PSH
May 19	Harry Wills	Panama	L TKO	7 PSH
Jun 6	"Battling" J. Johnson	Atlanta, GA	W PTS	10 AC
Aug 5	"Battling" J. Johnson	Atlantic City, NJ	W NWS	8 PR
Aug 6	Jack Thompson	Philadelphia, PA	W NWS	6 PR
Aug 19	"Roughhouse" Ware	Tulsa, OK	W KO	9 ARB
Aug 22	"Battling" J. Johnson	St. Louis, MO	D PTS	8 PP
Oct 31	Jeff Clarke	Lowell, MA	D	12 BG
Nov 16	Jeff Clarke	Atlanta, GA	D PTS	10 ARB
Nov 28	Jeff Clarke	Philadelphia, PA	D NWS	6 PPL
Dec 12	Jack Butler	Rock Is., IL	W KO	5 ARB
Dec 16	Jeff Clarke	Memphis, TN	W NWS	8 PR
Dec 27	Fred Fulton	San Francisco, CA	L PTS	4 SFC

1919

Mar 4	Willy Meehan	San Francisco, CA	L PTS	4 SFC
Apr 30	Billy Hooper	Columbus, OH	W KO	4 PR
Jun 19	"Big" Bill Tate	Minneapolis, MN	W DQ	5 ARB
Jul 4	Harry Wills	St. Louis, MO	L NWS	8 PR
Aug 4	Jack Thompson	Tulsa, OK	D PTS	15 PR
Aug 23	"Big" Bill Tate	Grand Rapids, MI	W KO	7 PP
Sep 17	"Roughhouse" Wilson	Battle Creek, MI	W TKO	4 PR
Sep 30	Harry Wills	Syracuse, NY	L NWS	10 PP
Oct 20	Jack Thompson	Tulsa, OK	D PTS	15 PR
Nov 5	Harry Wills	Tulsa, OK	L PTS	15 PR
Nov 17	"Mexican" J. Johnson	Sioux City, IA	W KO	9 CT
Nov 24	Jack Thompson	Duluth, MN	W TKO	6 CT
Dec 3	Dave McBride	Rockford, IL	W KO	1 CT

1920

Jan 16	Jeff Clarke	Kalamazoo, MI	W NWS	10	PR
Feb 16	Jeff Clarke	Terre Haute, IN	D NWS	10	CT
Feb 23	"Battling" Gahee	Memphis, TN	W KO	2	CT
Mar 29	Jamaica Kid	Columbus, OH	W KO	7	CT
Apr 5	Jack Thompson	Muskogee, OK	W PTS	15	MJ
Apr 9	Silas Green	Detroit, MI	W KO	3	CT
Apr 23	Harry Wills	Denver, CO	L PTS	15	CT
May 18	Marty Cutler	Windsor, Canada	W TKO	3	BCS
May 31	Jeff Clarke	Columbus, OH	W PTS	15	PR
Jun 7	"Roughhouse" Ware	New Orleans, LA	W KO	9	NOT
Jun 12	Pinky Lewis	Ft. Worth, TX	W KO	4	FWST
Jul 2	Jack Mitchell	Springfield, MO	W KO	3	SFC
Jul 26	Pinky Lewis	Memphis, TN	W TKO	7	ARB
Aug 14	Sam McVea	E. Chicago, IN	W NWS	10	CT
Aug 30	Ed "Bearcat" Wright	Walthill, NE	W PTS	10	MJ
Sep 2	Joe Borker	Gary, IN	L PTS	10	GEP
Sep 6	"Big" Bill Tate	Benton Harbor, MI	L NWS	6	CT
Oct 6	"Tiny" Jim Herman	Portland, OR	W KO	7	ARB
Oct 13	Frank Farmer	Seattle, WA	W PTS	4	TNT
Oct 20	Lee Anderson	Portland, OR	L PTS	10	CT
Nov 15	Jack Thompson	Memphis, TN	W PTS	8	CT
Nov 17	George Godfrey	Hot Springs, AR	W KO	2	CT
Dec 2	"Tiny" Jim Herman	Portland, OR	W TKO	7	PR
Dec 9	Terry Keller	Aberdeen, WA	W PTS	6	MJ
Dec 23	Clem Johnson	Marshfield, OR	W PTS	6	TL
Dec 29	Jim "Jam" Barry	Portland, OR	W PTS	10	MCA

1921

Jan 14	Bob Devere	Portland, OR	W TKO	7 LAT
Jul 20	Ed "Bearcat" Wright	Omaha, NE	W KO	9 MJ
Aug 12	Lee Anderson	Omaha, NE	W PTS	10 MJ
Aug 17	George Godfrey	Covington, KY	W KO	1 MJ
Aug 19	"Topeka" Jack Johnson	Topeka, KS	D PTS	10 TL
Sep 5	Lee Anderson	Ft. Worth, TX	L NWS	10 REG
Ssp 21	"Big" Bill Tate	Covington, KY	L NWS	12 IDS
Oct 18	"Young" Peter Jackson	Toronto, Canada	W KO	2 EJ
Nov 24	Lee Anderson	Phoenix, AZ	L PTS	10 AR

(Unpopular decision with the crowd on the part of the referee, Billy Murray of San Francisco.)

1922

Jan 17	Harry Wills	Portland, OR	L PTS	10 PP
Mar 17	"Cyclone" Smith	Huntington, WV	W KO	2 PP
Mar 27	"Big" Bill Tate	Memphis, TN	L PTS	8 PP
Apr 7	Jack Leslie	Indianapolis, IN	W PTS	10 FWJG
Apr 20	Kid Roscoe	Memphis, TN	W KO	2 PP
May 16	Kid Roscoe	Nashville, TN	W KO	4 CT
May 22	Ted Jamieson	Chicago, IL	D PTS	10 MJ
Jun 5	"Tiger" Flowers	Atlanta, GA	W KO	2 CT
Jun 19	Ed "Bearcat" Wright	Galveston, TX	D PTS	12 TL
Jul 17	Ed "Bearcat" Wright	Tulsa, OK	W KO	5 MJ
Aug 4	"Big" Bill Tate	Tulsa, OK	W PTS	12 MJ
Aug 11	Brad Simmons	Wichita, KS	W PTS	10 TL
Aug 21	Jack Taylor	Sioux City, IA	D NWS	10 MJ
Sep 22	"Battling" Owens	Juarex, Mexico	W KO	7 NS
Oct 6	"Cyclone" Smith	El Paso, TX	W KO	2 TL
Oct 20	Jack Taylor	Juarez, Mexico	W PTS	15 CT

Nov 5	Jack Taylor	Juarez, Mexico	D PTS	15 TL
Nov 10	Jim "Jam" Barry	Douglas, AZ	D PTS	10 TL
Dec 27	Sonny Goodrich	San Antonio, TX	W KO	5 TL

1923

Feb 15	Tom McCarthy	Albuquerque, NM	W TKO	2 BB
Mar 2	Jim Tracey	Mexico City	W KO	6 TL
Mar 17	"Chihuahua" Kid Brown	Mexico City	W KO	1 TL
Mar 31	Jim "Kid" Savage	Mexico City	W KO	1 CT

—Heavyweight Championship of Mexico

Apr 8	Andres Balsas	Mexico City	W KO	6 CT

—Heavyweight Championship of Mexico

Apr 13	"Chihuahua" Kid Brown	Torrean, Mexico	W KO	3 TL

—Heavyweight Championship of Mexico

May 6	Andres Balsas	Mexico City	W KO	3 CT

—Heavyweight Championship of Mexico

May 16	Art Surans	Mexico City	W KO	3 TL

—Heavyweight Championship of Mexico

May 19	Jack Voigt	Mexico City	W KO	11 TL

—Heavyweight Championship of Mexico

Jun 15	Jim Tracey	Mexico City	W KO	4 CT

—Heavyweight Championship of Mexico

Jul 27	Clem Johnson	Juarez, Mexico	L KO	13 TL

—Heavyweight Championship of Mexico

Oct 19	"Fireman" Jim Flynn	Mexico City	W KO	3 IDS
Nov 14	Andres Balsas	Mexico City	W KO	15 LA

1924

Jan 6	"Fireman" Jim Flynn	Juarez, Mexico	W PTS	8 TL
Jan 20	Tom Riley	Juarez, Mexico	W KO	2 TL

Apr 4	Jim "Jam" Barry	Huntington Bch., CA	W PTS	4 SFS
Apr 16	Jim "Jam" Barry	San Fernando, CA	W PTS	4 REG
Apr 18	Sammy Olson	Bakersfield, CA	W PTS	4 BDN
Apr 23	Eddie Trembley	Venice, CA	L PTS	4 CT

1925

Dec 7	Tim Sullivan	Fort Bliss, TX	D PTS	6 TL

1926

Jul 1	"Young" Jack Johnson	Shawnee, OK	W KO	2 TL
Aug 2	Brad Simmons	Drumright, OK	L KO	1 TL

THE FOLLOWING FIGHTS HAVE NOT BEEN CONFIRMED WITH A PRIMARY REFERENCE SOURCE:

1917

Sep 17	Andrew Johnson	Ardmore, MD	W KO	10 UC

1918

Aug	Jeff Clarke		W PTS	10 UC

1919

Nov 3	"Topeka" Jack Johnson	Sioux City, IA	?	10 TDW

1920

May	George Godfrey		D PTS	10 UC

1921

Jan 7	Lee Anderson	Omaha, NE	D PTS	12 UC
—	Brad Simmons	Cincinnati, OH	D PTS	12 UC
—	Jeff Clarke	—	W PTS	10 UC

—	Jack Thompson	—	D PTS	10 UC
—	"Big" Bill Tate	—	W PTS	12 UC
—	"Tiny" Jim Herman	—	W KO	2 UC
—	Alfred Johnson	—	W KO	— UC
—	Bill Watkins	—	W KO	— UC
Dec 7	Lee Anderson	Tucson, AZ	W PTS	10 UC
Dec 15	"Big" Bill Tate	Covington, KY	L NWS	12 UC

1922

Nov 21	James "Tut" Jackson	Juarez, Mexico	W KO	1 UC
Dec 1	"Big" Bill Tate	Juarez, Mexico	W PTS	8 UC
Dec 12	Jack Taylor	Juarez, Mexico	W KO	8 UC
Dec 24	Kid Roscoe	Juarez, Mexico	W KO	3 UC

1923

May	"Truck" Hannah	Mexico City	W KO	19 UC
Aug	Ed "Bearcat" Wright	Mexico City	L KO	9 UC
Aug	"Fireman" Jim Flynn	Mexico City	W PTS	10 UC
Dec 7	Homer Smith	Mexico City		UC
Dec 11	Kid Roscoe	Mexico City	W KO	1 UC
Dec 21	Sonny Goodrich	San Antonio, TX	L PTS	10 UC

1924

Feb 6	James "Tut" Jackson	Mexico	W KO	9
Mar 6	Kid Nolan	Venice, CA	W KO	5
Jul 7	Sydney Grant	Mexico City	W KO	4
Aug 17	Jim Briggs	Mexico City	W PTS	6
Sep 10	Kid Nolan	Mexico City	W KO	2
Oct 7	Jim Briggs	Mexico City	W KO	8

1925

Jan 1	Tim Sullivan		D PTS	6
Jan 14	Wolf Larsen	Juarez, Mexico	W KO	7
Feb 10	Jack Taylor	Juarez, Mexico	W KO	8
Mar 1	Tim Sullivan		D PTS	6
Apr 5	Frolin Gonzeles	Juarez, Mexico	W PTS	10
May 11	Jim Briggs	Juarez, Mexico	W KO	4
May 22	Wolf Larsen	Juarez, Mexico	W KO	13
Sep 25	"Battling" Gahee		L PTS	8

SOURCES: ABBREVIATIONS

AC = Atlanta Constitution
AR = Arizona Republic
ARB = T.S. Andrews Record Book
BB = Boxing Blade magazine
BC = Brisbane Courier
BCS = Border Cities Star
BG = Boston Globe
BH = Boston Herald
BMJ = Boston Morning Journal
Boxing (English magazine)
CT = Chicago Tribune
EJ = Edmonton Journal
FWJG = Fort Wayne Journal Gazette
GEP = Gary Evening Post
IBRO = International Boxing Research Organization
IDS = Indianapolis Daily Star
JH = John Hogg – Australian boxing historian
LA = La Aficio'n
LAT = Los Angeles Times
MCA = Memphis Commercial Appeal
MFP = Milwaukee Free Press
MJ = Milwaukee Journal
NOT = New Orleans Times

NS = Negro Star (Wichita, KS)
NWS = Newspaper decision
NYET = New York Evening Telegram
NYT = New York Times
PI = Philadelphia Item
PGRB = Police Gazette Record Book
PP = Pittsburgh Press
PPL = Philadelphia Public Ledger
PR = Philadelphia Record
PSH = Panama Star Herald
REF = "Referee" (Australian periodical)
REG = Reno Evening Gazette
RMN = Rocky Mountain News
SFC = San Francisco Chronicle
SFS = San Fernando Sun
SMO = Santa Monica Outlook
SY = Syracuse Herald
TDW = Tulsa Daily World
TL = Tim Leone – American boxing historian
TNT = Tacoma News Tribune
UC = Unconfirmed

BIBLIOGRAPHY

BOOKS

Alegria, Henry. *75 Years of Memoirs.* Caldwell, Idaho: The Caxton Printers, Ltd., 1981.

Ashe Jr., Arthur R. *A Hard Road to Glory: A History of the African American Athlete 1619-1918.* New York: Amistad Press, 1991.

Batchelor, Denzil. *Big Fight.* London: Phoenix House Ltd., 1955.

Bennison, Ben. *Giants on Parade.* London: Rich and Cowan Ltd., 1936.

Bettinson, A.F. and B. Bennison. *The Home of Boxing.* London: Odhams Press Ltd., 1923.

—*Famous Fights and Fighters.* Kingswood, Surrey: The World's Work Ltd., 1937.

Butler, James. *Kings of the Ring.* London: Stanley Paul & Co. Ltd., 1936

— *The Fight Game.* Kingswood, Surrey: The World's Work Ltd., 1951.

Chambers, Barrie. *Iron Hague, A Champion's Diary.* Privately published, 1997.

Corri, Eugene. *Fifty Years in the Ring.* London: Hutchinson & Co. Ltd., 1933.

— *Gloves and The Man, The Romance of The Ring.* London: Hutchinson & Co. Ltd., 1928.

Dartnell, Fred. *Seconds Out.* London: T. Werner Laurie Ltd., 1924.

DeLisa, Michael. *Cinderella Man.* Milo Books, 2005.

Dempsey, Jack (as told to Bob Considine and Bill Slocum). *Dempsey, By the Man Himself.* New York: Simon and Schuster, 1960.

Edney, Henry Grady. *Theodore "Tiger" Flowers.* Biltmore, North Carolina: Country Club Publishing Co., 1928.

Fleischer, Nat. *Fifty Years at Ringside.* New York: Fleet Publishing Corporation, 1958.

— *Black Dynamite IV – Fighting Furies.* New York: The Ring Athletic Library, 1939.

Fullerton, Hugh. *Two Fisted Jeff.* Chicago: Consolidated Book Publishers, 1929.

Gains, Larry. *The Impossible Dream.* London: Leisure Publications, 1976.

Goldman, Herb. *The Ring Record Book and Boxing Encyclopedia.* New York: The Ring Publishing Corp., 1987.

Grim, Joe. *"The Wonder Man" Biography & Ring Battles of the Greatest Living Italian Pugilist.* Publisher unknown, 1928.

Growden, Greg. *Snowy Baker.* Sydney, Australia: Random House, 2003.

Health & Strength. *The Life & Battles of Sam Langford.* London: 1909.

Heller, Peter. *In This Corner.* New York: Simon and Schuster, 1973.

Jarrett, John. *Dynamite Gloves.* London: Robson Publishing, 2001.

Kessler, Harry. *The Millionaire Referee.* St. Louis: Harkess Publishing, 1982.

Kilty, James. *Leonis of Vernon.* New York: Canton Press, 1963.

Liebling, A.J. *A Neutral Corner.* San Francisco: North Point Press, 1990.

Odd, Gilbert, ed. *Jack Johnson, In the Ring and Out.* London: Proteus Ltd., 1977.

Ottley, Roi. *Black Odyssey: The Story of the Negro in America.* New York: Charles Scriber's Sons, 1948.

Preston, Harry. *Memories.* London: Constable & Co., 1928.

— *Leaves From My Unwritten Diary.* London: Hutchinson & Co., 1936.

Rhoden, William C. *$40 Million Slaves: The Rise, Fall, and*

Redemption of the Black Athlete. New York: Crown Publishers, 2006.

Roberts, Randy. *Papa Jack.* London: Robson Books, 1983.

— *Papa Jack, Jack Johnson and the Era of White Hopes.* New York: The Free Press, 1983.

Saunders, Charles. *Sweat & Soul.* Hantsport: Lancelot Press, 1990.

Spink, Al. Spink *Sport Stories.* Chicago: The Spink Sport Stories Co., 1921.

Soutar, Andrew. *My Sporting Life.* London: Hutchinson & Co., 1934.

Sullivan, Edward. *The Fabulous Wilson Mizner.* New York: The Henkle Company, 1935.

Sullivan, Kenneth E. *Growin' Up on the Back Road.* Oxford, Maine: Western Marine Graphics, Inc., 1992.

Van Court, DeWitt. *Champions Made in California.* Los Angeles: Premier Printing Company, 1926.

Walsh, Peter. *Men of Steel, The Lives and Times of Boxing's Middleweight Champions.* London: Robson Books, 1993.

Ward, Geoffrey. *Unforgiveable Blackness: The Rise and Fall of Jack Johnson.* New York: Alfred A. Knopf, 2004.

Wignall, Trevor. *Ringside.* Hutchinson & Co., 1941.

— *Almost Yesterday.* London: Hutchinson & Co., 1949.

— *The Story of Boxing.* London: Hutchinson & Co., 1924.

— *The Sweet Science.* London: Chapman and Hall Ltd., 1926.

— *I Knew Them All.* London: Hutchinson & Co., 1938.

NEWSPAPERS

Afro-American Ledger
Appleton Post
Atlanta Constitution
Beloit Daily News
Border Cities Star
Boston American
Boston Globe
Boston Herald
Boston Morning Journal
Boston Post
Boston Traveler
Brisbane Courier (Australian)
Buffalo Courier Express

Buffalo Evening News
Chicago Defender
Chicago Journal
Chicago Tribune
Daily Province
Daily Telegraph (Australian)
Denver Post
Digby Courier
Evening Telegram
Evening World
Fort Wayne Sentinel
Galveston Daily News
Halifax Chronicle
Halifax Herald
Hamilton Spectator
Hamilton Times
Hammond Times
Indianapolis Star
Lincoln Daily Star
Lincoln Evening Journal
Los Angeles Daily Times
Los Angeles Examiner
Los Angeles Times
Lowell Sun
Melbourne Argus
Memphis Commercial Appeal
Milwaukee Evening
Milwaukee Free Press
Moncton Daily News
Morning Chronicle
Nashville Tennessean
Nevada State Journal
New York Evening World
New York Herald Tribune
New York Illustrated News
New York Journal
New York Times
New York World Telegram
News Journal
News Sentinel
Oakland Tribune
Ottawa Citizen
Panama Star
Philadelphia Evening News
Philadelphia Item
Philadelphia Public Ledger
Philadelphia Record
Pittsburgh Courier
Referee, The (Australian)
Register, The (Sandusky, OH)
Rocky Mountain News
St. Louis Dispatch
St. Louis Post
San Francisco Call
San Francisco Chronicle
San Francisco Examiner
Sandusky Star Journal
Savannah Tribune
Syracuse Herald
Sydney Daily Telegraph
Tamworth Daily Observer
Topeka Daily Capital
Topical Times
Toronto Daily Star
Trenton Times
Truro Daily News
Tulsa Daily Herald
Tulsa Daily World
Vancouver Province
Vancouver Sun
Vancouver World
Washington Post
Winnipeg Press
Winnipeg Tribune
Yarmouth Telegram
Zanesville Signal

INDEX

Adams, Dick 162
Allen, Bob 415
Almy, George "Doc" 76, 161
Aylwood, Kevin 69
Anderson, Andre 317, 422
Anderson, Eddie 377
Anderson, Lee 333, 337, 424, 425, 457, 428
Andrews, T.S. 247, 250, 430
Armstrong, Bob 103, 126, 162-3, **174**, 191-3, 203, 284
Attell, Abe 93-94, **175**, 404
Atwater, Fred 194, 196, 419
Austin, Gerard 288
Austin, Sam 218
Baer, Max 339, 386
Baker, Snowy 230-233, 239, 243, 432
Balsas, Andres 359, 361, 426
Barbanti, Phil 398
Barry, Jim 82-84, 87-88, 99, 101, 132-134, 161-162, **182, 183**, 210, 237-239, 244, 250-251, 263-265, 292, 301, 311, 332, **347**, 418-420
Barry, Jim "Jam" 361, 426-427
Baulknight, Jeff 373, 375
Baun, Eddie 142
Bell, Charley 90
Bell, Colin 257, 266, 268-269, 289, **349**, 420-421
Benton, B.H. 280
Berger, Sam 89-90, 162, **175**
Bettinson, A.F. "Peggy" 76-78, 81, 92, 96, 106, 108, 431
Bishop, "Biddy" 161
Blackburn, Jack 35-36, 44-47, 49, 54, **173**, 220, 288-289, 385, 388, **409**, 416-417
Blake, George 292, 294-295
Blow, E.A. 229
Borker, Joe 424
Bower, George 366

Boykin, Joe 373-374
Briggs, Jim 371, 428-429
Britt, Jimmy 202, 204
Britt, Willus 73, 100, 119, 138
Britt, Young 189
Brodsky, Alyn 388
Bronson, Edgar 141-142
Bronson, Jimmy 192
Brown, Aaron "The Dixie Kid" 56, 119-122, 220, 244, 418-419
Brown, "Chihuahua" Kid 357, 359, 426
Brown, Percy (P.A.) 369, 378-379
Burgo, Walter 415
Burke, Sailor 76
Burns, Farmer 162
Burns, Tommy 81, 89, 92, 94-97, 100-101, 157, 160, 195, 210, 227, 229, 233, 246, 250, 275, 382, 397
Burrell, Martha, see Langford, Martha
Butler, Jack 423
Butler, James **72**, 73, 78-81, 108, 204, 206, 431
Butler, John 415
Byers, George 33, **38**, 42, 63, 103, 142, **174**, 191-192, 284, 379
Calloway, Ralph 217, 419
Cameron, Jim 292, 421
Cameron, Lucille 252-254
Cannon, Ulysses, see Fitzsimmons, Black
Caponi, Tony 218, 224-225, 419
Carey, Jake 193
Carnera, Primo 339, 385
Carpentier, Georges 285-286, 289, 327-328
Carr, Harry 125, 130-132, 256
Carr, Howard 317, 327
Chisholm, Billy 415
Clabby, Jimmy 223
Clarke, Jeff "The Joplin Ghost" **188**,

435

192-193, 291, 306, 323, 325, 328, 330, 332, 419, 421-424, 427
Coffroth, James 101, 114, 134, 138, 140, 255, 292-293
Cole, George 47, 55, 142, 192, 417
Coleman, Vince 79
Collins, Mike 314-315
Conacher, Lionel 397
Conn, Billy 394
Considine, Bob 310, 431
Conway Jr., Jack 398
Cook, "Megaphone" 366
Corbett, James J. 25, 162, **175**, 210, 291, 220, 380, 405
Corbett, W.F. 255
Cornell, Roger
Corri, Eugene 80-81, 104-105, 108, 201, 205, 207-208, 213, **345**, 431
Cote, Arthur 416
Cotton, George 285, 289, 420-421
Craig, Frank 79, 265
Cross, Leach 367
Cuddy, Jack 384, 394
Curran, Matthew "P.O." **173**, 207-208, 283-284, 420
Cutler, Charley 296
Cutler, Marty 330, 424
Darcy, Les 256
Darmouth, Thomas 122
Davis, John "Liver" **174**, **184**, 246, 266, 284, **346**, **347**, **349**
Delaney, Billy 100-101
Delmont, Al **72**, 77-78
Dempsey, Jack 13, 132, 273, 291, 309-311, 317, 330, 374, 381, 388, 392, 404, **410**, 431
Depena, Dave 256, 266, **349**
Devere, Bob 312, 422, 425
Dewey, Nat 127-128, 419
Dickerson, Col. 152-153
Dillon, Jack 222
Dipley, Walter 152-153
Dixon, George 15, 39, 56, 63

Dorgan, Tad 50, 147
Dowling, Dowzer 29
Duane, Danny 35-36, 415
Dundee, Johnny 293, 381
Eaves, Eustace 387
Edgren, Bob 150, 153-154, 157, 224, 292-293
Edney, Henry 338, 431
Edwards, Harry 168
English, George 302
Erne, Frank 39
Fairbanks, Art 375
Farmer, Frank 424
Farr, Tommy 388
Felix, Peter 93, 195
Ferguson, Sandy 63, 66-67, 87, 103, **173**, 217, 244, 418
Firpo, Luis 309, 374
Fitzgerald, Jack 218-219, 419
Fitzpatrick, Sam 92, 93, 97
Fitzsimmons, Black 61, 87, 417-418
Fitzsimmons, Bob 15, 25, 82, 102, 143, 194, 200, 220-222, 247, 268, **342**, 380
Fitzsimmons, Floyd 374
Flaherty, Martin 325
Fleischer, Nat
Flowers, "Tiger"
Flynn, "Fireman" Jim
Flynn, Dan "Porky" 193, 226, 244-245, 262, 271-272, 300, **346**, **347**, 420, 421
Foley, Larry 268
Foley, Mike 27, 31-32
Foley, W.J. 380
Fowler, Gene 301
Frazier, Grant 369
Fulton, Fred 291, 313-317, 324-325, 330, 338, **354**, 369, 384, 392, 422-423
Gahee, "Battling" 328-329, 424, 429
Gains, Larry 334-335, 397, 432
Gallagher, Reddy 55-56

436

Gans, Joe 15, 17, 21, 36, 39-44, 49, 63, 142, 158, 313, 337, 399, 416
Gardner, George 221
Gibson, Harry 318
Gibson, William 116, 166
Gilmore, Marvin 7, 396
Godfrey, George 331-333, 339, 374, 381, 424-425, 427
Gonzales, Frolin 371, 429
Goodman, Danny 363
Goodman, Tom 334
Goodrich, Sam 361
Goodrich, Sonny 339, 426, 428
Goulder, Superintendent 249
Grant, Sydney 428
Greb, Harry 338, 403
Green, Silas 329, 424
Griffin, James 138
Griffo, Kid 416
Griffo, Young 268
Grove, Izzy 377
Gunther, George 55, 71, **173**, 416-417
Haack, Billy 328-329
Hague, James "Iron" **91**, 99, 102-109, **179-181**, 365, 418, 431
Haines, John "Klondyke" 114, 121, 418-419
Hales, A.G. 68
Hall, Nelson 53
Hannah, "Truck" 428
Harris, George 377-379
Harris, Herbert 288
Harris, Morris 99, 193, 418-419
Hartnett, Joseph 380
Hawkins, Cleve 306, 422
Herford, Al 40, 44
Herman, "Tiny" Jim 332, 424, 428
Holly, Dave 40, 49-50, 53-55, 416-417
Hooper, Billy 423
Howard, Kid 319, 369-370, 373
Hughes, Ed 40, 376-377

Hughes, Sam 373
Humphrey, Joe 377
Hurdman-Lucas, F. 282
Hyde, Bogardus 55, 417
Igoe, Hype 18, 134, 140, 262, 405
Jack, Beau 392
Jackson, James "Tut" 339, 428
Jackson, Peter 15, 55, 268
Jackson, "Young" Peter 55-57, 62, 70-71, 83, 220, 293, 333-334, 417-418, 425
Jacobs, Mike 392
Jamaica Kid 329, 424
Jamieson, Ted 425
Jennette, Joe 21, 57-58, **60**, 61-62, 75, 87-88, 168, **177-178**, 194, 196, 211, 222-224, 245-246, 248, 250, 255, 265-266, 268, 271, 273-274, 281, 283, 286-287 289, 299, 301, 307-309, 312, 317-318, **352**, 365, 377, 417-422
Jeffries, James J. 67, 97, 100-101, 115-121, 138-139, **156**, 157, 159-165, 167, 169, **175**, 192, 200, 224, 256, 258, 326
Jennings, Sadler 415
Jerome, Jerry 420
Johnson, Alfred 332, 428
Johnson, Andrew 304, 421, 427
Johnson, Charlie 416
Johnson, Clem 332, 359-360, 424, 426
Johnson, Etta Duryea 395, 250
Johnson, "Mexican" J. 423
Johnson, Jack 13, 14, 16, 21, 56, 58, 61-70, 73, 81, **86**, 87, 89, 91-97, 99-103, 106, 108-109, 114-116, 119-121, 126-127, 132, 138-139, 141, 150, 157-169, 189-194, 196, 199, 200-201, 205, 208, 210-211, 215, 217, 220, 223-225, 227, 237, 245-248, 250-253, 255-256, 258, 261-262, 266-268, 270-271, 273, 279, 285-286, 288-290, 292, 295-296, 299, 304, 308-312,

437

326, 370, 380-381, 392, 394, 395, 417, 432-433
Johnson, "Topeka" Jack 332-333, 425, 427
Johnson, "Young" Jack 427
Johnson, "Battling" Jim 157, **186**, 285, 288-289, 296, 299, 302, 312, 324, 419-423
Johnson, John Lester 272-273, 286, 310, 420
Johnston, James 364, 366
Jones, Edna 305
Joplin Ghost see Clarke, Jeff
Jordan, Billy 415
Kanner, Jack 301
Kaufmann, Al 74, 100-101, 114, 166-168, 194, 196, 210, 215, 223-224, 292
Kearns, Jack "Doc" 310
Kearns, Tim 415
Keller, Terry 332, **346**, 424
Kelly, Hugo 73-74, 191, 222
Kelly, Jimmie 142
Kelly, "Honest" John 137, 150
Kelly, W.C.J. 251-252
Kessler, Harry 307, 432
Ketchel, Stanley "The Michigan Assassin" 21, 73, 88-89, 92, 96, 99-102, 114-121, 134, *136*, 137-154, 157-158, 164, **174**, 191, 193, 204, 220, 222, 279, 404, 419
Kiecal, Stanislaw, see Ketchel, Stanley
Kilty, James 275 432
Klaus, Frank 138-139, 143, 191
Koven, Eddie 377
Kubiak, Al 101, 158-159, 292, **349**, 418-419
LaGuardia, Fiorello 387-388, **412**
Landis, Kenesaw 270
Laney, Al 391-394, 123
Lang, Bill **cover**, 93, 194-196, 199-210, 224, 227, 247, **343, 344-345,** 419

Langford, Charlotte (mother) 21
Langford, Charlotte (daughter) 88, 247, 269, **352**, 396, 399-400, 403, **413**
Langford, Martha 54, 88, 247, 269, 303-304, 307, **352**, 396, 399-400, 403
Langford, Robert (father) 21-22, 24, 269
Larsen, Ivoy 226
Larsen, Wolf 371, 429
Lawless, Will 243
Lawrence, George **184**, 269, 359, 361
Lee, "Canada" 377
Leonard, Benny 403
Leslie, Jack 425
Lester, Jack 227-228, 274-275, **353**, 420
Levinsky, "Battling" 289
Lewis, Bill 416
Lewis, Pinky 330, 424
Lewis, Willie 49, 397
Liebling, A.J. 42, 222, 432
Loughran, Tommy 374
Louis, Joe 13, 44, 47, 201, 309, 311, 329, 385, 388, 392, 394, 397, 399, 404, **409**
Lumley, Arthur 49, 51, 53
Machen, Walker 327
Magee, Bull 331
Maher, Peter 220
Malone, Jock 374
Mandell, Sammy 47
Manuel, Luther 415
Mathison, Charles F. 97
McBride, Dave 423
McCarey, Tom 126-127, 255, 293
McCarthy, Tom 256, 426
McCarty, Luther 246, 258
McClain, Billy 233
McCoy, Kid 74, 220-221
McFadden, George "Elbows" 50, 416
McFarland, Packy 223
McGeehan, W.O. 73, 75, 382
McGoorty, Eddie 191
McGovern, Terry 313, 377

McIntosh, Hugh 92, 95, 100, 195-196, 200-206, 209-210, 215, 222-224, 226-229, 233, 237-239, 242-243, 245-248, 250-255, 261-263, 265-268, 271, 365
McKettrick, Dan 250, 308
McLarnin, Jimmy 397
McMahon, Tom 292, 295, 397, 421
McQuillan, Jim **72**, 77-80, 82
McVea, Sam 21, 94, 104, 152, 194-195, 210-215, 226-234, **236**, 261, 265-266, 237-243, 246-255, 257, 286, 300-306, 308-309, 312, 330, **341-342**, 404, 419-422, 424
McVicker, Jack 31-32, 415
Meehan, Willie 326, 423
Mellody, Honey 53
Menke, Frank 290-291
Miller, Charlie 271
Mills, Dave 306, 422
Mitchell, Jack 330, 424
Mizner, Wilson 134, 140, 164, 433
Moir, "Gunner" 82, 102, 244, 247
Monahan, Chick 415
Moran, Frank 291, 313
Morgan, J.P. 57
Morris, Carl 215, 270, 314
Morris, "Shadow" **356**, 416
Muldoon, William 366, 378-379, 382
Mullen, Jim 370
Muller, Eddie 90
Muller, Nick 142
Mullins, Duke 64, 93-94, 103-104, 106-108, 141, 227-228, 232, 237, 247, 255, 263-264, 267-268, **346-347**
Murray, Billy 425
Murray, Miah 190
Murray, Michael 383
Naughton, W.W. 96, 137, 274-276, 279-280
Nelson, "Battling" 40, 43
Nolan, Kid 428

Norfolk, Kid 286, 318-319, 337, 422
O'Brien, Jack "Philadelphia" 56, 82, 89, 119, 196, 219-222, 419
Olson, Sam "Sammy" 361, 427
O'Rourke, Tom 56
Owens, "Battling" 339, 425
Owens, Jesse 388, **410**
Papke, Billy 73-74, 114-115, 117, 137-138, 191, 220, 223
Peterson, "Big Boy" 335
Pelkey, Arthur 270, 289, 333
Phillips, A.D. 65
Picasso, Pablo 283
Pollock, Abe 301
Pratt, Arthur 34, 415
Preston, Harry 107-110, 432
Read, Jack 266, **349**
Reed, Joe 416
Reisler, John 373, 310
Rickard, Tex 164, 374
Riley, Tom 361, 426
Roberts, Randy 253, 432
Robertson, Homer 376
Robinson, George 376
Romero, Baldomero 357
Root, Jack 221, 439
Roscoe, Kid 339, 361, 425, 428
Ross, Tony 88, 101, **175**, 222, 418-419
Ruecroft, Agnes 102
Runyon, Damon 331
Ruth, Babe 279
Savage, Jim "Kid" 358-359, 426
Schreck, Mike 121, 419
Schreiber, Belle 253
Scott, Arthur 239, 242-243, 249
Scott, Fred 395
Scozza, Lou 375
Sharkey, Jack 375-376
Sharkey, Tom 220, 359
Shaw, George Bernard 282
Sherry, Mike 139-140
Shore, Toots 392
Simmons, Brad 332, 339, 373, 425, 427

Slattery, William 271
Slavin, Frank 269
Slocum, Bill 310, 431
Smith, "Cyclone" 339, 425
Smith, Dave 229
Smith, Goldie 152-153
Smith, Ed "Gunboat" 270, 273, 275-276, 279-281, 288-291, 310-311, 365, 420, 421
Smith, Harry 325-326
Smith, Homer **356**, 428
Smith, Dr. James 362, 367-369, 385
Smith, Jim "Farmer" 219, 419
Smith, Kevin 7-8, 35, 49, 56, 61, 192, 285, 328, 338
Smith, Mick **349**
Smith, S. Fawes 22
Smith, "Tiger" 76-77, 79-82, 417
Soutar, Andrew 195-196, 205-207, 432
Suggs, Chick 376
Sullivan, Ed 164, 381-382, 433
Sullivan, Jack 193, 244
Sullivan, John L. 16, 39, 82, 113, 115, 210, 261, 266, 405
Sullivan, Kenneth 400, 433
Sullivan, Tim 371, 427, 429
Sullivan, Tommy 34-35, 54, 307, 416
Surans, Art 359, 426
Sweeney, Patsy 416
Tate, "Big" Bill 18, 312-313, 323, 332, 339, 422-425, 428
Taylor, Bud 47
Taylor, Jack 339, 371, 425-426, 429
Taylor, Major 14
Temple, Larry 56-57, 61, 82, 87, 417-418
Tessin, Frank 362
Thomas, Joe 88
Thompkins, Sim 55
Thompson, Jack 300-302, 312, 323, 327, 329-330, 332, 421-424, 428

Thompson, Johnny "Cyclone" 226, 289, **346**
Thorne, Geoff 82, 417
Toland, Jim 383, 407
Townsend, Jack 376
Tracey, Harry **198**, 202
Tracey, Jim 357, 359, 426
Trembley, Eddie 363, 427
Tunney, Gene 374, 380-382, 398, 403
Turner, Eugene 55-56
Van Court, DeWitt 292-294, 433
Voigt, Jack 359, 426
Walcott, Belfield 36, 416
Walcott, Joe 15, 21, 36, 46, **48**, 49-53, 56, 63, 120, 158, 219-220, 383, 386, **407-408**, 416
Walker, Beany 127, 129-130
Walker, Mickey 338-339, 403
Walsh, Jimmy 31, **184**, 189, **342**
Walsh, Peter 191, 433
Ware, "Roughhouse" 285-286, 330, **353**, 420, 423-424
Watkins, Bill 285, 288, 332, 420, 421, 428
Watson, Andy 35, 54, 63, 415-416
Wells, "Bombadier" Billy 247
Wheatcroft, Irving 226
White, Charlie 168, 169, 221
Wignall, Trevor 120, 201-202, 208, 212, 433
Wilkins, Grace 400-401
Willard, Jess 270, 273, 279, 291-293, **298**, 299, 301, 304, 306-307, 310-311, 313, 317, 320, 324, 326, **410**
Wille, John 88, 99, 418
Williams, Ike 391
Williams, Joe 310-311, 328, 376, 404, 405
Williams, Kid 76, 417
Wills, Harry 21, 286-288, 291-295, 303-306, 312-313, 318, 323-324, 327-330, **355**, **356**, 370, 374-376, 392, 421-425

Wilson, George 369
Wilson, "Roughhouse" 369, 423
Wilson, Ruth 22
Woodman, Joe 21, 29-33, 35, 45, 49, 75-76, 82, 89, 96, 100, 102-105, 109, 123, 126-127, 134, 137-139, 159-160, 162, 165, 167-168, **184**, 190-192, 195-196, 202, 214-215, 222, 227, 239, 244, 247, 261-263, 265-266, 270-271, 273, 275, 281, 284, 286, 295-296, 299-300, 307, 310-311, 316, 327, 330, **346**, 366, 368, 391, 397, 403, 408
Wright, "Bearcat" 332, 338-339, 424-425, 428
Ziskin, Joseph 383
Zivic, Fritzie 392

ABOUT THE AUTHOR

Clay Moyle is a member of the International Boxing Research Organization (IBRO), created in 1982 for the purpose of establishing an accurate history of boxing and compiling complete and accurate boxing records.

He is also a passionate collector of boxing books with over 4,000 titles in his personal collection, many dating back to the 1800s. He has a personal website from which he sells boxing books, autographs, programs, and other forms of boxing memorabilia (www.prizefightingbooks.com).

In 2011, he published *Billy Miske: The St. Paul Thunderbolt*.

He lives in Edgewood, Washington.

CPSIA information can be obtained at www.ICGtesting.com
Printed in the USA
LVOW08s1817090914

403241LV00028B/976/P